WITHDRAWN

D1071006

NORFOLK IN THE CIVIL WAR

A Portrait of a Society in Conflict

by the same author

THOMAS GRAY
Cambridge University Press

HORACE WALPOLE
Methuen

FELBRIGG: THE STORY OF A HOUSE
Rupert Hart-Davis

NORFOLK ASSEMBLY

COUNTRY NEIGHBOURHOOD

A NORFOLK GALLERY

NORFOLK PORTRAITS

THE EARLY LIFE AND DIARIES OF WILLIAM WINDHAM

NORFOLK
in the Civil War

A Portrait of a Society in Conflict

R. W. KETTON-CREMER

SHENANDOAH COLLEGE
LIBRARY
WINCHESTER, VA.

ARCHON BOOKS
Hamden, Connecticut

*First edition published
in the United States
1970*

DA   Ketton-Cremer, Robert
670   Wyndham
.N6
K292   Norfolk in the Civil War
1970
942.062 K51n

23379

© *Robert Wyndham Ketton-Cremer 1969*

PRINTED IN ENGLAND

TITLE IL

12-29-70 goldberg

To
James Fergusson of Kilkerran
and
Gyles Isham of Lamport
historians of their shires
in gratitude for long friendship

Preface

This book deals with people and events in Norfolk during the Civil War and the preceding decade. It attempts to tell the story of a single English county through those memorable years. It is concerned primarily with individuals, with men and women caught up in the tragic circumstances of their time.

I am a biographer rather than a historian; and I had at first intended the book to consist of a series of biographical studies. But I was influenced by the wishes of my publishers, and resolved to embark upon a continuous narrative. Even so, the narrative will be seen to have a strongly biographical slant throughout. I hope it may suggest lines of more detailed research to other workers in the same territory. The study of history grows ever more specialized; and it would be a particular satisfaction to me if specialists, present and future, at the University of East Anglia would follow up some of the paths which I have sought to indicate.

There is room in that territory for many explorers. I would greatly like to see full studies of Matthew Wren the Laudian Bishop of Norwich, of Miles Corbett the Puritan doctrinaire and regicide, of Sir John Holland the moderate Parliamentarian, and of several others who figure in my pages. Much work remains to be done on the lives of the sequestered clergy during the Civil War and the Commonwealth. The Royalist composition papers in the Public Record Office would justify years of study. The Tanner manuscripts in the Bodleian Library include a unique store of seventeenth-century Norfolk material, which I have used extensively but have by no means exhausted. The British Museum also contains material which deserves examination in greater detail than I have been able to achieve. Uncertain health and other circumstances have somewhat limited my opportunities for research, and the book was planned from the start with these limitations in mind.

Certain aspects of the Civil War have already been treated in some of my earlier books—four chapters of *A Norfolk Gallery* (1948), two chapters of *Norfolk Assembly* (1957), several essays in *Forty Norfolk Essays* (1961). A good deal of this material is now reproduced, sometimes in the same words; for when a writer has done his best to narrate an event or to describe a human being, he seldom prefers a different choice of words thereafter. The descriptions of the King's journey through Norfolk in Chapter XV, and of the Royalist riot in Norwich in Chapter XVI, have been taken almost in their entirety from *A Norfolk Gallery* and *Norfolk Assembly* respectively.

My debt to the writings of several living historians is acknowledged in the bibliography; and certain friends, with whom I have discussed various aspects of this book, will recognize their influence upon it. A special word of gratitude is due to Dr. Bertram Schofield for his edition of the letters of Thomas Knyvett, the most valuable historical discovery relating to seventeenth-century Norfolk that has appeared for many years.

My principal manuscript sources have been the Bodleian Library, the Department of Manuscripts at the British Museum, and the Norfolk and Norwich Joint Record Office. I wish to express my sincere gratitude to these institutions; and in thanking their officials for much valued help, I would especially mention Dr. W. O Hassall at the Bodleian and Miss J. M. Kennedy at Norwich. For the use of unpublished manuscripts my thanks are also due to the Earl of Leicester and to Marguerite, Lady Hastings. To Lady Hastings I am further indebted for permission ro reproduce the splendid portrait of Sir Jacob Astley; and for the use of other portraits my thanks are due to Mr Bryan Hall, the National Portrait Gallery, Norwich Castle Museum, the Corporation of King's Lynn, and the Master and Fellows of Pembroke College, Cambridge. Mr. Norman Scarfe has helped me with kindness and authority on several matters connected with Suffolk. Mr. D. W. Boorman has allowed me to read and quote from the unpublished thesis to which reference is made in the bibliography. On particular points I have had assistance from the Rev. R. S. C. Baily, Mr. A. L. Bedingfeld, Dr. Alan Everitt, Mr. Richard Martineau, Miss Sophia Mottram, the Rev. H. J. Paine, and the late Eric Pursehouse. Finally Miss E. F. Herbert has typed the book with unfailing patience and skill.

Felbrigg Hall
Norwich   R.W.K.-C.
November 1968

Contents

Contents

Illustrations

As is often the case in the field of seventeenth-century portraiture, there must be a measure of uncertainty regarding some of the above attributions.

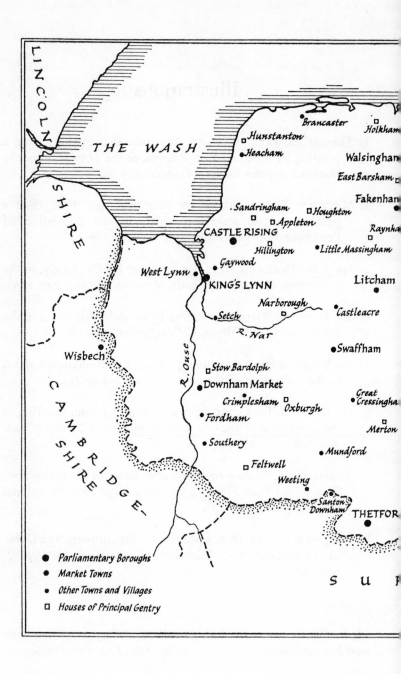

LINCOLN SHIRE

THE WASH

Brancaster

Holkham

Hunstanton

Walsingham

Heacham

East Barsham

Fakenham

Sandringham

Houghton

Appleton

Raynham

CASTLE RISING

Little Massingham

Hillington

Gaywood

West Lynn

Litcham

KING'S LYNN

Narborough

Castleacre

Setch

R. Nar

SHIRE

Wisbech

Swaffham

Stow Bardolph

Downham Market

Great
Cressingham

Crimplesham

Oxburgh

R. Ouse

Fordham

Merton

CAMBRIDGE-

Southery

Mundford

Feltwell

SHIRE

Weeting

Santon
Downham

THETFORD

● Parliamentary Boroughs
● Market Towns
• Other Towns and Villages
□ Houses of Principal Gentry

S U F

ffkey
Blakeney
Saxlingham
Holt
Baconsthorpe
Felbrigg
Cromer
Overstrand
Barningham Norwood
Melton Constable
Barningham Town
Aldborough
Wolterton
Swafield
ursford
Mannington
Erpingham
North Walsham
Heydon
Blickling
Foulsham
Sall
Aylsham
Burgh-next-Aylsham
Oxnead
Reepham
Hevingham
R. Wensum
Swannington
Potter Heigham
R. Bure
Ludham
Elsing
Horsham St Faith
East Dereham
Honingham
Costessey
NORWICH
Sprowston
South Walsham
R. Yare
Thorpe
Blofield
Kimberley
GREAT YARMOUTH
Hingham
Ketteringham
Little Ellingham
Wymondham
Loddon
Ashwellthorpe
Raveningham
Somerleyton
Attleborough
Kirby Cane
Stockton
Lowestoft
Tibenham
R. Waveney
Quidenham
Earsham
Beccles
East Harling
Gissing
Alburgh
Bungay
Kenninghall
Redenhall
West Harling
Harleston
ddlesworth
Diss
Dickleburgh

F   O   L   K

0   5   10   15
Miles

CHAPTER I

Introductory

I

The structure of Norfolk early in the seventeenth century was much as it remains today—a large industrial city, two important seaports, and a vast agricultural countryside. It was, as it still is, an exceptionally self-contained province, isolated by natural boundaries of river and breckland and fen, and surrounded northwards and eastwards by the sea.

Norwich, in population and wealth, was probably the third city in the land.[1] It had long been the greatest centre of the textile trade in all England. During the previous century a large influx of refugees from Spanish persecution in the Low Countries— Dutch, Flemings and Walloons—had brought new techniques and new prosperity to the city. The great Norman castle on its high mound looked down on a mass of crowded roofs, interspersed with many trees and the towers of thirty-six churches, with the river busy with craft and the Cathedral standing aloof in its close. The walls and gates were complete and defensible. The people took great pride in their gardens, and here again the Dutch had given the lead, 'bringing hither with them not only their profitable crafts, but pleasurable curiosities'. Norwich was, in fact, 'either a city in an orchard, or an orchard in a city, so equally are houses and trees blended in it, so that the pleasure of the country, and populousness of the city, meet here together'.[2]

Some twenty miles away was Great Yarmouth, the seaport for Norwich, the base of much coastwise and seagoing traffic, and the headquarters of a vast fishing trade. For centuries the herring had remained the economic mainstay of the town, and three silver herrings formed its earliest coat-of-arms. It was ruled by an

[1] Possibly at this time it ranked second only to London (Hoskins, *Local History in England*, 174–8).
[2] Fuller, *Worthies*, ii, 274.

oligarchy of rich merchants, with two bailiffs instead of a mayor at the head of the corporation; and it firmly maintained its traditional rights against the Cinque Ports and all other rivals. Remotely placed on its long and narrow spit of sand, at the easternmost point of England, its size and opulence invariably surprised the newcomer. Travellers down the winding river, or along the bleak flat road from Norwich, were unprepared for the fine houses, the spacious market-place, the unending quay, the crowded population in the 'rows', the largest parish church in the land. King Charles II, later in the century, was to exclaim on his only visit that 'he did not think he had had such a place in his dominions'.

On the opposite side of the county, at the point where the river Ouse flows into the Wash, lay King's Lynn—a seaport of the same antiquity as Yarmouth, but smaller, less self-contained, very much the capital and the meeting-place of the western hundreds of Norfolk. It had an extensive sea-borne trade, and served a wide area of the surrounding countryside; but its greatest days were to come in the second half of the century. Like Yarmouth it was governed by a group of leading merchants, but was more susceptible to the influence of the neighbouring gentry.

Norwich, Yarmouth and Lynn were borough towns, each returning two members to Parliament. So was Thetford, at the south-west extremity of the county. It was now small and decayed, retaining scarcely a vestige of its importance in earlier centuries; but it was still the only assize town besides Norwich, and remained so, to the general inconvenience, for two centuries to come. An even smaller borough was Castle Rising, four miles north of Lynn. It consisted of a few cottages scattered round the huge ruinous castle of the Howards; but its handful of voters returned the same number of members as the county of Norfolk or the city of Norwich.

Along the coast there was a string of little seaports. Those perched on the cliffs, such as Cromer and Sheringham, built jetties which were frequently washed away by the scouring tides. Cley and Wiveton and Blakeney, and other villages further to the west, possessed havens protected by the shingle-banks. Some of them were soon to be threatened by speculators who saw more profit in well-drained marshland than in ventures on the sea. All were engaged in the coastwise import of Newcastle coals and Sussex timber, or the import from across the sea of Flemish bricks and salt and barrel-staves. They exported the corn and malt of their hinterland, cloths woven on village looms, fish and butter and coney-skins and other local produce. Heavy goods from London invariably reached Norfolk by sea.[3]

Scattered over the countryside were some thirty market-towns and more than six hundred villages.[4] Many of these market-towns —Aylsham, Swaffham, East Dereham, Fakenham, North Walsham, Wymondham, Diss—still act as centres of local life: others have become reduced in population and importance, and are no more than large villages. Each market-town was the metropolis of its neighbourhood, and many people never went farther afield throughout their lives. Within the borders of the county, the fourth largest in the realm, there was a remarkable diversity of soil and cultivation. 'All England may be carved out of Norfolk', wrote Thomas Fuller. 'Here are fens and heaths, and light and deep, and sand and clay-ground, and meadows and pasture, and arable and woody . . . so grateful is this shire with the variety thereof'. The richest land, growing impressive crops of barley and wheat, lay at the eastern and western extremities, in the Flegg hundreds and in Marshland. Other important corn-growing areas lay around Fakenham and Walsingham, and between Dereham and Swaffham. There had already been a certain amount of enclosure; but in most villages the open-field system of cultivation, with its innumerable strips and their attendant disadvantages, continued to be practised. Sheep were folded everywhere, the golden hoof steadily enriching the land, the wool-clip going off to the looms in towns and villages, or in consignments further afield. On the areas of enclosed pasture cattle were reared, with dairying and cheese-making on a considerable scale. Great droves of cattle were annually brought down from the north, from Scotland and Yorkshire, to be sold at the fairs at Hempton and St. Faith's, and subsequently fattened on the rich meadows and marshes. Root and clover crops, although introduced earlier than is generally

---

[3] *Stiffkey Papers*, 1-8. N.R.S. viii, 17-37.

[4] Camden, *Britannia* (1607), 346, gives 27 market-towns and 625 villages. There seem to have been 35 places which at various times during the 16th and 17th centuries were regarded as market-towns (*Agrarian History of England and Wales*, Cambridge, 1967, iv, 474-5).

supposed, were still some decades away. Coney-warrens were carefully managed on the lighter soils, and decoys for wildfowl on the Broads.[5]

The interests of the countryside were not wholly agricultural, since the textile industry had spread from the towns into the remotest villages. There were occasional groups of weavers dwelling among the farmers and farm workers. But the spinning-wheel was more usual than the loom, and wives and daughters would be busy with rock and distaff while their menfolk worked in the fields. It was still so at the very end of the century, when Celia Fiennes made her journey through Norfolk. 'The ordinary people . . . knit much and spin', she noticed soon after she had crossed the Waveney: 'some with the rock and fuseau as the French does, others at their wheels out in the streets and lanes as one passes'. It was the same as she journeyed from Wymondham to Attleborough, 'through lanes where you meet the ordinary people knitting four or five in a company under the hedges'; and as far as Thetford she still found 'the country full of spinners and knitters'.[6]

2

Within this relatively isolated province, this rather closed society, certain marked characteristics had developed. The Norfolk man, gentle or simple, tended to be dour, stubborn, fond of argument and litigation, strongly Puritan in his religious views. The type was far from universal, as this book will show; but it was a type to which the majority in all classes to some degree conformed.

The litigiousness of Norfolk people was proverbial, and was emphasized by contemporary writers to the point of boredom. According to Camden the county 'is at present, and always has

[5] For an excellent account of the agriculture of East Anglia during the early seventeenth century, see Joan Thirsk in *Agrarian History of England and Wales* (Cambridge, 1967), iv. 40–9. The most valuable contemporary source is the account, almost certainly by John Norden, in *The Chorography of Norfolk*, ed. C. M. Hood (Norwich, 1938). See also Fuller, *Worthies*, ii, 246; and (for some details of the droves from the north) my *Felbrigg: The Story of a House* (1962), 37.

[6] *Journeys of Celia Fiennes* (ed. Morris), 146, 150. Such passages recall *Twelfth Night*—'the spinsters and the knitters in the sun'—although the allusion to a stage-play might not have pleased the Puritanically-minded Miss Fiennes.

been reputed, the most fruitful nursery of lawyers; and even among the common people you shall meet many who . . . if they have no just quarrel, are able to raise it out of the very quirks and niceties of the law'.[7] These same people, said Fuller, 'will enter an action for their neighbour's horse but looking over their hedge'.[8] Aubrey had heard much the same of them: 'they are good clear wits, subtle, and the most litigious of England: they carry Littleton's Tenures at the plough tail.'[9] And everyone quoted the proverb, 'Norfolk wiles many a man beguiles.'

These litigious country folk could quote familiar examples of the rewards the law could bring. Norfolk had as yet produced no greater national figure than Sir Edward Coke. Bacon, Hobart, Gawdy, Yelverton were names of power throughout East Anglia. All their great fortunes, their widespread manors, their stately houses were founded on the practice of the law. The lesson was not lost on their humbler neighbours.

The ideas of the Reformation had met with a prompt and enthusiastic reception in East Anglia, and had spread rapidly amongst all classes. The Marian reaction entirely failed to check them. In the diocese of Norwich more men and women died in the flames for their faith than in any other save London and Canterbury. During Elizabeth's reign Protestant sentiment was strengthened by the refugees from the Low Countries, with their horrifying stories of torture and persecution. This climate of opinion was favourable to the development of extremist sects—Anabaptists, Brownists, the Family of Love. Robert Browne himself lived for some years first at Aylsham and then in Norwich, and drew a large following in both places. These separatist elements never became deeply rooted in Norfolk; but they continued to exist, and were to make their contribution to the more militant aspects of seventeenth-century Puritanism.

The Puritan movement, in the stricter sense of the term, was gathering strength in Norfolk throughout the reign of Elizabeth. Its development was not spectacular; but its ministers formed a compact and single-minded body, determined to advance their cause by every means in their power. The first of the Elizabethan

---

[7] Camden, *Britannic* (1695 ed.), 383.
[8] Fuller, *Worthies*, ii, 247.
[9] Aubrey, *History of Wiltshire* (1847), 12.

Bishops of Norwich, John Parkhurst, was well disposed towards them—so favourable, indeed, that he more than once incurred the personal displeasure of the Queen. They had sympathisers among the leading gentry and the principal merchants in the towns. They professed their desire to remain within the Church, and their abhorrence of 'Papists and other heretics, and the late schismatics of the faction of Browne'; but they were rigid in their Calvinist opinions, and on many points of doctrine and observance they refused to yield to higher authority.[10] Above all they stressed the importance of preaching, the constant exposition of the word of God, as against those ceremonies which savoured of the Mass and the iniquities of Popery.

In 1596 the Puritan leaders had drawn up lists of the clergy in eleven counties, mainly in order to prove the unfitness for the ministry of the vast majority of their brethren in Christ. Norfolk was one of the counties thus dealt with: and the investigators concluded that it contained 'parishes served by unfit ministers not able to preach above 400 at the least'. Virtually every clergyman in the list was recorded as 'no preacher'; and many more were also stigmatized as ignorant, incontinent, drunken, idiotic or infamous. Others again were 'old mass priests', or 'a conjuror suspected', or 'consumed by carding, dicing and gaming'. The rector of Bawburgh was 'a great hunter', the vicar of East Harling 'an old ruffian', the rector of Carleton and Claxton had been 'a painter and an interlude player'.[11] It is a self-righteous and ill-tempered document. On the question of preaching, in particular, it must always be remembered that no clergyman might preach without a licence from his Bishop; and these licences were granted sparingly and after due examination. Nevertheless the propaganda of the Puritans should not be lightly dismissed. There were many shortcomings in the Church which Elizabeth and her Archbishops had striven to establish and consolidate during those years.

On the opposite flank of the Church, the Catholics were by no means a negligible force. Their strength in East Anglia lay mainly among the gentry: there were few Catholics, as Father John Gerard found, in the ranks of 'the ordinary people, for they are unable to live in peace, surrounded as they are by most fierce

[10] *The Seconde Parte of a Register* (ed. Peel), i, 143–6, 157–60, 223–5, 244.
[11] Ibid., ii, 146–56.

Protestants'.[12] Several families of note had remained steadfast to
the old faith, and others were 'Church Papists', extremely lukewarm in their Protestant allegiance.[13] Furthermore, new converts
were coming forward. The arguments of the counter-Reformation
appealed strongly to intelligent young men at the Universities and
the Inns of Court.

The most striking example of this trend occurred in the Walpole
family, and almost led to its extinction. In the sixteenth century
there were two main branches of the Walpoles, at Houghton and
at Anmer. Henry Walpole, the eldest son of the Anmer house, had
been one of a circle of Catholic-minded friends at Peterhouse and
at Gray's Inn. He witnessed the execution of Edmund Campion,
some of whose blood spurted upon his clothes. This was for him
a clear indication of his own path. He went abroad, was admitted
to the Society of Jesus, was sent in due course to England, captured almost immediately, tortured atrociously in the Tower and
finally executed in 1595. Three of his brothers likewise became
Jesuits: so did his cousin Edward, the heir of Houghton. The
Anmer house was extinguished; and the same fate would have
befallen the Houghton branch had not Edward's brother Calibut,
alone of his entire generation, remained a Protestant.[14] It was due
to Calibut, who married and continued the line, that the Walpole
achievements of the eighteenth century in politics and in letters,
these achievements still recalled to our minds by the survival of
Houghton and Wolterton and Strawberry Hill, ever occurred at all.

Another Jesuit from Norfolk who died for his faith was the
poet Robert Southwell. His family had done well out of the
dissolution of the monasteries, and he himself was born in a
former priory, Horsham St. Faith's near Norwich.[15] But he was
given a Catholic education abroad, after which his career ran
parallel to Henry Walpole's—the return on the English mission, capture, imprisonment, torture, death. When Gerard, a
few years later, made his breath-taking escape from the Tower,
he first commended himself 'especially to Father Southwell,
who was imprisoned near here until he was taken out to

[12] Gerard, 33.
[13] N.A., xxxii, 27–46.
[14] The story of the Catholic Walpoles was admirably told by Augustus Jessopp in
One Generation of a Norfolk House (1878).
[15] *The Book of Robert Southwell*, ed. C. M. Hood (1926), 6–7.

martyrdom, and to Father Walpole and to all our martyrs'.[16]

Gerard's narrative gives a vivid impression of the Catholic network in East Anglia at the close of the sixteenth century. He was landed near Happisburgh at the commencement of his mission, and made his way, after various adventures, to the house of Edward Yelverton at Grimston on the other side of the county. Here he stayed for several months, living with his Catholic hosts in the guise of a gentleman of moderate fortune and sporting inclinations, his knowledge of hunting and falconry enabling him to mix with the local Protestant gentry without incurring suspicion. During these months he made some spectacular conversions, and restored many of the lapsed and lukewarm to the duties of their religion.[17]

Between these two extremes of Puritan and Papist, a succession of Bishops of Norwich had endeavoured to control their large and difficult diocese. Instructions on a wide range of matters, secular and ecclesiastical, came down from the Privy Council and the Archbishops, and were carried out with varying efficiency. None of these bishops were men of great ability, none possessed the spiritual gifts which might have won them a substantial measure of love and obedience from their clergy and people. On the other hand, the path of an Elizabethan or Jacobean bishop was not an easy one, especially in an impoverished see such as Norwich. Some degree of episcopal state had to be observed; hospitality was expected; a married man was obliged to make provision for his family; there were bound to be unseemly wrangles about leases and dilapidations. Freake, Scambler, Redman, Jegon—they have all suffered in reputation from aggrieved or hostile witnesses. With all their faults, they managed to hold together the organization of the Church within their diocese, and gradually but perceptibly to raise the standard of learning and conduct among their clergy.[18] By the early years of the

[16] Gerard, 135.

[17] Ibid., 9–23.

[18] Augustus Jessopp (*Diocesan History of Norwich*, 175) described these bishops as men 'whom it is impossible to think of with veneration'. Perhaps so; but recent research suggests that under them the affairs of the diocese were conducted reasonably well. See *Bishop Redman's Visitation*, 1597, ed. J. F. Williams (N.R.S., 1946), especially the editor's introduction and his conclusions on pages 27–8; and *The Registrum Vagum of Antony Harison*, ed. T. F. Barton (N.R.S., 2 vols., 1963–4). Harison was secretary to Bishop Jegon.

seventeenth century, in Norfolk as elsewhere, the Church of England was firmly established, with the greater number of its ministers contentedly treading their middle path, equally averse from Calvinism and Popery.

Nevertheless, and more especially amongst the laity of every class, there persisted a bias in the Puritan direction. The dread of Catholicism was ineradicable. The plots against Elizabeth, the massacre of Saint Bartholomew, the Spanish Armada, the Gunpowder Treason had only served to enhance the memory of the Marian flames. Several important families among the gentry were openly Puritan in their sympathies. Even the Anglican-minded gentry were disposed to regard their Catholic neighbours with suspicion, no matter how loyal they might appear and how acceptable in private intercourse. And they looked with misgiving upon any ceremony or usage that might bear the least suggestion of a return to Popery.

The churches of East Anglia, in town and countryside, bore many traces of the Reformation of the previous century. Almost everywhere the rood had gone, the crucified figure above the screen, with its attendant Virgin and Saint John. The vestments had gone, the copes and chasubles of damask and silk and sarcenet, and the richly embroidered altar-cloths. The altar-plate had gone; the gilt and silver chalices and patens with their Popish emblems had been replaced in every parish by a simple cup and cover. The eager commissioners had impounded almost everything of metal, precious or otherwise—crosses and lamps and candlesticks, censers and pixes, the little sanctus bells and most of the greater bells in the towers.[19] The illuminated service-books, missals and psalters and graduals, had of course long since vanished. There was whitewash over the painted walls, with texts replacing the familiar figures, Saint Christopher bearing the holy child through the river, the three young huntsmen confronted by the grinning skeletons in the wood.[20] Yet much remained still to affront Puritan eyes—saints and angels in roofs and screens, crucifixes and crosses, inscriptions with prayers for the souls of the

[19] H. B. Walters, *Inventories of Norfolk Church Goods* (1552), N.A. xxvi, 245-70, and in several subsequent volumes.

[20] The theme of *Les Trois Vifs et les Trois Morts* was frequent in Norfolk churches, and is still to be seen, in company with Saint Christopher, at Wickhampton, Paston and Seething.

dead, a wealth of painted glass. All these things were relics of Popery; and those clerics who sought to maintain them, or to enhance the beauty and dignity of their services in any way, were stigmatized as Papists too.

3

Norfolk was a county with slender connections with the Court. The influence of its gentry was not overshadowed by the presence of any resident peer. The Howards, Dukes of Norfolk, had been in eclipse, and their dukedom in abeyance, since the execution of the fourth Duke in 1572. They still owned much land around their mansion at Kenninghall, in the extreme south of the county, besides a good deal of property in other areas. They controlled the two little boroughs of Thetford and Castle Rising. Their Palace in Norwich was an imposing structure, described by Fuller as the greatest house he had seen in a city outside London.[21] But they disposed of little effective power in Norfolk until their gradual return to favour under James I. In 1605 the King appointed the fourth Duke's brother, Henry Howard Earl of Northampton, as Lord Lieutenant of Norfolk; and when he died in 1614 his great-nephew, the famous collector and connoisseur Thomas Howard Earl of Arundel, was chosen to succeed him. But their personal appearances in the county were rare; and they exercised their authority by a somewhat remote control.

No other peer had a residence or any substantial property in Norfolk. The local affairs of the county were in the hands of its gentry, the small group of Deputy Lieutenants and the larger but still carefully selected body of Justices of the Peace. They faithfully carried out the behests of the Privy Council, and looked after their own neighbourhoods responsibly and well. The papers of Sir Nathaniel Bacon of Stiffkey provide a complete and most valuable picture of the multifarious duties of a conscientious Justice of the Peace early in the seventeenth century. As a leading figure in the county, Sir Nathaniel was often employed on special commissions to deal with a wide variety of civil and ecclesiastical matters. Living on the coast and within easy reach of the north Norfolk

[21] Fuller, *Worthies*, ii, 275.

ports, his services were constantly required in connection with the maintenance of embankments and piers, the export of corn and wool, the impressment of seamen, the good order of the beacons. But he also undertook his full share of the routine work that fell to the lot of every Justice—the supervision of the local constables and overseers, the administration of the laws affecting the poor, the licencing of alehouses, the taking of endless depositions on every kind of offence and dispute.[22]

Some of the older mansions in the county, secluded within their moats, were already growing venerable. The lovely brickwork of Oxburgh, and the stages of its soaring gate-tower, were already mellowed by a century and a half of wind and sunshine. There was lichen on the carstone of Hunstanton and the flint of Manning-ton. Newer manor-houses, Tudor and Jacobean, rose all over the countryside, with their stepped or shaped gables, elaborate chimneys, mullioned windows, and above the entrances the arms or intertwined initials of their builders. Heydon, Barningham, Felbrigg are amongst those which survive with little external alteration. The material was invariably the local brick or flint or a patterned combination of the two, with stone dressings imported by sea or river from the nearest counties where stone abounded.

Of the greater houses, some have long since vanished. Not a trace remains of the palace of the Howards in Norwich, or of their splendid mansion at Kenninghall. Baconsthorpe, where the Hey-dons maintained high state and hospitality through most of the Tudor era, is a fragmentary shell. One wing is left of Oxnead, the finest of all the Paston houses; the foundations of the rest, and the terraced gardens sloping down to the little river, are ghosts beneath the turf and the meadow-grass. Blickling survives, one of the supreme examples of Jacobean architecture, the last master-piece of the designer of Hatfield, Robert Lyminge, who died in 1628 while the work was in its final stages, and was buried in the church nearby. The completion of Blickling coincided with the commencement of Raynham, where a novel and sophisticated classicism, already favoured in the circles of the Court, was first introduced into Norfolk. Raynham was long attributed to Inigo

---

[22] *Stiffkey Papers*, ed. H. W. Saunders (Camden Society, 1915). *Supplementary Stiffkey Papers*, ed. F. W. Brooks (Camden Society, 1936).

Jones; and parts of it may well have been the work of John Webb or some other disciple of the King's great architect.[23]

Apart from the Pastons at Oxnead, the gentry of East Anglia were not conspicuous patrons of the arts, even though they produced in Sir Nathaniel Bacon of Culford in Suffolk an amateur painter of marked distinction. Their taste in painting was confined to portraiture, or perhaps to an occasional flower-piece or a 'drollery' brought back from a visit to the Low Countries. Religious art for most of them had a disturbing savour of Popery. Landscape-painting meant those meticulous and now invaluable representations of their family houses, surrounded by knot-gardens and bowling-greens, peopled with stiff little groups of visitors and retainers. Monumental sculpture, on the other hand, was lavishly patronised. The leading sculptor of the day, Nicholas Stone, was employed by several families, and repeatedly by the Pastons and the Cokes. One of Stone's ablest assistants, John Hargrave, was a son of the parson of Blickling, and was buried there after his early death. He carved the noble effigy of Sir Edward Coke in Tittleshall Church. For this he received £15, a somewhat meagre sum in comparison with the £400 that Stone was paid for the whole monument.[24]

Of all the arts, it was music that most appealed to these country gentlemen. The Puritan prejudice against organ-music in churches did not extend to the melody of viols and lutes in the privacy of their own houses. The composer John Jenkins, for example, was domiciled for the whole of his long life in the households of East Anglian squires—the L'Estranges at Hunstanton, the Norths at Kirtling, the Wodehouses at Kimberley—and was equally welcome to Royalist and Puritan masters.[25] The library of a Norfolk gentleman, Edward Paston of Appleton, has lately been made the subject of study. It was remarkably rich in lute-books and song-books, printed and manuscript, the works of Byrd and Lassus and Ferrabosco. All these volumes, together with many other books in a variety of languages, were carefully particularized in his will and bequeathed to his several sons. Edward Paston was a Catholic;

[23] Lees-Milne, *The Age of Inigo Jones* (1953), 111–15. Hill and Cornforth, *English Country Houses: Caroline* (1966), 57–60.

[24] *Notebook and Account Book of Nicholas Stone*, ed. W. L. Spiers (Walpole Society, 1919), 75, 122. M.I. in Blickling Church.

[25] *Lives of the Norths*, iii, 78–80.

but in his love of music, at least, he probably did not differ greatly from his Protestant neighbours.[26]

4

There were many links between the gentry of Norfolk and the citizens of Norwich, Yarmouth and Lynn. Most of the gentry sent their sons to the big grammar schools in those towns, or to the lesser schools which existed in many of the market-towns. There they mixed on equal terms with the sons of merchants, shopkeepers and artisans. Such contacts often persisted in later life. As in every age of English history, the townsman liked to invest a portion of his profits in land, and sometimes purchased or founded an estate. The gentleman was often glad to marry his son to the merchant's daughter, and to establish his younger boys in trade. Class distinctions were recognized, but they allowed for a great deal of intercourse and familiarity. Reference will be made in later chapters to the collection of *Merry Passages and Jests*, compiled by Sir Nicholas L'Estrange, a work which reveals the extent to which gentleman and cleric, lawyer and doctor, shopkeeper and yeoman mingled and rubbed shoulders in Jacobean and Caroline Norfolk.[27]

Norwich was a community with a deep sense of civic pride, very conscious of its ancient rights, in no way dependent on the gentry of the county or under their influence. There was a famous incident in 1617 when Sir Augustine Palgrave of North Barningham, the High Sheriff, sought to mislead the judges of assize on a question of precedence. This attempt at encroachment, on the part of the county, was 'very discreetly and stoutly' resisted by John Mingay, apothecary and Mayor. It ended with the High Sheriff, standing bare-headed, receiving a public reprimand from the judges, with the victorious mayor seated beside them.[28] It will be seen in later chapters that the merchants of Norwich were by no means all Puritan and Parliamentarian in their inclinations. The

[26] Philip Brett, *A Norfolk Gentleman and his Musical Collection*, in Transactions of the Cambridge Bibliographical Society, iv, I (1964), 51–69.

[27] B. M. Harley MS. 6395. A selection was printed in *Anecdotes and Traditions*, ed. W. J. Thoms (Camden Society, 1839).

[28] Blomefield, iii, 367.

Royalists among them were in a minority, but that minority was far from negligible.

Below the principal merchants in the towns came a host of shopkeepers, tradesmen, artisans. Below the gentry in the countryside came the yeomanry. Robert Reyce, the Suffolk commentator, remarked how the yeomen, by virtue of their thrift and the advantages of an obscure station, were able to rise and prosper. Their 'continual under-living, saving, and the immunities from the costly charge of these unfaithful times, do make them so to grow with the wealth of this world, that whilst many of the better sort . . . do suffer an utter declination, these only do arise, and do lay such strong, sure, and deep foundations that from thence in time are derived many noble and worthy families.'[29] The process has been at work all through English history, but never more noticeably than in the first half of the seventeenth century.

As for the mass of the population, the workers in the fields, the wrights and smiths in the villages, the weavers and dyers and fullers in the towns, the seamen and fishermen and fowlers, they have left little memorial of their lives and their toil. 'They took their wages and are dead'; and seldom, outside the pages of parish registers and parish accounts, can even their names be recovered. Their lives were harsh and often brief, with hardship and poverty never far away. But they played their part in the communal life of their parish, whether in country or town, a life intimately bound up with the church at which they worshipped. Their horizon was narrow, and in their alehouse discussions it may well be that less was said about affairs of state than of matters of religion. But the church was central to their lives, and what the parson said and did there was the subject of endless interest and speculation. Many of them, probably a substantial majority, were sympathetic to the Puritan point of view; and from their ranks the troops of the Eastern Association were to be recruited. Nevertheless the only spontaneous proletarian uprising that will be recorded in this book was in support not of the Parliament but of the King.

[29] Robert Reyce, *The Breviary of Suffolk*, ed. Lord Francis Hervey (1902), 58.

CHAPTER II

The Lord Lieutenant and the Gentry

I

In the seventeenth century the most important personage in every county was the Lord Lieutenant. In earlier times the armed forces of the shire had been under the control of the High Sheriff during his year of office. But in the reign of Edward VI it was thought expedient to create the office of Lord Lieutenant, the duration of which was at the sovereign's pleasure, but normally for life. The Lords Lieutenant replaced the Sheriffs at the head of the local forces, and became responsible for the defence of their county against invasion or rebellion. They appointed their own Deputy Lieutenants, to whom the organization and training of the militia was entrusted, and who exercised considerable influence in county affairs in addition to their military duties. The Lords Lieutenant were also largely responsible for the annual choice of a High Sheriff; and they recommended suitable gentlemen for the office of Justice of the Peace, on whom the main burden of day-to-day local administration ultimately rested.

It was obviously to the public advantage that the Lord Lieutenant should be a peer with property and connections within the county over which he presided. The house of Howard, alone of the peerage, held substantial property in Norfolk; but the political unreliability of the family had disqualified them from the office during the greater part of Elizabeth's reign. In 1605, however, Henry Howard Earl of Northampton was appointed Lord Lieutenant of Norfolk. He died in 1614 and was succeeded in office by his great-nephew, Thomas Howard Earl of Arundel and Surrey.

The new Lord Lieutenant was the grandson of the fourth Duke of Norfolk, who had aspired to marry Mary, Queen of Scots, became involved in the Ridolfi plot, and was attainted and executed in 1572. He was the first of his line to be restored to the royal favour and to some portion of the family honours—at first his two earldoms, and in due course the high office of Earl Marshal. Even so, the Dukedom was withheld from him to the end of his days, despite his loyal service to two Kings.

Arundel had been brought up by his mother in the Catholic faith. His father had undergone a lifetime of imprisonment in the Tower for that faith, and the boy had never known him. Throughout his childhood years the family had lived in comparative poverty and under the shadow of disgrace; and it was only with the accession of James I that his fortunes began to mend. He recovered his alienated properties, married a rich wife, figured prominently at Court, and learnt the enjoyments of display and power. In 1615, greatly to his mother's distress, he was received into the Church of England. He brought up his own children as Protestants, and his younger son was educated for some years in the household of Bishop Harsnett at Norwich. Clarendon regarded him as wholly indifferent in matters of belief. 'He was rather thought not to be much concerned with religion, than to incline to this or that party, if any.'[1]

He was a lover and patron of the arts, a famous collector of paintings and sculpture, a brusque haughty man to his equals, with a vein of familiar kindness to humbler men. Mytens depicted him seated calm and grave in his gallery of statues; Van Dyck in armour, his hand resting on his little grandson's shoulder, and again seated with his wife examining an enormous globe. Rubens painted him several times—heads of extraordinary power, with hair and beard grandly dishevelled, for he cared little for appearances. One of his fellow-peers used to remark, 'Here comes the Earl of Arundel in his plain stuff and trunk hose, and his beard in his teeth, that looks more like a nobleman than any of us.'[2]

From 1616 onwards Arundel was a member of the Privy Council, and he held other important offices besides that of Earl Marshal. He was often sent on missions abroad, and to escort royal personages on journeys to and from this island. Clarendon remarked that he 'had little other affection for the nation and the kingdom, than as he had a great share in it, in which like the great Leviathan he might disport himself'. To some extent this may

[1] Clarendon, i, 44.
[2] Hervey, 358.

THOMAS HOWARD, EARL OF ARUNDEL AND SURREY
from a painting by Sir Peter Paul Rubens, in the possession of the
National Portrait Gallery

have been so, although Clarendon's strong personal dislike of the
Earl is never concealed.[3] But there is nothing to suggest that he
neglected that somewhat minor branch of his duties, the Lieutenancy of Norfolk. He seldom visited the county in person; but he
kept himself fully informed of all that went on there, and maintained close touch with his Deputy Lieutenants. From the later
sixteen-twenties he frequently sent his elder son down to Norfolk
as his representative, to spend a few days at Kenninghall or at the
Palace in Norwich. In 1633 this young man, who bore the title of
Lord Maltravers, was formally appointed Lord Lieutenant jointly
with his father. While sharing to the full Lord Arundel's love for
the arts, he also showed himself active and businesslike in public
affairs.

A volume has survived which contains copies of much correspondence that passed between these two Lords Lieutenant, singly
and jointly, and their Deputy Lieutenants.[4] It also includes a
number of communications between the Privy Council and the
Justices of the Peace for the county. Sir Charles Firth pronounced
that 'no single book gives so good a picture of the militia system
in the first part of the seventeenth century as this collection of
documents'. On the whole the system appears to have been func-
tioning smoothly and well. There were eight Deputy Lieutenants
at the outset of King Charles's reign—Sir John Hobart, Sir
Thomas Wodehouse, Sir Roger Townshend, Sir Charles Cornwallis, Sir Arthur Heveningham, Sir William de Grey, Sir
Anthony Drury and Sir John Hare. It is evident that Arundel had
chosen them carefully, and that they were able and conscientious
men. They did not hesitate to put their own point of view, to
raise objections and offer suggestions for Arundel's consideration.
He was equally ready to listen. It was an arduous business to levy
and muster some five thousand men, provide them with weapons,
train and exercise them—to do all that was requisite, in the King's
words to his Council, 'for the settling of a perfect militia'. The
militia was far from reaching perfection, in Norfolk as elsewhere;
but by consultation and goodwill much was achieved.

[3] Clarendon, i, 44.
[4] *State Papers relating to Musters, Beacons, Ship Money, etc., from 1626 chiefly to the
beginning of the Civil War*, ed. Walter Rye, with a preface by C. H. Firth (Norwich,
1907).

Below the Deputy Lieutenants were the captains of the companies of foot raised in each hundred, and the captains of the troops of horse, in each of which the horsemen of three or four hundreds were joined together. The lists of the captains contained many names of men who were to be bitterly opposed in the coming war—Sir Thomas Wodehouse, Sir Hamon L'Estrange, Sir John Holland, Thomas Knyvett, William Heveningham, John Potts. But at present they were all united in the King's service, faithfully carrying out the behests of the King's Lieutenant. Arundel took great pains over the appointment of these officers; and when one of them asked to be relieved of his duties on grounds of ill-health, he sent the papers, including a doctor's certificate, down to Norfolk for the Deputy Lieutenants to consider the case and report their conclusions to him.[5]

The only note of disharmony in the smooth working of the militia, if we may judge from this volume, was provided by Sir John Hobart. In 1627 three of his fellow Deputy Lieutenants had to take him to task, in a strongly worded letter, for saying in public that there had been injustice and corruption over the impressment of soldiers at Lynn. They felt 'an extraordinary resentment to have been in so proclamatory manner traduced, especially by the report of you our associate in the Lieutenancy, our countryman, our neighbour, and to some of us in the esteem of a dear and professed friend, whereby in our county our reputation receives so great a blemish, and by consequence the King's future services to be executed by us no small detriment, when in the eyes and opinions of the people our faith and sincerity shall be made so doubtful, and by consequence our authority with them so much diminished'.[6] It is not known whether Sir John climbed down. It would have been unlike him to do so.

2

An immense amount has been written about the seventeenth-century gentry, and historians have arrived at widely different conclusions as to their opinions and their motives. So far as

[5] Ibid., 6–7, 76, 116–7, 129.
[6] Ibid., 102–3.

Norfolk is concerned, it is impossible to generalize about them as a class. It may indeed be a mistake to describe a body with so many gradations as a class at all. They were a large and varied company, professing every shade of opinion, differing greatly in fortune and circumstance. They ranged from families with centuries of history to families which had but lately risen from the status of yeomen. Their ranks included fervent Catholics such as the Bedingfelds, and rigorous Puritans such as the Hobarts. Some of them, for example the Pastons, were at the zenith of their fortunes. Others, like the Heydons and Knyvetts, had advanced far into decline. Some were avid purchasers of land, eager graspers at local power. Others were without ambition; in the words of one of them, 'they loved the shade'.

These diverse elements were connected by an intricate network of marriage and cousinship. Except among the grandest gentry, and of course the closed circle of the Catholics, wives were seldom sought far afield. In an age, moreover, when daughters were many and their fortunes often small, matches between the varying grades of gentry, between old families and new, between landowner and citizen, were by no means infrequent. In consequence almost everyone was related in some degree to everyone else, and a connection three or four generations back was sufficient for a family to 'call cousins'. It would be easy to pursue these ramifications all over East Anglia, and to trace family relationships between the most committed Royalists and the most obdurate Puritans. But relationship need not be taken to imply agreement. Bitter quarrels between kinsmen and within families have occurred in every century. This widespread cousinship did little to prevent personal animosities or political rivalries, and should never be emphasized in any consideration of the seventeenth-century gentry.

To illustrate the diversity of which I have spoken, the profound differences within the ranks of their class, it may be well to devote a few pages to four of the leading gentlemen of the county. All four were Deputy Lieutenants or Captains of Militia under Lord Arundel during the sixteen-thirties. All were living during the Civil War years and will play some part later in this narrative. Two of them, Sir Thomas Wodehouse and Sir John Hobart, became supporters of the Parliament; two, Sir Hamon L'Estrange and Sir William Paston, adhered to the King.

The Wodehouses had been seated at Kimberley since the fifteenth century, and for two hundred years had figured prominently in Norfolk affairs. Sir Thomas Wodehouse, the second baronet, was born in 1585, and passed his early manhood at the court of James I, where he was high in the favour and friendship of Henry Prince of Wales. After the death of that much-loved prince he withdrew to a quiet life in Norfolk, to hunting and hawking, books and music, and the composition of poetry. In that art he was by no means an adept; but his verses include the only original statement I have discovered, by any Norfolk gentleman, of his private sympathies during the sixteen-thirties.

The passage occurs in *Nocab and Calydon*, a hitherto unpublished eclogue which he addressed to his friend Sir Edmund Bacon of Redgrave in Suffolk. Nocab (Bacon in reverse) and Calydon are shepherds, and discourse in the archaic language employed by Spenser in his *Shepherd's Calendar*. Calydon, as his name suggests, purports to be a Scot, and the Spenserian jargon of the eclogue is therefore besprinkled with Scotticisms. It is a long and rambling affair, in which Calydon, the shepherd of the impoverished north, voices the complaints of his nation, while Nocab, the shepherd of the comfortable south, defends the existing order. Ostensibly Calydon is presenting the grievances of contemporary Scotland; but much that he says was the voice of Puritan and Presbyterian England as well, the voice of Sir Thomas Wodehouse. Nor should too much weight be attached to Nocab's justification of things as they were. Sir Edmund Bacon was an elderly man, several years older than Wodehouse, and did not take much part in public life; but his influence throughout the Civil War was on the side of the Parliament, and his name figured on most of the committees for Suffolk. The eclogue was, in fact, a private joke between the two friends, full of allusions which must now escape us. There may well be an undercurrent of humorous reference to the situation of one man in rugged Norfolk, the other in 'sweet and civil' Suffolk. But it would be a mistake to interpret any phrase too literally.

The poem opens with Calydon envying Nocab's happiness 'in southern vales, so free from our unrest', and Nocab somewhat complacently acknowledging God's goodness to him:

'His altars therefore daily when I rise
Shall have my Lamb, or Lauding sacrifice.'

After further dialogue, Nocab speaks of that best of shepherds,
their 'great Pastor' now no more, their good King James, and
the happiness of the whole isle under his watchful care. Calydon
breaks in to eulogize those prosperous days, and to contrast them
with his present discontents. Blessed were the times, he says,

When our gude Jeamy more than twenty Mays
Did guide his flocks still in halcyon days.
Woe, woe is me! now liggs he wrapt in lead,
And Caroline there stayes all in his stead,
Ne cares to see our silly swains, ne sheep;
But sets proud Conducts o'er them to take keep,
Who with a soothing mouth and surly mind
Seek'n our zealous Gospellers to blind,
And wad imposthume with their papish quirks
The sincere discipline of our pure Kirks,
Where to high Altar-Worship they applaud
With low-Wren-loutings, and loud-organ-Laud.
Then add they quibbles to our books of prayer
With oaths and articles of Romish air.
They als' erect Courts of Commission high
Where magpie Prelates sett in surquedry,
And as them list, cite, silence, censure, sway
Our Presbytries and elders of the lay . . .

Nacob warns him not to provoke the wrath of Caroline, their
present great pastor, and the 'stout shepherds of the southern
plain' who have subdued the Scots before and may well do so
again. Calydon retorts—

Tush, Nocab, we not dread those lubbers now;
Long calm has made them lazy as a cow.
They loll at home in ease, ne con they skill
To lead 'gainst us, gif they had hearts or will
Which siker now they want, for all does see
They suffer grievance too, as well as we;
For their gude swayns and kirkmen bid adieu
Unto Old England, and flee'n to a New.

37

> The people-commons, als' may give good-night
> To Parliament petitions of right;
> They mun give ear now to a new-taught lecture
> Of getting money by a good projecture.
> The servile law-men too feign law for clipping
> Poor shepherds' fleeces, to pay royal shipping.

Nocab again rebukes Calydon, and brings the eclogue to a close with a long speech denouncing rebellious thoughts, and enjoining loyalty and submission—

> Lo how by loyalty we still enjoy
> The fruits of fields and flocks without annoy,
> And while in peace our flocks and lambkins feed
> We sit securely piping on a reed,
> Which jolly state of ours, so safe and good,
> Accurs'd be they who'd change for broil and blood.

The speeches of Calydon touch upon all the main grievances which were afflicting so many Englishmen besides Sir Thomas Wodehouse—the long intermission of Parliament, the rule of courtiers and prelates, the Laudian injunctions on matters of religion, the imposition of Ship Money. Even Laud's henchman Matthew Wren, whose activities as Bishop of Norwich are described in a later chapter, is not forgotten—'Low-Wren-Loutings and Loud-organ-Laud'. They show how a gentleman of moderate but firmly-based Puritan views was thinking in the sixteen-thirties, and helped to explain why he acted as he did in the decade which followed.[7]

Of more recent establishment in Norfolk than the Wodehouses, the Hobarts were a family of distinguished legal stock. Their fortunes had been founded by Sir James Hobart, attorney-general and privy councillor in the reign of Henry VIII. His great-grandson, Sir Henry Hobart, himself became attorney-general in 1606, and Chief Justice of the Common Pleas seven years later. He pursued a moderate but independent line, with

---

[7] The poems of Sir Thomas Wodehouse and of his son Sir Philip (which will be quoted in a later chapter) are contained in a manuscript volume brought into the Astley family by Sir Philip's daughter Blanch, who married the younger Sir Jacob Astley in 1662. I am enabled to quote from this volume by the kind permission of Marguerite, Lady Hastings.

none of the dramatic triumphs and reverses that befell his great contemporaries Bacon and Coke, and amassed the considerable fortune which enabled him to acquire the Blickling estate. The later years of his life were devoted to the building of his fine new house at Blickling, and there he died in 1625.

It is strange that Blickling, with its richness of decoration and its air of aristocratic grandeur, should have been the centre of the anti-Court and Presbyterian party in Norfolk for the greater part of the seventeenth century. We have already seen Sir John Hobart, Sir Henry's elder son and successor, at odds with his fellow Deputy Lieutenants. He was a hot-tempered and masterful man; and although his Puritan bias did not in earlier years extend to his private life, both he and his brother Sir Miles, who inherited the family property at Intwood, were wholly out of sympathy with the Court and all that pertained to it. The family already had a political hero in a kinsman, another Sir Miles, member for Great Marlow in the Parliament of 1627-8, whose action in locking the door of the House, to prevent members leaving during the angry debate of 2 March 1629, had earned him two years' imprisonment in the Tower. Sir John Hobart had likewise sat for various boroughs in the earlier Parliaments of Charles I.

Sir John's first wife was Lady Philippa Sidney, a daughter of Sir Philip Sidney's younger brother, Robert Earl of Leicester. After her early death he married in 1621 Lady Frances Egerton, the eldest daughter of the first Earl of Bridgewater. They had one daughter, Philippa, who married her father's heir, her cousin John, the son of Sir Miles Hobart of Intwood. This second Sir John was destined to become a member of Cromwell's House of Lords, and to maintain the Blickling tradition of opposition to the Stuarts throughout the reign of Charles II. Lady Frances was a formidable personage, who played a notable part in the religious life of Norfolk for many years to come. She had been much at Court in her youthful days, and had loved revels and masques. Her brothers and her sister Alice had played leading parts in the first performance of *Comus* at Ludlow Castle. But she had been greatly influenced by her father, who 'seasoned her against Arminian principles', and by a Huguenot governess, under whose tuition she became 'a Calvinist in point of doctrine, and a Presbyterian as to discipline'.

In Norfolk she became a great sustainer of Puritan clergymen, and towards the close of her husband's life she installed the eloquent and voluminous Dr. John Collinges as their private chaplain at Blickling. After her death in 1664 he published a discourse entitled *The Excellent Woman*, based on a famous passage in the Book of Proverbs, to which he added a memoir of his patroness and a panegyric upon her virtues. From this we may learn how she converted her husband to her own Calvinistic beliefs, and taught him 'to abhor the things wherein he had formerly delighted; to inquire after, choose, be acquainted with, and to delight in those good ways of God, with which formerly he had no acquaintance, and against which (for want of a due knowledge of them) he had formerly taken up a prejudice'. She disburdened his estate of debt; she regulated his household affairs with vigilance and severity; she even stopped him from swearing. He had contracted this habit in his youth, and 'found it yet difficult wholly to leave it, and as a means in order to it enjoined his lady privily to pinch his arm, when she heard any oath slip from him, to which reproof he would ordinarily with a great deal of kindness reply, *I thank thee my dear saint*; and by this means was at length able wholly to abstain from that vice'.

In the coming troubles Sir John was to play a leading part in his county, organizing the Parliamentarian forces, active on all the committees despite increasing ill-health. As Collinges said, 'he did remarkably serve his generation'; and I do not think he exaggerated when he described Sir John as a man 'of that nobleness of temper, height of courage and spirit, that he never valued cost, nor wanted an heart to go through with any thing of the goodness and justice of which he was convinced, and to whom . . . nothing was wanting which could constitute, adorn and accomplish a brave and gallant man'.[8]

There was probably no Norfolk family in longer continuous possession of their estates than the L'Estranges of Hunstanton. They had been there since the twelfth century, and no other family rivalled their prestige in the north-west of the county and the areas bordering the Wash. Their head during the early seventeenth century was Sir Hamon L'Estrange. He was born about 1583, and was brought up under the care of his guardian and

[8] John Collinges, *Par Nobile* (1669), 3–20.

kinsman Sir Henry Spelman, the great jurist and antiquary. He
was in a sense the Royalist counterpart of the Puritan Sir Thomas
Wodehouse. He too was fond of books and liked to employ his
pen, producing 'a short discourse of Taprobane, and a far longer
of Solomon's Ophir', and later a commentary on Dr. Thomas
Browne's *Vulgar Errors* and at least one controversial pamphlet.
Like Wodehouse he was also fond of music. As has already been
mentioned, the composer John Jenkins was domiciled with the
L'Estranges at Hunstanton for many years, and died at a great
age while still occupying a similar position with the Wodehouses
at Kimberley.

Sir Hamon had been Knight of the Shire for Norfolk in the
Parliaments of 1614 and 1620, and had sat for Castle Rising in
that of 1625. In 1616 he was concerned in the arrest of the only
Catholic, so far as I know, who suffered for his faith in Norfolk.
A priest named Thomas Tunstal escaped by a rope from Wisbech
Castle, for decades a famous prison for recusants, and made his
way in disguise to the house of some Catholics not far from King's
Lynn—perhaps the Cobbes at Sandringham or the Pastons at
Appleton. The rope had 'grievously galled and wounded' his
hands; and his hosts advised him to have them dressed by their
neighbour Lady L'Estrange, who was both skilful in medicine
and charitable to the distressed. Afterwards the lady spoke to her
husband of her mysterious visitor, so superior in bearing to his
poor apparel. Sir Hamon at once concluded that he was the Popish
priest lately escaped from Wisbech, and despite his wife's entreaties
had him pursued and apprehended. He was tried at Norwich on
a charge of attempting to convert certain good Protestants to the
superstitions of Rome, and condemned to death. At his execution
Sir Hamon 'alighting off his horse, came and spoke to him in a
courteous manner, with his head uncovered, to this effect. "Well,
Mr. Tunstal, I find then you are determined to die, and I hope you
are prepared for it." "Indeed, Sir Hamon," says the holy man,
"die I must, neither do I repine at it: on the contrary, I have great
reason to rejoice that I am to die in so good a cause, and therefore
I cannot but be thankful to Sir Hamon L'Estrange, for being
chiefly instrumental in bringing me to this place. I do heartily
forgive you, Sir, and I beseech God that my guiltless blood may
not lie heavy upon you and yours." Sir Hamon thanked him, and

so departed.'[9] In years to come, in common with all adherents of the Royalist and High Church party, Sir Hamon was no doubt accused of Popish sympathies. This sad and dramatic story shows the gulf that in fact separated the Papist from the Anglican.

Sir Hamon's sons were men of the same type as himself, cultivated, articulate, musical. All three left writings of various kinds behind them. The eldest, Nicholas, assembled over the years a manuscript volume of *Merry Passages and Jests*, many of them dull and more of them dirty, which nevertheless give a most vivid impression of seventeenth-century provincial life—the gossip of the dinner-table and the family parlour, the talk at quarter sessions and at hawking parties along the cliffs and heaths of that remote corner of Norfolk. This was of course a private undertaking, and even now only a selection of Sir Nicholas's collection of anecdotes has been printed. The interests of the second brother, Hamon, were theological and historical, and he published in later years a number of works that aroused some controversy. The youngest, Roger, became one of the most prolific writers of his time. Pamphleteer, journalist, translator, incessantly embroiled in controversies, a master of vigorous and downright English, he was to continue his stormy career into the next century, and to die in extreme old age in the reign of Queen Anne.

William Paston was a considerably younger man than Wodehouse, Hobart and L'Estrange. They were all born during the last two decades of the sixteenth century, in the days of Queen Elizabeth. He was of the succeeding generation. Born in 1610, he inherited in early manhood what may well have been the richest estate in Norfolk. Over the years the wealth of his family had become proverbial. 'There was never a Paston poor, a Heydon a coward, or a Cornwallis a fool.' At the age of nineteen he married Lady Katherine Bertie, a daughter of the Earl of Lindsey. They settled at Oxnead, the finest of all the Paston properties, a noble Tudor house built on rising ground above the Bure, with gardens descending in a series of terraces to the little river.

William Paston was a lover of art and poetry, a friend and patron of writers and painters throughout his life. The great sculptor Nicholas Stone visited him in Norfolk, carved the remarkable memorials to his parents in the church at Paston,

[9] Quoted in E.A., ii, 17–23, from Challenor's *Memoirs of Missionary Priests*.

furnished him with busts for his house and statuary for his gardens. The chambers and galleries of Oxnead were filled with treasures—vessels of crystal and agate and cornelian and amber, paintings in their richly carved frames, miniatures and enamels, cupboards of gold and silver plate. And there he lived in hospitality and contentment until his wife died in childbirth after seven years of happy marriage.

The poet Ralph Knevet lamented her in a volume of elegies. Stone carved the exquisite portrait-bust which may still be seen in Oxnead church. William Paston sought to assuage his grief in a long period of travel abroad. He spent many months in Italy, and journeyed as far afield as Egypt and Palestine. Then he returned to England; and gradually the gaieties and hospitalities of Oxnead were resumed. Those were the years when King Charles was assembling his incomparable collections at Whitehall, Van Dyck painting the Queen and her court, Rubens adorning the Banqueting House, the buildings of Inigo Jones rising in city and countryside. Alone among the mansions of Norfolk, Oxnead reproduced something of the atmosphere of the Court, the refinement and luxury, the sympathy with every aspect of art. When the Civil War began, William Paston was to hope and work for some form of accommodation until the latest possible moment; but inevitably, when that moment was reached, he rallied to the side of the King.

Here, then, were four leading figures of the Norfolk gentry, comparable in wealth and estate, all of high local influence and widespread connection, two destined to support the Parliament and two the King. It is difficult to see how their opinions and their actions can have been influenced by any economic motive, or to explain their differing standpoints except as the result of their personal convictions on matters of church and state.

3

The same diversity of opinion is visible all through the ranks of the gentry, and appears to follow no pattern of any kind. It will be seen later that the majority inclined to a moderate Puritanism, and in due course supported the Parliament. But within every economic grouping and social grade, and within many family connections, there were enough of the opposite persuasion to ensure a sizeable minority.

Some families were enabled by a fortunate chance to remain neutral. The Townshends were perhaps the most nearly comparable to the Pastons in wealth and estate. For years Sir Roger Townshend had been building his grand new house at Raynham, which excelled Blickling and Oxnead both in size and architectural refinement—'the noblest pile among us', as Dr. Thomas Browne was to describe it.[10] Through his mother, the daughter of Sir Nathaniel Bacon, he was also the owner of Stiffkey Hall and the surrounding lands. But Sir Roger died in 1635; his heirs were children, too young to take any part in the war, and their estate was steered quietly through the troubled years. His eventual successor Sir Horatio was to show decided Royalist sympathies under the Commonwealth, and did much to influence opinion in Norfolk in favour of the King's return.

Amongst other prominent and long-established families, whose representatives had been included in Arundel's selected groups of Deputy Lieutenants, the de Greys of Merton were sympathetic to the Royalist cause; while William Heveningham of Ketteringham became a Parliamentarian extremist, who sat in judgment on the King and received sentence of death, presently commuted to lifelong imprisonment, after the Restoration. The important and widespread family of the Gawdys, whose fortunes, like those of the Hobarts, were founded on the law, with a single exception consistently supported the Parliament. Other families with a legal background such as the Spelmans, with the illustrious Sir Henry Spelman at their head until his death in 1641, were predominantly Royalist, though here again there was an exception in John Spelman of Narborough, an active Parliamentarian.

The heads of two ancient families of declining fortunes, the Heydons and the Knyvetts, were Royalist too. The greatest days of the Heydons, and of their impressive houses at Baconsthorpe and Saxlingham, had been during the sixteenth century, when Sir Christopher Heydon is said to have feasted at Christmas thirty master-shepherds of his flocks. Then, towards the close of that century, disaster had come upon them. They had fallen hopelessly into debt. Their support of the Earl of Essex in his attempted

10 Dedication of *Urn Burial* (1656).

rising of 1601 had plunged them into further trouble. Their behaviour grew extravagant and unpredictable; they engaged in frantic duels and scribbled astrological pamphlets while their estates foundered in decay. Some measure of recovery was achieved by two brothers of the last generation of the family, Sir William, who was killed during the expedition to the island of Rhé, and Sir John, who succeeded him in the ownership of the family estates. Both rose to prominence in the royal service, holding high places in the Ordnance Office; and Sir John was Lieutenant-General of the King's Artillery throughout the Civil War. But the family had virtually abandoned Norfolk before the war began. Their estates had shrunk to a meagre remnant, and Baconsthorpe was already collapsing in ruin.[11]

The Knyvetts of Ashwellthorpe, through no fault of their own, had likewise fallen upon difficult times. Thomas Knyvett was born to an encumbered estate, and was plagued with debts and lawsuits all his days. He was the rightful inheritor of the dormant barony of Berners, but never considered himself wealthy or influential enough to press his claim. He married the youngest daughter of an impoverished peer, Lord Burgh of Gainsborough, a lady who brought him much happiness but a negligible dowry. All his troubles, and all his consolations, are set down in the remarkable correspondence with his wife which will be frequently quoted in later chapters. Knyvett was an outstanding letter-writer, and his letters have been discovered and admirably edited in recent years by Dr. Bertram Schofield. They reveal the exceptional charm of his character, his courage and fortitude and sweetness of temper; and they show most vividly the predicament of a gentleman of Royalist sympathies in a strongly Parliamentarian area. The Royalist temperament could not have found a more attractive exponent than Thomas Knyvett. Perhaps one day, from the ranks of the Puritans of East Anglia, an equivalent representative of their own cause may emerge. The *Autobiography* of that learned and self-righteous Suffolk gentleman, Sir Simonds D'Ewes, is scarcely comparable with the letters of Knyvett.

The middle and lesser ranks of gentry partook of the same division of opinion as those of greater estate and more distinguished ancestry. Again the Puritan predominance is noticeable;

[11] H. R. Trevor-Roper, *The Gentry*, 19. G. E. Aylmer, *The King's Servants*, 289-91.

but there were a good many exceptions. The committee lists will in due course serve us as a guide to those who actively supported the Parliament; and the sequestration lists will tell us something about those, such as the Holls of Heigham, the Pecks of Spixworth, the Anguishes of Great Melton, who took the opposite course.

The disagreements within families were sometimes very marked. William Heveningham had a younger brother Arthur, as resolutely engaged for the King as he himself was for the Parliament. Sir Jacob Astley, a younger son of the family long established at Melton Constable, had spent most of his life as a soldier in foreign service. When the troubles with Scotland began, he returned to serve his own King, and continued to serve him with great distinction throughout the Civil War. By this time he was an elderly man, and two of his nephews, Sir Isaac and Sir Edward Astley, represented the family in Norfolk. Both actively supported the Parliament, although Sir Edward was married to the daughter of his Royalist uncle. The Corbett family of Sprowston was similarly divided. Sir Thomas Corbett served with the King's forces from the outbreak of the war; while his uncle, Miles Corbett, Recorder of Great Yarmouth and several times Member of Parliament for that borough, was a Puritan doctrinaire of the most fervid and vindictive type. He was the only Norfolk man to sign the death-warrant of the King, and to be executed as a regicide under his successor. In a still older generation, Clement Corbett, the elderly uncle of Miles, was a strict High Churchman and the Puritan-baiting Chancellor of Bishop Wren. Naturally his sympathies were Royalist, and he got into trouble for them despite his venerable age.

Still more remarkable were the divergences of view among the children of that steadfast opponent of royal prerogative, that mighty assertor of the rights of Parliament, Sir Edward Coke. The great Chief Justice died in 1634. Of his three sons who were alive at the time of the Civil War, two supported the royal cause. There was no youthful romanticism about their choice, no suggestion of children reacting against the precepts of an over-mastering parent. Both were steady middle-aged men—Sir Robert Coke of Huntingfield in Suffolk and the Durdans in Surrey, Henry Coke of Thorington in Suffolk—with fine estates, the product of their father's hard-won gains, at the mercy of their Puritan neighbours. Both were to suffer imprisonment and sequestration for their defiance of Parliament. Only John Coke, the second surviving son of the Chief Justice, acted as his father would have wished. His principal inheritance had been the Holkham property in Norfolk, which he had much increased by marrying an heiress of that neighbourhood. From the outset of the troubles he was a prominent figure in Parliamentarian activities in Norfolk, and a formidable upholder of the cause. Sir Nicholas L'Estrange in his book of anecdotes described him as 'a great fellow in large folio', and spoke of 'his loud vociferation and bawling at all conferences and meetings'. Not surprisingly he became a member of every Parliamentarian committee in the county.[12]

Sir Edward Coke's daughters were similarly divided in their sympathies. The elder, Anne, the wife of a Hertfordshire gentleman, Ralph Sadleir of Standon Lordship, was a most fervent upholder of the King's cause, a great succourer of imprisoned Royalists and ejected clergymen. Her younger sister Bridget married William Skynner of Thornton College in Lincolnshire, and became associated with the two greatest poets of the age, poets who were whole-hearted supporters of the Parliament, John Milton and Andrew Marvell. It was to the former that she entrusted the education of her youngest son Cyriack. The friendship of master and pupil is commemorated in two of Milton's noblest sonnets.[13]

4

Conspicuous amongst the moderates in the Parliamentarian ranks was a Norfolk member, Sir John Holland of Quidenham. The Hollands had come into the county a century or so before, as dependants of the Dukes of Norfolk, and had risen to prominence through their services to successive generations of the Howards. They had built up a fair-sized estate in south Norfolk, and had acquired widespread family connections among their fellow-gentry. Sir John was created a baronet in 1629.

[12] *Anecdotes and Traditions*, 61.
[13] James, 50–77, 82–90, 112–19.

He was a man of firmly-held Puritan and Presbyterian convictions; and it was a matter of some surprise to his associates when he married a Catholic wife. She was Alathea, the daughter and coheiress of a Denbighshire gentleman named John Panton, and the widow of the fourth Lord Sandys of The Vyne in Hampshire. She bore him six sons and five daughters, none of whom she was allowed to bring up in her own faith. They were all instructed and catechized, on rigid Puritan lines, by Sir John. One of the daughters, who became a Catholic and a nun later in life, wrote sourly of her father that 'self-interest, and to advance his fortunes, made him take to wife a Catholic lady, whose riches made her religion tolerable'. However this may have been, it will be seen later that the Popish opinions of his lady caused Holland much difficulty and embarrassment in his political career. Nevertheless the marriage was an extremely happy one, with Sir John telling his children that she was the mirror of wives, and admonishing them to imitate her in all things but her religion.[14]

In all the years that followed, Sir John's influence was consistently exercised in the cause of moderation. He was frequently a member of the commissions which were appointed to treat with the King, both before and after his defeat. He greatly disliked the measures of sequestration and confiscation which were put into force against local Royalists, several of whom were his relations and friends, and took as little part in such matters as he possibly could. He was, in short, a man of kindly and reasonable temper, sometimes provoked to anger, but in essence an exponent of tolerance and conciliation. It was perhaps the result of his equable nature that when he died in his 98th year, at the outset of the next century, he was the last survivor of all the members of the Long Parliament.

5

The Catholic gentry alone behaved with absolute consistency. During the reign of King Charles, thanks largely to the influence

[14] C. S. Durrant, *A Link between Flemish Mystics and English Martyrs* (1925) 272–305—a fascinating account by Sister Catherine Holland of her upbringing and conversion.

of his Queen, they had been relieved from the most burdensome of their disabilities. Many of the laws and regulations against them fell quietly into disuse. They had nothing whatever to hope from a change of régime, nothing but persecution to expect from a Puritan ascendancy. They supported the Royalist cause to a man.

Fifty years had wrought changes in the Catholic network that Father Gerard had known; but many of the recusant families still remained. Fines and imprisonment had eaten deep into some of their estates. The Lovells of East Harling, the Cobbes of Sandringham, Thomas Downes of Bodney, John Paris of Pudding Norton, were ill equipped to face the renewed and greatly enhanced penalties which would presently be exacted from them. Soon their ancient homes would know them no more. Others, such as the Bedingfelds of Oxburgh, the Jerninghams of Costessey, Sir Edward Waldegrave of Stanninghall, the Catholic branch of the Yelvertons, still disposed of considerable resources, and were able to survive the coming storm.

There were, moreover, some newcomers to the Roman fold, in particular amongst the Paston family. The Pastons had been outwardly conformist during Elizabeth's reign, although that notable soldier, seaman and courtier Clement Paston, the builder of Oxnead, had more than once fallen under suspicion. Margery Paston, a nun of Barking, had returned home at the Dissolution with a pension of eight marks a year. In the parish register of Oxnead occurs the entry of the burial of *Margeria Paston generosa*, in December 1589. I do not think it is fanciful to suggest that this gentlewoman may have been the former nun, living into extreme old age in an utterly changed world, carrying her memories of choir and cloister into the Armada year, and perhaps helping to influence the members of her family towards the older faith.

Clement died childless, and Oxnead passed to the senior line of the Pastons, faithful adherents of the established Church. But his younger brother Sir Thomas founded another line which spread widely in Norfolk. Edward, the son of Thomas, built Barningham Hall in the north of the county and Appleton Hall near the Wash. He settled his eldest son William at Appleton, Thomas at Binham, Clement at Thorpe near Norwich, Edward on a property in Gloucestershire, and John at Barningham. At some unknown date, early in the seventeenth century, the entire family became

D   49

Catholic. The youngest son, Wolstan, entered religion under the name of Augustine Beeston. Two daughters, Katherine and Frances, became nuns of the Order of Saint Benedict at Brussels. At the outbreak of the Civil War the sons one and all, together with the widow of Thomas at Binham and her second husband, were plunged into trouble for their recusancy. Clement was taken into custody, by special order of the House of Commons, as one of the most dangerous among the Papists. John joined the forces of the King, and served with him until the close of the war. The estates of all were sequestered, and heavy compositions exacted. Early or late into the fold, the Catholic families met with the same hard measure.

CHAPTER III

The Bishops of Norwich from Jegon to Corbett

I

The Bishop of Norwich during the first fifteen years of King James's reign was John Jegon, previously Master of Corpus Christi College, Cambridge. In his diocese, as in his college, he was a noted disciplinarian; and his unpopularity in both is attested by satirical rhymes that have come down to us. On the other hand, Sir John Harington and Thomas Fuller spoke well of him; and the recently published *Registrum Vagum* of his devoted secretary, the Rev. Antony Harison, gives an unexpectedly favourable impression of this much-abused man, at any rate in his earlier years. He was no more a favourer of the Puritans than any of his predecessors since Bishop Parkhurst's death in 1574. But it does not appear that he was unduly harsh to them, or required more than a proper measure of conformity. His instructions about weekly sermons in the Norfolk and Suffolk market-towns show an intimate knowledge of his clergy, and a readiness to appoint as preachers such active Puritans as Samuel Otes of Southrepps and Nicholas Ayland of Coltishall.[1]

Later in life he seems to have grown extremely parsimonious. He had married a wife a good deal younger than himself, and was accused of neglecting charity and hospitality in order to enrich his family. He built up an estate of his own at Aylsham and Buxton, and economised by living not in his Palace at Norwich but in the episcopal manor-house at Ludham. In 1614 there was a disastrous fire at Ludham, which destroyed much of the house and its outbuildings. He would not rebuild it, but moved to his own house at Aylsham, where he died four years later. He was

---

[1] Harington, *Nugae Antiquae* (1804 ed.), ii, 170. Fuller, *Worthies*, i, 326. Harison, *Registrum Vagum*, i, 96–103.

buried in the church there, and his monument is in the chancel, a good deal damaged but still bearing his mitre carved in alabaster.

His widow remarried Sir Charles Cornwallis of Beeston near Norwich, who had been Ambassador in Spain for some years, and Treasurer to Henry Prince of Wales. His son Robert Jegon built himself a house at Buxton, and was in trouble for his Royalist sympathies in the next reign. So was Robert's half-brother, Francis Cornwallis, Sir Charles's son and successor at Beeston.[2]

Bishop Jegon was followed by Dr. John Overall, Bishop of Lichfield and Coventry, and formerly Dean of St. Paul's. Dr. Overall was an experienced theologian, and had been a notable figure at the Hampton Court Conference and as prolocutor of the lower house of Convocation. He is perhaps more vividly remembered through Aubrey's account of his wife, 'the greatest beauty of her time in England . . . not more beautiful than she was obliging and kind, and so tender-hearted that truly she could scarce deny anyone'. Aubrey quotes an enchanting ballad about her and one of her lovers, and comments that 'the good old Dean, notwithstanding he knew well enough he was horned, loved her infinitely: in so much that he was willing she should enjoy what she had a mind to'.[3] I do not know whether this lovely creature ever adorned the Palaces at Lichfield and Norwich; the last verse of the ballad suggests that she may have died comparatively young. Bishop Overall himself died in 1619, barely a year after his appointment to the see of Norwich.

His successor was Dr. Samuel Harsnett, a former Master of Pembroke College, Cambridge, who was translated from Chichester. Harsnett was a man of learning and conviction, a vigorous administrator and a determined High Churchman. He had written strongly against Popery, which did not save him from being accused of Popish practices by the fellows of his college and the Puritans of his diocese. He set himself at once to remedy the damage, material and spiritual, that had resulted from the laxity of Bishop Jegon's later years. The Palace at Norwich and the country house at Ludham were repaired at a cost of £2000,

[2] Blomefield, iii, 564. Mason, 299, 317-8.
[3] Aubrey, 161-4.

mainly from his private resources.[4] In his relations with his clergy he showed himself resolved to enforce conformity, and was soon deeply embroiled with the Puritan elements throughout Norfolk and Suffolk.

Puritanism was growing ever stronger in the principal towns, Norwich, Ipswich, Great Yarmouth; and the corporations tended always to appoint well-known Puritan divines to the preacher-ships or lectureships under their control. At Ipswich the preacher since 1603 had been Samuel Ward, who was frequently in trouble with Bishop Harsnett and his successors. Respected even by his adversaries, a man of blameless character and obstinate convictions, Ward exemplified the Puritan temperament at its best. He was, rather unexpectedly, an accomplished caricaturist, and the title-pages of his tracts were often adorned with emblems of his own designing. In 1621, at the time of the proposed marriage between Prince Charles and the Infanta, he produced an admirable plate entitled *The Double Deliverance*. This was printed in Amsterdam, but there was nothing furtive about its authorship— 'invented by Samuel Ward, preacher at Ipswich' appeared on the plate for all to see, and no doubt it had a wide circulation. In the centre the Pope, the cardinals and the King of Spain are seated in solemn conclave with the Devil. On one side the Armada is dispersed by the winds, *ventorum ludibrium*; on the other, Guy Fawkes with his lantern approaches the Parliament House, his fell designs revealed by a beam from the eye of God. Not surprisingly the Spanish ambassador Gondomar complained, and Ward was committed to prison for a spell by the Privy Council.[5]

Next year the Bishop himself took proceedings against Ward in the consistory court at Norwich. Ward appealed to the King, who referred the matter to Lord Keeper Williams. According to Williams's biographer, Bishop Hacket, 'the Lord Keeper found Mr. Ward to be not altogether blameless, but a man to be won easily by fair dealing. So he persuaded Bishop Harsnett to take his submission, and to continue him in his lecture at Ipswich . . . and

---

[4] C.S.P.D., 1634/5, 102. In a dilapidations dispute with his successor, Bishop White, Harsnett claimed that the Bishopric had been worth to him '£800 per annum and no more'. White asserted that during Harsnett's time, and in his own, the profits were £1,200.

[5] M. Dorothy George, *English Political Caricature* (1959), i. 15–16. *The Double Deliverance* is reproduced as plate 3. See also Browne, 139–41 and footnotes.

I aver it upon the faith of a good witness, that after this Bishop Harsnett acknowledged that he was as useful a man to assist him in his government, as was in all his diocese.'[6] This may have been so; nevertheless it appears that Ward was still in trouble the following year, when the corporation of Ipswich received a letter from the King to inhibit him from preaching.[7]

The Bishop's policy was just as displeasing to the Puritan citizens of Norwich. Sir Edward Coke took up their grievances, and accused him before the House of Commons of all kinds of tyrannous and Popish practices. He had, it was alleged, forbidden morning sermons except in the Cathedral, suppressed other sermons and lectures, commanded images—even 'one of the Holy Ghost fluttering over the font'—to be set up in churches, prosecuted people for not praying with their faces to the east, extorted undue fees and neglected to keep registers. The matter was remitted to the House of Lords, where he was able to furnish a convincing defence to all the charges against him. Some of them, he said, came from Puritans 'whom he has vainly endeavoured to bring to conformity', and others from a disgruntled cleric whom he had refused to make one of his archdeacons. He abhorred Popery, a religion of juggling and feigned miracles. He never spoke with a priest or a Jesuit, and never invited a known recusant to his table. As to praying to the east, he never enjoined it, and until this charge was made had never heard of it. When King James addressed Parliament at the close of the session, he said he would rather commend than punish the Bishops of Norwich and London—the latter was Mountaigne, the immediate predecessor of Laud—for setting up and adorning images in churches, and for putting down popular lay lectures; but that he would frown on any suppression of popular ministers.[8] In less than a year the old King would be dead, and such moderate policies were not to survive him long.

Bishop Harsnett also kept a watchful eye on the factious town of Yarmouth. In 1624 he had a good deal of correspondence with the Bailiffs about the suppression of conventicles, and the committal to prison of an obstinate little band of sectaries,

---

[6] John Hacket, *Scrinia Reserata* (1693), i, 95.
[7] D.N.B. *sub* Samuel Ward. See also C.S.P.D., 1619–23, 431.
[8] C.S.P.D., 1623–5, 238, 246, 249, 252, 265.

indifferently described as Anabaptists and Brownists. Soon afterwards there began a series of disputes about the appointment of a
minister, which continued to plague Harsnett's successors for
years after he had left the diocese of Norwich.[9]

The Bishop was a lifelong friend of Lord Arundel, and they
co-operated closely in Norfolk affairs. According to Fuller it was
to Arundel's recommendation that Harsnett owed his later preferments, the Archbishopric of York and a seat on the Privy
Council.[10] The Earl entrusted his youngest son William to the
Bishop's care, and the boy was for some years a member of the
episcopal households at Norwich and London. A letter from his
father has survived, telling him how he should behave there.
'You shall in all things reverence, honour and obey my Lord
Bishop of Norwich, as you would do any of your parents, esteeming whatsoever he shall tell or command you, as if your grandmother of Arundel, your mother, or myself, should say it; and in
all things esteem yourself as my Lord's page; a breeding, which
youths of my house far superior to you were accustomed unto, as
my grandfather of Norfolk, and his brother, my good uncle of
Northampton, who were both bred as pages with bishops.' Inigo
Jones, an inmate of Arundel House, wrote to the Earl on one
occasion that 'Mr. William was very merry at his departure, and
the bishop and he are the greatest friends that may be.' William
Howard's tuition during his time at Norwich was undertaken, at
least in part, by Henry Peacham, who dedicated *The Compleat
Gentleman* to him.[11] But the effects of this Anglican upbringing
soon wore off, and in early manhood he returned to the religion
of his forebears. He was created Viscount Stafford, a title belonging
to his wife's family, and was beheaded in 1680, one of the innocent
victims of the so-called Popish Plot.

Bishop Harsnett became Archbishop of York in 1628. In the
north he continued his opposition to the Puritans, and his last
years were saddened by their ever-growing numbers and influence. He was at York for less than three years, dying in the spring
of 1631. He was buried at Chigwell in Essex, which had been his
first living, and where his brass may still be seen—one of the

[9] Browne, 74–8. Swinden, 827–43.
[10] Fuller, *Worthies*, i, 326.
[11] Hervey, 169–70.

latest examples of that type of memorial, and a work of exceptional dignity.

2

The next Bishop of Norwich was Francis White, who was translated from Carlisle. He was known as a writer against the Papists, and had been engaged, together with Laud, in the famous disputations with Fisher the Jesuit. His rule at Norwich was brief and uneventful. At the end of 1631 he was promoted, like so many Bishops of Norwich in the seventeenth and eighteenth centuries, to the smaller but more remunerative see of Ely.

Next year he was succeeded at Norwich by Richard Corbett, who had been Bishop of Oxford for the past three years, and before that Dean of Christ Church. Corbett was a distinctly unclerical figure, much addicted in earlier life to wine and merriment and practical joking, and far from disdaining such things during his episcopal years. He was also one of the most admired and popular poets of his day. Good-natured and indolent, he acted with moderation in matters of ecclesiastical discipline. He much disliked the Puritan temperament, so far removed from his own; but to act with severity against individual Puritans was not in his nature. In Fuller's words, 'he was an high wit and most excellent poet, of a courteous carriage and no destructive nature to any who offended him, counting himself plentifully repaired with a jest upon him.'[12] The most memorable of those jests was his poem *The Fairies' Farewell*, with its enchanting levity and its half-affectionate glances back to the old religion. The wittiest was perhaps *The Distracted Puritan*—

> Am I mad, O noble Festus,
> When zeal and godly knowledge
> Have put me in hope
> To deal with the Pope,
> As well as the best in the college?
> Boldly I preach, hate a cross, hate a surplice,
> Mitres, copes, and rochets:

[12] Fuller, *Worthies*, iii, 83.

> Come hear me pray nine times a day,
> And fill your heads with crochets . . .

His policy of moderation was sometimes rewarded. He found himself obliged to proceed, as Harsnett had done, against Samuel Ward of Ipswich, and by mild courses obtained his submission. He then sent him, in October 1633, a letter full of kindness and consideration.

MY WORTHY FRIEND,

I thank God for your conformity, and you for your acknow-ledgment. Stand upright in the Church wherein you live; be true of heart to her governors; think well of her significant ceremonies: and be you most assured I shall never displace you of that room which I have given you in my affections. Prove you a good tenant in my heart, and no minister in my diocese hath a better landlord. Farewell; God Almighty bless you with your whole congregation.

From your faithful friend to serve you in Christ Jesus.

RICH. NORWICH.[13]

In short, it was well said by another bishop that Corbett had 'learned the way of that diocese of Norwich, and found that, though it were skittish and would not always come to the pail, yet the Puritan cow gave the best milk'.[14]

The Bishop brought with him to Norwich his favourite chap-lains, William Strode and Thomas Lushington, both of whom he presented to benefices in Norfolk. Strode was an excellent minor poet; his prologue for one of the Florists' Feasts in Norwich, those occasions so frowned upon by the Puritan citizens, will be mentioned on a later page. Lushington was a convivial character, much beloved by his patron. Aubrey describes how 'the Bishop would sometimes take the key of the wine-cellar, and he and his chaplain would go and lock themselves in and be merry. Then first he lays down his episcopal hat—"There lies the Doctor." Then he puts off his gown—"There lies the Bishop." Then 'twas, "Here's to thee, Corbett," and "Here's to thee, Lush-ington." '[15]

[13] B.M. MS. Harley 464, f. 13.
[14] B.L. MS. Rawlinson D.1104, f. 3.
[15] Aubrey, 287–8.

At the time of Corbett's translation to Norwich, Abbot was still Archbishop of Canterbury, excluded from affairs and deep in the King's disfavour. The real power at the head of the Church was Laud, with his exacting standards of discipline and order, and his determination to enforce them. In these circumstances the appointment of so easy-going a bishop as Corbett to the Norwich diocese, a key position in the struggle against the Puritans, may have caused some surprise. But Laud had his own reasons for promoting him, as Mr. Bennett and Professor Trevor-Roper have explained in the introduction to their edition of Corbett's poems. He had 'resolved, as part of his general policy, to solve the anomaly of bishoprics without palaces, and he was determined to have a bishop of Oxford who would pay for his promotion by providing himself and his successors with an episcopal house. By moving Corbett to Norwich he was able to achieve this result: the vacant diocese of Oxford was granted to the King's candidate, John Bancroft, on condition that he converted the next suitable parsonage house that should fall vacant into a bishop's palace; and thus four years later, when Laud visited Oxford in state, he was able to spend the night in Bancroft's new episcopal house at Cuddesdon'.[16]

Laud became Archbishop of Canterbury in September 1633, and took immediate steps to enforce his policy of order and conformity throughout the southern province. He was already aware of the casual fashion in which Corbett administered his diocese, although it was some while before he discovered the full measure of his laxity. In 1634 he began a metropolitan visitation of his province, through the agency of his Vicar-General, Sir Nathaniel Brent. The turn of the diocese of Norwich came in the spring of 1635, only three months before Corbett's death. Brent's official report makes no direct criticism of the Bishop, although Laud told the King later that the whole diocese had been found much out of order, even more so at Ipswich and Yarmouth than at Norwich. 'But I hope that my Lord that now is will take care of it, and he shall want no assistance that I can give him.'[17] The town

[16] J. A. W. Bennett and H. R. Trevor-Roper, *The Poems of Richard Corbett* (1955), xxxiv-v. I am indebted to this introduction for other points in my account of Corbett.

[17] Laud, *Works*, v. 334.

of Ipswich, according to Brent, was 'exceeding factious'; and there were evidently good reasons why Corbett's successor, 'my Lord that now is', the efficient Matthew Wren, gave his earliest attention to the county of Suffolk.

In Norfolk a good deal of Brent's report was devoted to the manner in which he was received by the various corporations. At Lynn 'the Mayor and his brethren showed very great respect unto your Grace's visitation in visiting me and feasting me twice. They likewise went with me to the town quay, where they caused all their ordnance to be shot off'. At Yarmouth he was likewise 'entertained by the magistrates with very great solemnity'. At Norwich, on the other hand, 'the Mayor and his brethren came not to visit me at my coming in. Afterwards I convented them for walking indecently in the Cathedral Church every Sunday in prayer time before the sermon, and I admonished them to forbear for the future . . . After this they visited me often, and gave me ample satisfaction for their former neglect, protesting they will be always ready to desire your Grace's good opinion of them.'

He found that Norwich Cathedral was much out of repair. 'The hangings of the choir are naught, the pavement not good, the spire of the steeple is quite down, the copes are fair but want mending. The churchyard is very ill-kept; there is a necessary house at the west end of the Church.' The phrase 'quite down' in fact gives a misleading impression of the condition of the spire. Other evidence shows that the topmost five or six feet were missing; and the Dean and Chapter had lately appealed to their tenants for assistance over 'the ruins fallen upon the spire of our Cathedral Church by time and tempestuous weather'.[18] At Lynn the three churches were 'exceeding fair and well kept, and the three ministers are very conformable and agree exceeding well'. At Yarmouth there was more to put in order—the roof of the great church was ruinous, the churchyard kept very indecently: but 'I made as much haste out of the town as I could, because the plague was there very hot'.

As for doctrinal matters, at Norwich 'many ministers appeared

[18] N.A., v. 122-3. See also Bishop Corbett's comments on this matter in W. Sparrow Simpson, *Documents illustrating the history of St. Paul's Cathedral* (Camden Soc., 1880), 138.

without priests' cloaks, some of them are suspected for noncon-
formity, but they carry themselves so warily that nothing could
be proved against them'. At Lynn 'since the Court of High
Commission took in hand some of their schismatics, few of that
fiery spirit remain there or in the parts thereabout'. But there were
'divers Papists who speak scandalously of the scriptures and of
our religion', and order was given that they should likewise be
brought into the Court of High Commission. At Yarmouth 'the
town is now in quiet, and the chiefest promise absolute obedience
to the laws of the Church'. On the other hand 'the magistrates
desire a lecturer, but I find no inclination in them to give the
choice of him to your Grace'. At Swaffham he noted that there
were few Puritans, but much drunkenness, 'accompanied with all
such vices as usually do attend upon it'.[19]

A matter which particularly exercised Laud's mind, in his desire
for ecclesiastical conformity throughout the land, was the position
of the congregations of immigrant foreigners, still worshipping
in their own languages and under their own discipline. During
his stay at Norwich, Brent saw to it that 'the Dutch and Walloon
congregations are admonished according to your Grace's directions, and an act is made of it'. Laud's admonition took the form
of requiring that the 'native' members of those congregations—
those who had been born in England and were subjects of the
King—should henceforth attend the churches of the parishes in
which they dwelt; and that their ministers and those others who
were not born subjects of his Majesty, while continuing to enjoy
their own church discipline, were to make use of the English
liturgy translated into their own tongues, 'for the better settling
of their children to the English government'.[20]

Ever since the great immigration from the Low Countries in
1567, the Walloon congregation in Norwich had been allowed
by successive Bishops to use the chapel attached to the Palace for
their own worship. When they first arrived, in Parkhurst's time,
they found it 'more like a dovehouse than a church, full of muck
and ordure, the roof decayed and the windows broken'. They had
repaired it at considerable expense, so that the Bishops had begun
to avail themselves of it again 'for baptizing their children,

[19] Quoted from Mason, 410.
[20] Moens, 92. Trevor-Roper, *Laud*, 197–202.

ordaining English ministers, and other uses at their pleasure'.[21] All had gone happily for many years: then on 26 December 1634 they were told by Corbett, in the most peremptory tones, to quit the chapel before Whitsuntide. 'Your discipline, I know, cares not much for a consecrated place, and any other room in Norwich that hath but breadth and length may serve your turn as well as a chapel. Wherefore I say unto you, without a miracle, *Lazare, prodi foras*! Depart, and hire some other place for your irregular meetings . . .'[22]

This curt notice of dismissal was addressed to the Walloon congregation some months before Brent's visitation, and suggests that Corbett, had he lived longer, might have been at some pains to enforce Laud's policies in his diocese. But his health was failing and it was in fact left to his successor to eject the Walloons two years later. He died on 28 July 1635, and was buried in his Cathedral. His words were whispered to his much loved chaplain, the companion of his pleasures—'Good night, Lushington.'[23]

[21] C.S.P.D., 1637/8, 356. *Remonstrance and petition of the Walloon congregation to Bishop Wren.*
[22] B.M. MS. Harley 464, f. 15.
[23] Aubrey, 288.

CHAPTER IV

Bishop Wren and his Clergy

I

The new Bishop of Norwich, from whose reforming zeal Laud
had hoped so much, was Matthew Wren. He had been Master of
Peterhouse, that seminary of High Churchmen, for a number of
years, and before his appointment to Norwich was for a few
months Bishop of Hereford. In 1623 he had accompanied the
King, then Prince of Wales, on his journey to woo the Infanta of
Spain, in the capacity of his chaplain; and he held several offices,
such as Dean of Windsor and Clerk of the Closet, which brought
him in contact with the Court. He was one of Laud's most loyal
supporters, and in complete agreement with his views—a lover of
ceremony and good order, a rigid disciplinarian, resolute and
energetic in all that he undertook. He was also a man of deep piety
and learning, and of an unfaltering courage. But he shared with
his Archbishop a sharp tongue, a peremptory manner of speech
and writing, and an attention to detail which even their well-
wishers often regarded as meddlesome and undignified. Clarendon
wrote of his 'severe, sour nature';[1] and a diocese accustomed to
Corbett's easy ways soon knew that it had a master of a very
different temper.

Wren was Bishop of Norwich for two years and a few months.
During that time he worked with single-minded devotion to establish order and conformity throughout his diocese, and aroused a
quite exceptional degree of hostility. Next to Laud, he became the
most hated of all the Bishops, the most obvious target for Puritan
recrimination and abuse. Few men can have made themselves so
widely disliked in so brief a space. A great mass of his papers has
been preserved among the Tanner manuscripts in the Bodleian
Library, covering every phase of his episcopal activities, together
with his very detailed answers to the articles of impeachment later

[1] Clarendon, i. 83.

MATTHEW WREN, BISHOP OF NORWICH AND ELY
from a painting by an unknown artist, in the possession of Pembroke
College, Cambridge

drawn up against him. From this material the ensuing account of his period at Norwich might easily be extended to several chapters; and it is my hope that before long someone will undertake a full biography of this redoubtable man.

2

Bishop Wren was well aware, from Brent's visitation of the previous year, that the southern half of his diocese was in the worst disorder, and most needed his presence. He therefore obtained the King's leave to spend several months of 1636 at Ipswich, rather than in his episcopal houses at Norwich and Ludham, and set himself to subdue the non-conforming ministers and stiff-necked lecturers of Suffolk.[2] This was probably his longest period of continuous residence within his diocese, since his offices of Clerk of the Closet and Dean of the Chapel Royal kept him much at Court. For the greater part of his episcopate he directed matters from his house at Westminster through the agency of his Chancellor, Dr. Clement Corbett, of whom more will be heard presently. As a general rule Dr. Corbett conducted the visitations of the diocese; and other duties were entrusted to the group of High Church clergy whom he appointed as his commissioners.

The 'orders, directions and remembrances', issued by the Bishop at his primary visitation in 1636, comprised twenty-eight articles. All were designed to promote the reverence, decency and good order for which Laud and his followers consistently strove. The forms of the Prayer Book were to be scrupulously observed. There were detailed instructions about the services, the Liturgy, the ordering of baptisms and marriages, prayers for the sick, the churching of women, and above all the administration of the Holy Communion. The minister was to catechize regularly. The Clerk must be able to read sufficiently, and lead the people in audible responses. There must be clean water in the font, and no wicker bottles or tavern pots were to be brought to the communion table. The parish perambulation was to take place on the rogation days, and at no other time.

[2] Laud, *Works*, v. 339.

Certain of the articles were more controversial. The third required 'that the communion table in every church do always stand close under the east wall of the chancel, the ends thereof north and south, unless the ordinary give particular direction otherwise, and that the rail be made before it (according to the Archbishop's late injunctions) reaching across from the north wall to the south wall, near one yard in height, so thick with pillars that dogs may not get in'. Since Elizabethan times the communion table in most parishes had stood in the main body of the church; and none of the Laudian reforms caused deeper suspicion and resentment than this. To Puritans it suggested unqualified Popery, especially as another article required communicants to 'come up reverently and kneel before the rail', instead of receiving the sacrament from the minister in their seats. It roused John Milton to thunderous indignation. 'The table of communion, now become a table of separation, stands like an exalted platform upon the brows of the choir, fortified with bulwark and barricado, to keep off the profane touch of the laics, whilst the obscene and surfeited priest scruples not to paw and mammock the sacramental bread, as familiarly as his tavern biscuit.'[3] To many churchwardens the altar-rails themselves were a formidable and unnecessary expense. Dogs had roamed free in churches ever since they could remember, with the legs of the holy table no more exempt from their attentions than any other piece of furniture. At Hadleigh in Suffolk a dog had run away with the communion bread in its mouth.

Another article ordered 'that no man do presume to have his hat on his head in the time of service; and that due and lowly reverence be visibly done by all persons present, when the blessed name of the Lord *Jesus* is mentioned; and that every one of the people do kneel devoutly when the confession, absolution, commandments, or any collect or other prayer is read'. Bowing and genuflexion were abhorrent to the Puritan mind; and such Popish practices were a stock accusation against Wren and the clergy who supported him. Wren indeed took every opportunity to encourage the use of ceremonial by his own example. When articles of impeachment were drawn up against him in 1641, it was asserted that 'he did in his own person use superstitious and idolatrous

---

[3] Milton, *Works* (1753 ed.), *Of Reformation in England*, i, 8.

actions and gestures in the administration of the Lord's supper, consecrating the bread and wine standing at the west side of the table with his face to the east, and his back to the people, elevating the bread and wine so high as to be seen over his shoulders, bowing low either to or before them, when he, after the elevation and consecration, had set them down on the table'.[4]

Some of the injunctions were especially irksome to Puritan gentlemen who had been accustomed to have their own way in their own parishes. It was ordered 'that none of what rank soever do keep any chaplains, schoolmasters, ministers or scholars in their houses to read prayers, and expound scriptures, or to instruct their family, unless they be thereunto enabled by law'. So much for those unbeneficed inmates of the manor-houses, who ranged from scholars and preachers such as John Collinges to the thread-bare 'trencher-chaplains' whose lot was described in an early satire by the future Bishop Hall. Nor was the squire allowed his accustomed privacy in church. Seats which encroached upon the chancel and aisles were to be removed. No pews were to be built 'so that they which be in them cannot be seen how they behaved themselves'; and all existing pews which much exceeded a yard in height were to be taken down to that level.[5]

At the same time Wren issued a formidable series of articles addressed 'to the Churchwardens, and any other of every parish, that shall be sworn to make presentments'.[6] Printed as a pamphlet in black letter, it consisted of nine chapters of inquiries, containing in all 142 sections, with each section including half a dozen or more questions. In the articles of impeachment against Wren the total number of questions was reckoned to be 897, many of which were there described as 'ridiculous and impossible'.[7] The most searching inquiries were made into the conduct of the services, the condition of the church, the demeanour of the minister, and the morals of the parishioners. The document must have been a nightmare to any conscientious churchwarden, and its requirements most unwelcome to those who were negligent or parsimonious.

Most of them were full of good, pious and charitable intent.

[4] *Articles of Impeachment against Wren* (1641), art. 18.
[5] B.L. MS. Tanner 68, ff. 33-6.
[6] *Articles to be inquired of within the Diocese of Norwich: in the first year of ... Matthew, Lord Bishop of Norwich* (1636).
[7] *Articles of Impeachment*, art. 22.

Wren was no respecter of persons; he was as anxious to remove the intrusive or over-lofty pews erected by private grandees as he was to reduce the swearing and alehouse-haunting of the vulgar. But an impossibly high standard was required of everyone; and many of the questions were meticulous to the point of triviality. 'Doth your minister usually wear a gown with a standing collar, and sleeves strait at his hands, and a square cap? doth he in journeying use a cloak with sleeves, commonly called a priest's cloak, without guards, buttons or cuts? doth he at any time in public wear any coif or wrought night-cap, but only a plain cap of black silk, satin or velvet? doth he at any time go abroad in his doublet and hose without a coat or cassock, or wear any light-coloured stockings? is he in any way excess in his apparel, either himself or his wife?' This sort of thing, carried into every department of parish life, cannot have been very acceptable even to the orthodox; and the Puritan element greeted it with mingled exasperation and ridicule.

Another frequent source of trouble was the question of the proper observance of Sunday. The Puritans, with their traditional emphasis on the preaching and exposition of the word of God, believed that the Sabbath should be a day of austerity, mainly occupied in listening to the sermons which they loved. The Laudians, with an equal devotion to the Book of Common Prayer, considered that when divine service had been fully and reverently performed, the rest of the day might be given to innocent recreation. They also thought that the young were better employed in archery, wrestling and dancing than in hearing sermons of dubious theological or political content. To this end the King had reissued in 1633 the controversial *Book of Sports* first published fifteen years before under the auspices of his father, and ordered his clergy to read and commend it from their pulpits. Wren gave the Book every encouragement; in the words of another of the articles against him, 'the more to hearten and confirm the people in profaning the Lord's day, he enjoined the ministers to read publicly in their churches a book published touching sports on the Lord's day . . . by which knowledge was suppressed, and ignorance and profaneness introduced into the diocese.'[8] Many of his clergy welcomed the Book warmly, and were later in trouble

[8] Ibid., art. 8.

for doing so. John Lewthwaite, the vicar of Stow Bedon, to take one of many examples, was denounced by the Parliamentarians because he 'read the Book of Sports and applauded at Sunday games'.[9] The clergy of Puritan sympathies, on the other hand, refused to read the Book at all, in defiance of anything that Wren and his local officials could do.

The lecturers were a particular offence to Wren. There were many unauthorized lectures within his diocese, and more especially in Suffolk, some endowed and supported by the corporations, others by private gentlemen. 'Not a market, or a bowling green, or an ordinary could stand without one,' he wrote to Laud.[10] The lecturers were men without benefices, and to that extent were outside episcopal authority and control. Most of them were strongly Puritan in temper, as were the corporations and individuals who maintained them. They were a law unto themselves in the doctrine they preached, the political views they advanced, the form of service that accompanied their sermons. High Churchmen regarded them as the most dangerous channels of Puritan propaganda. Dr. Clement Corbett, Wren's outspoken Chancellor, wrote to him that 'if his Majesty shall in his princely care abolish that ratsbane of lecturing out of his churches, the virulency whereof hath intoxicated many thousands of this kingdom, we shall have such a uniform and orthodox Church, as the Christian world cannot show the like'.[11]

Under the Laudian régime, certain measures had been introduced which enabled bishops to deal more effectively with the lecturers within their dioceses. Wren took full advantage of these powers, and was able to bring most of the lecturers in Norfolk and Suffolk, at any rate for a time, to submission and conformity. His visitation articles laid down certain requirements which all lecturers were to fulfil, and which were by no means agreeable to many of them. They were to read divine service, in surplice and hood, before every lecture. They were to behave themselves modestly in their discourses, preaching faith, obedience and good works. They were not to 'meddle with matters of state, news, or questions late in difference, nor favour or abet any

[9] B.L. MS. Walker c.6, f.44.
[10] William Prynne, *Canterburies Doome* (1646), 374.
[11] B.L. MS. Tanner 68, f.2.

schismatics or separatists, either by special prayer for them, or otherwise approving of them'. Laud reported to the King at the close of 1636 that only three lecturers had been inhibited in Norfolk and three in Suffolk, 'of which one is no graduate, and hath been a common stage-player'. But a great deal of ill-feeling was stirred up. It is unlikely, for example, that the corporation of Bury St. Edmunds accepted Wren's injunctions 'with very good content', as Laud asserted.[12] At Ipswich the veteran preacher Samuel Ward, who had submitted for a while both to Harsnett and to Corbett, had relapsed once more. In November 1635 he had 'preached against the common bowing at the name of Jesus, and against the King's Book of Sports, and further said that the Church of England was ready to ring changes in religion, and the gospel stood on tiptoe, as ready to be gone'—an interesting echo of a famous couplet of George Herbert.[13] For this he was suspended and imprisoned by the Court of High Commission. The corporation of Ipswich stood firm for his reinstatement, and would not ask Wren to allow them another in his place. Deadlock ensued, and eventually Ward, on his release from imprisonment, crossed the sea to Holland.

He had already been preceded there by William Bridge, the most recalcitrant of the Puritan preachers of Norwich. Bridge was rector of St. Peter Hungate, and had a considerable following in the city. He persistently refused to conform; and Laud told the King that he 'hath left his lecture and two cures, and is gone into Holland'. The King, who was in the habit of annotating Laud's reports, scribbled in the margin, 'Let him go: We are well rid of him.'[14] Both he and Ward joined the English church at Rotterdam, which had flourished for several years as a Presbyterian body, and which Laud was vainly trying to bring under his own authority. A number of their more devoted adherents, men and women, followed them across the sea.[15] There they remained until the turn of events brought them back in triumph once more to their own land.

Laud's report for 1636 went on to say that 'his Lordship's care hath been such, as that though there are about 1500 clergymen

[12] Laud, *Works*, v. 340-1. *Canterburies Doome*, 374-5.
[13] Rushworth, II., 301.
[14] Laud, *Works*, v. 339-40.
[15] C. B. Jewson, *The English Church at Rotterdam*, N.A., xxx, 324-37.

in that diocese, and many disorders, yet there are not thirty excommunicated or suspended; whereof some are for contumacy, and will not yet submit; some for obstinate denial to publish your Majesty's declaration; and some for contemning all the orders and rites of the Church, and intruding themselves, without licence from the ordinary, for many years together'.[16]

William Prynne described these suspensions from the opposite point of view in a pamphlet entitled *News from Ipswich*. Under the feigned name of Matthew White of that town, he wrote of 'our Norwich diocese, where little Pope Regulus hath played such Rex, that he hath suspended above sixty of our sincerest, painfullest, conformable ministers, both from their office and benefice, so as many of our churches (as the like was never seen since King John's days) are quite shut up, and *Lord have mercy upon us* may be written on their doors: the people cry for the bread of their souls, and their ministers are prohibited to give it them . . .'[17] The whole of *News from Ipswich* was written with extraordinary vehemence, and with an unstinted wealth of libels upon Wren and Laud. For this and other works Prynne was condemned in the Court of Star Chamber to life imprisonment, an exorbitant fine, pillory, branding and the loss of that portion of his ears which had remained uncropped after an earlier sentence.

Admiration for Prynne's courage, and compassion for his savage punishment, should not blind us to the fact that his denunciations of the bishops were inaccurate as well as vindictive. Nevertheless Wren's proceedings aroused immense bitterness and resentment in the Puritans of East Anglia, and a good deal of anxiety and heart-searching among moderate men. Archbishop and King, however, were warm in their approval. Laud wrote, with *News from Ipswich* and the general Puritan reaction in mind, that Wren 'hath deserved very well of the Church of England, and hath been very ill rewarded for it. His humble suit to your Majesty is, that you will be graciously pleased in your own good time to hear the complaints that have been made against him, that he may not be overborne by an outcry for doing service.' The King noted in the margin, 'His suit is granted.'[18]

[16] Laud, *Works*, v, 341.
[17] Quoted from Browne, 96–7.
[18] Laud, *Works*, v, 341–2.

3

Clement Corbett, Doctor of Laws and a former Master of Trinity Hall, had been Chancellor of the diocese of Norwich since 1625. He was a younger son of Sir Miles Corbett of Sprowston, and consequently an uncle of Miles Corbett the regicide. Although their political and ecclesiastical views were poles apart, uncle and nephew possessed the same biting tongue and the same inquisitorial temper. During the long periods when Bishop Wren's duties kept him at Court, Corbett was his principal representative in the diocese. Many eminent men have been undone by the conduct and demeanour of their subordinates. It was unfortunate for Wren that his chief legal officer should have been this harsh and ill-spoken man.

Their association had begun with a clash of wills. At the end of a long letter, dated 31 March 1636, on certain points of difference between them, Wren wrote: 'I will not end till (once for all) I tell you, that whatsoever you think good to do touching yourself, where anything touches me, or any orders from me, you cause your officers to know themselves and to count honest obedience the sum of their duty. I give them all this warning, that I shall watch with many eyes and long ears; and if I meet with aught to the contrary it will prove too hot for some of us. So God have us all in his blessed keeping.'[19]

This storm seems to have cleared the air. Thereafter Corbett carried out the Bishop's instructions faithfully, and indeed with an excess of zeal. Wren had said, 'I shall be right glad, if obedience may be had with love and mildness.' But one has the impression that love and mildness were weapons seldom employed by Corbett. Wren caused a clerk to copy out a series of passages which he marked in the Chancellor's reports, dealing with important matters to which he might need to refer again. These he annotated and indexed himself. In his index no fewer than eleven entries were included under the heading of 'Chancellor's fierceness', and one under 'language ill given'.[20]

This last entry was endorsed again by Wren in the margin,

[19] B.L. MS. Tanner 68, f. 39.
[20] B.L. MS. Tanner 68, ff. 1-12.

'shrewd and sour language'. The letter in question related to two especially unruly clergymen, George Cook of Fritton in Norfolk and William Greenhill of Oakley in Suffolk. It was reported to Wren that his Chancellor had used threats against both, and he had asked for an explanation. Corbett replied: 'For the term of hanging, to that savoury ignorant 'pothecary Cook of Fritton, upon an audacious affront of language given me, fairly mentioning his usual neglect of the rites and ceremonies of the Church, his ridiculous and silly expositions in his preaching, having set up a lecture in his own parish without authority, disgracing the Universities, and sundry other things which be here *apud acta* and proved, I told him he did not merit an ecclesiastic but a laic suspension and hanging.' As for Greenhill, 'for the matter of pistoling and bloodshed, I never used the term to any . . . he and his seeming smooth brethren have been long since branded with the badge of lying.'[21]

Corbett's rich vocabulary of abuse was not confined to his personal encounters with clerics such as Mr. Cook and Mr. Greenhill. In his letters to Wren he used the same violent language, describing the Puritan clergy as owls, mushrooms, anything that came into his head. Jeremiah Burroughes of Tivetshall, a popular young preacher whom he particularly disliked, was 'a factious schismatic princox, a bold beardless fearless fellow'.[22] In short he seized every opportunity of harassing those who would not conform, and more than once exhorted Wren to greater severity. 'I know your Lordship's favourable inclination, because they are your brethren, but they are false brothers, and ever have and will, by their fanatical and insidious discourses public or private, machinate against the good foundation of doctrine and discipline of the Church established.'[23]

Whatever his reservations as to Corbett's methods and language, Wren was no less determined than his Chancellor that conformity should be enforced throughout the diocese. Quite apart from major questions of doctrine and discipline, he took the closest interest in the fabric and the furnishing of every parish church. He did not intend his articles and injunctions to be ignored, either by the clergy or the churchwardens. A great

[21] Ibid., f. 6.
[22] Ibid., f. 8.
[23] Ibid., f. 5.

number of his notes and memoranda survive, attesting the thoroughness with which he knew his diocese, and the care with which he studied the reports of visitations, and sent down instructions to his commissioners in the various archdeaconries.[24]

There was much to be reformed, wherever he looked. Sir Thomas Wodehouse's seat in the chancel of St. Peter's in Thetford was over-high. Sir Thomas Gawdy's pew at Redenhall was 'of monstrous height, curtained like a bedstead, and encroaches upon the aisle'. The church at Holt was much decayed, and not ceiled within, though Mr. Claxton the incumbent was a rich man. Waxham church had been made a hogsty. The chamber over the porch at Blofield was used for the storage of gunpowder. At Marsham the church from the porch to the altar was strewn with foul rushes.

At Saxthorpe there was no catechizing, nor at Heydon, nor prayers on Wednesday. At St. Faith's and at Sall the curates were still keeping schools, although they had been often admonished not to do so. At Acle it would be necessary to 'call the midwife, but admonish and dismiss her upon submission'—perhaps she had been exceeding her traditional function of baptizing newly-born children who were weakly and unlikely to live. The incumbent of Wolterton, Paul Amyraut, 'runs up and down to private houses, crying out of Popery and timeserving'. Amyraut was a German by birth, a native of the Palatinate, and a noted Puritan, much encouraged by a local squire, John Potts of Mannington. At Denton 'old Mr. Thomas Pert, a weak man, is much led by his parishioners'. And so on for page after closely-written page.

An affair which caused Wren great concern was the ill conduct of the Rev. Nicholas Sherwood, rector of Earsham. 'It will be known to you,' he wrote wearily to Corbett, 'what time I have spent, and what patience I have had in sifting the business against the parson of Earsham'; and his notes bear witness to the immense trouble he took over this case. Sherwood was at loggerheads with his leading parishioners, a father and son both named Robert Gooch; and they accused him before the Bishop of an extraordinary variety of misdemeanours—persistent misconduct with Prudence Clark; adultery with at least two other women; attempting the chastity of several more; frequenting inns and alehouses; playing at cards and tables; swearing, cursing and railing; fomenting discord in the parish; ungodly, profane and sophistical speech. Eventually the Bishop decided that all these charges were proved, with some reservation as to those which related to women. 'As to the crimes of enormous incontinencies wherewith they have charged him . . . I cannot take the proofs as full and irrefragable, yet they are such as draw upon him a necessity of purgation.' Sherwood was suspended for a period from his cure. Then he was to do penance in his own church, expressing publicly his deep contrition 'in a due, lowly and reverent manner . . . with such behaviour of himself, and in such words of submission and deprecation as I have prescribed'. His words of contrition covered all his offences in full detail, and were to be uttered in the presence of four prominent local clergy, and four laymen, 'men of good reputation, of the gentry or the head of the yeomanry within that hundred'. This was what was known as a 'purgation of eight hands'; and Wren added that it would not mislike him if Prudence Clark were also to be summoned, and put to a purgation of four hands.[25]

Local Puritans cannot have failed to contrast Wren's lenient treatment of Sherwood with his severity towards clergymen of their own persuasion. Men of upright life and blameless character were deprived of their livings for refusing to conform in matters of ceremony and ritual. The scapegrace rector of Earsham, once his penance had been carried out and his escapades duly purged, was allowed to resume the charge of his unhappy flock. But Sherwood was a conformist; and one of the charges against him, when he was ejected by the Parliamentarians a few years later, was that he was a faithful observer of Bishop Wren's injunctions.[26]

4

According to Clarendon, Wren exercised particular severity towards the foreigners within his diocese. He 'passionately and warmly proceeded against them: so that many left the kingdom, to the lessening the wealthy manufacture there of kerseys and

[25] Ibid., ff. 252–66.
[26] B.L. MS. Walker c. 6, f. 48. Cf. *post*, p. 243.

narrow cloths, and, which is worse, transporting that mystery into foreign parts'.[27] For many years the Dutch congregation in Norwich had worshipped in Blackfriars Hall, the chancel of the former Dominican priory; while the Walloons, as we have seen, were allowed to use the chapel attached to the bishop's palace. They were led by able and respected pastors, the Dutch by Jan Elison and the Walloons by Pierre de Laune. The two pastors addressed a petition to the Archbishop, explaining their point of view in moderate and reasonable terms. His somewhat peremptory reply contained one important modification, that only 'native-born subjects of the second degree'—the second generation born on English soil—were required to attend their parish churches. This reply was read by the pastors from their pulpits, 'with thanks to his Majesty for granting the continuance of their congregation, and allowing those of the first descent to remain members.'[28]

No doubt Wren did his best to enforce Laud's injunctions, and took steps against any members of the congregations who disobeyed them. But I do not know whether Clarendon's story of a drastic persecution of these foreigners is supported by evidence. Nothing was said of it in the articles of impeachment against Wren in 1641, whereas the suppression of the immunities of other foreign churches figured prominently in the articles against Laud. Nothing was said in Laud's reports to the King about any steps taken by Wren against the foreigners in his diocese. In such lists as survive of those who left Norfolk for Holland or New England in these years, there are few Dutch or French names, certainly not enough to suggest an exodus of the kind described by Clarendon.

In 1637 Wren gave the Walloons notice to leave his chapel, as Corbett had done two years before, but in terms that were far less peremptory than those employed by his predecessor. On 7 March 1638 he addressed a courteous letter to their pastor Pierre de Laune, asking him and his congregation to reply within a month to the report of the commission on the dilapidations of that building. He continued, in the same friendly and unauthoritative tones: 'I cannot also but heartily wish, that you in your wisdom and true

[27] Clarendon, ii, 74.
[28] Moens, 93–5.

fidelity to the Church of England, would lay before you the example of the French congregation in the isle of Axholme, who though but lately settled in this land, yet have already entertained the liturgy of the Church of England (as it is set forth in French) and with great alacrity do conform themselves to the rites of that Church, in the protection whereof they live. I speak unto wise men, God give you all a right understanding in it. So heartily remembering myself unto you, I recommend you and us all to the blessed protection of the Almighty.'[29]

There is nothing to show that the Walloons of Norwich followed the example of the congregation at Axholme, a colony of French-speaking workmen engaged in the draining of the Lincolnshire fenland. But in the following month they reported to Wren with a 'remonstrance and petition' on the question of dilapidations. This document in no way suggests a harassed or persecuted body. They addressed the Bishop deferentially but without timidity. About a year since, they said, they had yielded up the keys of the chapel, together with twenty nobles by way of gratitude. Although they were 'a poor decayed congregation', they had been to the expense of £160 'to repair a poor little forlorn church granted them by the city's favour'. They besought him to hold them excused from doing more.[30] There the matter seems to have rested. The little forlorn church was St. Mary the Less, at the south-west corner of Tombland. It continued to serve as the church of French-speaking Protestants in Norwich for centuries to come, and sermons in French were still preached there in the reign of Queen Victoria.

In fact, apart from the ejection of the Walloons from their long-established place of worship, it would appear that the foreign congregations in Norwich rode out the Laudian storm. Elison and de Laune, by their meek reception of the Archbishop's reply to their petition, had at least made a show of obedience. I know of no evidence as to their use of translations of the English liturgy, nor any details of the extent to which the younger members attended their parish churches, as was required of them. A very few years were to bring about the collapse of everything for which

[29] B.L. MS. Tanner 68, f. 311.
[30] C.S.P.D., 1637/8, 356.

Laud and Wren had striven. Until then, I think, the two pastors and their flocks possessed their souls in patience, and awaited the coming of better times.[31]

But there can be no doubt that Wren's policy drove many English-born nonconformists across the seas, some for a few years, others for the rest of their lives. One of the articles against him alleged that 'by reason of the rigorous prosecutions and . . . the continual superstitious bowing to and afore the table set altarwise, the suspending, silencing, driving away of the painful preaching ministers, the suppressing and forbidding of sermons and prayer; the putting down of lectures, the suppressing means of knowledge and salvation, and introducing ignorance, super-stition and profaneness, many of his Majesty's subjects, to the number of three thousand, many of which used trades of spinning, weaving, knitting, and making of cloth and stuff, stockings, and other manufactures of wools, that is to say Daniel Sunning, Michael Metcalfe, John Berant, Nicholas Metcalfe, John Derant, Busby, widow Mapes, Richard Cock, John Dicks, Francis Lawes, John Senty and many others, some of them setting an hundred poor people on work, have removed themselves, their families and estates into Holland, and other parts beyond the seas, and there set up and taught the natives the said manufactures to the great hindrance of trade in this kingdom, and to the impoverish-ing, and bringing to extreme want, very many who were by those parties formerly set on work, to the great prejudice of his Majesty and his people'.[32]

The figure of three thousand exiles seems a formidable total; but it must be remembered that families were large, and often included servants and dependants as well as children. A paper has survived, presumably the work of someone concerned in prepar-ing the articles against Wren, giving the number of persons who emigrated from the various hundreds of Norfolk; and this bears all the signs of factual accuracy. It is headed 'The number of families whereof divers ministers and the most being tradesmen, considerable and useful persons, enforced to leave the diocese of Norwich by reason of Bishop Wren's innovations'.[33]

[31] Moens, 94–7.
[32] *Articles of Impeachment*, art. 16.
[33] B.L. MS. Tanner 68, f. 332.

PERSONS

Imprimis, out of the city of Norwich above fifty families besides 7 or 8 without families, which may contain by estimation about 500 persons	500
Item, out of Depwade Hundred, 2 families	18
—————— Earsham, 4 families	62
—————— Shropham, 8 families	35
—————— Taverham, 2 families	15
—————— Forehoe, 21 families	134
—————— South Erpingham, 2 families	6
—————— Holt, 1 family	5
—————— Lynn and near it, 7 families	33
—————— Yarmouth and Humbleyard	500

Families about 200	Persons about 1350

If a similar number emigrated from the Suffolk half of Wren's diocese, the total does not fall far short of the three thousand stated in the articles of impeachment.

Some registers have also survived, containing the names and other particulars of all travellers who embarked at Great Yarmouth during the three years 1637–9. Men and women of every rank and condition were crossing to Holland—tradesmen to sell their wares or collect their debts, craftsmen to learn the latest Dutch techniques, soldiers to take service in the armies of the States-General, maidservants to seek employment, the majority just to enjoy a holiday abroad, 'to see the country and return within a month'. But a certain number, whatever they may have said to the official who examined them, were going there to stay, at any rate until the coming of better times. In Holland they would find William Bridge and others of the deprived clergy; and the names of several men and women in the Yarmouth lists soon appear among the members of the English congregational church at Rotterdam. These lists only cover the last year of Wren's episcopate, and only one minister deprived by him, Jeremiah Burroughes, is included in them. But we obtain from them some idea of the steady stream of men and women, with their children and servants, who took

77

up their abode in Holland during Wren's years at Norwich.[34]

The lists include two large parties bound for New England. In April 1637 two ships sailed from Yarmouth, the *John and Dorothy* of Ipswich, whose master was William Andrews, and the *Rose* of Yarmouth, in charge of his son of the same name. In May a further group left in the *Mary Anne* of Yarmouth, the master being William Goose. The emigrants came from all over Norfolk and Suffolk, and the total number of passengers in all three ships was nearly 200. They were mostly family parties, weavers and husbandmen, craftsmen and tradesmen of all kinds, with their wives and children, the more prosperous taking several servants or employees with them. John Baker, grocer of Norwich, was accompanied by his wife, three children, three maids and a man-servant. Richard Carucar, husbandman of Scratby, a man of sixty years, took his wife, two children, two men and a maid. The first party included three of the Norwich master-weavers mentioned in the article against Wren which has been quoted, Michael Metcalfe, Francis Lawes and Nicholas Busby. With Lawes went a servant or apprentice named Samuel Lincoln, aged eighteen. He married in New England, and Abraham Lincoln was his direct descendant.[35]

At the time of his threatened impeachment in 1641, Wren prepared full answers to each of the 25 articles against him.[36] He denied that he was in any way responsible for the migration of clothiers beyond the seas. He pointed out that 'the humour of separating themselves from the Church of England into foreign parts' was of a much earlier date than 1636. Puritans had gone in plenty to New England from the dioceses of Lincoln and Exeter, whose Bishops had never been so much as accused of persecution, and had named the towns of Boston and Plymouth after their old homes. The emigrants named in the article were not master-clothiers with numerous employees, as his accusers suggested. Francis Lawes, for example, was 'a poor and mean weaver', John

[34] C. B. Jewson (ed.), *Transcript of Three Registers of Passengers from Great Yarmouth to Holland and New England, 1637-1639*. Introduction, especially 8-14. (N.R.S., 1954.)

[35] Ibid., 20-2, 29-30.

[36] B.L. MSS. Tanner 220, ff. 67-115; 314, ff. 149-79. His answers to the articles of impeachment were also printed in full in *Parentalia: or Memoirs of the Family of the Wrens* (1750), 73-114.

Dicks 'a poor joiner', Richard Cock 'a draper newly set up that kept but one prentice'. Michael Metcalfe, a dornix weaver, was the only emigrant 'of some estate'.

The exodus to Holland, he explained, was due not to persecution but to low wages. 'This defendant humbly conceiveth, that the chiefest cause of their departure hence was the small wages which was given to the poor workmen, whereby the workmasters grew rich, but the workmen were kept very poor. And then that occasioning the slight and ill making of those manufactures, the Hollanders desirous to learn the trade, as well for their own advantage as for the better making of those commodities, did for a time invite our people thither by giving much greater wages for work than was given here, so that it was generally reported in Norwich, that they could have fifteen shillings in Holland, for that work which here yielded not ten shillings. To which is to be added that in the year 1636, the danger of plague in London stopped the weekly intercourse of stuffs and other commodities from Norwich, and thereby men forbore to set so many on work as before . . . and that forced the poor to complain, and to go seek the means of living abroad.'[37]

5

The group of active Puritans in East Anglia was not a large one; but its members were sustained by an abundant sense of their own righteousness, and conscious of a good deal of local support. The articles against Wren gave the number of fifty 'godly, faithful preaching ministers' whom he had 'excommunicated, suspended, or deprived and otherwise censured and silenced'.[38] In his reply the Bishop asserted that this figure could not possibly stand, even if it were taken to include the quite considerable number of clergymen, such as Sherwood of Earsham, whom he had been obliged to discipline for reasons of misconduct or negligence. Only twenty sufferers are named in the article, but there were certainly others who were in trouble with Wren on doctrinal or ceremonial grounds. Mr. D. W. Boorman has found the names of 69 ministers

[37] B.L. MS. Tanner 314, f. 192.
[38] *Articles of Impeachment*, art. 13.

who clashed at some time with Wren and his officials on these matters, out of a total of 1081 clergy in the whole diocese. Some of these were brought to submission; and we may perhaps estimate the hard core of committed Puritan recalcitrants as thirty or forty.[39]

In Norfolk they included four prominent Norwich clergy—William Bridge of St. Peter Hungate, Thomas Allen of St. Edmund's, John Ward of St. Michael at Plea, and John Carter, curate of the great church of St. Peter Mancroft. Bridge, as we have already seen, withdrew to Rotterdam in 1636, and Allen and Ward joined him there before the close of the following year.[40] Carter adopted a different line. In June 1636 he disappeared for a time from view, but Corbett wrote that 'he is latitant in the town; I hear, if it be true, that he intends to turn schoolmaster. He will do more mischief in that course than he hath done in his snuffling practices in the Church'. In December it was reported that 'he still juggles in his conformity'. Later in the month he resigned his curacy, but two months afterwards he sought to be re-elected. (The appointments at St. Peter Mancroft were, as they still remain, in the gift of the parishioners.) Corbett wrote: 'He is come up with some overture from many of his parish, but not all, to obtain your Lordship's favour. Your Lordship will not forget that he hath played fast and loose and peepbo with you.' For all that, Wren appears to have accepted his submission; and he was elected the chief minister at St. Peter Mancroft in 1638.[41] In more congenial times he became one of the most vociferous of all the Puritan preachers. We shall meet him again.

Jeremiah Burroughes of Tivetshall also retired to Holland in 1637. Later in the year, according to Corbett, he and his friend William Greenhill of Oakley, disguised as soldiers, were on a ship which docked at Yarmouth, and attempted to smuggle 'parcels of books entitled *Dr. Bastwick's Library*' into the country. But this may have been only a rumour. He seems to have remained in Holland until 1641, when he returned to a London cure and eventually to prominence in the Assembly of Divines.[42]

[39] D. W. Boorman, *The Administrative and Disciplinary Problems of the Church on the Eve of the Civil War*. (Unpublished thesis in Bodleian Library), 82–3.
[40] B.L. MS. Tanner 68, f. 3.
[41] B.L. MS. Tanner 68, ff. 4–5.
[42] Ibid., ff. 9, 10. Cf. *Parentalia*, 95.

Another leading Puritan was Robert Peck of Hingham, who for thirty years had exercised great influence in his large parish with its noble church. He was constantly in trouble with Wren, as he had been with earlier bishops, and left Hingham towards the end of 1637. For a time his son took his place, without any authority, and Corbett was soon on his trail. 'For young Peck that officiated in his father's church at Hingham and did *patrisare* and perform nothing in order, I sent an express for him to appear at Wymondham, but he is returned to Essex from whence he came, and it is rumoured that the old fox is kennelled there.' When John Lewthwaite, vicar of Stow Bedon and one of Wren's commissioners, came to take a service at Hingham, the Bishop noted sadly that 'there ran 200 at once to other churches'. Early next year Corbett wrote: 'Reverend Mr. Peck of Hingham *parat se ad fugam in Novam Angliam*, and many households in that and other towns adjacent, as I heard.' He and a number of his neighbours did in fact depart for New England, where earlier settlers had already founded the community of Hingham in Massachusetts. In 1646 he returned to England and to his old parish, dying at a great age ten years later.[43]

Other non-conforming clergy who appear much in the correspondence of Wren and Corbett, and were eventually deprived, were Paul Amyraut of Wolterton and Thomas Case of Erpingham. They were supported in their recalcitrance by prominent local Puritans, Amyraut by John Potts of Mannington and Case by Sir John Hobart of Blickling. On the other hand George Cook of Fritton, the object of Corbett's frequent gibes because he had been an apothecary, made his submission after a period of suspension, and was restored to his living.[44]

There were not a few clerics whose sympathies inclined towards Puritanism, but who pursued a moderate course and never incurred the displeasure of their bishops. One of these was John Rous, who lived at Weeting in the heathlands of south-west Norfolk, and was vicar of Santon Downham, just across the Suffolk border. He was a quiet observant man, with an interest in the affairs of the day and a liking for satirical poetry. At intervals he kept a diary, dealing mainly with the political and religious

[43] Ibid., ff. 3, 11, 210. Browne, 103-4.
[44] Browne, 99-100. Blomefield, v, 309.

issues of the time, in which it is possible to trace the growth of his Puritan opinions under the pressure of events.[45]

In 1627 he was prepared to defend the policy of King Charles against the subversive criticism of his neighbour, Mr. Paine of Riddlesworth. 'I saw hereby that which I had seen often before, viz. men be disposed to speak the worst of state businesses, and to nourish discontent, as if there were a false carriage in all these things, which if it were so, what would a false heart rather see than an insurrection? a way whereunto these men prepare.' But as the years passed by, he grew ever more disillusioned. He preserved his moderation and his scrupulous fairness of judgment; but he was quite certain that things were going wrong in church and state. On a more familiar level, he was irritated and perplexed by the doings of his High Church neighbours—'Ceremonious Buck' of Stradbroke, for example, or Mr. Garey of Beachamwell, who 'mouthed it *Je—sus*, with a low congie; and in his sermon upon Matthew iii, 10, among those whom he made liable to God's fearful judgment, against whom the axe is threatened, he named adulterers, oppressors, atheists, those that bowed not at the name of Jesus, and (I think also) those that were covered at divine service . . . *O tempora, qui pastores?*'[46]

A vivid description of this type of divine, so antipathetic to an old-fashioned clergyman like Rous, is given in a poem entitled *The New Churchman*, which he transcribed into his diary in 1635.

> A ceremonious, light-timbered scholar,
> With a little dam-me[47] peeping over his collar;
> With a Cardinal's cap, broad as a cart-wheel,
> With a long coat and cassock down to his heel.
>   See a new Churchman of the times,
>   O the times', the times' new Churchman!
>
> His gravity rides up and down
> In a long coat or a short gown;
> And swears, by the half football on his pate,
> That no man is predestinate.

[45] *Diary of John Rous*, ed. Mary Anne Everett Green. (Camden Society, 1856.)
[46] Rous, 12, 69.
[47] In a marginal note, Rous explains this word as being derived 'from the soldier's band, who usually sweareth God dam me'.

See a new Churchman of the times,
O the times', the times' new Churchman!

His Divinity is trussed up with five points,
He dops, ducks, bows, as made all of joints;
But when his Roman nose stands full east,
He fears neither God nor beast.
See a new Churchman of the times,
O the times', the times' new Churchman![48]

Such were Wren's active supporters in the diocese, as seen in caricature through the eyes of their adversaries. By this time a succession of High Church bishops had ruled the diocese for many years, and had tended to appoint clergy whose views reflected their own. These now formed a considerable party, outnumbering the active Puritans; and they supported the Laudian reforms with enthusiasm. From among their number Wren appointed commissioners to carry out his behests in the diocese. We know the names of many of his principal adherents, since his lists of the commissioners have been preserved. 'He was one of Bishop Wren's rural deans,' and 'he was a great maintainer of Bishop Wren's injunctions,' were to figure often among the charges preferred against the Royalist clergy of the two counties in a few years' time.[49]

In each Archdeaconry of his diocese, Wren nominated sixteen reliable clergymen to serve as his standing commissioners. There were then two Archdeaconries in Norfolk, and in both the Dean of Norwich was named at the head of the commission. The Dean at this time was John Hassall, who has lately cherished great hopes of being appointed a bishop himself. He had been chaplain to the King's sister Elizabeth, the Electress Palatine and Queen of Bohemia, and had delivered to Laud a letter of recommendation from his august patroness, at an interview during which 'he carried it so high upon his own merit' that he made a very bad impression. In any case the King and the Archbishop had already determined upon the appointment of Wren, and Laud replied to

[48] Ibid., 78–9.
[49] Wren always described his assistants as commissioners, not as rural deans. In his articles of defence he said that he never used the latter term, 'nor did constitute any such'. *Parentalia*, 106.

the Queen of Bohemia to that effect with considerable firmness.[50]
Hassall accepted his defeat with a good grace, and did all he could
to give support to Wren. He wrote to the new bishop at the time of
his first visitation: 'I thank God, and God's gracious instrument
your Lordship, for these fair beginnings. Good luck have thou
with thine honour, ride on. What furtherance your Lordship's
humble servant the Dean of Norwich can give to this great
work shall never be wanting.'[51]

Several Doctors of Divinity with cures in the diocese were
appointed commissioners in one or other Archdeaconry, and most
of the prebendaries of Norwich Cathedral. For the rest, the commissioners were prominent High Churchmen such as Matthew
Brooke of Great Yarmouth, John Lewthwaite of Stow Bedon,
Edmund Duncon of Swannington, Stephen Hurry of Aldburgh and
Thomas Thexton of Trunch.[52] Those who survived into the years
of the Civil War were ejected from their livings almost without
exception.

Wren had his adherents too among the clergy of the city of
Norwich. As we have seen, the ministers of some of the principal
churches were strongly Puritan. But fourteen Norwich clergymen,
including the rectors or curates of St. Andrew, St. Mary and
St. Lawrence, set their hands to a declaration of support for the
Bishop, 'by whose pious care and great pains herein, the public
worship and service of God is much advanced amongst us already,
and will doubtless, every day, more increase, as all moderate and
truly religious men will fully testify.'[53]

Among the citizens of Norwich he likewise had a substantial
body of sympathizers, although the majority of the Corporation
were disposed towards Puritanism. The King had sent written
instructions that the Mayor, Sheriffs and Aldermen should repair
to divine service and sermon at the Cathedral, and his wishes were
on the whole well observed. Nevertheless, it was reported, Alderman Shipdham 'useth no reverence at all in the Cathedral, neither
in standing up at the creeds, nor at the hymns, nor at the blessed
name, and standeth not up at the Gospel'; and a 'factious and

[50] Laud, *Works*, vii, 167–8.
[51] B.L. MS. Tanner 68, f. 86.
[52] Ibid., ff. 219–20.
[53] Ibid., f. 164.

dangerous' councillor named Thomas King was often absent from the services. Moreover the swordbearer of the Corporation wore the cap of maintenance on his head in the Cathedral, whereas he ought to have held it in his hands.[54] But when in the autumn of 1636 the Mayor and a majority of the Corporation petitioned the King in favour of the non-conforming ministers, no fewer than twelve of their civic brethren addressed a letter to Wren in which they recorded their dissent. 'Whereas it is come to our knowledge that a petition is preferred to his Majesty in the name of the whole Corporation of the City of Norwich: we whose names are subscribed thought it our bounden duty to certify under our hands that our assent was not thereunto.' They signed themselves as 'your Lordship's ever devoted'; and several of their names occur among the Royalist minority expelled from the Corporation by their Puritan colleagues a few years later.[55]

6

Laud's report on the state of the southern province during 1637, delivered to the King in the early months of 1638, has a good deal to say about the diocese of Norwich. There were now only six lectures in the diocese, at Norwich, King's Lynn, North Walsham, East Harling, Wymondham and Bungay; 'but they are all performed by conformable and neighbouring divines'. As for the 'single lecturers', presumably those maintained by private individuals, 'my Lord hath a special eye over them.' Of the Puritan clergy who were under episcopal censure, or had fled to avoid it, not more than three or four had submitted themselves; and the Bishop, who had patiently awaited the submission of the rest, must now proceed to deprivation, 'or suffer scorn and contempt to follow upon all his injunctions'. The King wrote in the margin, 'Let him proceed to deprivation'.

Mention was made of churches that had become ruinous, often through the depopulation of villages, where nothing had been left standing but the manor-house and the church, 'and that turned to the lord's barn, or worse use'. Along the coast 'divers,

[54] Ibid., ff. 82, 238. Laud, *Works*, v, 350.
[55] B.L. MS. Tanner 68, ff. 151-3.

not only churches, but townships themselves, are in danger of utter ruin by a breach of the sea'. In the larger towns the church-yards were often profaned by the neighbourhood of inns and alehouses. At Carrow, on the outskirts of Norwich, there were twelve houses 'reported to be of no parish, and so an ordinary receptacle for recusant papists, and other separatists, to the great prejudice of that neighbouring city'.

Nevertheless, despite these various shortcomings, Laud was well pleased with what had been achieved by Wren during the past two years. 'Divine service, both for prayers, catechism and sermons, is diligently frequented; and that beyond what could suddenly be hoped for in such a diocese, and in the midst of the humorousness of this age.'[56] Wren had his implacable opponents and his ardent supporters; but it is likely that most of his clergy were quiet conformists, willing to accept the measure of cere-monial that he enjoined, and in many cases welcoming his call to repair and beautify their churches.

We may take as an example the parish of Melton All Saints, now known as Great Melton, where entries in the register show parson and patron and other well-wishers working together to this end all through the sixteen-thirties. The leading people at Melton at this time were the Anguishes, a Norwich merchant family who had invested in land and were now established among the gentry. The Rev. William Yonger was presented to the living by Edmund Anguish in 1631, and thereafter scarcely a year passed without some improvement to the fabric and furnishing of the church. In 1632 the old communion cup was melted down and refashioned into two, one of which was bestowed upon the church of Melton St. Mary, which then stood close to All Saints though served by another incumbent. In 1633 the high altar was provided with rails; and the commandments, the creed and the Lord's Prayer were set up. In the same year there is mention of a painted ceiling set above the altar, 'formerly taken from the rood loft'. In 1635 the chancel was new paved at the charge of Mr. Anguish, and in 1639 it was new tiled at the charge of the rector. In 1638 a cushion for the communion table was given by the squire's kins-man, the Rev. Richard Anguish, the rector of Starston. In 1640 the seats of the church were planchered with deal at the cost of one

[56] Laud, *Works*, v, 349–52.

of the churchwardens, and Mr. Anguish had two sundials set up, one over the porch and one on the chancel wall. Then these entries abruptly cease.[57] Mr. Yonger the rector, despite his Laudian inclinations, seems to have gone with the altered times and remained undisturbed in his living. But his brother of the cloth, Mr. Anguish of Starston, was ejected and sequestered; and several of the Anguishes of Melton joined the King's forces, or otherwise displayed their Royalist sympathies.

But despite the measure of order and conformity that he had managed to achieve in his diocese, Wren was fighting a losing battle. The machinery of church discipline was cumbrous and antiquated. It could no longer be enforced with any degree of effectiveness or justice. In theory every sort of offence, from adultery and fornication to drunkenness and absence from church, came within the cognisance of the ecclesiastical courts. But in the eyes of the laity, the courts had lost much of their authority, and were no longer held in awe. The penalties they were able to impose, such as excommunication and penance, were often disregarded or evaded. They could be vexatious enough, especially in a diocese ruled by a bishop with the energy and conviction of Wren; but they were seldom effective, and their shortcomings lent force to the incessant Puritan attack on the Church.[58]

None of this is likely to have been apparent to Wren. He believed, as Laud believed, that the blessing of God rested on their labours, and that despite 'the humourousness of this age' the Church would prevail over all her adversaries. He continued on his course, determined and inflexible, until the spring of 1638, when he was appointed to take charge of the neighbouring diocese of Ely. 'I am right sorry,' wrote Dr. Corbett, 'that we shall lose you before your Lordship hath perfected this diocese in all respects, which a year or two more would have reduced to a good pass by your Lordship's indefatigable diligence and vigilancy.'[59]

[57] Register of Melton All Saints, kindly made available to me by the Rev. H. J. Paine.
[58] This subject is fully treated in two remarkable chapters, 'The Bawdy Courts' and 'The Rusty Sword of the Church', in Christopher Hill's *Society and Puritanism in Pre-Revolutionary England*. Its East Anglian aspects are described in detail in Mr. D. W. Boorman's valuable thesis, to which reference has already been made.
[59] B.L. MS. Tanner 68, f. 11.

Ely was in area a smaller diocese than Norwich; but it was greater in standing and in revenue, and the supervision of the University and town of Cambridge was paramount among the functions of its bishop. A few hundred yards from Wren's new Cathedral and Palace was a modest house occupied by a country squire who in the last Parliament had been member for Huntingdon, and who had lately succeeded an uncle as farmer of the Cathedral tithes. His name was Oliver Cromwell.

CHAPTER V

Ship Money

I

The decade of the sixteen-thirties was a time of peace and prosperity, and within a few years men were to look back to it as to a golden age. There was, wrote Clarendon, 'so excellent a composure throughout the whole kingdom, that the like peace and plenty, and universal tranquillity for ten years was never enjoyed by any nation.' But it was also a period of bitter and ever-growing discontent. Beneath the apparent calm and felicity of England, so envied by the warring nations of continental Europe, lay 'the inward reserved disposition of the people to murmur, and unquietness'.[1]

The decision of the King to govern without a Parliament, which alone could control the customary sources of supply, led to a variety of new expedients to raise money. These caused much resentment, but in general their effects were confined to property-owners of some standing. In 1634, however, the ancient levy of Ship Money was revived, by which in earlier centuries coastal towns had been required to furnish ships for the Navy. And next year it was extended to cover not only the maritime counties, but the whole of England.

Its legality was uncertain, a subject for endless judicial and antiquarian dispute. In the famous case of John Hampden the judges were divided, and a decision was given in favour of the King by an extremely narrow majority. It was assessed on very comprehensive lines, so that its effects were felt by a multitude of small occupiers, more burdensomely indeed than by the larger landholders. It was by far the most rewarding of the financial measures introduced during the period of the King's personal rule. But, as is the way with taxes, its undoubted effectiveness did nothing to mitigate its unpopularity.

[1] Clarendon, i, 52, 58, 60, 71.

Norfolk was a maritime county with a long seafaring tradition. It had also been very conscious, all through the centuries, of the danger of attack from across the sea. The presence off its coasts of the piratical 'Dunkirkers' is a recurrent theme in Norfolk history. Nevertheless its people as a whole were no more ready to pay Ship Money than the people of any other county, especially after the Hampden case had shown its probable illegality and the further dangers implicit in its principle. The duty of collecting this highly unwelcome tax was laid upon the Sheriff of each county; and the experiences of successive Sheriffs of Norfolk tell a tale of progressive difficulty in their unenviable task.

Early in his year of office, a writ would be delivered to the Sheriff, requiring him to collect a given sum for the construction of a ship of a specified burthen, 'with the men, victuals, munitions and equipment of the same'.[2] The Sheriff would then hold a meeting with the authorities of the various boroughs within the county, at which proportions of the total payment were allocated to the boroughs, and the responsibility for the remainder was undertaken by the county. In due course he assessed the contribution required from each parish, including the payment expected from each clergyman on his ecclesiastical and temporal estate. It then became the duty of the chief constables of the hundreds to collect the sums due, and remit them to the Sheriff.[3]

The writ issued in 1635, for Ship Money to be collected and delivered by the Sheriff appointed for 1636, assessed Norfolk at £8000. Of this sum Norwich was required to find £1100, King's Lynn £300, Great Yarmouth £220, Thetford £30, and Castle Rising £10. The remainder was to be provided by the county. This was duly collected by the Sheriff for that year, Sir Edward Barkham of Southacre. The writ for 1637 was for £7800. In this year the Norwich contribution was drastically reduced to £500, the other boroughs remaining as before: so an extra £400 was required from the county. The new Sheriff was William Paston of Oxnead, who likewise remitted the full sum to the Privy Council, although he met with a certain amount of resistance. On 4 Nov-

[2] H.M.C., Great Yarmouth Corporation, 311.

[3] See especially C.S.P.D., 1637–8, 220, in which Sir Francis Astley describes the allocation between the boroughs and the county at a meeting at the Guildhall of Norwich on 16 November 1637.

ember 1637 he wrote to Secretary Nicholas that 'I have paid all the Ship Money to Sir William Russell, but I have not levied so much as the sum amounted to. I beseech you petition the Lords to grant their mandate to my successor to collect the arrearage, £16 12. 9.' He was a rich man, well able to adopt this casual attitude over a comparatively small balance, and if necessary to meet it from his own pocket.[4]

His successor in 1638 was Sir Francis Astley of Melton Constable, who was required to raise the sum of £7800. He soon ran into difficulties. Resentment against Ship Money was increasing, and the case of John Hampden was being determined during these very months. Hampden, in the words of Clarendon, 'grew the argument of all tongues, every man enquiring who and what he was that durst at his own charge support the liberty and property of the kingdom, and rescue his country from being made a prey to the Court.'[5] The Hampden case, even though the verdict was ostensibly favourable to the King, added greatly to the unpopularity of the tax. Local Hampdens made life a burden to the Sheriffs and their underlings.

On 1 May 1638 Astley wrote to the Privy Council complaining of his difficulties. He mentioned the neglect of several chief constables, including Matthew Stephenson and Roger Reynolds of the hundred of Blofield. Two attorneys, Edward Holt and Edmund Hilton, had refused to pay, and encouraged others to stand out. And a clergyman, Henry Nowell, curate of Great Plumstead, had proved especially recalcitrant. He had 'braved the Sheriff in a great assembly', and in the end Astley had been obliged to commit him. 'He had not been in gaol above an hour before he wrote a submission; whereupon, out of respect for his submission, the Sheriff discharged him, but he has not paid, and goes about boasting and encouraging others to withstand payment.' Later in the month Nowell was sent for by warrant to appear before the Council, and was discharged 'upon his acknowledgement of his error and promise of conformity in all the King's services'. There were many others to be complained of, but the Sheriff had only certified these few, 'not desiring to draw up multitudes before the Lords'. The corporations, with the

---

[4] C.S.P.D., 1637, 284, 511, 515.
[5] Clarendon, ii, 205.

exception of Thetford, were all backward in their payments. 'The parts of the county adjacent to them have an eye to them, and upon their delay are not so forward as otherwise.' He prayed that the Lords of the Council would write to remind these laggard corporations of their duty.[6]

Only a few days after writing this letter, Sir Francis Astley unexpectedly died. Before the end of May a patent had gone down to Norfolk, appointing John Buxton of Tibenham as his successor. It was accompanied by a copy of the instructions to Astley about Ship Money, and by special injunctions that the new Sheriff was to use his utmost diligence in its speedy collection.

2

The Buxtons of Tibenham, and later of Shadwell, are not to be confused with the present family of the name, who did not appear in Norfolk until the beginning of the nineteenth century. They were minor landowners who for some generations had stood in a confidential relationship to the Dukes of Norfolk, looking after their local affairs, and themselves gradually attaining wealth and standing in the county. John Buxton himself was a somewhat diffident and retiring character, a man made for quiet times. It was bad luck that he should have to take over the duties of Sheriff at this juncture, since Astley had already collected such of the Ship Money as was readily proffered by men of good will, and he was left to cope with the reluctant and recalcitrant.

There is a tendency among certain historians, preoccupied with the concept of 'status', to assume that the office of Sheriff was always eagerly sought. It is true that a thrusting and ambitious man could greatly advance his own interests and those of his friends during his year of office. But in the eyes of many country gentlemen, the trouble and expense far outweighed any advantage that could be obtained in terms of influence or social prestige. Sometimes the office could be imposed on a man, by an unfriendly cabal amongst the dominant figures of a county, wholly against his wishes and to the serious detriment of his estate. Buxton's mother-in-law, Mrs. Pert, wrote to him on 14 August 1638,

[6] C.S.P.D., 1637–8, 295, 444.

probably at the close of the summer assizes: 'I am very glad to hear that you have found such noble friends to bring you off of your fearful business with so much honour. I hope that you will be careful to retain the King's favour, and also to keep the love of your countrymen, which I confess as the times are now is a very hard task to be performed; yet I hope you will endeavour it, so that in the conclusion of your office, your enemies shall find that they did you a courtesy, though they intended a mischief. I was told that one of their faction should say that you should continue your office another year. I did intend to give you notice of it that you might use means to prevent it when the time shall serve, and I would wish you to be careful to look unto it and not to rely too much on great men's promises.'[7]

The identity of this hostile 'faction' remains undisclosed; and it is clear from Buxton's papers, which his last descendant recently bequeathed to the Cambridge University Library, that in general his neighbours rallied to support him in his duties of ceremony and hospitality. It was no light task for a country gentleman to organize his tenants and servants into the retinue necessary at assizes—the trumpeters, the ushers, the footmen, the cooks, the helpers in kitchen and buttery. Men and horses were freely borrowed for the cavalcade which was to escort Buxton into Norwich, and to attend upon the judges. He found 26 men, and his neighbours provided 32 more. They were all furnished with liveries in his own colours. Sir John Holland, Sir Robert Kemp, Thomas Knyvett, various members of the D'Oyly family, uncles and cousins in all directions came to his aid. Knyvett, his closest friend, delighted to address him as 'Noble Mr. Shreeve'; and Holland, genial and kindly as always, wrote that 'I salute you with the constant affections of a faithful heart, which shall be ever ready to do you service'.

Not only men and horses were supplied by Buxton's friends during the summer assizes: lavish gifts of provisions also flowed in. Venison was sent by every well-wisher who owned a park with deer—Sir John Hobart, Sir Thomas Wodehouse, Sir Robert Kemp, Thomas Knyvett, Mr. Berney, Mr. Bacon, Captain Havers, Mr. Ward of Bixley. Others sent partridges and capons, perch and

[7] Cambridge University Library, Buxton MSS., Box 96.

bream. Every gift is listed in a notebook kept by one of Buxton's assistants, together with his innumerable outgoings. There were presents to the judges' officers, and payments to a multitude of attendants and servants and helpers of all kinds. His purchases of meat and fowls were formidable in amount, together with every sort of fish and shellfish, from salmon and sturgeon down to lobsters, crabs and cockles.[8]

3

But the proper entertainment of the judges of assize, however expensive and burdensome, was secondary to the great task of gathering in the Ship Money. All through the summer and autumn months Buxton rode to and fro, 'with daily labour and travail, besides great expenses in journeying up and down the county'. Some of the chief constables were still refractory. Those of Walsham and Clavering, and the Blofield pair of whom Astley had already complained, were in arrear for the whole amount assessed upon their hundreds, and refused to distrain. These were the worst defaulters; but everyone engaged in collecting the tax was heartily sick of it. The under Sheriff, George Bayfield, made bold to address some sensible words of advice to the new Sheriff. He counselled him to suggest 'to their Lordships' consideration that somewhat may be allowed to the clerks and collectors, which will make them more cheerful in the service. No man goes a warfare of his own purse. The King hath had almost £30,000 out of this county, and no penny allowance given, which makes every man weary of his place'.[9]

Buxton may or may not have acted upon this suggestion. But the problem of the recalcitrant constables remained; and he asked that they should be summoned up to London by a pursuivant, which 'will much advance the service, and put spurs to the rest, who are not so forward as they ought to be'. At some stage not only the Blofield constables, but Buxton himself, appeared before the Privy Council. Lord Arundel, mindful of the long connection between the Buxton family and his own, spoke of him to the

[8] Cambridge University Library, Buxton MSS., Box 96.
[9] H.M.C., Buxton MSS., 252.

other Councillors with particular commendation; and his reception at this interview gave fresh encouragement to the exhausted Sheriff. He wrote that 'although many of the chief constables have assured me they will execute the warrant I have given them for distress, yet I am glad to assist them by my presence, labour and authority. Truly it is a work of that difficulty and excessive charge to me, besides the hate I have incurred of my county for executing those commands imposed upon me, that were I not supported by his Majesty's acceptance of my service it were insupportable, and I should sink under the burden. But I thank his Majesty for his goodness to me, and the Board when I was convented before them, which if I may have still it will be no small comfort to me'. And again, that he 'must ever gratefully acknowledge the gracious acceptance of his Majesty of his humble and dutiful endeavours. Had he not been encouraged and honoured beyond his merits, the task of collection of the arrears would have so far daunted him that he would have distrusted his spirit and stoutness in the execution of those commands . . . He was enforced, with his daily attendance on the service, to levy by force to that severity as he is become the most odious despicable man to his county that can be imagined'.[10]

The Blofield constables, Matthew Stephenson and Roger Reynolds, were no doubt severely admonished; and they were required, before they were dismissed by the Council, to enter into bond to pay Buxton the arrears that were due. Nevertheless, when they were safely back in Norfolk, Buxton was told that 'they have bragged and boasted of their coming off at the Council Board, and how well they spoke there, which has retarded all others that were in arrear'. By the end of October he had collected the whole amount but for £110, of which £78 was due from Blofield hundred. Stephenson and Reynolds were still up to their old tricks. 'They are such factious, peremptory fellows that their ill example, besides their persuasions in a secret way, has retarded others from the execution of the warrants I daily sent out for distress . . . and Stephenson more especially has bragged since his return from the Board that God strengthened him in a marvellous way, and that he answered boldly and undauntedly for himself. I have been much perplexed to hear of his daily ostentations in that kind, and am

[10] C.S.P.D., 1638/9, 48-9, 61.

persuaded that such spirits have caused it to be a work of such difficulty. Such hundreds as bordered upon Blofield were so infected by the vicinity that I had more to do to collect and levy their arrearages than in all the county beside.'[11]

Stephenson and Reynolds were now committed to the custody of a messenger. On 25 November they addressed a petition to the Privy Council, claiming that their hundred had been much overcharged, and the tax levied on many people who could not possibly afford to pay it. They 'thought it was not his Majesty's pleasure that such poor as these [should be compelled to pay], who cried out when the petitioners came to them for money, that they and their children were starving, and who had nothing to distrain but their bedding or some poor household stuff of no value'. They had already spent £20 out of their own estates, and would sell their whole estates rather than incur his Majesty's displeasure. They begged to be discharged from custody. It was ordered that they should be discharged, and Buxton was to answer the petition; but they were to attend upon the Council next term if the money in arrears had not been paid in the meantime.[12]

The next document in the affair is a further petition, bearing no date, from Stephenson and Reynolds. Their previous petition, they said, had been shown to Buxton. 'He could not deny the same, but said, "for all this I shall make you know that I am a man of worth and wisdom, and have many good friends at court, and make no doubt that I shall so far prevail with the Archbishop of Canterbury to lay you fast by the heels, where, for anything I know, you may lie all the days of your life, and these are but so many pricks in my side to make me use my best wits to accomplish the same". Saying also, that he would make the petitioners an example to all chief constables in England.' Harking back to the events of the summer, they asserted that Buxton had given them six weeks to collect the money; and after they had gathered £110, a fortnight before the time limit, 'he procured a messenger to be sent for them in harvest time', so that they had to spend £100 out of their own estates, and if they have to pay the further £78 they will be utterly undone. By this time Reynolds was apparently out of custody, but was sick of an ague and so disabled from collecting

[11] Ibid., 67.
[12] Ibid., 121–2.

more money. Stephenson again begged for release out of prison.[13]

Buxton's reply to the petition of 25 November was sent up to the Privy Council in January 1639, by which time his harassing period as Sheriff had come to an end. Since he was afflicted with an ague, and was much preoccupied with his militia duties, he asked the Council to excuse his personal attendance. He answered all the charges of the petitioners in considerable detail. He agreed that the charge laid upon Blofield was a high one, 'the greatest yet laid upon the hundred'. But the constables were themselves to blame for the rating of poor men. 'I conceive they discover their own carelessness in the service, for having received warrants from my predecessor (who died in the time of his Sherrifwick) for the assessing of £188 2s. 11d. upon the towns and persons within that hundred . . . they should not, according to the terms of the warrant, have assessed any poor men, but rated every man according to the most usual rates within that hundred; and had they complained of that in its season, I am confident [Astley] would have eased the poor, and laid the burden upon the better sort, as well in that hundred as in the rest.' In any case, the total of the sums of 3s. 4d. and under, which the constables described as so afflictive to the poorer men, amounted only to £22 3s. 10d.; and many of these little sums were rated upon 'able men' who had parcels of land in several different places. He therefore besought the Lords, 'there being in the whole county not one penny besides unlevied', that he might be discharged from collecting the outstanding £78 2s. 11d., since the constables still refused to inform him who had paid and who had not paid within their hundred. 'Lastly, I do certify the Lords that these petitioners confessed to me that they had sums in their hands of the Ship Money which they had collected, but have neither tendered nor paid it to me.'[14]

This official reply was accompanied by a private letter, presumably addressed to Secretary Nicholas, in which Buxton asked his correspondent's good offices with the Privy Council, and repeated his complaints against Stephenson and Reynolds. 'I have with extreme difficulty, incessant labour, and with the expenses of well nigh £200, without any allowance for it, collected, levied, and paid in all those sums which my predecessor dying left for me to

[13] Ibid., 233-4.
[14] Ibid., 401-3.

G

collect, and there is at this present under four score pounds to levy, all the rest being paid, which sum in arrear is within Blofield hundred; the chief constables of that hundred, Stephenson and Reynolds, being appointed the collectors, with whom I have had more trouble than with all the county besides.' They had refused to execute his distress-warrants, or to co-operate with him in any way. And as they stood bound to his Majesty, since their appearance before the Privy Council in the previous autumn, to collect and pay the money, he urged that direct proceedings should be taken against them.[15]

On 30 January the Privy Council issued a warrant committing Matthew Stephenson to the Gatehouse,[16] from which he was later discharged. But they continued to press Buxton as well; and a further letter from him, bearing no date, repeats his view of the matter, and again urges that he may be discharged from all responsibility for the unpaid £78. Stephenson and Reynolds had given bond to his Majesty to pay it. 'In the end of my year I again complained, and they or one of them were the second time committed and after discharged . . . and now Stephenson is dead, but Reynolds living and of good ability to pay a far greater sum. I do verily hope his Majesty (having good security) will be graciously pleased to look to them and not to me for the money, having collected little of the money paid in for that short time I abode in my place, but by distress; and for the poor, though rated by my predecessor, I have paid their rates of my own purse. My humble desire is, his Majesty having good security, I may be discharged and not be put to any further attendance, assuring you if you put the bonds in suit the debt is good and will be paid.'[17]

It would be possible to portray Stephenson as a village Hampden, dying soon after his release from the Gatehouse, worn out by the strain of his contest with an overbearing Sheriff. It would be equally possible to regard him as a stubborn and cross-grained fool, deliberately refusing to perform the duties which he was appointed and paid to carry out. Probably the truth lay somewhere in between. During these years there were plenty of such collisions between unpopular authority and local intransigence. In the end,

---

[15] H.M.C., Buxton MSS., 252–3.
[16] C.S.P.D., 1638/9, 382.
[17] H.M.C., Buxton MSS., 255.

it would seem that the £78 remained unpaid by anyone.[18] Buxton's protestations to the Privy Council had their effect, and he was able to return thankfully to the quiet tenor of his private life. Many Sheriffs had collected a far smaller proportion of the assessment on their counties, and had made far less strenuous efforts to do so. Within a few years he was to regret the conscientious way in which he had carried out the distasteful functions of his office.

4

Buxton was succeeded as Sheriff by Augustine Holl. The Holls, originally a merchant family in Norwich, had lived for several generations at Heigham, then a village in the countryside just outside the city walls. Augustine's father had been Sheriff of the county in 1626; and Augustine himself was married to a daughter of Sir William Wodehouse of Waxham, an ancient family apparently unconnected with the Wodehouses of Kimberley. His period as Sheriff was an easy one, since in 1639 the Ship Money assessments were much lighter than in past years. The counties of Norfolk and Suffolk were this year rated together at £5500, so that the total formerly paid by each was reduced by more than one half. Holl and the Sheriff of Suffolk, John Clench, held a joint meeting at Bungay, to which the boroughs of both counties likewise sent their representatives. It was decided that Suffolk should raise £2800 and Norfolk £2700. Of the latter sum, Norwich was rated at £150, Yarmouth at £80, Lynn at £72, Thetford at £12 and Castle Rising at £4. The rest of the county was to find £2382.[19] Holl managed to collect the whole of this with the exception of £78. It is probably a coincidence that this was the same amount that Buxton had been unable to extract from the hundred of Blofield. Despite the lower assessments, resistance to Ship Money was growing everywhere; and over the country as a whole, more than a third of the required sum remained unpaid.[20] In the eyes

---

[18] N. D. Gordon, *The Collection of Ship Money in the Reign of Charles I* (Trans. Roy. Hist. Soc. 1910), 159. It seems clear from the table on this page that the official county total for 1638 fell short by this amount.

[19] C.S.P.D., 1638/9, 403.

[20] Gordon, op. cit., 143.

NORFOLK IN THE CIVIL WAR

of the Privy Council, therefore, the performance of Norfolk and of its Sheriff was a highly creditable one.

The next Sheriff was Thomas Windham of Felbrigg. Of his three immediate predecessors, Paston and Holl may be assumed to have felt at least some measure of sympathy towards the aims of the government, since both actively supported the royal cause in the troubles to come; and Buxton was to preserve throughout the war a cautious neutrality. But Windham was a man of decided Puritan views. He had been bred to the law, and had shown considerable promise in his early years at Lincoln's Inn. He was of the school of Edward Coke, a friend and associate of the group of families connected with the law—Hobarts, Bacons, Gawdys—who gave unswerving support to Parliament. He can have felt no enthusiasm whatever for the task of collecting Ship Money. When he entered upon his term of office at the beginning of 1640, the ill-success of the first Scottish War had brought the administration to a new level of unpopularity. More and more people, in all walks of life, refused to pay the tax. Some Sheriffs indulged in various forms of obstruction, and a few virtually refused to collect it at all. Thomas Windham did not go to these extremes, but he was remarkably unsuccessful in his efforts to gather in the sum required.

Once again the county and boroughs of Norfolk had been assessed at £7800, an amount that the most devoted and energetic Sheriff, in the existing state of public opinion, could have had little hope of collecting. On 1 April, Windham told the Privy Council that 'I have with all industry applied myself to the service of Ship Money, and have not without extreme difficulty drawn the county to make and give up their rates and assessments, their defects therein having been much supplied by myself. Now by several reiterated warrants, all officers coming to make their collections and levies are so surcharged with multitudes of distresses, for which neither keepers nor buyers may be found in the county, that notwithstanding my good example and advice, I am now forced to appeal to the Lords for further directions and advice for my proceedings in so important a service'.

Early in April the Short Parliament was summoned, and, having failed to vote any subsidies, was dissolved after a life of three weeks. As a result the Council ordered the levying of Ship Money to be pursued with redoubled vigour. By 28 May, however, Windham had only gathered £1100. 'This has been collected with inexpressible difficulty and levied by distresses of which there were few buyers. There is in the county a general damp of industry and commerce, with a despicable ebb and depression of the price of commodities.' On 4 June he wrote again. He had 'earnestly incited' the chief and inferior constables of the various hundreds. 'Some have laboured diligently in this service and brought in a good part of the money chargeable on their hundreds, whilst others are so abounding in their remissness and obstinacy that they have done very little or nothing. I should have committed some of them, had it not been probable that their freedom from attendance on other services, especially in matters of arms at this present, would have rendered them and many of the inhabitants more conceitedly obdurate.' He once again sought the advice and assistance of the Council, 'that so the tractable subject who has paid his assessment may not be deeper contributory than the obstinate even in this expensive year, wherein his Majesty has no other known supply'.[21]

Lighter relief was furnished by the case of the Rev. Roger Howmans, rector of Sall, which Windham thought it necessary to transmit to the Privy Council. Thomas Baldwin, constable of that village, went to the parsonage house and 'in civil manner' demanded 15s. for Ship Money. The rector, 'being much moved', asked him 'if the Devil had sent him to him for the said Ship Money'. The constable replied that 'he received no warrant from any such'. 'I think verily the Devil sent you to me', was the rector's rejoinder, and he 'reiterated the same passionate words several times, saying he was not yet resolved whether he would pay or no'.[22]

Windham received no comfort from the Council in answer to his letters, nothing but rebukes and threats. The point he repeatedly tried to make, that there were few or no buyers at the sales forced by distress-warrants, was brushed aside as a mere excuse. Eventually a letter was sent under the King's sign-manual. After a lengthy preamble, Windham was told that 'contrary to the faith and allegiance which you owe unto us, you have hitherto

[21] C.S.P.D.,, 1640 1, 230, 266.
[22] Ibid., 222. Cf. H. A. Wyndham, *A Family History, 1410–1688*, 191–2.

neglected to perform that service in manifest contempt of our Crown and dignity, and thereby have much incurred our high displeasure and indignation, and as much as in you lies have exposed this state and kingdom to the danger of a foreign enemy, for the want of those timely supplies which are necessary for the safety and preservation thereof. We have therefore to leave you the more excuseless thought fit by these our own letters to signify our express pleasure to you that, without further delay, you perform that service according to the tenor of the said writ . . . and this upon your peril of incurring the uttermost of such forfeitures and punishments as by the laws of the realm may be inflicted upon you for so high a contempt and misdemeanour.'[23]

Despite all this sound and fury, Windham only collected less than one quarter of the amount that was due—£1659 in all, leaving £6141 unpaid. But none of the threatened consequences fell upon him. At the end of the year, before his term of office had expired, a second Parliament, destined to be known as the Long Parliament, was returned to Westminster. One of its earliest measures was a declaration that the raising of Ship Money was wholly contrary to the laws of the realm. The situation was completely reversed; and those Sheriffs who had been especially active in the collecting of the hated tax, and had incurred exceptional unpopularity during their term of office, now found themselves liable to be called to account before a committee specially set up to consider cases of 'the rigorous levying of Ship Money'.

A Norwich lawyer lost no time in petitioning Parliament against John Anguish, Mayor of Norwich in 1635, for his rigorous levying of Ship Money. During the winter Thomas Knyvett met John Buxton out hunting on Larling Heath, and they discussed the present situation out of earshot of others in the open field. 'Poor Jack is very matt,' Knyvett told his wife, 'and, I believe, much afraid his turn of being questioned for Ship Money will come.' But just at that moment Anguish's son rode by, on his return from London, and consoled Buxton with the news that his father 'came off very well'. In March a letter from Knyvett in London told Buxton that he had met his cousin Henry Elsing, the Clerk of the House, 'who tells me that there have not yet been any tittle of motion against you, but withal tells me he verily believes

[23] Wyndham, op. cit., 192–3. H.M.C., Corporation of Great Yarmouth, 312.

that all shreeves that have been active by distraining for Ship Money will be questioned and forced to good sore damages'. Elsing advised that 'it would be much better for any man (if he can) to make his peace at home with such as he fears will complain, than to run the hazard of the House'. Sir William Paston was in danger of being summoned before Parliament 'on the complaint of parson Frier'. In the event no retribution seems to have befallen Anguish, Buxton or Paston; but the very possibility is enough to show the dramatic suddenness with which the times had changed.[24]

[24] Rushworth, III, i, 88, 151. Knyvett, 96. H.M.C., Buxton MSS., 260-1, and further material in Buxton MSS., Cambridge University Library.

CHAPTER VI

The Summoning of Parliament

I

Virtually no members for the county of Norfolk, or for any of its five boroughs, had been at all conspicuous in the Parliaments of King James and the three first Parliaments of King Charles. The Knights of the Shire were members of families long established in the county, bearing such names as Cornwallis, L'Estrange, Drury, Townshend, Heveningham. The independent boroughs of Norwich, Great Yarmouth and King's Lynn almost invariably chose influential merchants, members of their own corporations, and on occasion their recorder. At Thetford and Castle Rising the Howard influence was paramount, and was usually exercised in favour of suitable gentlemen within the county, though sometimes a nominee was selected from farther afield.

A few exceptions to this pattern may be noted. That indomitable figure Sir Edward Coke was returned for his native shire in the Parliaments of 1625 and 1626. His activities in the first of these Parliaments greatly angered the King, who disabled him from sitting in the second by the neat device of appointing him High Sheriff of Buckinghamshire. In the 1628 Parliament, the Parliament of the Petition of Right and his last great speeches, he sat for Buckinghamshire, having also been returned for Suffolk.

Another figure of more than local importance was the antiquary and book-collector Sir Robert Cotton, a close friend of Lord Arundel, who enabled him to sit for Thetford in 1625 and for Castle Rising in 1628. In both these Parliaments he adopted a strong anti-Court line, and incurred the deep displeasure of the King and his advisers, which resulted later in an accusation of concealing treasonable pamphlets and the virtual confiscation of his library.

At the opposite extreme, Norwich provided a seat in 1626 for a nominee of the Court, Sir John Suckling, the Comptroller of the Household. This might appear an unexpected choice; but Sir John was the son of a former Mayor of Norwich and the brother of its present Dean, and had maintained close ties with the city throughout his career. He had prospered greatly at Court, both through his own abilities and his opportune marriage to the sister of the rich magnate Lionel Cranfield, Earl of Middlesex. But he had buried his wife in the city of his birth, under a splendid monument in St. Andrew's Church, a very sophisticated affair with its recondite emblems and its mottoes in French, Italian and Spanish. And on the monument was carved the kneeling figure of his son John, a demure boy with his hair combed stiffly backwards, soon to become the gay and flamboyant poet who embodied, in Puritan satire and propaganda, all the most frivolous and reprehensible aspects of the Court.

2

In the summer of 1639 the King embarked upon the first of the 'Bishops' Wars', those misguided attempts to impose an episcopal system upon the Scottish people. The expedition proved wholly ineffective, and was soon brought to a close by the truce signed at Berwick in June. In this campaign Lord Arundel was in command of the royal forces, and had raised a volunteer troop of horse from amongst his supporters and well-wishers in Norfolk. A stately letter from the King, written from his Court at Berwick on 27 June, acknowledged the services of his loving subjects in Norfolk, 'not only in sending your sons, allies and friends in this service, but also of your and their voluntary charges therein'. His thanks, and the assurance of his favour, were to be expressed at 'your next public meeting or as you shall find convenient'. A letter from Arundel, hardly less stately in tone, brought his own appreciation of 'your zeal and devotion to his Majesty's service in sending to attend me in this late expedition so brave a troop of horse, which his Majesty hath seen with much satisfaction and thereby received a great impression of your hearty affections unto his service, no other county having given so free and worthy a testimony thereof.'[1]

[1] Holkham MSS., 684. The two letters are copied into a manuscript volume compiled by William Heveningham of Ketteringham, which descended to the Coke family through his daughter Abigail, the grandmother of the first Earl of Leicester.

But despite these magniloquent phrases, the campaign had been an ignominious failure. It left the King virtually without financial resources, and certainly with no funds with which to resume an unnecessary and highly unpopular war. 'That summer's action,' wrote Clarendon, 'had wasted all the money that had been carefully laid up; and to carry on that vast expense, the revenues of the Crown had been anticipated; so that, though the raising of an army was visibly necessary, there appeared no means how to raise that army. No expedient occurred to them so proper as a Parliament.'[2] Through the authority of Parliament the King hoped to raise fresh supplies, and bring the Scots to their proper obedience. There had been no Parliament in England for eleven years; yet neither the King nor his advisers seem to have expected that the newly-elected assembly would prove other than tractable. They remained wholly unaware of the real temper of the nation.

The decision to call Parliament was taken in December 1639, and it was summoned to meet early in the following April—'the notice of it,' wrote Clarendon, 'being welcome to the whole kingdom.'[3] Norwich returned two prominent members of its civic body, Thomas Atkins and John Tolye; and Lynn returned a similar pair, William Doughty and Thomas Gurlyn, both of whom had represented the borough in earlier Parliaments. Thetford chose Sir Thomas Wodehouse, whose verses were quoted in an earlier chapter, and Framlingham Gawdy of nearby West Harling, who had already been their representative five times. The members for Castle Rising were Thomas Talbot and Nicholas Harman.

At Yarmouth the Court interests attempted to apply a little pressure. The High Steward of the borough, Edward Earl of Dorset, wrote at the end of 1639 to recommend the younger Sir John Suckling, 'a very noble gentleman and of able parts', as a highly suitable person to serve as one of their burgesses. The courtier-poet, incidentally, had made himself conspicuous during the late expedition against the Scots, for which he had raised at immense cost a troop of horse—'a hundred very handsome young proper men, whom he clad in white doublets and scarlet breeches, and scarlet coats, hats and feathers'—the splendour of whose

[2] Clarendon, i, 103.
[3] Ibid., 104.

equipment was scarcely matched by the valour they displayed.[4]
The Bailiffs of Yarmouth replied that Sir John's name would be
included 'amongst such others as are to stand for it to the general
vote of the Assembly, leaving the success to divine providence,
by which all the actions of men are governed'. At the same time
the Lord High Admiral, Algernon Earl of Northumberland,
wrote that in earlier days the ports and sea-towns of England had
been accustomed to give the Lord High Admiral the nomination
of one of their burgesses, and commending to their notice the
suitability of Sir Henry Marten, Judge of the High Court of
Admiralty. He received a similar reply. But in the following
March the two Earls were informed, without any further references to divine providence, that the Assembly had chosen neither
of their nominees, having preferred to be represented by two of
their own townsmen who had served them in former Parliaments.[5]
The two burgesses thus chosen were Miles Corbett, their recorder,
and Edward Owner, a citizen noted for his enterprise and
obstinacy. There could have been no more suitable representatives
for that self-reliant and independent town.

The name of Miles Corbett will appear frequently in this book.
He was a younger son of Sir Thomas Corbett of Sprowston, and
nephew of Dr. Clement Corbett, the Chancellor of Bishop Wren.
Uncle and nephew shared the same authoritarian temperament,
but exercised it in contrary directions. Miles Corbett was a lawyer
of rigid Puritan convictions, a future regicide and Rumper. A
grim-faced, swarthy, saturnine man, he developed into a vindictive extremist, hated and feared by the Royalists, and regarded with
mistrust by the more moderate elements of his party and class.
'This Inquisitor General,' Clement Walker called him, 'this prologue to the hangman, that looks more like a hangman than the
hangman himself.'[6] He became chairman of the dreaded Committee of Examinations, and many accounts have survived of the
hectoring and bullying in which he delighted to indulge.

There was considerable disagreement over the choice of the
two Knights of the Shire. It might have been supposed that
the gentlemen of Norfolk, whatever line they may have taken

[4] Aubrey, 59–61.
[5] H.M.C., Corporation of Great Yarmouth, 311–2.
[6] Walker, *History of Independency* (1661), 63.

individually in years to come, were at this juncture virtually unanimous in their dissatisfaction with the existing state of affairs. They might have been expected to agree among themselves, at so critical a moment, on the return of two of the most forceful and effective of their number. But it was not so. A clash of personalities occurred, and a contest took place. There was no doubt as to the general acceptability of Sir Edmund Moundeford of Feltwell, who had sat in the last Parliament for Thetford. But there was disagreement as to whether the other seat for the county should be filled by Sir John Holland of Quidenham or Mr. John Potts of Mannington.

Both men were to play a leading part in Norfolk affairs in the years ahead, and there would seem to have been no great difference in their political views. Both were strongly opposed to the policy of the Court, but later adhered to the moderate wing of their party. The families of both were of comparatively recent standing in Norfolk; and their personal qualities, rather than prestige or wealth, had brought them to the fore at this time.

The background and the personal character of Sir John Holland were discussed in an earlier chapter.[7] He was there described as a man of outstandingly moderate temperament, much in demand as a negotiator and conciliator, and regarded with some suspicion by the extremists of his party. It was also mentioned that despite his Puritan views he was married to a Catholic wife, a circumstance which involved him in much trouble and misunderstanding throughout his career.

Mannington Hall, the romantic moated manor-house in north Norfolk, built and embattled by William Lumnor in the fifteenth century, had come into the possession of the Potts family during the latter part of Elizabeth's reign. John Potts, a London lawyer, had married Anne Dodge, the half-sister of the last of the Lumnors, and had bought Mannington after his death. Their son, another John Potts, inherited the property; but in the meantime his mother had become the second wife of Sir Christopher Heydon, the impoverished and eccentric representative of that declining family. Young John Potts became Sir Christopher's ward, and was hustled into a marriage with the daughter of 'a favourite at Court with a small fortune'. After the death of his

7 See above, pp. 47-8.

wife he married a lady more to his mind, Ursula, daughter of Sir John Willoughby of Risley in Derbyshire, and widow of Sir Clement Spelman of Narborough. John Potts was a member of Gray's Inn before he retired to live in Norfolk, and was close on fifty years of age when he first aspired to a seat in Parliament, ten years older than his rival Holland.[8]

Much of the opposition to Holland was aroused by suspicions of his Papist wife, and therefore of his own possible unsoundness in religion. In the Long Parliament he would be required to give a full explanation of these matters to the House. But there were private cross-currents also at work. The two members for Thetford, Wodehouse and Gawdy, were particularly anxious that Potts should be chosen. Their influence lay mainly in the south of Norfolk, as did Holland's, and local rivalries may have caused them to take this line.

On 13 March Wodehouse wrote from Thetford to Potts, urging him to come forward as a candidate.

Sir

I doubt not but you have heard of my desires (amongst many others) that you might be elected to serve our county as a Knight of this ensuing Parliament, and so I wished it might be intimated unto you by your son-in-law [i.e. stepson] my cousin Spelman long before the declaration of those that now rise up to be solicitors for the same; since which time I have had much conference and approbation of your just merit by a comfortable number of honest men, so as there is probable hopes you may carry it, if so be you would express your willingness to undertake the work, and not neglect such ordinary ways as may be fairly used by laws of modesty.

In these bad times all good men ought to seek such means as might enable them to enterprise good matters; and you, Sir, are the man, accounted one of those few we can now find to settle our hopes upon for this employment; wherefore it is not reasonable you should delay us any longer without divulging of your willing forwardness herein.

I was enforced to find excuse for your absence at this late

[8] C. S. Tomes, *Mannington Hall and its Owners* (1916), 14–16; MSS. at Mannington, Narborough and Baconsthorpe. Brunton and Pennington, 75.

assizes here in Thetford, where I wish you had been for divers good respects. I had some full occasion given me there, besides what else I took, to tell your competitors of my own devotions unto yourself, which I do not now tell you to beg a thanks, for thus I would have done unto my open adversary if I had thought him so sufficient to serve his county; which consideration hath made me and others to resolve upon our best endeavours for your election, and therefore we will be confident (until you say to the contrary) that you will not refuse the suffrages of many honest men, nor of myself who am

Your ever loving kinsman and servant
THOMAS WODEHOUSE.[9]

Potts's draft of his reply is much torn and stained, but the legible sentences convey a modest yet resolute acceptance.

That I have not sooner acknowledged the favour of your good opinion was my unwillingness for an undertaking too heavy for my strength. I must confess my own unfitness ever deterred me from the thought of Parliament, especially in this high road, so full of envy, toil and hazard; and more than ever had I cause to decline it, when all in me grows weaker, save my affections to the public good . . . Though I shall be ashamed to accept a charge much above my abilities, and should have been much more ashamed to beg it, yet your noble offer prevails; and since it pleaseth you and my friends, to cast the uninvited honour of your votes upon me, I will not ungratefully neglect the opportunity of service, nor be wanting in a modest way, to further your good aims . . . The die is cast and we come to the trial, where I expect the strongest opposition, which cunning, scorn and anger can invent, to disgrace myself or defeat others' freedom; but the mischief is foreseen, and the remedy prepared. If the work be God's, he can effect it; if it be not his will (more than my own) to employ me, I shall find ease in the loss, and comfort in discharge of my duty. The issue I leave to my Master; and whatever the success be, I hope still to approve myself an honest man to all the world, and to yourself, Sir,

Your humble kinsman and servant
JOHN POTTS.[10]

[9] B.L. MS. Tanner 67, f. 176.
[10] Ibid., f. 178.

Wodehouse wrote again on 23 March:

Sir

I found your letter newly come to my house on Friday night last, returning home out of Norfolk, where I had been negotiating for you, or rather for myself and county, which are the only objects of our endeavours for your election.

It is likely there will be the greatest noise and confluence of men that ever have been heard or seen on Norwich Hill, for never do I think was there such working and counterworking, to purchase vulgar blasts of acclamation. I have not been negligent in preparing minds and mouths about those parts imparted by your letter, yet I find some people ravished away by strenuous importunities, so as you must expect a rival of high stomach as well as stature, and yet I cannot fall in my belief, but do assure myself (by God's good favour) we shall obtain a prosperous wind to bring us to our wished port of Parliament.

I had some correspondence with my cousin Heveningham at the assizes. He seemed but cold; my hope is, it was cunning and discretion not to discover his intentions unto me; as I remember he said that Sir John had sent unto him, and that he had never heard from you at all about the business.

If you please to persevere by your self and friends in divulging your intent, content and willingness, I will not dread nor doubt the influence of any infatuated Procyon that may be elevated.

Sir, I shall not fail (by God's permission) to meet with you on Saturday at your house before dinner, where we may freely communicate our thoughts, and direct our course for a fair procedure according to his holy pleasure, who will and only can conduct us to a happy issue.

I remain, Sir,
　　　　Your entirely loving kinsman to serve you,
　　　　　　THOMAS WODEHOUSE.[11]

The election must have taken place within a couple of weeks after the writing of this letter, since Parliament assembled on 13 April. No record of the voting appears to have survived.

[11] Ibid., f. 189.

We do not even know whether a poll of the freeholders was taken, or whether the election was settled privately at a meeting of the gentry of the county. But some meeting was held at Norwich Castle, when Moundeford and Holland were returned as the Knights of the Shire, despite efforts made on behalf of Potts by his friends. There was much wrangling and disagreement, and Holland's opponents did all they could to cast doubt on the sincerity of his religious views. Their accusations wounded him deeply, and at the close of the meeting he reproached them in very downright terms.

Two manuscript volumes have survived into which Holland copied the speeches he delivered on various occasions. We do not know the date of the compilation of these volumes, or to what extent, if at all, he altered and amended the words which he had delivered. His speech at the Castle 'to the county of Norfolk, upon their electing me Knight of the Shire', began with the usual thanks for his election and the usual protestations of future service. He then continued: 'It is late, we are all weary, and I ought to ease you and bid you goodnight. And yet, gentlemen, now I think on't [clapping on my hat] a word to you in opposition before we part; and more especially to those, who have endeavoured to traduce me in the tenderest part of my reputation, in that of my religion—in the point of my faith, the faith I was brought up in, the faith I have publicly, constantly and sincerely professed, which faith I have ever bounded and guided by the established doctrine of the Church of England, and in which faith I hope by the favour of God to live and die . . . Then let all men judge how unjustly, how injuriously I have been dealt with: so unjustly, so injuriously as well might I here break out and say the poison of asps is under their lips, that you are a generation that cares not whose good name you traduce, so you may but thereby advance your own envious ends. But I will not lose myself in your offence. I will rather choose to heap coals of fire on your heads . . . Calumnies that are cast upon me undeservedly I shall value but as the barking of dogs in the street; well may they a little offend my ears, but never suffer them to come near my heart. But I forgive you all; go your ways and sin no more, lest God visit you for such practices, such offences; I have now only to thank the generality of my county, that they would not receive any

SIR JOHN HOLLAND
from a painting by Sir Peter Lely, in the possession of Norwich Castle
Museum

impression to my prejudice. And so, gentlemen, once more I bid you all goodnight.'[12]

Moundeford and Holland did not have to remain long at Westminster. The new Parliament, instead of voting the supplies that the King required, gave its attention solely to the grievances and illegalities which had so long afflicted the nation. They refused to grant the subsidies in exchange for which the King offered to discontinue the levying of Ship Money. He might well have attempted further conciliation or negotiation; but to the dismay of the moderate elements, and the satisfaction of those implacably opposed to him, he dissolved Parliament on 5 May.

'There could not a greater damp have seized upon the spirits of the whole nation,' wrote Clarendon, 'than this dissolution caused; and men had much of the misery in view, which shortly after fell out. It could never be hoped that more sober and dispassionate men would ever meet together in that place, or fewer that brought ill purposes with them; nor could any man imagine what offence they had given, which put the King upon that resolution. But it was observed, that in the countenance of those men who had most opposed all that was desired by his Majesty, there was a marvellous serenity; nor could they conceal the joy of their hearts: for they knew enough of what was to come, to conclude that the King would be shortly compelled to call another Parliament, and they were as sure, that so many, so unbiassed men, would never be elected again.'[13]

3

Without sufficient pay or supplies for his untrained and disorderly forces, the King embarked upon the second Bishops' War. In this adventure, as in that of the previous year, one of the few efficient and creditable commanders was the veteran Norfolk soldier Sir Jacob Astley. After a lifetime of campaigning all over northern Europe he had been recalled to England, and in the Bishops' Wars had held the important post of Serjeant Major General in the Army of the North. His letters and reports tell us much about his

[12] B.L. MS. Tanner 321, f. 3.
[13] Clarendon, i, 110.

efforts to set the northern defences in order, to train the local
levies, and to instil some measure of discipline into the troops
which reached him from other parts of the kingdom.

He was beset with all sorts of problems, and above all the
constant anxiety about the lack of equipment and money. 'I am
tortured in mind to think that I have not means to do what I
would,' he had written to Lord Arundel in the spring of 1639;
and in the summer of 1640 his note was the same. 'God help us!
I fear a good occasion will be lost for lack of money.' Indiscipline
was rife amongst the troops. He wrote from Selby to Secretary
Conway at the end of June 1640 that 'the men already come are
good bodied but extremely unruly, so that they break open all
prisons and are ready to strike their officers and do great mischief
in the country. So I have taken here a house for the prison to
commit offenders, and cast up a good trench before it, and have a
guard of forty men in it day and night'. In his next letter, written
from York early in July, he lamented that 'now I am to receive all
the arch knaves of the kingdom, and to arm them at Selby'. When
men were haled before him by the country people for stealing
geese, his penalty was to 'hang the geese about their necks in
irons'. Graver offences, brought to his notice by the officers, were
punished by confinement in his prison in irons, 'neck and heels
together'.[14]

The result of the King's second expedition was an invasion of
the northern counties by the Scots. They out-flanked Berwick,
occupied Newcastle, met with little resistance anywhere. In
October the King was compelled to sign the humiliating treaty
of Ripon. Under the terms of this treaty the Scots were to remain
in occupation of the northern counties, and to receive a payment
of £850 a day, until a final peace was concluded. Obviously so
huge an indemnity could not be met without the calling of
another Parliament. The Long Parliament, as it was to be known
in history, was accordingly summoned for 3 November.

In the Norfolk seats there were several changes from the representation in the Short Parliament. The members for Thetford,
Sir Thomas Wodehouse and Framlingham Gawdy, were returned
once more. So were Miles Corbett and Edward Owner for Great
Yarmouth. But at King's Lynn the previous members, William

[14] C.S.P.D., 1638-9, 566-7; 1640, 365, 462, 468, 490, 519, 558-9.

Doughty and Thomas Gurlyn, were replaced by two other merchants and former mayors of the borough, John Percival and Thomas Toll. Here there was an attempt on the part of Lord Arundel to influence the election. He had written to the Mayor and Corporation, and also to the Mayor in his private capacity, 'the effect of both letters being to elect a burgess to serve in the next ensuing Parliament one whom his Lordship hath nominated in his said letters'. The Hall Book discreetly passes over the name of Arundel's nominee; but it was 'unanimously agreed by the house that they will choose no other burgesses to serve in Parliament but only such as are resident and inhabiting within the Corporation'.[15] The newly chosen members, Percival and Toll, were both men of strong Puritan convictions; whereas Gurlyn, one of those now passed over, was to be prominent among the Royalist sympathisers when in 1643 the town declared for the King.

Norwich also changed both its members. Thomas Atkins was not this time a candidate, presumably at his own request, although he was elected again to fill a vacancy in the city's representation five years later. The other member in the Short Parliament, John Tolye, came bottom of the poll, a long way below the two members who were elected, Richard Harman and Richard Catelyn. Harman was a hosier, and Mayor of Norwich in 1639. Catelyn, although his family came originally of Norwich merchant stock, was the owner of two properties in the countryside, Lakenham on the outskirts of the city, where he usually resided, and Kirby Cane in the south-east of the county. The Sheriff of Norwich, whose function it was to act as returning officer, pronounced that Catelyn was 'a freeman, inhabiting in the county of Norfolk, but not in the city'. He therefore felt some doubt as to his qualifications to represent the city, and sent up a double return to Parliament: Harman and Catelyn, but 'if they be not duly chosen', then Harman and Tolye, as the House in its wisdom should decide. The matter was referred to the Committee of Privileges, which pronounced that Harman and Catelyn were 'well elected, and well returned to serve as the two citizens for the city of Norwich'. The scruples of the conscientious Sheriff nearly landed him in serious trouble. The Committee 'took into consideration the punishing of the Sheriff; yet, because there appeared no corruption or

[15] King's Lynn Hall Book, 12 October 1640.

practice in the managing of the election, they passed that point by'. And the House itself, when accepting the Committee's report, took notice 'that this carriage of the Sheriffs, in returning more than two burgesses for the said city of Norwich, is a great misdemeanour in him'.[16]

There was also a complete change in the representation of Castle Rising. For one of the seats the little borough, on the instructions of Lord Arundel, returned a courtier and Northamptonshire landowner named Sir Christopher Hatton. But Sir Christopher had also been elected for Higham Ferrers in his own county, another small borough which he had represented in the Short Parliament; and he now chose to sit for that borough. In his place Castle Rising elected his uncle Sir Robert Hatton, a man of similar background, but with interests also in Cambridgeshire and Kent. Neither of the Hattons had any connection with Norfolk, and both adhered to the Royalist cause in years to come. The other seat for Castle Rising was filled by Sir John Holland, who had this time been rejected by the county electors in favour of John Potts.

As the likelihood of a new Parliament became evident, feeling throughout the county had grown steadily in favour of stronger measures. This was presumably the reason why Potts, who had attracted much support at the earlier election and had not the handicap of a Papist wife, was now preferred to Holland, and was returned to Westminster in conjunction with Sir Edmund Moundeford. It may well be that Holland, resenting the asperities of the earlier contest, and anxious to preserve unity at this critical time among the gentry of the county, voluntarily withdrew in favour of Potts on this occasion. It was much grander to be a Knight of the Shire than a member for a little private borough, but it was also a good deal more troublesome and expensive. And Lord Arundel's willingness, by virtue of his family's long-standing association with the Hollands, to offer him a seat at Castle Rising, presented an opportunity for a graceful withdrawal from the county election.

[16] C.J., ii, 22. Keeler, 56–7, 128, 203–4. Brunton and Pennington, 81, state that Richard Harman had represented Castle Rising in the Short Parliament; but it seems certain that the member in that Parliament was named Nicholas Harman, and was a different person.

Some such action is suggested by certain phrases in letters from Holland to Framlingham Gawdy, Sir Thomas Wodehouse's colleague at Thetford. Gawdy had dismissed the steward of his manor, John Howse, for supporting Holland in the contest for the Short Parliament; and Holland twice wrote asking Gawdy to forgive the offence. The letters, which are undated, reveal the moderation and good feeling that Holland almost invariably displayed.

Sir

I am sorry John Howse's integrity and entireness to me at the former election is become a fault, and that the loss of your favour must be his punishment for this offence. He hath warning from you I hear to bring in your court rolls, and depart your service, and all for this cause. It would much trouble me to have so just provocation to revive the discourtesies of that business from some friends. I hitherto (what to satisfy the desires of Sir Edmund Moundeford, what to quiet discontents, and avoid all sidings and faction of the gentry of this county, incident to businesses of this nature) have passed by, as well the injuries I have received from some, as unkindness from others. And I hoped to find all the gentlemen of this county of the like constitution. Sir, you have hitherto given all testimonies of a quiet and peaceable nature. Depart not now I pray from your own principles and former practice, by casting him off for the expression of his faithfulness to me; which will *male audire* in the county, and give too public cause of fraction with him, that hath always desired to hold good correspondence with all men, and to you, Sir, have ever been an affectionate and faithful friend, and loving neighbour,

JOHN HOLLAND.[17]

This appeal seems to have met with no response, and the second letter was still more urgent in tone.

Sir,

There is no man living delights more in unity, and the progress of my life I hope assures it, the necessity of the times I am sure requires it. Why should we stick at trifles? If John Howse's over-zeal in the promoting of my cause hath made him forget some part

[17] B.M. MS. Egerton 2716, f. 333.

of that respect you expected from him, it is not a fault unpardon-
able I hope. Let him acknowledge it, and you cannot do yourself
and me more right than in the forgiveness. It is the glory of man's
nature to pass by offences! Be you, Sir, I pray, as worthy and wise
as you would have me in this business; nor do I desire in one tittle
from you, what I would not practise towards you.

Sir, the desertion of John Howse (whatsoever you think) will
have a clear reflection upon me in the eye of the county. His
sufferings herein cannot but be taken for my sake; and how can I
then avoid the sense of that discourtesy, that all men sees?

Sir, he lives not, and I can truly profess it, that have been, aye
and should be more troubled to desert that true and ancient
affection which have ever been preserved towards you in the
bosom of

JOHN HOLLAND.[18]

'Sidings and faction of the gentry . . . the necessity of the times
I am sure requires unity'—such words are not conclusive evidence
that Holland withdrew to Castle Rising to avoid further disunity,
but they suggest that it may have been so. In any event he and
those who had been opposed to him at the previous election—
Potts, Wodehouse, Gawdy—worked together harmoniously in
the Long Parliament for years to come. But there is nothing to
tell us of the success or failure of his plea on behalf of John Howse.

4

The new Parliament assembled on 3 November 1640. The
members representing the Court interests, the committed supporters of the King, were wholly outnumbered by ranks of impatient and resolute men, united in the pursuit of certain well-
defined aims. This unity was not to prevail for long. Amongst the
knights and gentry from the shires, the lawyers and merchants
from the boroughs, there were many who would range themselves
on the Royalist side when the great cleavage occurred. But at this
stage the great majority were of one mind as to what was amiss in
church and state. The grievances of the past two decades, the

[18] Ibid., f. 335.

resentments that had accumulated during the eleven years without a Parliament, were about to be remedied. They would put an end to the personal rule of the King, and sweep away the courtiers and churchmen who were his advisers. Above all, they would bring the towering figure of Strafford to the dust.

Under the dynamic leadership of Pym, they embarked at once on a great programme of innovation and reform. On 7 November a number of members presented petitions from their counties or boroughs, reciting the burdens and oppressions under which they had laboured during the long intermission of Parliament. Among them was Sir Edmund Moundeford, who delivered a petition from the freeholders of Norfolk. On the same day speeches were made by Pym and others, in which the measures to come were clearly outlined. A notable contribution was made by Sir John Holland, who alone of the Norfolk members figured with any prominence during those early debates.

'Times of action,' he began, 'are not for rhetoric and elocution, which emboldens me to rise; and though I must acknowledge myself one of the youngest scholars, and meanest proficients in this great school of wisdom, yet I conceive it a great part of my duty at this time, both to deliver my suit and conscience. We are called hither, Mr. Speaker, by the royal power, we sit here by the King's Majesty's grace and favour; and since his Majesty hath been graciously pleased to leave the government of all in our hands, I doubt not but that we shall lay such a foundation in the beginning of this Parliament, that we shall make it a happy age, a long lasting one, since the dangers of these times, the present distempers of this state, and therein his Majesty's and our necessities, yea, and the whole kingdom's safety do require it.'

He then proceeded, as other speakers had done, to list the grievances which were oppressing church and commonwealth— the usurping prelates; the sufferance of priests and Jesuits, 'by which means the number of the Roman Catholics is dangerously multiplied, idolatry increased, and God's heavy judgements highly provoked'; the extensions of the royal prerogative; the 'over-potency of some great ones, councillors of state, by whose advices . . . these present distempers do derive their originals'; the monopolists and projectors, 'the very moths and cankers that have fretten and eaten out all trade and commerce, the very beauty, strength and health of this famous island'; the favouring of foreigners and strangers.

As for the course that Paliament should now pursue, he thought that his Majesty's wants should be supplied 'with as much loyal duty and liberality as ever any people expressed towards their Prince'. The removal of the Scots army should be undertaken 'with a soft and gentle hand of mediation, pacification and reconciliation, if possibly it may be wrought with his Majesty's honour, and the kingdom's safety; if not, then to repel and repulse them with stout and resolute spirits, with valiant and united hearts and hands, such as shall best suit with our duty to God, our King, our country'. The affairs of the Church should be regulated 'with all true piety and well-grounded zeal to God's house and his truth ... Yet in all, Mr. Speaker, I do humbly desire we may proceed as best suiting the matter and condition of these distempered times, and as best becoming the honour, dignity and wisdom of this so great a court, so great a council, with all temper, modesty, and all due moderation'.[19]

Temper and moderation were words a good deal used, and sincerely meant, at this early stage of the Parliament. There were plenty of members who felt, with Sir John Holland, that a new era of peace and happiness was about to dawn. His speech is interesting as a summary of their point of view, and as the only detailed expression in Parliament of the personal attitude of any of the Norfolk members.

In spite of this speech, with its harsh words about the Catholics and their priests, there were still those who regarded Holland with suspicion. Pym gave expression to his view by moving that all those who had married recusants should cease to be Deputy Lieutenants of their counties. On this Holland rose and 'admitted the disaffection of my wife in point of religion', but protested his own entire loyalty. After some debate, John Hampden moved that since Holland had dealt 'so frankly and ingenuously' with the House, he should continue as a Deputy Lieutenant, to which the House agreed by vote. However, the matter was presently raised again, and on this occasion Holland made a longer speech, of

[19] Rushworth, III, i, 27–8. The speech was reprinted as a pamphlet in 1641, in a somewhat garbled form, without a publisher's imprint and without the authority of Parliament.

which a copy survives in his own hand. 'I must with ingenuity confess that notwithstanding the best of my endeavours to draw my wife to our Church, she yet withdraws herself from the communion of our Church. Consciences, Mr. Speaker, are in the hands of God, and he governs and guides them according to his good will and pleasure. They are not to be compelled, they are not to be enforced, they are only to be fairly treated and persuaded; and herein I have not been wanting, nor shall I, nor do I doubt but God in his good time will open her eyes and she shall see the light. In the mean time I think it part of my duty with patience and humility to wait God's leisure.' He had himself always been a faithful son of the Church of England. He was prepared to make a further attestation of his faith in any form the House might desire.

Once again the generous-minded Hampden used his influence in Holland's favour. On his proposition the House declared full confidence in their colleague; 'which was done unanimously,' wrote Holland, 'and stands to this day entered at large upon the journal of the House of Commons, and was my shield and buckler in those dangerous times.'[20]

5

'And now reformation goes on again as hot as a toast,' wrote Thomas Knyvett to John Buxton at the end of November, when the Parliament was less than a month old. 'I pray God the violent turning of the tide do not make an inundation. If thou didst but hear what sermons are preached to the Parliament men, thou wouldst bless thyself, and I go to Church now to learn the old way to heaven.'[21] Knyvett was to be an active and Buxton a passive Royalist, and these misgivings were soon amply justified. Nevertheless most of the earlier undertakings of the Parliament would have met with their approval—the abolition of the Courts of Star Chamber and High Commission; the declaration of the unlawfulness of Ship Money; above all, perhaps, the attack upon Strafford.

[20] Holland's own account of these episodes is in B.L. MS. Tanner 239, f. 12. See also Rushworth, III, i, 58.
[21] H.M.C., Buxton MSS., 259.

Correspondence between the Norfolk members is scanty during 1641; but a letter of Sir Thomas Wodehouse, who was ill and obliged to remain in the country, shows clearly enough their mood as the proceedings against Strafford reached a climax. On 21 April the bill of attainder had been passed by 204 votes to 59, with only one member from Norfolk, Sir Robert Hatton, the courtier representative of Castle Rising, voting in the minority. But the perplexed and hesitating King still stood between his faithful Commons and their victim. On the 23rd Wodehouse wrote to Potts, thanking him first for his frequent letters—'there be so few who will descend to love their lame and decrepit friends'—and continuing:

'It also gives no small content to us in your county, to be assured of such constant patriots as yourself, that will persevere faithfully in the defence of Church and Commonwealth affairs, especially in this heretical age, wherein there lives so many sublapsarians—

> Quos aut ambitio impotens,
> Aut spes solicitat lucri.

But we are touched still with fears and fits of trembling at such indulgence used in stay of axe and execution upon that insolent Earl and artificer of mischief unto the public good and government of three kingdoms, which will receive no hope of cure until they be discharged from the doubts and dangers of his redintegration.'[22]

Thomas Knyvett's comments on the trial of Strafford were scarcely more merciful in tone, although he was moved to admiration by the gallant bearing of the fallen Lord Deputy. The charges, he wrote to John Buxton, had been 'bravely urged and borne by the House of Commons, and as cunningly and with as much art and eloquence defended by his Lordship as ever bad cause was by any mortal. Mr. Pym, Glyn, Maynard, the young Lord Digby, Mr. Whitelocke and Strode, members of the House of

---

[22] B.L. MS. Tanner 66, f. 65. I think the reference to 'sublapsarians' is taken rather too literally by Dr. Yule (*The Independents*, 127) who pronounces, on the strength of it, that Wodehouse should be numbered among the Independents. See p. 358, where I give my reasons for including him among the Presbyterian moderates. The Latin lines seem to be an echo of Seneca, *Thyestes*, 364 (information from Mr. Richard Martineau).

Commons, have so banged and worried his Lordship as it begets pity in many of the auditors, though they see him laid open to be so foul a man. I think there was never any man of so unmovable a temper, for in all this time, although his provocations sometimes have been great, yet he hath not discovered the least passion, but when he speaks he doth it with so much bravery and modest courtship of both Houses and in such language as begets admiration in all the beholders . . . But most are of opinion that his head must be the satisfactory sacrifice when he has showed all his skill.'[23]

The sacrifice was duly offered up. Despite his promises to Strafford and his anguished efforts to fulfil them, the King was gradually forced to give way. In the end he consented to the death of the ablest and most devoted of all his supporters; and Strafford was executed on 12 May. In the course of his speech upon the scaffold he said: 'I profess heartily my apprehension, and do humbly recommend it to you, and wish that every man would lay his hand on his heart, and consider seriously, whether the beginning of the people's happiness should be written in letters of blood? I fear they are in a wrong way.'[24] It was a warning that few men in England were then disposed to heed.

[23] H.M.C., Buxton MSS, 261–2.
[24] Rushworth, *Trial of Strafford* (1680), 759. Cf. Clarendon, i, 203.

CHAPTER VII

Bishop Montagu and Bishop Hall

I

Parliament now turned its main attention to ecclesiastical matters, and set in motion the long-planned attack upon the Bishops and the whole episcopal system. In this connection it is time to revert for awhile to the affairs of the diocese of Norwich.

When Bishop Wren was translated to Ely in April 1638, he was succeeded at Norwich by Richard Montagu, Bishop of Chichester. In earlier years this prelate had been a formidable controversialist, one of the most influential pamphleteers of the age, smiting Papist and Puritan alike. In his own words, it was his aim 'to stand in the gap against Puritanism and Popery, the Scylla and Charybdis of ancient piety'. This did not prevent the Puritans from accusing him of Romish tendencies, and his views had brought him into trouble with more than one Parliament at the outset of Charles's reign. But he held on his course unperturbed, and was extremely well qualified to defend himself against all attacks. Fuller wrote that 'his great parts were attended with tartness of writing; very sharp the nib of his pen, and much gall in his ink, against such as opposed him. However, such the equability of the sharpness of his style, he was unpartial therein; be he ancient or modern writer, Papist or Protestant, that stood in his way, they should all equally taste thereof'.[1]

At the time of his appointment to Norwich he was more than sixty years old, and grievously afflicted with a quartan ague, 'which accompanied him or rather brought him to his grave' less than three years later.[2] But he was in entire sympathy with the policy of Laud, and carried on Wren's work so far as his declining health allowed. In his first report to Laud he remarked that the churches in his new diocese were 'in very decent and good order

[1] Fuller, *Church History*, xi, 119.
[2] Blomefield, iii, 574.

generally'; and in 1639 he assured the Archbishop that the diocese was 'as quiet, uniform, and conformable, as any in the kingdom, if not more'.

He was, however, concerned at the unwillingness of the people to receive the sacrament at the altar-rails, as Wren had insisted they should do. On first coming to Norwich he had had some sympathy with the popular feeling on this matter, and wrote to ask Laud's instructions—'as it perplexeth them, so I must profess it troubleth me, wherein I desire resolution and direction'. Laud passed the letter on to Wren, who replied that 'it hath been neither perplexity nor trouble in that diocese ere now', and was wholly unsympathetic to the scruples of his successor. Montagu accordingly issued detailed directions to his clergy for the proper ordering of this portion of the communion service. All communicants were to come in a body into the chancel 'and as in course of civility and good order, it is seemly the best in the parish to come up first.' They were to place themselves in rows facing the altar, 'the first rank to stand, sit or kneel, near or close unto the rails, which being the most eminent place, the best in the parish may fitly be disposed there'. Then the priest was to walk along the rows, and so administer the sacred elements.[3]

There is more than a touch of his sharp pen in other instructions which he issued to his clergy. Many of them were backward in paying their tenths and their synodals. 'This is lewd and wicked dealing in clergymen. I must and will look into it; and on the word of a bishop I protest, that light where it will, I will make some an example for others to be more careful and honest afterward.' Others were accused of still more reprehensible conduct. 'I hear many complaints by men of worth, of great misdemeanour amongst divers of the clergy, especially for drunkenness, frequenting alehouses, taphouses and tobacco houses, especially in parts towards the seaside, to the foul scandal of their calling, offence of good men, and their own undoing in many ways . . . I must confess the laws are not strict enough for such malefactors, but if such men come under my fingers, what extremity law will afford they are like to find. It seems to me unreasonable to use rigour *in minoribus*, and to suffer these *majora* to pass unpunished. Those which are guilty I hope will amend; if not, it concerns their

[3] Laud, *Works*, v, 360, 364. Prynne, *Canterburies Doome*, 98–100.

brethren of honesty and worth to join with their Bishop to rid the Church of them.'[4]

A few weeks after the first assembling of the Long Parliament, Archbishop Laud was taken into confinement, impeached of high treason, and presently committed to the Tower. At the same time the solid phalanx of Puritan members from East Anglia joyfully seized the opportunity of calling to account their own detested bishops. A committee was set up to receive petitions against Wren, and to draw up articles of impeachment against him. Since there were 'great fears that he would fly away'—although nothing would have been more foreign to Wren's resolute temper—he was bound in the sum of £10,000 to remain and abide the judgement of the Parliament. Shortly afterwards Sir Simonds D'Ewes, who had been returned for the Suffolk borough of Sudbury, moved that the same committee should have its powers enlarged 'to receive likewise all petitions and complaints against the present Bishop of Norwich'.[5]

D'Ewes was a scholar and antiquary of great diligence, an enthusiastic member of the Puritan majority in Parliament, and in religion a fervent Calvinist. For years past he had been at logger-heads with Mr. Danford, the parson of his own parish of Stow-langtoft, and had brought Mr. Danford's 'exorbitant courses' to the notice of successive Bishops of Norwich without the slightest result.[6] So he was able to derive some righteous enjoyment from the meetings of the committee which was to investigate the conduct of Wren and Montagu. He recorded in his journal in some detail the petitions from parishes whose incumbents had been suspended or deprived by those prelates, and the examinations of clergymen who had been prominent in carrying out their injunctions.[7]

The attack was mainly directed against Wren; but Montagu came to the committee's particular notice over a petition from the people of St. Peter Mancroft in Norwich, accusing him of inhibiting their minister, John Carter, from preaching on Tues-days in his own church. A bill was drafted to deprive him of his

[4] E.A. (series I), i, 70–1.
[5] D'Ewes, *Journal*, 171, 251.
[6] D'Ewes, *Autobiography*, i, 274–5: ii, 27, 103, 107.
[7] D'Ewes, *Journal*, e.g. 200–1, 221–2, 234–5, etc.

bishopric, and make him incapable of any ecclesiastical promotion.[8] But the matter was carried no further. He was too ill to
appear before Parliament, and died within a few weeks—'went
a more compendious way', wrote Fuller, 'to answer all in the
High Court of Heaven.'[9]

The committee continued to investigate the numerous petitions
and accusations against Wren, and finally drew up twenty-five
articles of impeachment against him, relating entirely to his conduct during his three years as Bishop of Norwich. Some of these
have been mentioned earlier. They covered the entire range of
those activities which the Puritans found so distasteful in the
Bishop and his partisans—the raising of altars upon steps at the
east end of the church; the setting up of the hated altar-rails; the
removal of pews and seats from the chancels; the wearing of
surplices; the bowings and adorations and superstitious gestures.
The cases of the ministers whom he had suspended or deprived,
the lecturers whom he had silenced, the emigrants to Holland and
New England were all brought up against him. So were the
appointments as chaplains and commissioners of men 'who stood
affected to his innovated courses and to Popish superstition'. His
accusers did not even overlook the fact that 'the more to manifest
his Popish affection he caused a crucifix, that is to say the figure of
Christ upon the cross, to be engraved upon his episcopal seal
beside the arms of the see'.[10]

After much debate, in the course of which one member observed
with ponderous humour that 'the Wren is the least of all those
birds, but one of the most unclean ones', he was committed to the
Tower in December without his defence being heard. He was
released in the following spring, and spent the summer of 1642 at
Ely. Soon after the outbreak of war he was again taken into
custody, and remained a prisoner in the Tower until the Restoration almost eighteen years later. He was never brought to trial,
and during the Commonwealth he rejected several overtures
which might have led to his release. In adversity as in prosperity
he maintained the same unbending demeanour, the same courage
and resolution. After the Restoration he returned to his see of

[8] Ibid., 389-90.
[9] Fuller, *Church History*, xi, 194.
[10] *Articles of Impeachment*, art. 19.

Ely, and built the beautiful chapel at his old college of Pembroke, one of the earliest works of his nephew Christopher Wren. He died in 1667 at the age of eighty-two.

2

Bishop Montagu had died in April 1641, and no successor was named for several months, as was the case with other bishoprics which fell vacant during this year of confusion. The Church was in stormy waters, with Laud a close prisoner in the Tower, the bishops daily assailed in Parliament, and the 'Root and Branch' bill for the utter extirpation of prelacy introduced and received with enthusiasm. Finally the interregnum at Norwich was ended in November by the appointment of Joseph Hall, Bishop of Exeter.

The new Bishop of Norwich was sixty-seven years of age, and had held the see of Exeter for the past fourteen years. He had long been one of the most popular and prolific writers of the age. Sir Henry Wotton called him the English Seneca, 'from the pureness, plainness and fullness of his style'.[11] Long ago, when Queen Elizabeth was still on the throne, he had achieved his earliest fame with a series of harsh and crabbed satires in verse. Since then his output had been large and varied—devotional works, controversial works, epistles, sermons, the very strange fantasy called *Mundus Alter et Idem*, and those volumes of *Meditations* which were the best loved of all his writings.

He had been a scholar and a fellow of 'the house of pure Emmanuel', that nursery of Puritan divines, and throughout his life he remained sympathetic to the Puritan point of view. He loved tolerance and moderation, and when he became a bishop he practised these virtues and tried to enjoin them upon others. A remarkable degree of peace and harmony prevailed in the diocese of Exeter. The preachers and lecturers were allowed a liberty of expression that dismayed his severer brethren. 'What free admission and encouragement,' he wrote later, 'have I always given to all the sons of peace, that came with God's message in their mouths! How have I often and publicly professed, that as well

[11] Fuller, *Worthies*, ii, 130.

might we complain of too many stars in the sky, as too many orthodox preachers in the Church!'[12]

Such an attitude was highly displeasing to Laud. During his years of power he saw to it that no further promotion came to the Bishop of Exeter. Informers were placed in the diocese, by whom reports were sent up to Lambeth, accusing Hall of favouring Puritans, encouraging unorthodox and heretical preachers, indulging disaffected persons, and much besides. 'The billows went so high,' he wrote, 'that I was three several times upon my knee to his Majesty to answer these great criminations . . . Under how dark a cloud I was hereupon I was so sensible, that I plainly told the Lord Archbishop of Canterbury, that rather than I would be obnoxious to those slanderous tongues of his misinformers, I would cast up my rochet. I knew I went right ways, and would not endure to live under undeserved suspicions.'[13]

In spite of the divergence of his views from those of the Archbishop and most of his brother prelates, Hall rallied decisively to their side when the great storm broke against episcopacy. As a popular writer and formidable controversialist, and at the same time one of the most moderate and respected of the Bishops, he was well fitted to answer the attacks upon them. It was at Laud's request, and with his personal assistance, that he now strove to resist the torrent of pamphlets, sermons and Parliamentary denunciations with which their order was assailed. His most elaborate work of this kind, *Episcopacy by Divine Right Asserted*, was published at the beginning of 1640 with a preliminary address to the King. It was a long and learned treatise, written with the full weight of his age and experience. 'For me, I am now breathing towards the end of my race. The goal is already in mine eye. Young men may speak out of ambitious hopes, or passionate transportations; I, that am now setting foot over the threshold of the house of my age, what aim can I have, but of the issue of my last account?'[14]

But Hall still had sixteen years to live, and his polemical vigour was in no way abated. Two months after the Long Parliament had assembled, he addressed to its members a much shorter discourse,

---

[12] Hall, *Works*, i, xxxix.
[13] Ibid., xxxv-vi.
[14] Ibid., x, 145.

An Humble Remonstrance to the High Court of Parliament, by a Dutiful Son of the Church, an able and forthright defence of the liturgy and of the episcopal order. It is an eloquent and persuasive piece of writing, firmly asserting the Anglican standpoint, yet still voicing some hope of reconciliation with the opposing party. 'Alas, my brethren, while we do fully agree in all these, and all other doctrinal and practical points of religion, why will ye be so uncharitable, as, by these frivolous and causeless divisions, to rend the seamless coat of Christ? Is it a title, or a retinue, or a ceremony, a garment, or a colour, or an organ-pipe, that can make us a different Church, while we preach and profess the same saving truth?'[15]

The *Humble Remonstrance* was answered by five Puritan divines, Stephen Marshall, Edmund Calamy and others, whose initials made up the word Smectymnuus, a pseudonym used on the title-page of their rejoinder. A warfare of pamphlets, known as the Smectymnuus controversy, now raged for several months. Hall defended his *Remonstrance* in two further tracts, and one of his sons also came to his aid. The fray was presently joined by John Milton, who lavished his store of vituperative eloquence on father and son alike. He made special play with certain of the Bishop's early writings, the absurdities of *Mundus Alter et Idem*, and the indiscretions of the youthful satires written all those years ago.

Early in 1641, on the second Sunday in Lent, Bishop Hall preached before the King at Whitehall a sermon entitled *The Mischief of Faction and the Remedy of it*. His discourse was a plea for sanity and tolerance, a memorable statement of the moderate's point of view. He knew he would be censured by both the opposing factions in church and state, and welcomed their censure. 'Therein I joy, yea and will joy. I am for the peace of both, for the humour of neither. How should the mortar or cement join the stones together, if it did not lie between both? And I would to God not you only, that hear me this day, but all our brethren of this land were alike-minded.' Were his countrymen to divide into warring camps because of differences on minor points of observance? ' "This man is right," ye say; "that man is not right: this sound; that rotten." And how so, dear Christians? What! for ceremonies and circumstances, for rochets, or rounds, or squares?

[15] Ibid., x, 285.

Let me tell you, he is right, that hath a right heart to his God, what forms soever he is for. The kingdom of God does not stand in meats and drinks; in stuffs, or colours, or fashions; in noises or gestures: it stands in holiness and righteousness; in godliness and charity; in peace and obedience: and if we have happily attained unto those, God doth not stand upon trifles and niceties of indifferences; and why should we?'[16]

But the time for such wise and gentle counsels had gone by. The scene was changing fast even in his own diocese, where until lately he had always known 'peace and comfort in the happy sense of that general unanimity, and loving correspondence of my clergy'. He returned to Exeter for the summer of 1641, when Parliament was in recess, and was 'cheerfully welcomed with some hundreds'; but he was never to see the west country again. Soon after his return to Westminster came the news of his appointment to Norwich.[17]

In sending a prominent sympathiser with the Puritan viewpoint to this unruly and resentful diocese, the King may have had in mind some thoughts of conciliation. Certainly no bishop could have been a greater contrast to Wren and Montagu. But it was now too late for measures of appeasement; and in any case Hall's recent writings in defence of episcopacy, and the furious recriminations of the Smectymnuus controversy, had brought him into great disfavour even amongst the milder Puritans. He was completely involved in the general unpopularity of his order.

He did not set out for Norwich at once. Parliament had assembled, and it was his duty to attend the House of Lords. Before he could visit his new diocese, to use his own words, 'I took the Tower in my way.' This was the first of the tribulations which he described in the little tract entitled *Bishop Hall's Hard Measure*. His measure was not very hard in comparison with that meted out to Laud or even to Wren; but for an elderly man, who until lately can have expected nothing but a peaceful close to his long and honoured career in the Church, the experiences of his remaining years were harsh enough. He bore them all with patience and dignity.

During the course of 1641 the pristine zeal of the Commons

[16] Ibid., ii, 446.
[17] Ibid., i, xxxvi.

had faded, and a measure of reaction had set in. A King's Party was formed; members of lukewarm sympathies withdrew to the country; the Grand Remonstrance was only carried in November by a very small majority. Petitions were even organized by faithful churchmen in some counties in favour of episcopacy: these, according to Hall, 'though signed by many thousand hands, were slighted and disregarded'. But no echo of these developments within Parliament reached the angry mobs outside. Hall described how he and his brethren had to make their way to the House of Lords through a rabble shouting 'No Bishops, no Bishops', and threatening to pull them in pieces. After a particularly alarming demonstration they decided 'it was not for us to venture any more to the House without some better assurance'. At a meeting convened by the Archbishop of York, Laud's old enemy and rival John Williams, they were persuaded by him to petition the King and the House of Lords for security against further affronts, and to protest that during their enforced absence from the House all legislation must be regarded as null and void.

Such a claim on the part of the Bishops, at this time of their greatest unpopularity, was the height of imprudence. It embarrassed their well-wishers, annoyed the King's party in both Houses, and was a most welcome gift to their adversaries. The protest was deemed to be a matter for impeachment, and the twelve prelates who had signed it, Hall among them, were consigned to the Tower on a dark December night 'in all the extremity of frost'.

In the Tower they remained for several months, until the next Whitsuntide. A bill depriving bishops of their votes in Parliament was passed through both Houses; and although the charge of High Treason was eventually dropped, they were declared delinquents 'of a very high nature', and all their revenues were sequestered. Each bishop was allowed a certain sum for his maintenance, Hall's own portion being set at four hundred pounds a year. He vividly described in *Hard Measure* the anxieties and discomforts of their imprisonment in the Tower: how they were examined before Parliament, in circumstances of contumely and humiliation: how they were released on bail, and almost at once hauled back to the Tower once more: how they would preach on Sundays to gatherings of the more sympathetic citizens. One of his own sermons, preached during the penitential season of Lent, is a fine example of his eloquence, and not without references to the times through which they were passing. 'Hath not God for these many years crossed us in our public designs, both of war and peace? Hath he not threatened to stir up evil against us out of our own bowels?'[18]

They were released at Whitsuntide, upon bail of five thousand pounds apiece, 'with a clause of revocation at a short warning if occasion should require'; and Hall was at last able to take up residence in his new diocese. He was no stranger to East Anglia. As a young man he had spent some happy years as rector of Hawstead in Suffolk, and his wife was one of the Winyeves of Brettenham in that county. When he reached Norwich, he tells us, 'I was at the first received with more respect, than in such times I could have expected; there I preached the day after my arrival to a numerous and attentive audience.'[19] In his Palace at Norwich, in the hush before the storm, we must for the present leave him.

[18] Ibid., ii, 488.
[19] Ibid., i, l–li.

CHAPTER VIII

The Outbreak of War

I

After the execution of Strafford, and almost until the close of 1641, there came a period of uncertainty and a considerable measure of reaction. The first objectives of a virtually united Parliament had been attained; and now enthusiasm began to wane, and unity to disappear. Moderate counsels were heard, and moderate men reviewed the whole situation. A King's Party formed in the House of Commons, and members such as Falkland and Hyde, who had been among Strafford's foremost opponents, gave it their adherence. At the end of November the Grand Remonstrance, that tremendous summary of all the grievances of the past decades, was only passed by the narrow majority of eleven votes.

The King did what he could to encourage these moderate elements, and if possible to win them over to his side. In Norfolk, as elsewhere in the kingdom, his new policy was signalized by the creation of an unprecedented number of baronetcies. No one in the county had received this mark of royal favour since 1629, when it was conferred upon Sir Hamon L'Estrange and Sir John Holland. Now, in the summer months of 1641, five Norfolk gentlemen were created baronets, and three more in the first half of 1642. The acquisition of a baronetcy involved the payment of a substantial fee, and the money helped to replenish the royal coffers. By the bestowal of these distinctions, the King was aiming at the same time to rally new supporters and to raise fresh revenue. At this time of crisis, furthermore, a reduced rate of payment was offered to the gentlemen on whom the honour was conferred.

Of the newly created Norfolk baronets, only one, Sir John Potts of Mannington, was a member of the House of Commons; and the King's gesture made no difference to his future line of conduct. Two others, Sir John Palgrave of North Barningham and Sir Isaac Astley of Melton Constable, were likewise to be uncompromising in their support of Parliament. Four of the new baronets actively supported the royal cause—Sir William Paston of Oxnead, Sir Thomas Pettus of Rackheath, Sir Robert Kemp of Gissing, and Sir William Denny of Gillingham. I have found no evidence that the eighth, Sir Ralph Hare of Stow Bardolph, espoused either side.

At the end of the year the King determined on a trial of strength with his adversaries in the House of Commons, and gave orders for the impeachment of five of its members—Pym, Hampden, Hazelrigg, Holles and Strode. On 4 January 1642 he took the fatal step of entering the House with an escort of his guards, and making a vain attempt to arrest them in person. There could have been no more disastrous infringement of the rights of Parliament, no action more certain to bring unity and strength to the opposition. Six days later he was obliged to withdraw from London, never to return until he was brought there in another January seven years later, a prisoner on trial for his life.

2

All this was watched with the deepest interest and anxiety throughout the country. There were now two authorities in the land: Parliament at Westminster, and the King who gradually moved further northward, and finally established his court at York. It was a situation without precedent, and to all men of moderate views it brought perplexity and heart-searching.

The control of the militia was a vital necessity to both sides; and one of Parliament's most forceful acts was to nominate, on 12 February 1642, its own Lords Lieutenant from among the peers who supported its cause. It will be remembered that in Norfolk this office was held by Lord Arundel, and that his son Lord Maltravers had been joined in commission with him. In their place Parliament now appointed Robert Rich, second Earl of Warwick. For many years past Warwick had been closely identified with the opposition party, in politics and in religion. He had been active for much of his life in the affairs of New England and Bermuda, and had long experience of the sea. At this juncture Parliament also appointed him Admiral of the Fleet;

and it was mainly due to his efforts that virtually the entire navy came under Parliamentarian control at the very outset of the war.

There were now in effect two Lords Lieutenant in Norfolk, Warwick and Maltravers, who had lately been granted his father's barony of Mowbray and called to the Upper House by virtue of that peerage. Lord Arundel had faded from the English scene. He was given no active command in the second expedition against the Scots, being appointed General of the forces south of the Trent. He was an ageing man, in indifferent health. There was little he could do to forward the royal cause; and in this same month of February 1642 he crossed the sea to Holland, escorting the Queen and her eldest daughter, Princess Mary, the child wife of the youthful Prince William of Orange. He never returned to England again, but lived first in Holland and then in Italy, dying at Padua in 1646. His son Lord Mowbray, as he must henceforth be called, now assumed the full duties of the Lord Lieutenancy of Norfolk; and he and Warwick presently began to issue, on behalf of the rival authorities which they represented, entirely conflicting instructions to the bewildered officers of the local militia.

As an important landed proprietor in Essex, Warwick was well known in the eastern counties. His familiar and genial manner was in marked contrast to the aloof grandeur of Arundel, and he was popular with all classes. As the war developed, he became too much occupied with other duties to pay close attention to Norfolk, and probably kept in touch with local affairs through Edward Montagu, Lord Kimbolton, who had married one of his daughters. Kimbolton, presently to succeed his father as Earl of Manchester and to be better known by that name, was a prominent member of the opposition group in the House of Lords, and had been impeached by the King along with the five members of the House of Commons. Next year he was placed in charge of the Association formed by the eastern counties, and will thus figure prominently in this narrative.

During the spring of 1642 the breach between King and Parliament continued to widen, and a resort to arms seemed inevitable. Proclamations, declarations and ordinances issued from Westminster, and were at once countermanded from York. At the beginning of June, the full demands of Parliament were laid before the King in the form of the Nineteen Propositions. In a long and closely-argued rejoinder he rejected them absolutely. If he consented to such terms, he said, the monarchy would be reduced to a puppet institution. 'As to real and true power, we should remain but the outside, but the picture, but the sign of a King . . . and by this means the splendid and excellently distinguished form of government [would] end in a dark equal chaos of confusion, and the long line of our many noble ancestors in a Jack Cade, or a Wat Tyler. For all these reasons, to all these demands our answer is, *Nolumus leges Angliae mutari*.'[1]

Later in the same month of June, the King issued to the Lords Lieutenant of each county his Commissions of Array, whereby they were ordered to disregard the Militia Ordinance of the Parliament and the Parliamentary Lords Lieutenant, and to 'array and train our people, and to apportion and assess such persons as have estates and are not able to bear arms'. Parliament immediately voted that the Commissions of Array were illegal. 'By the constitution and policy of this kingdom, the King by his proclamation cannot declare the law, contrary to the constitution of any of the inferior courts of justice, much less against the High Court of Parliament.'[2]

The Commission of Array was duly entrusted by the King to Lord Mowbray, as the rightful Lord Lieutenant of Norfolk. He does not appear to have taken any immediate steps to rally the King's supporters in the county. But a good deal of private negotiation and quiet manœuvring was undertaken by both sides, and East Anglian gentlemen of Royalist or moderate views found themselves in a very difficult position. The dilemma with which such men were confronted is vividly portrayed in the letters written by Thomas Knyvett from London to his wife at Ashwellthorpe during the spring of this year.

It seems probable, from one or two passages in these letters, that he had gone to London to avoid committing himself on the militia issue. Certainly his cousin Sir William Paston had done so. 'He hath told me since he came that he left Norfolk to avoid employment. He is intended to be at the cost of the best counsel

[1] Rushworth, III, i, 725–35.
[2] Ibid., 657–9, 679.

in point of law, which he hath promised me privately I shall partake with him in.'[3] The tone of some of his letters is cautious— 'I know how my heart stands, but 'tis not safe to write any of these high distractions'—but his long letters of 18 and 24 May would seem to have been sent by some trustworthy private messenger, and confide his perplexities and fears without restraint. On the 18th he wrote: 'I would to God I could write thee any good news, but that is impossible so long as the spirit of contradiction ranges between King and Parliament higher still than ever; and 'tis to be feared this threatening storm will not be allayed without some showers (I pray God not a deluge) of blood. The one party now grows as resolute as the other is obstinate.' He went on to describe how pressure had lately been put upon him to obey the militia ordinance issued by the Parliament. 'Oh sweetheart, I am now in a great strait what to do. Walking this other morning at Westminster, Sir John Potts, with commissary Mutford, saluted me with a commission from my Lord of Warwick to take upon me (by virtue of an ordinance of Parliament) my company and command again. I was surprised what to do, whether to take or refuse. 'Twas no place to dispute, so I took it and desired some time to advise upon it. I had not received this many hours, but I met with a declaration point blank against it by the King. This distraction made me to advise with some understanding men of what condition I stand in, which is no other than a great many men of quality do. What further commands we shall receive to put this ordinance in execution, if they run in a way that trenches upon my obedience against the King, I shall do according to my conscience. And this is the resolution of all honest men that I can speak with. In the meantime I hold it good wisdom and security to keep my company as close to me as I can during these dangerous times, and to stay out of the way of my new masters till these first musterings be over.'

However firmly Knyvett was resolved to support the King, the royal cause seemed a forlorn one in the insurgent atmosphere of London. 'Poor King, he grows still more in contempt and slight here every day than other; and no wonder when the reverence and worship of the King of Kings comes to be construed superstitious and idolatrous, yet no worship too much for

[3] Knyvett, 105.

the sons of men.' It was a weary time, and Knyvett longed for the peace of his country home. 'Dear Mother, I wish myself in thy arms every night most cordially, and all the Potts in Christendom shall not keep me from thee long.'

The next letter strikes the same note of perplexity. 'Dear heart, still to be at the pen distance doth not a little trouble me, but such is the sad condition of these times, as no man knows how to dispose himself, for now there is so much declared as makes all officers in the kingdom traitors of one side or other; neither are standers-by in any better condition. I think it fit amongst a great many here in town, which are in the like strait, to keep awhile out of the dint of my new commanders. You may see in print what the King declares concerning the putting the militia in execution without him. Here's nothing but remonstrances and declarations, and all exasperations one against the other, not a tittle of hope of accommodation, so that we can foresee nothing but a public phlebotomy, if God in mercy doth not in time cast out those evil spirits from amongst us.' He looked forward to the approaching contest with nothing but misgiving, and was by no means enthusiastic over the King's preparations in the north. 'They are extreme bad counsellors that shall excite the King to begin a war against his people . . . I think we have no peacemakers left.' Nevertheless, if war were to come his course of action would be clear. He would retain command of his militia company, and if possible bring them into the conflict on the Royalist side. 'I would I were quit of this new commission though not of my company, for whatsoever comes there's no policy to decline them, if I can keep them close to go that way I mean to go myself. But say nothing of this one way or other.'

The last of this series of letters was written on 31 May. Knyvett proposed to return to Norfolk next week, and in the meantime sent his wife word of the release of the twelve bishops after their long seclusion in the Tower. 'Only Canterbury is still a-fatting,' he wrote somewhat heartlessly. The careless phrase well shows how lukewarm even convinced Royalists could be in their attitude towards Laud. But the times were too grave for jesting. 'God Almighty send a happy conclusion of these high and fearful distractions.' Knyvett returned to Norfolk as he intended, and there are no more letters from him for a period of ten months.

When he wrote to his wife again, in March 1643, it was as a prisoner of war.[4]

3

It is difficult to gauge the strength of feeling at this time among the ordinary people of Norfolk and Norwich. Excitement ran high, although there can be little doubt that the great majority, then as always, only wanted to go quietly about their daily business and enjoy their family life. The Puritan element, in town and village, sought to pursue the ideals which had sustained them for so long. Their opponents regarded them as hypocritical and 'precise', and were considered in return to be worldly, godless, or 'Popish'. Those convenient terms of opprobrium, Cavalier and Roundhead, were to come into use only after the outbreak of war.

The Florists' Feasts, which took place annually during the sixteen-thirties, provide an illustration of the two conflicting points of view within the city of Norwich. These festivities, said to have been first introduced by the flower-loving Dutch immigrants, were organized by a body called the Society of Florists, and generally included a flower-show, a banquet and a play or masque. Any kind of stage performance was displeasing to the Puritan members of the Corporation, who sought to suppress the Feasts altogether. People who liked gaiety and enjoyment, amongst them certain poetry-loving churchmen, rallied to the defence. On one occasion the Puritans accused the Florists of grave impiety, in celebrating the rites of Flora, a heathen goddess. Thereupon William Strode, Bishop Corbett's chaplain, wrote a delightful prologue for one of the plays, asserting that

'our feast we call
Only from flowers, from Flora not at all',

and pointing out that the beauty of flowers is a gift from God, and not the least of 'his various works of excellence'.[5]

Another warm supporter was the poet Ralph Knevet, who wrote a play in five short acts, *Rhodon and Iris*, for the Florists'

---

[4] Knyvett, 100–109 *passim*.

[5] Corpus Christi College, Oxford, MS. 325. I am grateful to Miss Margaret Crum for bringing this prologue to my notice.

Feast of 1631. Little is known about Knevet's life, but he appears to have been domiciled for a number of years in the household of Sir William Paston at Oxnead, and eventually took orders and became rector of Lyng. His only work published earlier was a long poem entitled *Stratiotikon: or a Discourse of Military Discipline*, a performance chiefly notable for the addresses in verse which preceded the main text. These were 37 in number, and celebrated, in the most high-flown terms, the transcendent merits of all the principal officers of the militia, and other leading gentlemen of the county.[6] *Rhodon and Iris*, the Rose and the Lily, was a pastoral, with the scene laid in Thessaly. The characters are shepherds and shepherdesses, and most of them bear the names of flowers. There are also two evil beings, Poneria the witch and her satellite Agnostus the impostor, who seek to bring discord into peaceful Thessaly; but all is set to rights in the last act by the descent of Flora, brought from her distant bower by 'the noise of these tumultuous broils'.

Several of the more comic passages, and especially the character of Agnostus, were undoubtedly aimed at prominent local Puritans. In the opening scene there is mention of 'a schismatical self-conceited coxcomb in an ancient corporation'. Later on Poneria dresses up Agnostus in a disguise—beard, cap, gown—which is clearly intended to resemble some particular member of the corporation. Later still he is fitted out as a militia officer, though he protests that

'I am altogether ignorant in the words of command,
    And know not one posture neither of musket or pike.'

And in his opening address to the Society of Florists, Knevet like Strode defends the whole concept of the Feast from Puritan imputations. ' 'Tis true, many sanctimonists, that like the men of China, think themselves wiser than all the world beside, do inveigh against it . . . If I did think it might be any way prejudicial, either to politic or moral society, I should detest it as deeply as the most zealous heteroclite of them all. If it had any affinity with Bacchanalian riot, if gluttony and drunkenness ever found any

---

[6] *Stratiotikon* has lately been reprinted, from the only known copy now in the Huntington Library, by Professor Amy M. Charles in her excellent edition of *The Shorter Poems of Ralph Knevet* (Ohio State University Press, 1966).

entertainment there, I should utterly loathe to name it. But since it is a meeting so civil, so unspotted, that malice herself, had she a brazen face, might blush to detract from it; since it is a feast celebrated by such a conflux of gentlemen of birth and quality, in whose presence and converse (I think) your city's welfare partly consists; I cannot but commend it (though not so highly as it deserves) in spite of ignorance or envy.'[7]

Puritan feeling in Norwich gathered strength as the years went on, although there were still plenty of citizens who supported the established order, and the Corporation itself continued to be much divided. The attack on the bishops naturally drew men's thoughts and eyes towards the Cathedral. The splendid building, standing proudly aloof in its Close, became a symbol of the episcopal system and all that it implied—a Bishop, a Dean, a body of well-endowed dignitaries, elaborate ceremonial, chants, anthems, the music of organs. Once the 'Root and Branch' bill had been introduced into Parliament, with its proposals for the abolition of bishops, deans and chapters, the murmurings of the Puritans against the Cathedral turned to menaces. This was welcome enough to the rowdier elements, and especially to the apprentices, ever glad of a respite from long hours and hard work. On the Shrove Tuesday of 1642 the Cathedral authorities had reason to expect an organized attack, and took precautions accordingly.

The story appears only in a satirical pamphlet, *True News from Norwich*, written by someone who signed himself 'T.L.', and designed to ridicule the preparations made by the 'Cathedral blades' against an attack which never took place. According to the pamphleteer, the Dean and prebendaries were told that the apprentices were going to invade the Cathedral and destroy the altar-rails and the organs. They therefore removed the rails, but resolved to stand fast in defence of the organs. Two days before Shrove Tuesday they shut the gates of the Close and mustered that morning in full strength. There were the learned prebendaries; 'great store of parsons and priests'; the singing-men, ready to 'blow the rebels away with their profound sounding roaring voices'; the humbler choristers, one of whom was heard to say that 'if I do but go into church and say my prayers, and hear the organs go, they make the water run down my cheeks, they are so

[7] *The Shorter Poems of Ralph Knevet* (ed. Charles), 169–242.

sweet and so good a music'. Then there were the guards who had been hired for the occasion, musketeers and halberdiers, all eager to fire a shot or strike a blow at the apprentices; and finally a force of about five hundred persons, armed with swords and pistols. This whole assembly stood about all day, 'like so many Abraham ninnies, doing nothing but tell how many crows flew over the pinnacle'; while the godly apprentices 'had no intent to come, but were at home about their masters' occasions, and did not intend to foul their fingers about such a company of rakeshames'.

The whole affair may have been a false alarm, or it may really have been an intended attack which was frustrated by the precautions of the Dean and Chapter. Those dignitaries still exercised some influence in Norwich, and commanded some support. 'Oh how loath they are,' complained the pamphleteer, 'to part with their Dianas, their altars, images, crucifixes, copes, surplices and Romish vestments; no (as some of them said) they would rather lose their lives than their organs, so fast they are glued to their pipes and Popish trinkets.' But the Puritans had not long to wait. Next year all these idolatrous things were to be swept away.[8]

4

All through the spring and summer of 1642 the Norfolk members of the House of Commons were greatly occupied with the affairs of the local militia. They suggested suitable candidates for commissions to Warwick, the new Lord Lieutenant, and did their best to ensure that every key position was held by a man who might be relied upon when the critical moment arrived.[9] Pressure was put upon officers whose sympathies were thought to be uncertain, as we have already seen in the case of Knyvett. Every precaution was taken to safeguard the stores of arms, ammunition and equipment belonging to the militia of the county and the trained bands of the city.

At the same time members set an example by offering 'to advance horse, money and plate for the defence of Parliament'.

[8] *True News from Norwich*, written by T.L. (London, 1641/2).
[9] Letters from Sir Edmund Moundeford in London to Sir John Potts in Norfolk, B.L. MS. Tanner 63, ff. 32, 43.

Sir Robert Hatton had already joined the King; and although Richard Catelyn, one of the members for Norwich, had not yet withdrawn from the activities of Parliament, his crypto-Royalist sympathies are indicated by his failure to subscribe. Apart from these two, every Norfolk member figured in the list of contributors which was opened on 10 June. Sir Thomas Wodehouse offered two horses and £200 in plate or money; Moundeford two horses and their maintenance; Potts one hundred pounds. A number of others—Gawdy, Corbett, Owner, Percival and Toll—volunteered £50 apiece. Harman was willing to provide a single horse. Holland worded his offer with some care, in contrast to the laconic entries of most of his colleagues—'Sir John Holland will bring in two horses ready furnished and an hundred pounds in money or plate, for maintenance of the true Protestant religion, the defence of the King's person, his royal authority and dignity, our laws, liberties and privileges conjunctive.' A somewhat similar formula, mentioning King and Parliament 'conjunctively', was used by several other members of moderate views, though by no one else from Norfolk. It may be mentioned, for purposes of comparison, that Cromwell volunteered £500, and Hampden three horses, with their maintenance, and £200 in plate.[10]

The King did not actually raise his standard at Nottingham until 22 August, although manœuvring and skirmishing had been going on in some areas for months before. Norfolk remained quiet; but on 1 August it was ordered by Parliament that all its most influential members—Wodehouse, Holland, Potts, Moundeford, Heveningham and Gawdy—were to repair forthwith into the county. (Heveningham had been returned to Parliament, through the influence of his wife's family, the Wallops, for the Hampshire borough of Stockbridge; but he was frequently called upon to play a part in Norfolk affairs.) They were instructed to propagate throughout the county the declaration of both Houses that the royal Commission of Array was contrary to the laws of the realm; to enforce contributions of arms, money and plate for the defence of the kingdom; and to require the Sheriff, the militia and the trained bands to assist them in their task.[11]

[10] Ibid., ff. 51-61.
[11] Ibid., f. 110.

There had already been an attempt to raise forces for the King in Norwich. On 29 July a certain Captain Moses Tresswell appeared in the city, bearing a commission from the Earl of Lindsey, the General-in-Chief of the royal forces, for the levying of a hundred volunteers and conducting them to Newark. 'The Mayor and Court of Aldermen being informed hereof, convented him before them, and advised him not to beat his drum; he went out notwithstanding, and did beat up his drum: Mr. Mayor sent the sword-bearer unto him, to require him not to beat up his drum: he answered, if he could not have their good wills for beating up his drum, he would beat it up against their wills.' On this the Mayor caused Captain Tresswell to be apprehended, and sent up as a prisoner to Parliament, together with his man Gilbert. Their two horses were seized, as well as the Captain's sword and dagger, his scarlet coat, his cloak-bag and a bag of money. He duly appeared before Parliament and was committed to the Gate-house, 'there to remain during the pleasure of the House'. From this durance he managed to escape with two other captains six months later.[12]

More disturbing to the Parliamentarians in Norfolk was the sudden appearance of Lord Mowbray, the King's Lord Lieuten-ant. He arrived at his ancestral seat at Kenninghall, probably some time early in August, bearing with him the Commission of Array, and evidently made some attempt to rally the Royalist sym-pathisers in the county. His visit is unrecorded apart from some passages in the correspondence of Potts, and it is difficult to make out exactly what took place, beyond the fact that his efforts were wholly unsuccessful.

A great burden of responsibility lay upon Potts at this time, since his fellow Knight of the Shire, Sir Edmund Moundeford, was taken ill at Newmarket on his way down to Norfolk. He was suddenly seized with a cough, fever and spitting of blood, probably the onset of the illness of which he died in the following May. The doctor sent him to Cambridge, whence he wrote to Potts that 'I resolve never to give myself the lie by deserting the path you tread, though bugbeared by all the neutrals in the county'. He found that Cambridge was 'a place as malignant to the Parliament, as report can render it; if these fountains be not

[12] C.J., ii, 701, 1001. Norwich Court Book (1634–46), ff. 355–7.

purged, we are like to have bitter streams run all the kingdom over'.[13]

Potts acted with great circumspection. About this time he wrote to an unknown correspondent, presumably another member of Parliament: 'I am glad of your arrival in Norfolk, where your presence may help to continue what your persuasions helped to procure, the peace of this county. I can give you little account of myself more than that I remain in the same temper that you left me, studious of peace. My Lord Mowbray was not at the Assizes, nor the gentlemen of Array then with him, but were sithence appointed to meet him [at Kenninghall]. Some of them told me at Norwich that my Lord was willing to forbear executing his commands if I would undertake the militia should not be set on foot, nor preparation of arms be privately made; to which I was not authorized in way of bargain to answer, but bade them judge of my actions, which should rather hazard the censure of slackness than my county's quiet. My Lord's propositions to raise horse among the gentry, and the great recourse to his huntings, may give cause of suspect to weak judgments, and perhaps did beget those passages in Norwich concerning him.'[14]

Holland had also been ill. On 4 August he wrote to Potts from London that he was on his legs again, and they were able to carry him to the House. He was still under suspicion from the extreme wing of his party, and Strode had lately voiced those suspicions. 'Will Strode last day was so uncharitable to me, as he moved to have me sent down after you in advancement of the peace of the county, for the preservation whereof, I would willingly hazard my health, I protest my life. But I know in whose hands that work is now, nor can my assistance be wanted.' He had been able to satisfy the House that his ill-health was genuine and not an excuse. As for the great question of the hour, 'Sir, I know your wisdom, and no ways doubt of your prudent carriage in this business committed to your trust. I am confident you alter not that resolution you were pleased to communicate to me when

13 B.L. MS. Tanner 63, f. 116.
14 Ibid., f. 117. There are two drafts of this letter, with considerable variations. In the first draft the rather cryptic reference to 'the gentlemen of Array' reads: 'He required divers Commissioners of the Array to give him meeting at Kenninghall, which as they told me they forbare to avoid misconstruction, but have since performed.'

last you afforded me the favour of a visit; and which still appears to me, to be the sense of the most eager-bent of our countrymen remaining here—not to have the [Militia] Ordinance put into execution, but in case. All I study, Sir, and which I shall still with a faithful heart, is the peace of my county; and in order to this end, since my return to the House upon the occasion of Captain Tresswell (who is committed) I adventured to move, that in respect of the present constitution of our county, that the House would in their wisdom take order, that upon no commissions or directions whatsoever, the noise of a drum might for the present be heard in Norfolk; and which, I could not perceive but was well taken.' Similarly, he had written that week 'to most of the friends in whom I have interest, and such as I think are likeliest to be called to council in the execution of the Commission of Array, to persuade all they possibly may the suspension of the execution thereof, as the only means for the preservation of the peace of their county'.[15] In effect, this most moderate of Parliamentarians still believed that peace could be maintained in Norfolk if neither the Militia Ordinance nor the Commission of Array was put into effect. The war might yet be contained, might yet be prevented from spreading throughout the whole country. Compromise might still prevail.

On 18 August he went down to Norfolk, and wrote again to Potts next day. 'This last night brought me to Quidenham, where I hear of my Lord Mowbray's seating near me. I know what sleeps in his hand, the Commission of Array, and I hope it will still do so. You know, Sir, those relations ours have had to that family. I cannot but give him a visit; and by such correspondence I persuade myself I shall be the better able to advance your and mine own aims, the county's peace. But I pray your opinion herein, which is very persuasive to me. Sir, I gladly find the quiet of this county is so well preserved. I attribute much to your temper and wisdom herein. And assure yourself, Sir, that I shall be ready to contribute all I can that may any ways be in order to that end.'[16]

No more is known of Mowbray's stay at Kenninghall than is contained, or implied, in the following exchange of notes.

[15] Ibid., f. 121.
[16] Ibid., f. 126.

To his very loving friend Sir John Potts, Knight and Baronet, these.

Sir,

I have received information that certain letters to me were intercepted at Lynn and sent to you. If it be so I doubt not but you will send them to me, which I desire you to do by this messenger, and so I rest

Your very loving friend
MOWBRAY AND MALTRAVERS.

Kenninghall, 21 of August 1642.

My Lord,

There were not any letters which concern you brought unto me, neither do I know of any intercepted at Lynn, which being so remote it is unlikely they should bring them hither, my self having no acquaintance in that town. If it had been as your Lordship was informed, you needed not to doubt of such respect as 'tis fit to be performed by

Your Lordship's ready friend
and humble servant
JOHN POTTS.[17]

Mannington, 22 August 1642.

Whether the letters were intercepted or not, we shall never know. Probably they were, since the Parliamentarian organization was rapidly getting under way. The King had raised his standard on the very day of Potts' reply to Mowbray. On that day, also, orders were despatched by Essex 'for repairing unto Castle Rising and seizing all arms and ammunition in the said castle, and bringing them away and keeping in safe custody till further order'. [17a] Rising was a Howard possession, dangerously close to the politically divided town of Lynn: the Parliamentarians did well to disarm it. It was clear that Mowbray could achieve nothing effectual in Norfolk, and presumably he soon left Kenninghall, his hospitality offered in vain, the Commission of Array undelivered or disregarded. He went off to join the King's army, and

[17] Ibid., ff. 132, 134. Potts' reply is a rough draft.
[17a] Ibid., f. 135. The order is unaddressed, but it was probably directed to Potts and his fellow members of Parliament.

SIR JOHN POTTS
from a painting by Cornelius de Neve, in the possession of Mr. Bryan
Hall

fought gallantly throughout the war. He may have taken with him a few adherents, younger sons with no commitments and little to lose. But no gentlemen of influence or standing in Norfolk joined him; and he never attempted again to exercise his office of Lord Lieutenant in the county.

5

During the next months, preparations for war went steadily forward in town and countryside. Few men envisaged a long contest, and most continued to hope that some kind of settlement would soon be reached. But the Parliamentarian leaders in Norfolk had certain well-defined aims in view. They would ensure that their county was in a position to resist any attack by the King's supporters. They would disarm all Royalist sympathizers within their borders. And they would take precautions against the attempts that would probably be made, by the forces which the Queen was organizing in Holland, to seize one of the East Anglian seaports and use it as a base for invasion.

The members of Parliament, and their supporters among the Deputy Lieutenants, quietly but decisively assumed control of the militia; and in effect the county passed under their rule. Their policy was outlined at a meeting in Norwich on 6 September, when certain resolutions were passed. The Deputy Lieutenants were to meet the commanders of the trained bands, in order 'to provide for the safety and peace of the realm'. At this meeting 'such persons as are notified to have done or practised anything to the disservice of the Parliament shall be sent for to answer such complaint'. The Deputy Lieutenants should 'recommend to all such as are well-affected to King and Parliament' the support of the Parliamentary cause by contributions of arms, horses, plate and money. The magazines throughout the county should be put into safe custody. And 'such persons as shall appear by speech or action to have encouraged and practised any opposition to the proceedings of Parliament and disturbance of the public peace shall be disarmed for the service of the county'. These resolutions were signed by four members of Parliament—Holland, Wodehouse, Potts and Gawdy—and by five other Deputy Lieutenants,

Sir Thomas Richardson, Sir John Hobart, Sir John Palgrave, Sir Robert de Grey and John Spelman.[18]

On the same day, and above the same signatures, an order was despatched to the High Sheriff, instructing him, his under-sheriff, bailiffs and constables to apprehend William Lewyn, Doctor of the Civil Laws. Credible information had been received that this gentleman, a lawyer residing at Ludham, 'hath uttered dangerous words against the King and Parliament, and in many ways impedimented the public service and discouraged others from the payment of those moneys which ought to be levied by Act of Parliament, whereof we are commanded to render an account'. He was to be arrested and brought before the Deputy Lieutenants at the King's Head in Norwich on the 15th of the month.[19] There is no record of his apprehension, and probably he had already set out to join the King's forces. He later became Advocate General to Prince Rupert, and is recorded as having been present at the battle of Naseby. He seems to have been the first Royalist sympathizer in the county against whom active measures were taken.

On 15 September the proposed meeting of the Deputy Lieutenants with the commanders of the trained bands was duly held in Norwich. It resulted in the following declaration:

We whose names are hereunder written, having charge of several trained bands in this county, under the authority committed to the Right Honourable Robert Earl of Warwick, Lieutenant of the said county by ordinance of both Houses of Parliament, do hereby declare that we accept that charge, and will be ready from time to time to execute such commands, as shall be signified unto us by the said Earl of Warwick and his Deputy Lieutenants of this county to be for the service of his Majesty, and both Houses of Parliament, and for the peace of this county.

This document was signed by 28 captains and other officers of the militia. A few names were significantly absent. Not all those holding rank in the militia would accept the Parliament's appointment of Warwick in place of Mowbray, whom they still regarded as the rightful Lord Lieutenant. Amongst these absentees were

[18] Ibid., f. 152.
[19] Ibid., f. 151.

Sir Hamon L'Estrange and his sons, Sir John Spelman, Sir Robert Kemp, Thomas Knyvett and Augustine Holl. A letter of apology from Sir Nicholas L'Estrange happens to have survived, explaining to 'his ever honoured and noble kinsman' Sir John Hobart that for lack of horses he could not attend this or some similar meeting. His excuse was probably a polite form of words, masking his determination to absent himself from any such gathering. 'Noble Sir,' he wrote, 'I this last night received summons to attend you and other my honoured friends at Norwich on Thursday next, for a consultation about the peace and quiet of the county, a work most seasonable and worthy of every man's care; but my unhappiness is such, through a very ill-furnished and lame stable at this time, as I am necessitated to beg pardon for my failing, and your candid interpretation of this apology, and a communication of it to the rest of your grave senate . . . My wife presents her service; and we both kiss the fair hand of your noble lady.'[20]

A few of the signatories were men who within the coming months were to declare their Royalist allegiance, but who were hoping at this early stage that a compromise solution might yet be achieved. This group consisted of Sir William Paston, Sir Thomas Richardson, Sir William Denny, Sir Robert de Grey and Sir William D'Oyly. But they were far outnumbered by colleagues who never wavered in their support of Parliament.

On the reverse of this document is another list of signatures, 36 in all. It contains the names of those at the meeting who undertook to lend money 'towards the support of forces raised or to be raised, according to certain proportions set forth by both Houses of Parliament, for the maintenance of the true Protestant religion, the King's authority and his person in his royal dignity, the free course of justice, the laws of the land, the peace of the kingdom and the privilege of Parliament'. It was at first intended to ask the signatories to set down the amount of their subscriptions; but in the event this was done, no doubt for reasons of publicity and example to others, at a series of local meetings in various parts of the county.[21]

The people of England were now committed, after a century

[20] B.L. MS. Tanner 69, ff. 200–1.
[21] B.L. MS. Tanner 63, f. 165.

and a half of almost unbroken internal peace, to the waging of a civil war. Arms and ammunition of every kind were in short supply; and the collection of money and plate, by gift or loan, was the main preoccupation of the leaders on both sides. For this purpose the principal Norfolk members of Parliament—Potts, Wodehouse, Holland and Gawdy—were each entrusted with the supervision of a group of hundreds, ranging from five to eight in number. Seven hundreds were allotted to Sir Edmund Moundeford and William Heveningham jointly, presumably in view of Moundeford's ill state of health.

These members, with the assistance of the Deputy Lieutenants and Justices of the Peace, were to organize the collection of money, plate and horses for the Parliamentary cause. At the local meetings the collectors were expected to subscribe first, 'by way of encouragement and example'. In every area 'one able gentleman' was to be appointed receiver, and was to record the contributions 'for certainty of repayment'. All plate was to be delivered at Norwich, Lynn, Thetford and Yarmouth, and was to be tried and weighed by a goldsmith duly appointed for the purpose. This important duty was presently entrusted to Timothy Skottowe, a leading goldsmith of Norwich.[22]

Details survive of some of the meetings which took place in the ensuing weeks—two at Aylsham, one apiece at Walsingham and Holt. At Aylsham, on the first occasion, Sir John Potts volunteered to supply 'two horses furnished and ten foot arms', together with the sum of £100. Sir John Palgrave of North Barningham did the same, stipulating that his horses were 'for defence of this county'. Their lesser neighbours followed, with sums ranging from £60 to £20. At the second Aylsham meeting Sir William Paston offered 'in money and plate, to be sent up to the Parliament, two hundred pounds; and for the defence of this county, not to be sent out, six horses full furnished'. On this occasion the other contributors ranged from Roger Bulwer of Guestwick, who promised to give all his plate, 'one hundred pounds if it weigh so much', down to Robert Bacon, who 'out of my poor weak estate' was able to afford £5. At Holt there was a large attendance, with Sir Isaac Astley of Melton Constable subscribing £100, his brother Sir Edward £50, John Coke of

Holkham £50, and Thomas Lougher, the well-to-do rector of Letheringsett, another £50. The clerical subscribers at these meetings were few; but Nicholas Howlett of Reepham and John Martin of Edgefield contributed £10 apiece, and Henry Burton of Foulsham £5.

At Walsingham, James Calthorpe of East Barsham subscribed £100; Sir Thomas Guybon of Thursford and Robert Walpole of Houghton, £50 apiece. Thomas Windham of Felbrigg was also present at this meeting, and wrote down the terms of his subscription with some care: 'I do hereby undertake to deposit for the public service and good [illegible] score ounces of plate; and to be ready to furnish for defence of this county within itself two horses furnished and two foot.' This reservation, which Palgrave and Paston had also made—money and plate to be a loan or gift to the Parliament, but horses and arms to be devoted solely to the defence of the county—indicates an attitude that was widespread during the early stages of the war.[23]

Samuel Butler was to describe in *Hudibras* how the Parliamentarians

> . . . coin piss-pots, bowls and flagons
> Int' officers of horse and dragoons;
> And into pikes and musqueteers
> Stamp beakers, cups and porringers.[24]

A great deal of every man's capital was invested in his cupboard of plate; and in the lavish offerings of plate at these meetings we may see the very process that Butler described. Sir John Potts chose to pay his contribution of £100 in the form of plate; and Timothy Skottowe's receipt for the consignment has been preserved. It weighed altogether 371 ounces, and comprised 6 silver candlesticks, 2 banqueting dishes, 1 preserving ladle and dish, 8 plates, 1 basin, 1 'broath' standing bowl, 1 chafing dish, 1 vinegar cruet, 1 closet candlestick, 1 porringer and 3 trencher salts.[25]

The Deputy Lieutenants continued to meet in frequent session, and issued a variety of orders to strengthen and safeguard the militia. The captains were to tender to all their subordinate officers

[23] Ibid., ff. 30-2, 50-1.
[24] *Hudibras*, I., ii, 565-8.
[25] B.L. MS. Tanner 64, f. 88.

a form by which they undertook to serve under the authority of the Earl of Warwick, 'and to return the names as well of such as subscribe as of such as refuse'. Absentee or unreliable officers were replaced by others whose loyalty was beyond a doubt. Sir Thomas Hogan of Great Dunham was named captain of the troop commanded by Mr. Hovell—the Hovells of Hillington revealed their Royalist sympathies in the following year—and Mr. Rugg's troop of horse was taken over by John Windham, the son of Thomas Windham of Felbrigg. Captain James Calthorpe was promoted to be Colonel in place of Sir Nicholas L'Estrange, and his foot company was entrusted first to Sir Valentine Pell of Dersingham, and then to John Coke of Holkham. Thomas Knyvett was replaced by Robert Wilton of Wilby.[26]

Musters and exercises were arranged. Arms, equipment and stores were assembled at suitable points. For instance, the chamber over the porch of Hevingham Church, standing conveniently beside the highway from Norwich to Aylsham, was chosen by the authorities of South Erpingham hundred as the repository for their ammunition. A certificate signed on 1 November shows that it then contained 6 barrels of gunpowder, each weighing one hundredweight, and twelve hundredweight of bullets in their casks. There was also a large quantity of 'the best match' and a smaller amount of 'Flemish match'. The matchlock, not yet widely displaced by the flintlock, was a cumbersome weapon, and the lengths of smouldering 'match', which had to be kept dry at all costs, added much to the difficulties of seventeenth-century warfare. In addition the stores included implements for making trenches and emplacements—35 pickaxes, 30 'hodd sholves',[27] 30 mattocks, 15 axes and 15 beetles.

The Deputy Lieutenants kept a watchful eye on those who failed to contribute to the support of Parliament, and were empowered to bring pressure to bear upon them. Sir John Hobart and Sir Thomas Richardson were instructed to disarm all such persons, clerical or lay, within the Cathedral precincts 'who shall seem to them disaffected to King and Parliament, either by

[26] Ibid., ff. 9, 95-7, 99.
[27] B.L. MS. Tanner 311, f. 29. *Hodd sholves* were presumably the same as *hodding spades*, defined by Forby as 'a sort of spade principally used in the fens, so shaped as to take up a considerable portion of earth entire.'

refusing to contribute in some proportion according to their estates, or by other causes of suspect'. The rector of Great Cressingham, Dr. Edward Franklin, a leading adherent of Bishop Wren, came under suspicion; and 'if necessary he is to be conveyed up to the Parliament to answer the charges'.[28] Edward Heyward of Kerdiston wrote to Sir John Potts on 29 September: 'I beseech you . . . give me leave to keep myself, that am unfit for action, merely passive in this great difference. When any, how subordinate soever, employed by that honourable House shall come to me to that end, I shall clearly expose all the money and plate I have to their view and access, without any restraint by me of proportions or conditions, but only of my being merely passive.' His plate, he added, was worth £20 or £30. 'My ready money is only sufficient to supply my other present occasions, but not to pay my present debts, my rents and debts owing me not being at my command in these times. Your humanity, Sir, makes me presume this shall be private.'[29]

Edward Heyward was a lawyer of some distinction and an early friend of John Selden, who dedicated his *Titles of Honour* to him. He died in 1658 at the age of 64, 'laudable in his life, peaceable in his death', as his memorial in Reepham Church records. He was one of the six defaulters named in an order of Parliament dated 18 October, who were to be disarmed 'for not contributing with the good subjects to the common charge in this time of imminent danger'. The others were Sir Hamon and Sir Nicholas L'Estrange, Sir John Spelman, Sir Robert Kemp, and Erasmus Earle.[30]

Earle was also a lawyer, an able and ambitious man, of a family which had owned land in the parish of Sall for several generations. It is surprising to find him in this Royalist company, and his failure to contribute may have been due to other causes than Royalism. He will appear again in this book.

So far as the L'Estranges were concerned, this order to disarm them was not put into effect for two whole months. They were connected, by kinship or long family association, with virtually all the leaders on the Parliamentarian side. They were influential and popular, and the Deputy Lieutenants no doubt continued to

[28] B.L. MS. Tanner 64, f. 96. Cf. p. 245.
[29] Ibid., f. 25.
[30] Ibid., f. 70. Selden, 155, 187-8.

hope that they might listen to reason. It was not until 15 December that the chief constables of Smithdon hundred were instructed to remove all the arms, horse-furniture and ammunition at Hunstanton Hall to the magazine at King's Lynn. Even so, they were to proceed 'in a fair and respective way'; and they were given discretion 'to leave fit weapons for the defence of Sir Hamon L'Estrange his house against any rude or pilfering people'.[31] Although the sense of conflict was growing fast, there were still courtesies to be observed.

6

Even before the outbreak of war, precautions had been taken to safeguard and fortify the seaports of Lynn and Yarmouth, and the city of Norwich. Lynn was regarded as a particularly vulnerable point, as indeed it soon proved to be. Sympathies within the town were much divided, and the north-western area of Norfolk was more Royalist in outlook than any other. The authorities at Cambridge, with Oliver Cromwell already prominent among them, were directed by Parliament to maintain armed guards by day and night at all the bridges and ferries between Cambridge and Lynn, to intercept men, horses and plate sent from Norfolk to the King.[32]

At Yarmouth the two Bailiffs were empowered to muster and command the trained bands, and other persons able to bear arms. The town was to be fortified, the ordnance to be mounted, and everything done that might help to uphold the authority of Parliament. Anyone attempting to execute the Commission of Array was to be taken into custody; likewise anyone sending money, plate or arms to the King, 'for the maintaining of a wicked and unnatural war against his Majesty's good subjects'. Money and plate were to be collected for the defence of King and Parliament, and for 'the preservation of the town of Great Yarmouth and the towns nearby'. The people of Yarmouth responded generously to the call, as the lists of their contributions show. They brought along their gold rings, their double-gilt cups and

---

[31] Ibid., f. 111.
[32] B.L. MS. Tanner 63, f. 136.

covers, their silver tankards and beakers and spoons, together with quantities of their savings in cash, often in pieces of eight, sometimes in the foreign coinage which formed a part of their trade.[33]

It was also ordered before long that the trained bands of the two Flegg hundreds and the town of Yarmouth should be mutually bound to assist one another on occasions of danger; and a similar pact was arranged between Yarmouth and the trained bands of Lothingland, the nearest Suffolk hundred. There was, in fact, little Royalist sympathy in Yarmouth. But the town was acutely conscious of its exposed position as the easternmost outpost of England, and the nearest to the Royalist forces assembling across the sea in Holland. And this awareness was intensified when in October a ship, sent by the Queen from Holland with men and supplies to the port of Newcastle, sprung a leak and was driven by contrary winds into Yarmouth haven. The Yarmouth authorities promptly seized her and her crew and cargo. One account describes how the Royalists flung a packet of confidential letters into the sea, weighted with bullets, and how a nearby fisherman dived from his boat, rescued the letters and brought them to the bailiffs of Yarmouth. The soldiers in the ship, officers and men to the number of 140, escaped to shore, but were rounded up in Yarmouth and its neighbourhood and taken into custody, the cargo of wheat and beans being sold in order to maintain them. After some debate the ship was adjudged by Parliament to be the property of the town. She was renamed the *Adventure* and sent forth as a man of war 'for the taking of such prize, ships, vessels and goods, as belong to any persons or places, that are in hostility against the Parliament'.[34]

The vigilance of the Parliamentarian authorities in Norwich has already been shown in the episode of Captain Tresswell. 'In regard to the great distractions and dangers of the kingdom,' they ordered a double watch to be set each evening at nine o'clock during those summer nights, and the gates to be locked at that hour. The Guildhall was turned into a magazine, with arms and gunpowder in the armoury above the assembly chamber. The trained bands

---

[33] Swinden, 126-7, 555-6. H.M.C., Corporation of Great Yarmouth, 312-3.
[34] Swinden, 557-8. Manship, 383-4. H.M.C., Corporation of Great Yarmouth, 313.

were mustered, reviewed and enlarged, and much new equipment was purchased for them. The walls and towers were repaired and strengthened, and so were the booms on the river. Several of the city gates were blocked up. An experienced engineer named Christian was summoned from Lynn to advise on the defences, and was paid five pounds for his services. Two scouts were despatched to Barton Mills, and two to Bury St. Edmunds, 'to give speedy notice to the city of the approach of any cavaliers, or others that shall come in an hostile manner towards the city or county'. In November 'there were taken from Alexander Lawes thirty libellous and scandalous ballads, which he was singing of in this city and putting to sale, which were burned in the open market'. Whom did they libel, one wonders, and who was scandalized?[35]

Some of the Royalist sympathizers in the Corporation were already in trouble for not having contributed according to the propositions of Parliament. Others did not declare themselves at this stage, and indeed took an active part in the warlike preparations that were going forward. In December two of the aldermen, John Daniel and John Osborne, were named as delinquents, together with Justinian Lewyn, a Doctor of Laws who lived at Heigham; Stephen Knight, the Bishop's registrar; John Kettle, basket-maker, and Edward Wyer, mercer. These six were released on the 19th of the month 'from any trouble or molestation of the warrant, whereby they were sent for, as delinquents; they contributing upon the propositions as shall be thought fit by the Committee and Deputy Lieutenants'.[36]

We can only conjecture how the tides of opinion were running among the citizens as a whole—the discussions, the arguments, the conviction of some and the perplexity of others. A little of the atmosphere is suggested by the depositions, sworn on 3 December by some of the volunteer guard appointed to watch the city walls and gates. The guard had challenged two men, Robert Holmes and William Hardingham, who maintained that they were themselves the King's watch. Hardingham after many other words said that 'they would not be confronted by such a company of young

---

[35] Norwich Court Book (1634–46), ff. 355, 365, 368–9. Norwich Assembly Book (1642–68), f. 2.
[36] C.J., ii, 896.

fellows as this informant and his fellows were'. Holmes said to another informant, 'What, jackanapes, are you saying you are the King's watch?' and said further that they were none of the King's watch, since two of them carried no bills, and that 'he was a better man than this informant or any of his company'.[37]

Later in the month William Hardingham was one of twenty Norwich citizens named in the order of Parliament which dealt with the delinquent aldermen and their associates. None of them had so far subscribed under the propositions, and they were now given a final chance to do so. If they refused to subscribe, the Deputy Lieutenants and Committee for Norwich were to disarm and secure their persons; but 'if they shall submit and conform themselves', all would be well.[38]

The first in the list was Augustine Blomefield, a wealthy citizen of strong Royalist convictions. He presently joined the King at Oxford, whereupon his estate was sequestered and remained so until his death in 1645.[39] Another was Augustine Briggs, who also joined the Royalist forces, and survived to represent Norwich in Parliament in the reign of Charles II.[40] A third, Augustine Cullier —Augustine was a popular name in East Anglia at this time—was to be implicated in a Royalist attempt early in the following year. There were three clergymen, one of whom, the Rev. John White-foot, was to preach Bishop Hall's funeral sermon and to earn the warm regard of Sir Thomas Browne. Some of the rest were citizens of substance; some, like William Hardingham, of humbler station. Probably the greater number paid what was required of them, but we have no details. The Royalist element was decidedly outnumbered in Norwich, as in the county as a whole, but there can be no doubt that it existed, and in some strength.

[37] B.M. Add. MS. 22, 619, f. 40.
[38] C.J., ii, 896.
[39] *Cal. Com. Compounding*, 1012.
[40] Cozens-Hardy and Kent, *Mayors of Norwich*, 93.

CHAPTER IX

The First Months of the War

I

The first battle of the war was fought far away to the west, at Edgehill in Warwickshire, on 23rd October. Both sides claimed the victory, but in fact the result was indecisive. The Royalist cavalry, brilliant and undisciplined, at first nearly won and then nearly lost the day. The Parliamentarian infantry, steady and tenacious, at one moment almost prevailed. But they were in no position, when the battle was over, to prevent the King's forces from marching straight on London; and if an immediate advance had been made on the capital, all resistance might have collapsed. But the King determined otherwise. He asked the Parliament to send commissioners to treat with him, moved slowly as far as Brentford, and then withdrew to Oxford, which was to be his headquarters throughout the war. This failure to press home his advantage was an encouragement to the more militant party in Parliament, and the terms they offered were such as he could only reject. As the winter advanced, both sides set themselves to prepare for a long and costly war.

In December it was ordained by Parliament that the counties of Norfolk, Suffolk, Essex, Cambridgeshire and Hertfordshire, together with the Isle of Ely and 'the county of the city of Norwich', should henceforward 'associate themselves, and mutually aid, succour and assist one another, in the mutual defence and preservation of themselves, and of the peace of the said counties'. Wide powers were given to the Lords Lieutenant and Deputy Lieutenants to raise troops, levy contributions, disarm the ill-affected, imprison the recalcitrant, and in general to place the entire region on a war footing. A resolution was drawn up, whereby the representatives of the counties 'in pursuance of the said order, and the better to confirm a mutual confidence in one another . . . do hereby promise, testify, and declare to maintain with our lives, powers, and estates, the peace of the said counties . . . and neither for hope, fear, or other respect shall ever relinquish this promise'.[1]

Such was the beginning of the Eastern Association, which was to exert a decisive influence on the course of the war. A single block of united territory was formed, able to resist all attempts against it, and to provide an inexhaustible reservoir of manpower and supplies. Such a degree of unity was a new conception, and the committees of the various counties did not always work in harmony. But with headquarters established next year at Cambridge, and a fully representative joint Committee of the Association set up, an organization came into being which had no parallel on the opposing side.

All people, whatever their degree, were encouraged to support the Association. Meetings were held in every town and village, at which the inhabitants could sign a form of consent to its aims, and offer their contributions in arms or in money. Lists for certain Suffolk parishes have survived, which show three or four neighbours joining together to provide a musket, or a corselet, or a few days' pay for a soldier.[2] Recruiting was still on a voluntary basis, and the officers of the militia set themselves, with varying success, to draw in such young men from the districts under their command as might be attracted by the pay, the new clothes and the novelty of army life.

The popular enthusiasm was much sustained by the Puritan preachers, who were active and jubilant. For the past two years the Lord had blessed their cause and discomfited their adversaries; and surely He would continue to uphold them in the supreme trial of war.

The Rev. William Bridge had now returned from Rotterdam, was installed with acclamation as preacher at Great Yarmouth, and had been chosen a member of the Assembly of Divines. In January he addressed the volunteers of Norwich and Yarmouth in a rousing sermon, bidding them be of good courage, and smite the 'Popish malignant party' to the ground, and harbour no doubts as to the righteousness of their cause. 'I know it is

[1] Rushworth, III, ii, 94-8.
[2] Kingston, 81-5.

objected, *They take up arms against their King.* I am persuaded there is not such a thought in the bosoms of any of you all, and God forbid there should: but there is much difference between taking up of arms against the King's person, and taking up of arms for the defence of the Kingdom, without the King's command. David though he were God's anointed, yet was he a subject unto Saul his King, and he took up arms to defend himself; he took up arms indeed, but if you look into 1 *Samuel* xxvi. 19, you shall find that David does impute that unnatural war that Saul his King made against him, to those wicked malignants and wicked counsellors about him . . . He does not say the King had done it, but lays it upon those that were about him, and therefore took up arms to defend himself against the malignants; David's example is our practice . . . Put all together, your cause is good, your enemies weak, your victory certain, your service honourable, safe, warrantable; wherefore, *Be of good courage, and play the men, for your people, and the cities of our God, and the Lord do with you what seemeth him good.*[3]

2

At Edgehill the Royalist infantry were commanded by Sir Jacob Astley, the cavalry by Prince Rupert, whose governor or tutor in military science Sir Jacob had at one time been. Before the battle the veteran was heard to offer up 'a most excellent, pious, short, and soldierly prayer: for he lifted up his eyes and hands to Heaven, saying, *O Lord! thou knowest, how busy I must be this day: if I forget thee, do not thou forget me.* And with that, rose up, crying out, *March on, boys!*'[4]

He was born 63 years before, a younger son of Isaac Astley, whose family had already owned their estate at Melton Constable for close on four centuries. He had sought his fortune overseas, first in the armies of the States-General of the Netherlands, and later in the service of the Elector Palatine. He had served likewise with King Christian IV of Denmark, and with Gustavus Adolphus

[3] William Bridge, *A Sermon preached unto the Volunteers of the City of Norwich and also to the Volunteers of Great Yarmouth,* 17–18.

[4] Warwick, 229.

of Sweden. In the intervals of forty years of battles, sieges, skirmishes and marches he had been domiciled in the Netherlands, where he married a lady named Agnes Impel. It was at The Hague that he became a favoured member of the Queen of Bohemia's little court, and supervised the martial exercises of her son Prince Rupert.

The Winter Queen held him in high regard, and loved to direct her rather heavy royal badinage at the smallness of his person. He was indeed a very little man, as is attested by the clothes which his descendants still preserve—the plain buff coat which he wore on his campaigns, and beneath it the leathern vest with sleeves enriched with metal braid. But his small frame was charged with a fiery energy, and his courage and good humour surmounted every trial. His splendid portrait vividly depicts him—the martial features and upright active body, the vigorous greying hair and moustache and beard. Clarendon has protrayed him with equal vividness in words. 'Sir Jacob Astley was an honest, brave, plain man, and as fit for the office he exercised, of Major General of the Foot, as Christendom yielded; and was so generally esteemed; very discerning and prompt in giving orders, as the occasions required, and most cheerful and present in any action. In Council he used few, but very pertinent words; and was not at all pleased with the long speeches usually made there; and which rather confounded, than informed his understanding: so that he rather collected the ends of the debates, and what he was himself to do, than enlarged them by his own discourses; though he forbore not to deliver his own mind.'[5]

When the political skies became overcast, Sir Jacob was recalled to the service of his own King. He played an important part, as we have already seen, in the campaigns against the Scots. In those campaigns, and in the greater conflict that followed, he was one of the small number of officers on either side who had any experience of actual warfare. To the very end of the war, his services to the King's cause were invaluable.

His sons, Isaac and Bernard, likewise fought in the Royalist ranks, and Bernard was to die of wounds, a prisoner in the hands of Parliament. His only daughter, Elizabeth, was married to her cousin Edward, the younger brother of Sir Isaac Astley, the head

[5] Clarendon, ii, 373.

of the family and the owner of Melton Constable. Edward had accompanied Sir Jacob on the northern expedition in 1639, and married his young cousin—she was fifteen years his junior—in the little church at Melton Constable later in the same year. She had probably never been out of Holland before. Her spelling—*shortsh* for church and *shield* for child—suggests that her ear was attuned to Dutch rather than to English inflexions of speech; and she and her mother used by preference to correspond in the Dutch language. [6]She gave birth next year to a son, who was christened Jacob after his grandfather. Since Sir Isaac was childless, the little boy was heir to all the Astley estates.

Edward Astley was knighted at Hampton Court in December 1641, and Sir Isaac was created a baronet in the following month. But despite these marks of royal favour, and the unfaltering Royalism of their distinguished uncle, both brothers actively supported the Parliament. Such differences of allegiance within families were not uncommon in the Civil War. There were many instances of complete division between close relations, between father and son, brother and brother. Sometimes the sympathies of a woman would be cruelly torn between the claims of her husband and her own kindred. So it was with young Lady Astley. She remained in Norfolk with her husband, whom she devotedly loved. But she also loved her father, her mother, the brothers with whom she had passed almost the whole of her life, all now far away in the King's territory, hidden by the fog of war. The Astleys were more fortunate than many of these divided families, since no personal bitterness seems to have been involved, and the bonds of love and consanguinity held firm. Nevertheless Lady Astley was soon to see her husband march westwards with his company, perhaps, for all she knew, to encounter her father and her brothers on the field of battle.

Sir Jacob Astley was one of the two great Norfolk soldiers who played an outstanding part in the Civil War. The other was Philip Skippon. They fought on opposite sides, yet there were many resemblances between their careers. Skippon came from a family of minor gentry long established in the parish of Weasenham. He too sought his fortune abroad as a young man, and served with distinction in the Palatinate and in the armies of the States-

[6] MSS. now at Swanton House, Melton Constable.

General. He too married a Dutch wife, a lady named Maria Comes. He returned to England about 1638 and went to live at Foulsham, where he had inherited a house and property from an uncle.[7] He was a good deal younger than Astley, whom he would certainly have known abroad, and probably in Norfolk as well. But he was a man of deep Puritan convictions, and the two can have had little in common beyond the mutual respect of soldiers of their quality.

Skippon did not long remain in retirement at Foulsham. In 1639 the King recommended his appointment as 'Captain of the Artillery Garden'. In January 1642 Parliament appointed him commander of the trained bands of the City, with the rank of Major General—'an office never before heard of,' wrote Clarendon, 'nor imagined that they had authority to constitute'—and also commander of the Parliamentary guard.[8] On 12 November, when the King's forces approached London, he was at the head of the trained bands when they marched out towards Brentford. Whitelocke described how on this occasion Skippon, who now bore the title of Sergeant Major General of the Forces of London, 'made short and encouraging speeches to his soldiers, which were to this purpose: *Come my boys, my brave boys, let us pray heartily and fight heartily, I will run the same fortunes and hazards with you, remember the cause is for God; and for the defence of your selves, your wives, and children. Come my honest brave boys, pray heartily and fight heartily, and God will bless us.* Thus he went all along with the soldiers, talking to them, sometimes to one company, and sometimes to another; and the soldiers seemed to be more taken with it, than with a set, formal oration.'[9]

No blood was shed on this occasion; but Skippon was to fight heartily and pray heartily, in battle after battle, until the victorious close of the war. The Parliament had no finer soldier, no more trusted and loyal servant. And he uplifted the spirits of his men, not only with cheerful words, but by the manuals of soldierly devotion which he wrote for their benefit. He thought of himself as 'the Christian Centurion', an expression which occurs in the titles of all his pamphlets. Clarendon, while acknowledging that

[7] Rye, *Norfolk Families*, 803–7. Quarles, *History of Foulsham* (1842), 80–98.
[8] Clarendon, i, 298.
[9] Whitelocke, *Memorials* (1682), 62.

he was 'a man of order and sobriety', described him as altogether illiterate.[10] This was of course quite untrue. Probably Clarendon had never heard of the writings of the Christian Centurion, so homespun and unpretentious in style, yet with the power to fortify the hearts of simple men.

3

The winter months dragged on. The opposing sides continued to recruit men, assemble equipment and stores, and strive to meet their mounting expenses by the collection of money and plate. Until she returned to England in February, the Queen remained the centre of Royalist organization in Holland, and her forces were regarded by the Parliamentarians in Norfolk as a more immediate menace than those of her husband.

In December the Deputy Lieutenants summoned a meeting in Norwich to consider how to secure the county 'from being invaded by the Queen with foreign forces'. On this occasion certain Royalists were present, and openly declared their dissent from the purpose of the meeting, 'affirming that if the Cavaliers were in the county, they should account them their friends . . . which Sir John Palgrave, Sir John Holland and Sir John Potts took great exceptions unto; whereupon Sir John Spelman, Master Hamon L'Estrange and others were commanded to depart the meeting'.[11] The outcome of this was an order of Parliament that Spelman and L'Estrange, together with Sir William D'Oyly and two others, were 'to be sent for as delinquents, for affronting the Committees when they were met upon the service of the public; and thereby, as much as in them lay, obstructing and prejudicing the service of the Commonwealth'.[12]

Hamon L'Estrange was the second son of Sir Hamon, and later the author of several historical and theological works. Sir John Spelman was likewise an intellectual and a writer. He was the eldest son of the great Sir Henry Spelman, who had died in 1641,

[10] Clarendon, i, 298.
[11] Mason, 288–9. I have been unable to trace the pamphlet there quoted.
[12] C.J., ii, 884.

and the inheritor of his father's learning. His mother, incidentally, had been a L'Estrange, and his father had acted as Sir Hamon's guardian until he came of age. Sir John Spelman had travelled widely and associated much with foreign scholars. His own particular distinction was in Anglo-Saxon studies, and he wrote a life of Alfred the Great, not published until long after his death. He and his wife, one of the Townshend family of Raynham, lived at Stinton Hall in the parish of Sall, surrounded mainly by neighbours of the opposite persuasion.

Sir John had offered his services to the King, but had been bidden 'not to quit Norfolk or suffer himself to be carried thence; his personal services and residence there being especially needed'.[13] He did as he was ordered; but even before the contentious meeting at Norwich he had never concealed his views, and his comings and goings were closely watched. On 2 February 1643 he addressed a long letter, from the house of Robert Houghton at Wolterton, to his neighbour and kinsman Sir John Potts. It was an explanation of his actions on the previous night, which might otherwise be regarded as suspicious, and continued with a statement, adapted to the ear of a leading Parliamentarian, of his attitude to current events. I have printed the letter in full, since it gives so striking an impression of those early months of the war— the uncertainty and manœuvring, the evasiveness and suspicion between neighbours, while at the same time the accustomed social intercourse of the countryside was preserved, and ladies might still be expected to drive out to visit their friends despite their husbands' opposing views.

Honourable Sir,

It was my ill fortune, that coming late last night to my house to take order with my wife for some things that concern my own private, to be informed that my wife was gone to wait on you, in Mrs. Houghton's coach, and that she went from thence to Wolterton with her; I easily crediting it because it being past 6 of the clock, it was I thought too late for her to venture on horseback in the dark. I took my horse again and came about to

---

[13] N.A., ii, 402. The King's letter, from which only this single sentence is quoted, was then (1849) in the possession of Dawson Turner. I have not been able to trace it further.

Wolterton, and what by fetching about and missing my way made it so late that I found Mr. Houghton in bed, and much troubled at my so late coming to his house; as for my wife, I found she neither was nor had been there. I was sorry that I had exposed myself and my neighbour, to be had in jealousy for anything that such a nightly coming to him might (in these times) insinuate; and the more, because I understood by him that in conference with you, you affirmed there was a design and endeavour of some to raise forces and to procure the coming of his Majesty's army into the county and to join with the Papists here.

Sir, if I were not unjustly and without all colour publicly defamed for a malignant and Popishly-affected, I should never entertain any jealousy that I might be meant any share in such charges; but being by that crimination now made capable of partaking of every calumniation in that kind, I hold it my duty even to Christianity to protest my innocence. Sir, yourself knows well that at my Lord Mowbray's appearing with the Commission of Array I did really endeavour the surcease of it, as persuaded that the raising force, by either the one side or the other, would bring the war into the county, which (God is my witness) I have to my understanding and power faithfully sought and still shall seek to divert; and were that endeavour as well pursued on the one side as I persuade myself it has been and yet is on the other, I am confident our county, as it is privileged above all other by situation, so it would have enjoyed that privilege in immunity from the common calamity. In the same judgment hath Mr. Houghton ever concurred; and truly, Sir, it was and (I am persuaded) yet is your own judgment also. But to deal faithfully with you, Sir, how much soever your intention is to the contrary, it is too much feared that the courses that are set on foot will inevitably bring the war upon us, without any invitation at all. As for the Papists in this county, I think you believe them to be so inconsiderable a body as not to be able to move in any sort but to their own destruction, and to the prejudice, if not ruin, of them that should adhere to them.

Sir, I crave your pardon that I take this liberty to vindicate myself before anything particularly laid to my charge; but, Sir, I desire to give the character whereby you shall against all jealousies give yourself assurance upon what grounds I shall ever move, and committing that to you in confidence of your good acceptance, I commit you to God and rest

Sir,

> Your kinsman and servant in all dutiful affections
>
> JOHN SPELMAN

Wolterton in haste
2nd February 1643

My service to my Lady and to my cousin Potts and his lady.[14]

Certain points about this letter remain obscure. Why, for instance, did Spelman come to his own house to discuss private business with his wife? Had he evaded the Parliament's order of the previous December, and was therefore, at least technically, in hiding? If we did not know that the King had instructed him to remain in Norfolk, the letter might be taken at its face value as a genuine expression of moderate views, and not as a skilful piece of equivocation. Robert Houghton's own position was somewhat difficult, since his wife was a sister of Richard Catelyn, the crypto-Royalist member for Norwich. He had reason to be troubled when a known Royalist partisan came to his house unexpectedly under cover of darkness. He wished to retain the good opinion of his important neighbour at Mannington; and in fact he later became an active supporter of the Parliament.

Spelman, however, was not to remain much longer in Norfolk. Perhaps he was too conspicuous a figure, too closely watched by his adversaries, when any Royalist attempts in the spring would necessarily require an element of surprise. For whatever reason, the King soon summoned him to Oxford, appointed him to his private council, and intended still higher promotion for him. But he died at the end of July in this same year, a victim of 'the camp disease', an epidemic which had broken out in the overcrowded city and its neighbourhood. Such was the end of this 'religious, loyal and learned author', whom we have seen losing his way in the muddy Norfolk lanes in the darkness of a February night.[15]

---

[14] B.L. MS. Tanner 64, ff. 145–6.
[15] D.N.B., *sub* Sir John Spelman. *Life of Aelfred the Great* by Sir John Spelman, ed. Thomas Hearne (Oxford, 1709), 225–6.

4

'The East being an angle of this kingdom, and no thoroughfare into any other parts, and all as it were empaled and shut up by London, their good affections were stifled; but like a smothering fire, it was now and anon blazing out, but soon extinguished.'[16] The words of the Royalist writer Sir Philip Warwick describe accurately enough the events of the next few months. Throughout the counties of the Eastern Association the key positions were firmly held by supporters of the Parliament. But it seemed certain that the King's party, however disorganized and overborne, would make some attempt at a diversion early in the spring.

The forces of the Eastern Association were commanded first by Lord Grey of Werke, and later by the Earl of Manchester. But the driving force behind the Association, from the moment of its inception, was Oliver Cromwell, who had been returned to the Long Parliament for the town of Cambridge. Throughout those critical months he devoted all his energy and initiative to welding the levies from the five counties into a coherent force, to persuading the Deputy Lieutenants and Committees of those counties to work as a united body, and to rouse in them a full sense of the dangers and opportunities that lay ahead. As soon as the Royalist supporters began to show their hand, he acted swiftly and with complete success.

There was an alarm in January, when Cromwell received from Sir Philip Stapledon at Windsor the news that 'there is one gone into Norfolk . . . he carries a letter thither from Oxford, to encourage the Papists, generally, to take up arms'. It would be of great advantage, Sir Philip continued, if this man and his letter could be captured. He might be intercepted at Cambridge: 'but if he be gone into Norfolk, you are desired to use what means you can that the good party in that county do seize upon Gawdy and Bedingfeld, upon this just ground, that they intend to take arms.'[17]

Although the word Papist was used as a general term of abuse for the Royalist party, Sir Henry Bedingfeld of Oxburgh was in

[16] Warwick, 215.
[17] N.A., ii, 45–6.

fact one of the leading Catholics in Norfolk and a devoted supporter of the King. He was not apprehended on this occasion, and
there is reason to suppose that he had already withdrawn temporarily to Holland. The identity of Gawdy remains obscure. The
only Royalist in that strongly Parliamentarian family, so far as I
know, was Sir Charles Gawdy of Crow's Hall in Suffolk; but in a
letter addressed by Cromwell and his Cambridgeshire associates
on 27 January to the Deputy Lieutenants of Norfolk, passing on
the intelligence from Windsor, the man they were seeking was
described as Mr. Gawdy.

This letter, and one of the previous day, both invited the
Norfolk leaders to meet Cromwell and his colleagues at Milden-
hall in Suffolk on the 31st. 'The Parliament and the Lord General
have taken into their care the peace and protection of these eastern
parts of the kingdom; and to that end have sent down hither some
part of their forces, as likewise a commission, with certain instructions to us and others directed: all which do highly concern the
peace and safety of your county.' In the meantime they were
urged 'to have in a readiness, against any notice shall be given, a
considerable force of horse and foot to join with us, to keep any
enemy's force from breaking in upon your yet peaceable county.
For we have certain intelligence that some of Prince Rupert's
forces are come as far as Wellingborough in Northamptonshire,
and that the Papists in Norfolk are solicited to rise presently upon
you'. In the second letter they were assured that 'you shall find all
readiness and cheerfulness in us, to assist you to break any
strength that shall be gathered; or to prevent it, if desired, having
timely notice given from you thereof'.[18]

Everything remained outwardly quiet in Norfolk during February. In the meantime much important legislation was being
enacted in Parliament; and on 4 March an ordinance was issued,
imposing a weekly levy on every county and city for the purposes
of the war. The county of Norfolk and the city of Norwich were
jointly assessed at £1250 a week. The same assessment was laid
upon Suffolk; and from no other county was so much required
with the exception of Devon, which was to pay £1800—an
unrealistic assessment, as the greater part of it was at this stage in
Royalist hands.

[18] B.L. MS. Tanner 64, ff. 116, 129. Carlyle, *Cromwell*, iii, 228–30.

For the raising of this levy, committees were named by Parliament in each county. These were the first of the many local committees by which affairs of every kind were to be transacted during the coming years. In the main their members were active and convinced Parliamentarians, the hard core of the Puritan movement in each locality. The same names constantly recur on them, with occasional additions as the war went on; and although some committeemen came to find their duties burdensome or distasteful, they seldom appear to have withdrawn altogether. The Norfolk Committee appointed on 4 March was listed in the ordinance of Parliament as follows:

Sir Thomas Wodehouse, Sir John Holland, Sir John Potts, Sir John Hobart, Sir Miles Hobart, Sir Thomas Hogan, John Coke, John Spelman, Philip Bedingfeld, Samuel Smith, the Sheriffs of Norwich, the Bailiffs of Yarmouth, Thomas Toll and John Percival of Lynn, Thomas Windham, Francis Jermy, Robert Wood, Gregory Gawsell, John Houghton, Thomas Weld, Martin Sedley, Thomas Sotherton, Sir Edmund Moundeford, William Heveningham, William Cooke, Robert Rich, Sir Richard Berney, Sir Isaac Astley, Sir John Palgrave and Brigg Fountaine.

On 21 March a supplementary list of names was issued, by which the following were added to the Norfolk Committee:

Sir Edward Barkham, Sir Thomas Gawdy, Sir Edward Astley, Sir Thomas Guybon, Thomas Russell, John Walpole, Robert Wilton, Robert Jermy, John Guybon, Robert Sheppard and Philip Calthorpe.[19]

Many of these names have already appeared in the course of this narrative, and others will occur again later. It is necessary to distinguish John Spelman from his namesake and kinsman Sir John the Royalist. John Spelman was a strong Parliamentarian, a stepson of Sir John Potts: later he was to be nominated Member of Parliament for Castle Rising in place of Sir Robert Hatton, expelled for sitting in the King's Parliament at Oxford. It should also be explained that Philip Bedingfeld was the head of a Protestant family long established at Ditchingham, only remotely connected with the Catholic Bedingfelds at Oxburgh.

---

[19] Husband (1643), 932–4, 942; (1646), 10. I have corrected the spelling of several names. I think I am justified in rendering 'John Cook' as John Coke, although there was also a Puritan alderman named John Cook in the Corporation of Lynn.

There is significance in the absence from the Committee of certain prominent Deputy Lieutenants—Sir William Paston, Sir Thomas Richardson, Sir Robert de Grey. Until recently they had continued to work with their Puritan colleagues, and their signatures had regularly appeared at the meetings of the Lieutenancy.[20] Perhaps they had placed some hopes in the outcome of the negotiations between the King and the Parliament, which had been dragging on inconclusively at Oxford and were now clearly breaking down. They could no longer support the measures of Parliament; and each had lately, in one way or another, disclosed his Royalist sympathies.

All the names in the list of 4 March, with one addition, John Tolye of Norwich, reappear as committee men in the next important ordinance of Parliament. This was the Ordinance for Sequestering the Estates of notorious Delinquents, issued on 1 April. It gave the local committees the widest powers to take over the estates of their opponents, to impound their rents and revenues of all kinds, and to employ the money for 'maintaining of the army and forces raised by Parliament'.[21] It provided means by which all overt Royalist sympathisers in a Parliamentarian county such as Norfolk could be reduced to impotence and penury.

This unprecedented invasion of the rights of property may well have aroused some disquiet in Wodehouse and Holland, Windham and the Astley brothers and a number of others on the Committee —men of large property and moderate outlook, connected by ties of blood or neighbourhood with most of the leading figures on the other side. But as a measure of expediency, at a time of growing difficulty and danger, its advantages were obvious. And there was immediate work in Norfolk for the Sequestration Committee to do, since during the month of March a succession of Royalist attempts took place.

5

It is not clear whether these uprisings were part of a concerted plan, or whether they were the efforts of Royalist groups acting

[20] B.L. MS. Tanner 64, ff. 122–5.
[21] Husband (1646), 13–6, 19.

more or less in isolation. In any case they were sadly ineffective, and showed how firm was the control of the Parliament throughout East Anglia. The first open signs of trouble occurred in Norwich. During the past weeks the city had been active in furnishing men and horses to swell the forces of the Eastern Association at Cambridge; and on 1 March it was resolved to send a further hundred men and horses. By this time the voluntary supply of horses had been exhausted; and it was resolved, by the Parliamentarian majority in the Corporation, to seize all the horses of those citizens who could be comprised within the convenient term of 'malignants'.

The Mayor, William Gostlin, was undoubtedly a man of Royalist sympathies. It is significant that he had been among the prominent citizens who had signed the letter of support to Bishop Wren some years before;[22] and he must have assented reluctantly to many of the measures passed by his colleagues during his tenure of the mayoral chair. According to one account he now refused to confirm the order about the seizure of horses; and in any case he was regarded as politically unreliable at this time of crisis. On 2 March he was taken into custody by order of Lord Grey of Werke, and removed as a prisoner to Cambridge. Trustworthy members of the Corporation were allotted various wards of the city, in which they were authorized to seize all the horses of malignants. On 4 March it was 'this day ordered that Mr. Parmenter in the absence of Mr. Mayor shall supply his place until he shall return again'. Adrian Parmenter was a wealthy grocer descended from one of the Dutch or Flemish families which had sought refuge from Catholic persecution in Norwich a century before. He had been Mayor the previous year, and was an enthusiastic supporter of the Parliament.[23]

Gostlin's removal was soon followed by a purge within the Corporation. The record in the Court Book runs as follows: 'Forasmuch as several letters were written under the hands fo the greater part of the aldermen of the city and sent to the private dwellings of Mr. Henry Lane, Mr. John Daniel and Mr. John Osborne, three aldermen of this city, in regard that they have absented themselves from attending upon the Mayor and giving

[22] See p. 85.
[23] Norwich Court Book (1634–46), ff. 379–80. Blomefield, iii, 383–5.

counsel unto him according to the tenor of their oaths, and have neglected the pursuance of their places in their several wards . . . it was ordered that in the absence of the said Mr. Lane, Mr. Daniel and Mr. Osborne, and their total omission of performing the duties of their several places, is a sufficient cause for their removal and discharge from their places and degrees of aldermen.' Daniel and Osborne had already been in trouble some months earlier, as was mentioned in the previous chapter. A year later another alderman, Alexander Anguish, was similarly expelled; but in his case various accusations were brought against him 'touching fraud, deceit, corruption in the execution of justice and other misdemeanours', and he was adjudged 'a man unfit to continue any longer in the office, rank or degree of an alderman'.[24] Lane and Anguish had been signatories, as well as Gostlin, of the letter of support to Bishop Wren. Both were former Mayors of Norwich; and Osborne was to hold that office after the Restoration.

The vacant aldermanic seats were at once filled by trustworthy Puritans, most of whose names will appear later in this narrative—Matthew Lindsey, Livewell Sherwood, John Rayley and others. And this upheaval in the affairs of Norwich was completed on 18 April, when Parliament appointed a group of aldermen and councillors to act as committeemen for the weekly assessment and for the sequestering of the estates of malignants within the city boundaries. They were Adrian Parmenter, Christopher Baret, Samuel Smyth, Thomas Baker, Matthew Peckover, Samuel Puckle, Livewell Sherwood and Matthew Lindsey.[25]

One of their first tasks was to send a deputation to the Duke's Palace, as it was still called although there had been no Duke of Norfolk since 1572, to appraise and inventory the Earl of Arundel's goods, 'and to sequester the said house and goods, and Mr. Wright is also to attend them to open such locks, trunks and chests as shall not otherwise be opened for them'.[26] Similar treatment was to be meted out by the county committee to Arundel's mansion at Kenninghall later in the year. Nothing seems to be known about this, beyond the survival of a list of 'my Lord of

[24] Norwich Court Book (1634–46), f. 381. Norwich Assembly Book (1642–68), f. 16.
[25] Husband (1646), 38.
[26] Norwich Court Book (1634–46), ff. 381, 393.

Arundel's jewels and other things taken by Captain Vermuyden at Kenninghall' on 7 August 1643. They included many rings and other jewels, a looking-glass set in gold and silver, a crystal cup, two branches of coral, '26 rich jewels with precious stones in a brown paper sealed up.' They were to be sent up to Parliament and, if proved sequestrable, were to be sold and the money paid to the troops under the command of Sir Arthur Hazlerigg.[27]

Even before Gostlin's arrest, the leaders of the Eastern Association at Cambridge were expecting trouble in Norfolk. On 1 March an order was despatched by Lord Grey of Werke for measures to be taken against a number of named Royalists, together with 'all Papists, malignants and other persons whatsoever that have or shall refuse to appear at musters, or to contribute according to the propositions of both houses of Parliament, or to enter into the Association'. Their houses were to be entered, and forced in case of resistance; their horses, arms and ammunition were to be seized; their persons were to be secured till further order.[28]

The named Royalists were Sir Robert Kemp and Sir William D'Oyly, both of whom had by this time crossed to Holland; Sir John Spelman, who had now joined the King at Oxford; Sir Edward Waldegrave of Stanninghall and his son Henry, both Papists, who may also have been with the King; Sir Hamon L'Estrange, Sir Robert de Grey, Sir Thomas Pettus, Thomas Knyvett and Augustine Holl. The last-named gentleman lived at Heigham, just outside the walls of Norwich, and still maintained close connections with the city on which his family fortunes were based. His house was a suitable meeting-place for Royalist sympathizers, whether from Norwich or from the surrounding countryside; and a party of them assembled there during the first week of March, shortly after Gostlin's arrest.

The number of these malcontents is uncertain. Blomefield refers to 'many gentlemen and magistrates of the city, who had associated themselves in order to get the government of it out of [Parliamentarian] hands, and to hold it unto the use of the King'. On the other hand, only six gentlemen were named in the report

[27] Hervey, 442. The list is signed B. Vermuyden. The only son of Sir Cornelius Vermuyden, the drainer of the fens, of military age at this time was the eldest, another Cornelius.

[28] B.M. Add. MS. 22,619, f. 29.

presently submitted to Parliament. We only know that a group of Royalists 'stood upon their defence' in Holl's house, and 'wrote to another gentleman of the county to raise the county and come to their defence'. On this the Norwich volunteers, under the command of Captain John Fountaine and Lieutenant Hamond Craske, trundled their heavy guns out to Heigham, and declared that if the defenders did not at once surrender, they would 'demolish the house and them in it'. Whereupon they surrendered, and were all taken into custody.[29]

The six prisoners whose names are recorded were despatched, as the Mayor had been, to Cambridge, 'sent in safe custody to Colonel Cromwell, to be by him disposed of in such a place as the said Colonel Cromwell shall think fit and appoint'. Three of them were Norwich citizens of wealth and influence—Thomas Aldrich, John Payne and Augustine Cullier. The others, besides Holl, were two gentlemen of the county who had hitherto allowed it to be supposed that their sympathies lay with Parliament. They were Sir William Denny and Sir Thomas Richardson.

At the outbreak of the war, Sir William Denny had been regarded with some suspicion by Parliament, and had been summoned to attend the House. But he gave assurances to the Deputy Lieutenants in Norfolk which they decided to accept, and were prepared to convey to Parliament. Sir John Holland, as always tolerant and moderate in his outlook, had written in September to explain their attitude to Miles Corbett in London. Sir William, he said, 'applied himself to us, sought our favours . . . protested his innocence, and true affections to the Parliament . . . was one of the first of the militia that subscribed in obedience to the Lord of Warwick and his Deputy Lieutenants. So as we here were generally of opinion that if it might stand with your good liking there, not to call for his appearance, that he may awhile lie under the rod to see how he will behave himself in those public services that shall be required at his hand and of which we will not fail to give you a closer account, that it would advance the service . . . Thus much Sir John Potts and others declared they would signify to you in whose power I know it is, and to whose judgment I leave it, with this observation, that it hath still been the method of the House to be favourable to converts, of which number I

[29] Blomefield, iii, 384. B.M. Add. MS. 22,619, f. 33.

hope he will prove, and then I know he may be very useful to us, as having been most industrious in the knowledge of martial discipline of any captain of this county'.[30]

In these circumstances, Sir William Denny's defection probably came as less of a surprise to the local Parliamentarians than that of Sir Thomas Richardson. As lately as 24 January, Richardson had still been attending the meetings of the Deputy Lieutenants and ostensibly supporting all their measures. Now, suddenly and inexplicably, he had changed sides. He is a somewhat obscure figure, the son of an able but unpopular judge of the same name, who had bought the Honingham estate about 1600. The judge, by a somewhat unusual arrangement, had obtained for his second wife a Scottish peerage, the Barony of Cramond, with the remainder to Sir Thomas, the son of his first wife. In Scotland the son would have been styled the Master of Cramond, and his epitaph was to describe him as *Baro Scotiæ Designatus*. His stepmother, however, survived him; and he seems to have lived quietly in Norfolk, an amiable easygoing country squire, until the outbreak of war.[31]

The surrender at Holl's house took place on 7 March. On the 12th of the same month Sir Thomas Richardson died in custody. The Royalist journal *Mercurius Aulicus* told its readers that he was committed merely 'for being well affected to his Majesty, which is crime enough', and that 'he came to his death partly with grief in being so unjustly handled, but principally by the ill usage which he there received'.[32]

There are no suggestions elsewhere that the Royalist sympathizers captured at this time were subjected to physical illtreatment; and it is more likely that Sir Thomas succumbed to some sudden illness, perhaps in the circumstances a heart attack or a stroke. No details are given in the inscription on his monument at Honingham, where he is portrayed in full armour, grasping a truncheon and a sword, and looking a good deal more martial than probably he ever did in life.

After the dispersal of the gathering at Holl's house, and the purge of the Royalist sympathizers on the Corporation, the

[30] B.L. MS. Tanner 64, f. 33.
[31] *Complete Peerage*, iii, 489–91. Knyvett, 29, 86.
[32] *Mercurius Aulicus*, 18 March 1643.

Parliamentary party held undisputed control of Norwich until the end of the war. But they were taking no chances: so much so that on 26 March it was solemnly 'ordered that the boat belonging unto Mr. Holl, lying at Mr. Anguish's house without St. Martin's gates, shall be drawn into the city and there locked up by the marshals'.[33]

6

Between the neighbouring towns of Yarmouth and Lowestoft, only a few miles apart but in different counties, there was long-standing hostility. For centuries they had engaged in bitter disputes about their rights in the herring fishery, with petitions to monarchs and Parliaments, repeated commissions of inquiry, and an immense accumulation of ill-feeling.[34]

Yarmouth was the larger and wealthier community, with its fine harbour and anchorage within the mouth of the Yare, its spacious market, its crowded houses. Lowestoft was a much smaller place, with probably not more than two thousand inhabitants, living in houses strung out along the edge of its lofty cliff. Down below on the beach was a row of wooden fish-houses, where the herrings were smoked and cured.[35] There was no quay at all, for it was not until the nineteenth century that the cut into Lake Lothing was made, and Lowestoft became a seaport in the full sense of the term. Yarmouth, moreover, was a borough town, a status that Lowestoft never achieved, even though little townships further down the Suffolk coast, Dunwich and Aldeburgh and Orford, each returned their two members to Parliament.

Nevertheless Lowestoft was an active and thriving place, with a strong sense of its own independence. Its fishing and curing industry was a very considerable affair, and employed many ships and boats. Quite sizeable vessels were able to anchor close inshore. If the town could be seized and held for the King, it might be of valuable service despite the lack of harbour or quay. Since Yarmouth was wholly committed to the Parliament, there was a good

[33] Norwich Assembly Book (1642–68), f. 6.
[34] Gillingwater, sections 1–4 *passim*.
[35] Ibid., 50–4.

deal of Royalist sympathy amongst the Lowestoft townspeople. In the early days of March a number of Royalist gentlemen from Suffolk and Norfolk began to assemble there. News of their arrival was soon carried to Yarmouth, and messages were at once sent to Norwich and thence to the headquarters of the Eastern Association at Cambridge.

Cromwell, as it happened, was already in Norwich. On the 10th he had written from Cambridge to the Deputy Lieutenants of Suffolk, about the arrears of pay for the troop of one of their officers, Captain Nelson. He mentioned 'this business for Norfolk, so hopeful to set all right there', and ended with a postscript that 'with your conjunction, we shall quickly put an end to these businesses, the Lord assisting'.[36] Shortly afterwards he set out for Norwich, taking with him five troops of the Association's forces. He was there when word arrived from Yarmouth on the 13th that the authorities there had 'made stay of Sir John Wentworth and one Captain Allin of Lowestoft who came thither to change dollars, both of whom are yet secured; and that the town of Lowestoft had received in divers strangers and were fortifying'.

The fullest contemporary description of what took place at Lowestoft was given in a letter to Sir John Potts by John Cory, a Norwich merchant, presently to be appointed Treasurer of the Sequestration Committee. It was read out in Parliament, and copied by the industrious Sir Simonds D'Ewes into his journal of the proceedings of the House.[37]

'The Colonel [Cromwell] advised no man might enter in or out the gates [of Norwich] that night; and the next morning between 5 and 6 with his 5 troops, Captain Fountaine, Captain Rich and 80 of our Norwich volunteers marched towards Lowestoft, where he was to meet with Yarmouth volunteers who brought 4 or 5 pieces ordnance. The town [of Lowestoft] had blocked themselves up, only where they had placed their ordnance, which were three pieces, before which a chain was drawn to keep off the horse. The Colonel summoned the town and demanded if they would deliver up their strangers, the town and their army, promising them then favour; if not, none. They yielded to deliver up their

[36] Carlyle, *Cromwell*, i, 120–1.

[37] B.M. MS. Harley 164, ff. 340–1. There is another version, differing in a few minor particulars, in Carlyle, *Cromwell*, i, 121–5.

strangers, but not to the rest; whereupon our Norwich dragoons crept under the chain before-mentioned and came within pistol shot of their ordnance, proferring to fire upon the cannoneer, who fled; so they gained two ordnance and broke the chain, so they and the horse entered the town without more resistance, where presently 18 strangers yielded themselves.'[38]

No lives were lost, not a drop of blood was shed, in the affair at Lowestoft. Its eighteenth-century historian asserted that Cromwell 'suffered his soldiers, in a great measure, to plunder the town and live at free quarters'.[39] It is quite possible that the volunteers from Norwich, and more particularly those from Yarmouth, did indulge in some looting or other disorder at the expense of the townspeople. But the troops did not remain at Lowestoft more than a couple of nights; and the real sufferers on the occasion were the Royalist gentlemen, the 'strangers' who had yielded themselves when Cromwell entered the town.

Cory reported their names to Potts. Among the Suffolk prisoners were Sir Thomas Barker, a younger son of the family seated at Trimley, and Sir John Pettus of Chediston, not to be confused with his equally Royalist kinsman in Norfolk, Sir Thomas Pettus of Rackheath. From Norfolk there were Thomas Knyvett of Ashwellthorpe, John Hamond of Little Ellingham, and 'Mr. Richard Catelyn's son—some say his father was there in the morning'. Richard Catelyn was, it will be remembered, the member of Parliament for Norwich.[40] There was also 'Mr. Thomas Cory my unfortunate cousin, who I wish would have been better persuaded by his friends, and that it may so work with him that he may obtain what favour may be afforded him'.[41]

The ringleaders were immediately sent as prisoners to Cambridge. Three ministers were also mentioned by Cory as being taken into custody—Mr. Quash, Mr. Peters and Mr. Rous. Jacob Rous was vicar of Lowestoft at the time, and he too is said to have been despatched to Cambridge; but he seems later to have made his peace with the régime, and continued at Lowestoft

[38] B.M. MS. Harley 164, ff. 340-1.
[39] Gillingwater, 420.
[40] In a list of all the prisoners, subjoined to his letter, Cory confusingly named no fewer than four Catelyns—'Mr. Thomas Cattlin'; 'Mr. Thomas Cattlin juniors both of them'; and 'Mr. Edward Cattlin'.
[41] B.M. MS. Harley 164, f. 341.

throughout the Commonwealth years.[42] The other two were incumbents of nearby parishes in Norfolk, John Quash of Gillingham St. Mary and Richard Peters of Haddiscoe and Toft Monks.[43] Matthew Brooke, the former minister of Yarmouth, and a great supporter of Bishop Wren during his episcopate, had also been in Lowestoft, but with others he 'escaped over the river'.

At the same time there was a general round-up of local Royalist sympathizers, who may or may not have been directly concerned in the Lowestoft affair. 'Old Mr. Castell'—Roger Castell of Raveningham—had been arrested earlier in the week, and secured at the house of John Greenwood, the Sheriff of Norwich. Matthew Trott of Beccles was taken into custody by Cromwell, and sent off to Cambridge with the Lowestoft prisoners. Cory mentions further the arrest in Suffolk of Clement Corbett, Bishop Wren's redoubtable Chancellor; Henry Coke of Thorington, son of the great Sir Edward Coke, and Member of Parliament for Dunwich; and 'our old Daniel', the Norwich alderman who had recently been expelled from the Corporation of his native city. These were all elderly men, and were probably soon released.[44]

Some mystery surrounds the part played in this affair by Sir John Wentworth of Somerleyton, who had been apprehended, together with Captain Thomas Allin of Lowestoft, when visiting Yarmouth 'to change dollars'. Wentworth did not long remain in custody. He was, in fact, a member of several of the Parliamentarian committees in Suffolk, and was not even removed from them despite this unexpected lapse.[45] Cory, in his report to Potts, said that 'he is come off with payment of £1000 as is said; some report he hath a message or letter from Sir Henry Bedingfeld out of Flanders that he hoped to be with him ere long'. Despite his alleged association with this dangerous Papist, it would seem that Wentworth's riches saved him. Another report, in a contemporary pamphlet, states that he had offered 'to give the Parliament £1000, and to lend them £2000 more, and to surrender up all his arms, so as his person may not be seized on, and detained in custody'.[46]

[42] Gillingwater, 345.
[43] *Walker Revised*, 270–1.
[44] B.M. MS. Harley 164, f. 341.
[45] Information from Mr. Norman Scarfe.
[46] *Certain Informations* . . . 1643 (quoted in Knyvett, 111 n. 1).

No wonder that Thomas Knyvett, who had infinitely more diffi-
culty in making his peace with Parliament, wrote sardonically:
'They say he is like to pay well for the ransom of his baubles, and
Colonel Cromwell likes the seat [Somerleyton] very well.'[47]

The amount paid by Wentworth must remain a matter of
speculation; but there is evidence that Cromwell's troop, and
perhaps Cromwell himself, did in fact visit Somerleyton, and that
the place did undergo a measure of spoliation. The Rev. Alfred
Suckling, the nineteenth-century historian of Suffolk, quotes a
document which was presumably written by a steward or other
dependant of the Wentworth family. 'Upon the 14th day of March
1643, being Tuesday, Colonel Cromwell's troop, and Captain
Fountaine with his troop, and divers others, to the number of
140, came to Somerley [sic] Hall in the morning, and there they
quartered that night, and a great part of them all Wednesday and
Thursday till afternoon.'

The steward estimated the quartering of 100 men—'because
some of them went away in the morning'—for two days at
£3 6s. 8d. As always, their horses consumed a good deal more.
'They eat in that time, as by good proof is made manifest,' 35
coomb of oats, which at 5/– the coomb came to £8 15s. 0d. 'Item,
their horses eat and stroyed off the chamber, and out of the barn,
at least 4 coomb of wheat, besides rye: the price of such wheat
then, at least 16/– the coomb, comes to £3–4–0. Item, their horses
eat and stroyed at least 3 loads of grey peas in the straw, all of
which were very well worth £4. Item, they shot out of the sacks,
and gave to their horses, 9 bushels of barley: being then 2/– the
bushel, comes to 18/–.' The sum of all this free quarter came to
£20 3s. 8d., 'besides at least five loads of good hard-land hay
eaten, and stroyed, worth £5 at least.'

In addition, 'the 15th day of March 1643, Colonel Cromwell's
quartermaster took away from Somerleyton Hall, the house of
Sir John Wentworth, Knight, 6 muskets, worth 20/– the musket,
which comes to £6; and their bandoliers, and two rests, valued at
6/8; and one fowling-piece worth 22/–; and 12 head-pieces,
valued at 9/– the piece, comes to £5–8–0. So the total of these
arms comes to £12–6–8.' There is mention of goods and horses
also taken, but no details. Finally, 'at the same time from the

[47] Knyvett, 110–11.

same place was taken, but by whom we know not: in gold, £160'.[48]

Captain Thomas Allin, who had accompanied Sir John Wentworth on his errand to Yarmouth, was taken with Cromwell's other prisoners to Cambridge. He was released in due course, and managed to escape abroad. In the meantime the authorities at Yarmouth had seized a small vessel or 'pink' in which he owned a half share, and which was lying in their harbour. On the ground that he was 'in rebellion against the King and Parliament', they sold his share to a Mr. Wilde of Lowestoft. Allin forthwith became a kind of Royalist privateer. With a base at Ostend, and a band of Lowestoft fishermen under his command, he waged his own personal war on Parliamentarian shipping, but more especially on the fishing and trading vessels of Yarmouth. After the Restoration he became a captain in the Royal Navy, and rose to high distinction. He was knighted in 1665 after the great battle against the Dutch which was fought within sight of his native town, was promoted to the rank of Admiral in the following year, was appointed Comptroller of the Fleet in 1671, and Commander-in-Chief of the Fleet in 1678. In the meantime Sir John Wentworth had died without issue; and in 1672 Sir Thomas Allin purchased the house and estate of Somerleyton from the nephew, his sister's son, who had succeeded him there. Sir Thomas died in retirement at his new home in 1686; and in the chancel of Somerleyton Church the bust of his monument now looks across to the bust of Sir John Wentworth, his associate in the Lowestoft rising all those years before.[49]

7

The leading figures involved in this affair at Lowestoft stoutly maintained that no rising was ever contemplated, and no attempt made to seize the town. They had assembled there before crossing over to Holland, where they intended to join the Royalist forces. Certainly a number of East Anglian gentlemen, including Sir William Paston, Sir William D'Oyly and Sir Robert Kemp, had

[48] Suckling, ii, 48–9.
[49] Gillingwater, 111–2. Manship, 384. D.N.B. *sub* Sir Thomas Allin.

already reached Holland; and since Yarmouth was a Parliamentarian stronghold, Lowestoft was certainly the most obvious point of departure.

Years afterwards, when Thomas Knyvett was in trouble again under the Commonwealth, he gave the following version of his part in the business: 'In March 1643, being at Lowestoft purposing to wait an opportunity to go over into Holland, this being at the beginning of the fatal troubles of this nation, and at that time there being a high contest between the town of Yarmouth and the poor town of Lowestoft, which made them stand upon their guard to defend themselves against the threats of Yarmouth, but no way in opposition to the Parliament's authority and commands; but so it fell out, whilst I was in this town, Colonel Cromwell, the now Lord Protector, brought horses and foot against it, and upon his first summons all the gentlemen strangers walked out of the town and yielded themselves without the least opposition, whereof myself was one.'[50]

He took the same line in his letters to his wife during his imprisonment at Cambridge. He and his companions, he said, read with joy the accounts of the affair in the Parliamentarian newssheet, the *Perfect Diurnal*, 'because all false concerning dangerous plots for anything I ever was acquainted with. God of heaven forgive the devices of those horrible liars to wrong innocent men'.[51] But the large number of Royalists assembled, the barricading of the town, and the substantial quantity of arms captured there—fifty cases of pistols, according to Cory, besides other weapons—all seem to prove that something considerable was planned.

Whatever their intentions may have been, Knyvett and his friends were now at the mercy of the Parliamentarians, their persons in custody, their estates liable to sequestration. We can follow Knyvett's own experiences in detail in his letters to his wife. Humorous and indignant, sanguine and despondent by turns, they reflect his every mood. At first the prisoners were billeted in the Rose Tavern at Cambridge, and the atmosphere was not uncongenial until 'the malice of the townsmen by complaints to the Committee here have bereft us of the society of any scholar

[50] B.L. MS. Tanner 62, f. 317, quoted in Knyvett, 34.
[51] Knyvett, 109.

coming to us'. He sent directions to his wife about his horses, his clothes, all kinds of family matters. She was to write to John Hampden's wife, with whom they were acquainted, and ask her 'to use her interest to Colonel Cromwell that I may be fairly treated here till we be released'. He himself sent compliments to Cromwell, but no word came in return. He hoped they might all be moved to one of the colleges. 'Indeed I was never so weary of a tavern in my life. I think I shall get such a surfeit on't, I shall ne'er abide to come near one again. A fine song that. Well prithee be merry, and so will I as long as I can.'[52]

After several weeks at Cambridge, the prisoners, or at any rate those who were considered to be most dangerous, were transferred to Windsor Castle. Conditions were poor there at first, with only two rooms and a single bed for seven men. 'I was forced to leave all my clothes at Cambridge, so as I fear I shall be lousy before I shall get any change, but 'tis all our cases.' Presently things improved, but there were still seven of them crowded into two rooms and a shitting house. 'My fellow prisoners present their service to you, by name Sir William Denny, Sir Thomas Barker, Sir John Pettus, Mr. Holl, Mr. Hamond, Mr. Catelyn and thy dear bully boy—a knot of malcontents.' Evidently the ringleaders in two separate episodes, at Lowestoft and at Holl's house at Heigham, had been incarcerated together.[53]

By July Knyvett was at liberty once more. But his estates had been placed under sequestration, and a long perspective of trouble and anxiety stretched before him. Month after month and year after year, he and his wife were to struggle in the net of petty tyranny and heavy exaction which had entangled them. More will be said of this in a later chapter; but it is necessary at this point to return to the immediate aspects of the conflict in Norfolk.

---

[52] Ibid., 109–13.
[53] Ibid., 114–5.

CHAPTER X

The Summer of 1643

I

'We hear strange things from Lynn,' Thomas Knyvett had written to his wife early in April, when still in prison at Cambridge. 'Sure our wise intelligencers were much mistaken in the scene of the grand Norfolk plots, to carry Colonel Cromwell to Lowestoft when he should have gone to Lynn.'[1] Undoubtedly Royalist sympathies were stronger in Lynn and its surrounding country-side than anywhere else in East Anglia. All through the spring and early summer of 1643, the town was in a continual state of unrest, until in August it openly declared for the King, bringing the sound of cannon and musketry into Norfolk for the first and last time in the whole course of the war.

As soon as matters were settled at Lowestoft, Cromwell and his troopers rode back to Norwich, and almost immediately set out again for Lynn, 'because the malevolents in that town began to raise combustions there'. The nature and extent of these combustions is uncertain; but Thomas Toll, one of the members for Lynn, as early as 13 March had sent a letter to Parliament 'expressing some distractions, and some divisions, in that town, and some oppositions to those constituted officers and captains'. Cromwell arrived at Lynn on 20 March, and his presence temporarily over-awed the Royalist elements there. He was entertained at a civic feast by the Mayor, Thomas Gurlyn, at a cost to the town of five pounds. According to one account he seized a small barque laden with arms which had just entered port from Dunkirk.[2]

The only malcontents mentioned on this occasion were Francis Parlett, the Recorder of Lynn, and an attorney named Kirby. On 6 April, Parliament ordered the Norfolk members to inquire into

---

[1] Knyvett, 112.
[2] Kingston, 94–5, quoting *Certain Informations* and *Perfect Diurnal*. C.J., iii. 12. King's Lynn Hall Book, 17 April 1643.

187

their misdoings, and in general 'to consider the business of Lynn, and what ways are fittest to accommodate the matters there, and to reduce the town'. (The word *reduce* suggests the siege of a rebellious town. That was to come later: in the present context it meant the reduction of the townsmen to a proper obedience, to a reasonable frame of mind.) Five days later a local commission was appointed—Thomas Gurlyn the Mayor, Sir Thomas Hogan, John Spelman, Gregory Gawsell, John Coke, and the two members of Parliament, Toll and Percival—'to examine the state of the business of the town of Lynn, concerning the late distractions there . . . and to commit to safe custody, or send up to the Parliament, such as they shall find, upon full proof, to have disturbed the peace of the said town, and to have committed the late tumults and riots there.'[3]

It does not appear that any other delinquents were taken into custody at this stage, and presumably Parlett and Kirby were able to explain their conduct. But the town and neighbourhood remained unsettled; and on 5 May it was resolved in council that a letter should forthwith be sent from the Mayor and Aldermen to Miles Corbett, in his capacity as chairman of the Committee for Informations, 'desiring him in the town's behalf to present the sense of this house to the honourable House of Commons, to desire an order from them to authorize Mr. Mayor to examine all such persons strangers as now are lately or hereafter shall shroud themselves within this town, or which may be supposed to be malignants . . . and to remove or apprehend such of them as Mr. Mayor with the rest of his fellow justices shall think meet'. At the same meeting £36 was paid to carpenters and workmen for strengthening the drawbridge at the south gate of the town.[4]

Parliament responded promptly; and on 8 May the Mayor and Justices of Lynn were ordered to 'make diligent search for and apprehend' thirteen named Royalists: Sir Hamon L'Estrange, his sons Sir Nicholas and Roger, and his grandson, another Nicholas; Sir Robert de Grey of Merton; Sir Charles Mordaunt of Little Massingham; Arthur Heveningham, the younger brother of the prominent Parliamentarian William Heveningham; Lord Alington, a Cambridgeshire peer; Robert Bacon,

[3] C.J., iii, 32, 39.
[4] King's Lynn Hall Book, 5 May 1643.

at present unidentified; and Captains Clench, Goodwyn, Naunton and Havers. The order was extended to cover 'all such strangers and lodgers that have or shall come into the said town, or near the same, since the first of January last, and are now, or shall be, residing and being in the said town, as are Popish recusants, or that have endeavoured or shall endeavour to put into execution the Commission of Array . . . or that have or shall withdraw themselves into the said town, to avoid the contributions of King and Parliament'. When apprehended, these offenders were to be sent up to Parliament, or confined in Wisbech Castle; and their arms, horses, ammunition, plate and money were to be impounded.[5]

Once again there is no evidence that any of these Royalists were arrested; and several of them—the L'Estrange family, Sir Charles Mordaunt, Captain Clench—were to bring about the *coup* in August, when Lynn openly declared for the King. What happened to them during the three intervening months? After the issue of such explicit orders for their arrest, they can hardly have remained for the whole of that period in concealment, either at Lynn, or in their own homes, or at large in the countryside. Did they contrive to make their way into Royalist territory, perhaps by sea or river, until time was ripe for them to return to Lynn and head the uprising there?

After the Restoration it became necessary for the Rev. Thomas Thorowgood, formerly rector of Grimston and Little Massingham, and a member of the Assembly of Divines, to explain his activities during the preceding twenty years. Unkind people were accusing him of being a notorious upholder of the late régime; and he had undoubtedly sailed with prosperous winds through the whole period of the Civil War and the Commonwealth. In order to prove his moderate attitude, and his 'dovelike innocence' of the charges against him, he addressed in 1661 a lengthy *apologia* to Lord Townshend, the new Lord Lieutenant of Norfolk; and in this document he claimed that, 'so far from being an incendiary', he had sheltered many Royalist gentry and clergy in his house for considerable periods. He had harboured Sir John Spelman on his journey to join the King at Oxford, and had accompanied him a great part of his way thither. 'Sir Hamon L'Estrange came after

[5] C.J., iii, 76.

midnight to my house, hardly scaping the troopers; all the long day before he had wandered without food. The next morning I found him very ill in bed; I rode to Dr. Baron for his advice. Sir Charles Mordaunt lay in the same chamber the night before; he was then gone, but came again often in that squirrel-hunting time, as it was then called.' Thorowgood was anxious, of course, to emphasize his own beneficence to these hunted Cavaliers. But his statement, so far as it relates to Sir Hamon L'Estrange, is borne out by an entry in the account-book kept by Lady L'Estrange during these years. She always referred to her husband as 'Mr. Strange'. On 5 July 1643 she wrote: 'Laid out as appeareth by a bill of Mr. Strange's when he travelled to avoid the troopers £5. 5s. od.'[6]

Another disturbance during this spring took place at Aylsham and the neighbouring villages. We have no contemporary account of what happened; but there seems to have been a demonstration in April against the payments levied by the county committee for the prosecution of the war. A detachment of the trained bands was sent, presumably from Norwich, and some sort of opposition was attempted, although there is no evidence of any bloodshed or serious fighting. We only know of the affair because the estates of several local people, minor gentry and prosperous yeomen, were sequestered, and there is some record of their explanations when in due course they came to compound, as will be described in a later chapter.

Thomas Leman, an Aylsham attorney, was regarded as the ringleader and spent some time in prison, although he protested that his delinquency consisted in opposing only for an hour the Parliament's forces, 'not knowing them to be such'. Robert Burr, probably one of the family who farmed their own lands for centuries in the parish of Burgh, was constable at Aylsham, but was nevertheless 'a prime mover, and did disarm some of the well-affected to the Parliament'. Edward Colfer, another lawyer of Aylsham—his modest memorial slab is to be seen in Heydon Church—not only took part in this affair, but later joined the King at Oxford. Richard Curtis of Aylsham and Richard Allin of Tuttington admitted their delinquency 'in opposing the trained

[6] N.A., xxii, 311-37. N.N.R.O., L'Estrange MSS., P. 7. See also my book *A Norfolk Gallery*, 115-24.

band sent to Aylsham to appease a tumult about rates'. At least one clergyman, Richard Plummer of Alby and Sustead, also took a hand in the affair. In the following year, among many other misdemeanours he was accused of 'assisting by word or act the rising at Aylsham' many months before.[7]

2

Such men as Sir Hamon L'Estrange and Thomas Knyvett had been committed Royalists from the outset. They had no doubts whatever as to their course of action. In any circumstances they would support the King. The path of the moderates was, as always, more difficult. We have already seen how Sir Robert de Grey, Sir Thomas Richardson and Sir William Paston continued to act with their fellow Deputy Lieutenants for months after the King had raised his standard. They were still able to hope that matters might yet be accommodated, that even at this late hour the kingdom might not be torn asunder. Accommodation—the word was still being repeated, in accents ever less sanguine, all over England. A few months before, John Rous in his quiet parsonage had transcribed yet another poem into his diary. Its concluding lines admirably summed up the moderates' point of view.

> For if, by force of arms, the King prevails,
> He is invited to a tyranny;
> But if, by strength of Parliament, he fails,
> We heap continual wars upon posterity.
> Then he that is not for accommodation
> Loves neither God, nor Church, nor King, nor Nation.[8]

But for Paston and his friends all hope of accommodation faded during the early months of 1643, even before the breakdown of the peace negotiations, never very promising, which were conducted at Oxford at the beginning of April. They broke with their Parliamentarian colleagues, and gave what support they could to the King.

As related in the previous chapter, Sir Thomas Richardson

[7] *Cal. Com. Compounding*, 954, 993, 1271. Mason, 315-20. *Walker Revised*, 271.
[8] Rous, 124.

joined the Royalist gathering at Augustine Holl's house, and died almost immediately afterwards. The activities of Sir Robert de Grey are something of a mystery. We have seen that his arrest was ordered by Parliament on 8 May; yet he must somehow have cleared himself, for he was still in command of his militia company at the end of June. On 6 July a letter was read in Parliament, 'which he published at the head of his company, which occasioned a mutiny, and expressed disaffection to the Parliament'. It was resolved that he should be forthwith sent for as a delinquent, and that his estate in Norfolk and elsewhere should be sequestered. Moreover Sir John Potts and Sir John Holland were to go down at once into Norfolk, and 'take care that some severe punishment may be inflicted on the late mutineers in Sir Robert de Grey's company and others'.[9] Nothing more is known of this mutiny or its consequences; and Sir Robert's gesture in support of the King does not appear to have been repeated. He submitted to Parliament and took the Covenant in the following February, pleading that 'because he thought the forces raised by the King were destructive to the Commonwealth, he returned to his family, did not go out of the Associated Counties, and was never in arms, nor a contributor to the King'.[10]

Sir William Paston's attempts on behalf of the King were hardly more effectual than those of Richardson and de Grey. But it is possible to follow his movements more closely, and his story is perhaps worth recounting in detail. Something has been said of him in an earlier chapter—his exceptional wealth, his love of books and paintings, his travels abroad, the luxury and refinement of his great house at Oxnead. Thomas Knyvett described a visit there in a letter to his wife, at the outset of the ominous year 1640. 'One while we are Italians, another while Turks, by and by Egyptians, and eftsoons merry Greeks, but all very well and handsome, the mean reduced to a fine temper.' There was often a touch of friendly sarcasm when Knyvett spoke of Paston, his first cousin and so much his superior in fortune; and here I think he is referring to his host's accounts of his travels, which no doubt often enlivened the Oxnead dinner-table. 'I might spend another week,' he continued, 'and not see all the rarities. Indeed here is a

[9] C.J., iii, 158.
[10] *Cal. Com. Compounding*, 840.

world of curiosities and some very rich ones, as cabinets and jewels; but I must not forestall my own market, for if I enter into particulars I shall have nothing to talk of when I come home.'[11]

For a year or so yet, Paston had continued without much perturbation to adorn his house and gardens. Nicholas Stone sent down consignments of statues from his London workshop, Jupiter and Hercules, Juno and Diana and Apollo, to be placed on the terrace above the slow-flowing Bure.[12] It may have been at this time also that Paston married his second wife, Margaret Hewitt, a daughter of Sir Thomas Hewitt of Pishiobury in Hertfordshire. But in 1642 the worsening situation had begun to weigh deeply on his spirits, once so convivial and gay; and Knyvett told his wife that the company of 'my great cousin, Sir William', was by no means 'so liquid as it had wont to be'.[13]

The phrase 'my great cousin' was another of Knyvett's mild jests at Sir William's expense. It referred to his corpulence, hereditary in the Paston family, as well as to his worldly position. But this stout and comfort-loving man acted with considerable spirit when at length the crisis came. We have seen how he continued to carry out his functions of Deputy Lieutenant into the opening months of 1643, and so long as any hope of accommodation remained. Then, at some unknown date, he vanished from the Norfolk scene, and crossed the sea to Holland. A letter from Cromwell, dated 20 March, survives among the manuscripts at Holkham, in which the chief constables of the hundred of Holt were instructed to 'give warning to all such in their hundred as found cuirassiers under the command of Sir William Paston, Baronet, to appear at Thetford on Monday the 27th inst., completed, to march away under command of Captain Robert Rich, for the defence of their county'.[14]

The King was always generous in dispensing with the services of men of Royalist conviction whose estates lay in counties dominated by the Parliament. They were unable to bring to his aid any personal following of tenants and dependants. Their properties lay at the mercy of the local sequestration committees. For

[11] Knyvett, 94.
[12] *Note-Book of Nicholas Stone*, 128–9.
[13] Knyvett, 108.
[14] H.M.C., Earl of Leicester, 367.

example John Evelyn, whose family lands were mainly in Surrey, found that overt action would 'leave both me and my brothers exposed to ruin, without any advantage to his Majesty'. He tried to compose his mind by constructing a fishpond and 'some other solitudes and retirements', and his most militant effort was the dispatching of a horse and furniture to the King's army. But when in the summer of 1643 everyone was required to take the Covenant, 'I absented myself; but finding it impossible to evade the doing of very unhandsome things . . . I obtained a licence of his Majesty dated at Oxford, and signed by the King, to travel again.' He then embarked on a leisurely and protracted tour of France and Italy during the remaining years of the war.[15]

If a young man of twenty-two, in vigorous health, a younger son, unmarried and without dependants, could find it in his conscience to withdraw from the struggle in this way, Paston would have had every justification for doing likewise. In common with the majority of officers on both sides, he had no military experience beyond the almost formal duties of a captain of militia in a decade of unbroken peace. But his sense of duty impelled him to take some action, however ineffective. Kinsmen and friends had committed themselves to the war. His first wife's father, the Earl of Lindsey, had died of wounds after Edgehill, and her brother had been made a prisoner. There is no record of what he did in Holland, or what he had hoped to do. We only know that he was one of a group of East Anglian Royalists who assembled there in connection with some scheme of invasion or reinforcement of their own part of England.

Besides Paston, the party from Norfolk included Sir Henry Bedingfeld, Sir Robert Kemp, Sir William D'Oyly, Robert Jegon, and Robert Bacon, presumably the gentleman of the name who had already been in trouble at Lynn. There was also a 'Thomas Gross', probably the son of Sir Charles le Gros of Crostwight, one of the members for Dunwich in Suffolk, who never actually declared for the King but adopted a decidedly lukewarm attitude towards his Parliamentary duties.[16] All these, together with several Royalists from Suffolk, were listed in an order of the House of Commons on 14 June, as 'now residing at Rotterdam,

[15] Evelyn, *Diary*, ii, 78–82.
[16] Keeler, 248–9.

SIR WILLIAM PASTON
from a painting by an unknown artist, in the possession of the author

and other parts beyond the seas, doing ill offices to the Parliament, as this House is informed'. The order required them 'forthwith to return into England, within a month after notice hereof shall be left at their mansion houses; or otherwise, that all their estates, real and personal, shall be sequestered, and employed for the service of the Commonwealth'.[17]

At first these menaces were disregarded. The situation during the summer of 1643 seemed propitious to the Royalist cause. Newcastle's army was advancing southward into Lincolnshire, and might soon be expected to invade the territory of the Eastern Association. So the exiles in Holland ignored the summons to return home, and their estates were duly sequestered. But as the autumn and winter drew on, it became clear that the hopes of the Royalists would not be fulfilled. In particular the failure of the uprising at King's Lynn, which will presently be described, was a deep discouragement.

The efficiency of the sequestration committees varied from county to county, and their indulgence or severity depended greatly on the personalities involved. Many leading Parliamentarians derived small enjoyment from the harassing of their kinsfolk and neighbours, and were notable for leniency and sometimes for favouritism. A few withdrew from their distasteful duties altogether. Others, even if their motives were not actually malicious or vindictive, set themselves to exact reparation to the full. In any event, the sequestered Royalists in Holland felt ever more helpless as their rents and revenues were cut off, and at home their wives and families struggled to subsist on whatever proportion of their income, usually one-fifth of the whole, was grudgingly allowed them.

Lady Paston, left behind at Oxnead, sought assistance in her perplexities from her neighbour, the moderate and amiable Sir John Potts. The correspondence on this subject is scanty and difficult to interpret; but it would seem that in December 1643 she surrendered plate to the value of £1100, which the Earl of Manchester, who had by now become General of the Eastern Association, urgently required for the payment of his troops. In return for this very substantial sum, she received certain undertakings which remain obscure, but which included a promise of

[17] C.J., iii, 129.

security for the plate which remained. In reference to this transaction Manchester wrote to Potts: 'I am glad to have any occasion to express any respect to persons of quality, and esteem it a great happiness to be understood as one that desires to win by civility and not by harshness. I have sent you the pass and protection according to your desire, and shall be ready to serve my Lady Paston.'[18] Despite these fine sentiments, the loss of the plate was neither forgotten nor forgiven at Oxnead. Many years later, when Charles II paid a visit there, Paston's son told the King that he would have been able to serve him far more richly in plate, 'had not a Blue Ribbon, that attended on his Majesty with a white staff, plundered it from his father by trunksfull'. The reference was to Manchester, by then an elderly Lord Chamberlain and Knight of the Garter, in obsequious attendance on the monarch whose father he had defied and fought thirty years before.[19]

As the winter months passed by and the situation grew steadily worse, Paston felt that he had done his best and could now do no more. He and his family might well be reduced to penury, without affording any further help to the cause of the King. He too opened negotiations with Sir John Potts, and addressed to him from Rotterdam, on 15 February 1644, this letter of surrender.

Much honoured Sir,

I do infinitely acknowledge your manifold favours to me and my poor wife, for which, Sir, I shall never forget to be most thankful. Sir, I have a very great deal of reason to esteem you my very noble friend for your late advice to me by George, to which, Sir, I assure you I am very much inclinable, if you will be pleased to labour to set me out a way, how I may make my peace upon reasonable conditions with the honourable House, and to be assured of my liberty and estate, paying my proportions. I should gladder visit my own county than Oxford, and be subject to that authority under which I shall live, with fidelity and honesty. Sir, I have given George directions how your letters shall come to me, in which be pleased to give me the proceed of this my business;

---

[18] B.L. MS. Tanner 62, ff. 423, 431-2, 471-2, 489.
[19] John Hildeyard, *Sermon preached . . . at the Funeral of the Earl of Yarmouth* (1683), 25.

and the most faithful service of your servant shall never be wanting to express myself upon all occasions

Sir

Your most faithful and humble servant

WILLIAM PASTON.[20]

A month afterwards both Paston and Kemp were back in England, making solicitation to recover their estates.

3

During the spring and early summer of 1643, the organization of the Eastern Association went slowly forward. Lord Grey of Werke proved neither an effective nor an energetic commander. The committees of the five Associated Counties, to which Huntingdonshire was added in May, seldom worked in harmony, and were notably ungenerous in their contributions of money and supplies. Officers and men alike resented, and often resisted, any order to serve outside the boundaries of their own county. Cromwell strove against the prevailing inertia, raising and training his troops, the future Ironsides, and attempting by letter and exhortation to infuse into the reluctant committeemen something of his own passionate energy. The Royalists, though temporarily subdued, were heartened by the successes of their own party across the Wash in Lincolnshire, and were stirred by such episodes as the siege of Crowland—that fantastic combination of heroism and farce, during which Mr. Stiles, the Royalist parson of Crowland, kidnapped Mr. Ram, the Puritan minister of Spalding, and set him up on the Crowland fortifications to stand the fire of the besiegers.[21]

On 17 June the Committee of the Eastern Association, in session at Cambridge, wrote to the authorities at Norwich of the straits they were in, 'being constrained to guard Huntingdon with some companies, the enemy making many sallies upon our frontiers, coming down to Peterborough this last night'. They asked urgently for supplies of money, 'seeing we are debarred of

[20] B.L. MS. Tanner 62, ff. 543-4.
[21] Kingston, 102-9.

raising any monies, the ordinance of Parliament limiting the raising of monies by the particular committees in their several counties, which if you shall not speedily send us, our garrison will disband, our forces will be possessed by the enemies, and ten special piece of ordnance will be turned upon you and us, and repentance will be too late. A word to the wise is enough . . . Gentlemen, seriously consider the necessity of keeping this Committee together and supplying money for such forces as they need'.[22]

The Norfolk signatories of this appeal were Sir John Palgrave and Francis Jermy. Palgrave commanded one of the Norfolk regiments, at this time stationed at Wisbech. The other was commanded by Sir Miles Hobart, and had lately taken part in the siege and capture of Crowland. The discipline of Palgrave's troop in particular left much to be desired. In July a Huntingdonshire gentleman named Torrell Jocelyn, one of Cromwell's most reliable supporters, wrote to the Speaker that 'there are daily alarums given to Wisbech; the well affected there do much fear the fidelity of that Norfolk regiment under the command of Sir John Palgrave, from divers of which regiment they daily receive threats and disgraces, and do think themselves in less danger without them, than with them. But there is very lately four hundred of Sir John Holland's regiment of whom they hope well, unless the town of Wisbech in time may corrupt them'.[23] About the same time Adrian Parmenter of Norwich, who was also in Cambridge on the business of the Committee, reported to the authorities of his city that 'I have also sent you a copy of a letter which was sent to Colonel Palgrave, upon the receipt whereof his soldiers were in great fear, and many (to their great infamy) ran away; and the truth is that Colonel Palgrave hath not the courageous spirit of a brave commander, but is very timidous'.[24] Palgrave may have been an indifferent disciplinarian, but there is no reason to accept Parmenter's aspersions on his courage.

Palgrave's second-in-command was Sir Edward Astley; and Astley's letters to his wife, hitherto unpublished, give the same impression of indiscipline in the Norfolk forces. 'Dear Heart,' he

[22] B.M. Add. MS. 15,903, f. 40.
[23] B.L. MS. Tanner 62, f. 181.
[24] B.M. Add. MS. 22,619, f. 80.

THE SUMMER OF 1643

wrote on the 17th June, 'I am this morning riding post unto my Lord General, who we hear is at Northampton, to inform him of the condition of our regiment, which is very ill at this present, the soldiers doing what they list, having the power in their own hands.' Although a loyal Parliamentarian, he found the whole situation depressing and discouraging. His thoughts were always returning to his wife—whose father and brothers, it will be recalled, were serving with the opposing forces—and with his young family. 'I imagine Jacob doth sometimes ask for his dad, but poor Frank can say nothing. Sweet heart, thou shall hear from me as soon as I can. I prithee cheer up thy self, and I pray God send us a happy meeting.' Three weeks later he wrote again, 'I beseech God in his due time to put an end to these our miseries, and send us again if it be his blessed will a happy meeting.'[25]

The accounts of John Cory, in his capacity as Treasurer of the Norfolk Committee, show the steady accumulation of arms and equipment during these months—horses and horsemeat, oats and hay, saddles and shoeing; muskets, pistols, pikes, bandoliers, swords and belts; powder and bullets and saltpetre and match; coats and breeches, boots and shoes. Large orders were placed with the well-affected tradesmen of Norwich and Yarmouth. George Gaisford was paid £14 for saddles, David Cherry £11 18s. 0d. for swords, Posthumus Parker £3 16s. 10d. for powder and bullet. Edward Wyer supplied 400 shirts for £25. John Witherby charged £4 for making a coat for Captain Wild. Humbler men were less lavishly attired, and 'several tailors' received £35 for making 300 shirts at 2/4 apiece. Besides the large disbursements to the colonels, captains and other officers for the pay and subsistence of their men, there were lesser payments to such minor figures as corporals, cannoneers and cannoneers' mates. There were payments also to surgeons, preachers and chaplains.[26]

Week after week throughout the summer, Cromwell continued his work of raising troops. At Norwich the younger citizens, men and girls together, with the encouragement of the civic authorities

[25] MSS. at Swanton House, Melton Constable.
[26] B.L. MS. Tanner 66, ff. 1–11. These are Cory's disbursement sheets, and run from March 1643 until February 1644. His accounts of receipts for sequestration money, etc., are in B.M. Add. MS. 5508.

subscribed to raise their own particular troop under the command of Captain Robert Swallow. Cromwell wrote from Huntingdon to the Mayor of Norwich on 2 August, warmly encouraging this effort.

Sir,

I understand by these gentlemen the good affections of your young men and maids, for which God is to be praised.

I approve of the business: only I desire to advise you that your foot company may be turned into a troop of horse; which indeed will (by God's blessing) far more advantage the cause than two or three companies of foot; especially if your men be honest godly men, which by all means I desire. I thank God for stirring up the youth to cast in their mite, which I desire may be employed to the best advantage; therefore my advice is, that you will employ your twelve-score pounds to buy pistols and saddles, and I will provide four-score horses; for £400 more will not raise a troop of horse. As for the muskets that are bought, I think the county will take them off you. Pray raise honest godly men, and I will have them of my regiment. As for your officers, I leave it as God shall or hath directed to choose, and rest

Your loving friend
OLIVER CROMWELL.[27]

The Norwich authorities complied with Cromwell's wishes, and also made themselves responsible for the balance of the money required for the arming of the troop. On 18 August they paid £61 10s. 0d. to Captain Swallow, 'who raised a company of soldiers in this city, at the charge of the young men and maids of this city, who were horsed by Colonel Cromwell, for money which they fell short to complete them forth.'[28] Cromwell fulfilled the promise in his letter to take the troop into his regiment. It became in due course the eleventh troop of the Ironsides, and was always known as the Maiden Troop. Understandably its name and origin became the subject of Cavalier ribaldry; and a Royalist journal forecast dubious matrimonial prospects for 'these busy girls' who

[27] Carlyle, *Cromwell*, i, 145-6. The address has disappeared; but it was undoubtedly directed to the city of Norwich, and presumably addressed to the Mayor.
[28] Norwich Corporation MSS, 7k, f. 36.

had subscribed to it, since 'men will suspect those women to falsify their husbands, who are not true to their Prince'.[29] In 1644, or earlier, the troop was duly incorporated into Cromwell's regiment. Its commander, Captain Swallow, and his lieutenant Joseph Sabberton continued to serve in the army until the Restoration.[30]

To this month also belongs a letter written to Samuel Smyth, steward of the city of Norwich, by Cromwell's son and namesake the younger Oliver. He commanded the fourth troop of his father's new forces, and had cause to complain about the desertion of some Norwich men. 'Worthy Sir,' he wrote from Peterborough on 15 August, 'I am sorry that I should have an occasion to write to Norwich concerning those which they say came from that noble city, which hath furnished our armies (I can speak from experience) with godly men, but indeed I suppose them rather spurious offspring of some ignoble place. Sir, thus it is that among many honest men some knaves have been admitted into my troop, which coming with expectation of some base ends, being frustrated of them and finding that this cause did not nourish their expectations, have to the dishonour of God, my discredit, and their own infamy, deserted the cause and me their captain; therefore, Sir, look upon them as dishonourers of God's cause, and high displeasers of my father, my self, and the whole regiment. In brief I would desire you to make them severe examples by taking and returning the arms and horses of all that have not a ticket under my hand, and to clap them up into prison and inflicting of such punishment as you shall think fit, especially I desire you would deal severely with one Robert Waffe and Simon Scafe. Pray, Sir, cause to return speedily all that had liberty from me to go to their friends. And likewise I desire you would secure a good horse from some of your malignants to mount one of my soldiers, John Manning, now at Norwich, who was lately taken prisoner by the enemy, and by that means destitute . . .'[31] Young Oliver Cromwell was a vigorous and efficient soldier, but he was fated to die of smallpox early in the following year.

It was an anxious and disheartening summer for the Eastern

[29] *Mercurius Aulicus*, 487–8 (3 September 1643).

[30] Carlyle, *Cromwell*, i, 152n. Firth, *The Raising of the Ironsides* (Trans. Roy. Hist. Soc. n.s., xiii), 31–2.

[31] Firth, *Raising of the Ironsides*, 28 n. 1. The letter was first printed in Notes and Queries, 4th ser., x, 430.

Association, and for all supporters of the Parliament. The whole current of the war appeared to be running against them, with the death of John Hampden after Chalgrove Field, the defeat of the Fairfaxes at Adwalton Moor, the almost successful treachery of Sir John Hotham and his son at Hull. In the west country there had been a whole series of Royalist successes, culminating in the taking of Bristol at the end of July. The forces of the Eastern Association were conscious of increasing menace from the north, as the Earl of Newcastle's troops advanced southwards into Lincolnshire.

All this anxiety is vividly reflected in the letters from Sir Edward Astley to his wife. Rumours flew back and forth. In June the Queen, having landed in the north with reinforcements some time before, was on her way to join the King at Oxford. 'There is a great division in her army, the French and English cannot well agree together.' There was a plan that all the available Parliamentarian forces should join together to intercept her progress. Early in July the regiment in which Astley was serving had advanced to Peterborough, and was expected to join up with Sir Miles Hobart's regiment at Leicester. 'But I fear we shall have much trouble to get our men to march as far as Ashby de la Zouch, and the King hath sent Prince Rupert with 4000 horse and foot from Oxford to meet her and conduct her thither. The Earl of Essex we hear has likewise sent the like number after him, and since that the King hath sent more forces after the Earl's, and the Earl again hath sent as many after them, and is removed with the whole body of his army between the King's army and the way the Queen is to come with her forces unto him. What will be the issue God only knoweth.'[32] There was no interception of the Queen, and she was reunited with the King on the former battlefield of Edgehill on 13 July, the day when his troops won yet another victory over a Parliamentarian force on Roundway Down.

Towards the end of July the southward advance of Newcastle's troops was threatening Peterborough, and a party had occupied Burleigh House, the Earl of Exeter's great mansion on the outskirts of Stamford. At this point Cromwell counter-attacked, and Burleigh House fell to him on 24 July. This was the first

[32] Sir Edward Astley to his wife, 8 July 1643. (Swanton House MSS.).

action in which Astley and his men had taken part, and five days later he sent a full account of it to his wife.

My dear sweet heart,

Our regiment marched on Sunday last from Peterborough to Burleigh House within a mile of Stamford, where were gotten together about 400 of the cavaliers. We summoned them by trumpet on Sunday morning by break of day to deliver up the place, and we would give them quarter, which if they refused, if the ordnance were once bent upon them they were to expect no mercy but to be put all unto the sword. They answered us again that they would fight it out unto the last man before they would yield up the place. As soon as day appeared we began to play upon them with our ordnance, and gave them I believe above a hundred shot; but I believe it did no great execution by reason of the vastness of the house, for they still shouted upon every shot that was made upon them. About 12 o'clock we approached upon them in three several places, and our men assaulted them with such courage that by 3 o'clock in the afternoon they sounded a parley, and after some consultation our trumpet answered them with the like; but such was the madness of our soldiers for pillage that they broke in upon them and fell a-plundering. We took 300 prisoners whereof forty were officers, the commander in chief Colonel Welby, and a knight whose name I have forgotten. We lost not above four men, but we have some 20 or 30 sore wounded, and we cannot hear of many killed of theirs. We are at this present at Stamford, and we expect to return again shortly to Peterborough, and I hope then to see thee at Bale. I bought this horse of a soldier, which will serve thy coach if he had a little more flesh on his back. I prithee sweet heart send my man unto me as soon as thou canst. Thus with remembrance of my best affections unto thy self and our little ones, my humble duty unto my mother, and my kind love unto the rest of our friends I rest

Dear heart

Thy entirely loving husband till death

EDWARD ASTLEY.

Stamford this 29th of July.

After the storming of Burleigh House, Cromwell's forces

moved northwards to the relief of Gainsborough, in which a Parliamentarian garrison was surrounded by the Royalists. He put the besiegers to flight in a brilliant action, but was presently forced to retreat once more by the advance of Newcastle's main army. Gainsborough was taken, and the Royalist forces occupied virtually the whole county of Lincolnshire. Presumably Astley was involved in these events; but there are no more letters to his wife until the summer of 1645, when the war was drawing to its close.

4

On 10 August an ordinance was passed by Parliament which marked an important development in the organization of the Eastern Association. In view of the advance of 'several armies of horse and foot, consisting for the most part of bloody-minded Papists, Irish rebels, atheists, foreigners, and of the prelatical party, and especially that the Earl of Newcastle with his whole army, since the late surrendering of Gainsborough to him, is marching towards and ready to fall upon the Associated Counties', a joint Committee was to be formed from the most able and active figures in each of those counties. The committee was to be in permanent session at Cambridge, 'or at some other of the frontier towns of the Association'. Representatives of each of the six counties, and of the city of Norwich, were always to be in residence, changing over with colleagues after a fixed period of duty. The ordinance named Thomas Sotherton of Taverham and Martin Sedley of Morley as the first representatives for Norfolk, and Samuel Smyth for the city of Norwich.[33]

Although the county committees remained jealous of their rights, and individual members could still be laggardly or obstructive, the formation of this joint Committee undoubtedly brought about a greater sense of unity and purpose. Within the counties, moreover, a new enthusiasm and a broader basis of co-operation had already been achieved by an ordinance dated 1 June, which added a considerable number of fresh names to the local committees. In Norfolk several of the minor gentry now received a

[33] Husband (1646), 283–5.

new authority, and found themselves working on closer terms with the more important figures who had hitherto been in full control of affairs. By this ordinance Robert Gooch of Earsham and John Reymes of Overstrand, to name only two who happen to appear elsewhere in this book, first received some recognition of their zeal in the cause of Parliament.[34]

The formation of the new Committee coincided with the appointment of the Earl of Manchester as General of the forces of the Eastern Association, in place of the ineffectual Lord Grey of Werke. In January 1642 Manchester, at that time Lord Kimbolton, had incurred the King's particular displeasure, and had eluded the royal attempt at arrest, along with the five members of the House of Commons. His estates lay mainly in Huntingdonshire; and he had a further link with the Eastern Association through his marriage to the daughter of the Earl of Warwick, Parliament's nominee as Lord Lieutenant of Norfolk. He was a thoroughgoing Puritan, and in religion an ardent Presbyterian. Clarendon spoke of him and his father-in-law as the two pillars of the Presbyterian party.[35]

Clarendon's description of Manchester, written long after these events, and when their once intransigent opponent had amply made his peace with the Stuarts, is worded with great indulgence. 'The Earl of Manchester, of the whole cabal, was, in a thousand respects, most unfit for the company he kept. He was of a gentle, and generous nature; civilly bred; had reverence and affection for the King, upon whom he had attended in Spain; loved his country with too unskilful a tenderness; and was of so excellent a temper and disposition, that the barbarous times, and the rough parts he was forced to act in them, did not wipe out, or much deface those marks: insomuch that he was never guilty of any rudeness towards those he was obliged to oppress, but performed always as good offices towards his old friends, and all other persons, as the iniquity of the time, and the nature of the employment he was in, would permit him to do; which kind of humanity could be imputed to very few.'[36]

We have already seen Manchester, after plundering Lady Paston

[34] Ibid., 193-5.
[35] Clarendon, iii, 48.
[36] Ibid., ii, 160.

of the greater part of the family plate, expressing his respect for persons of quality, and 'esteeming it a great happiness to be understood as one that desires to win by civility than by harshness'. It may be doubted whether Lady Paston and her husband saw the matter in the same light, or would have subscribed to the eulogies of Clarendon. Certainly, in the next two years, scores of inoffensive clergy in the eastern counties were to take a very different view of his 'gentle and generous nature', as they were ruthlessly ejected from their livings by his commissioners, and saw their churches desecrated and despoiled by his chosen iconoclasts. Another Royalist writer, Sir Philip Warwick, while also granting Manchester's better qualities, was probably nearer the mark when he observed that 'with all his good nature or the facility of it, he did as much harm . . . as the worst-natured man could have done'.[37]

5

As Newcastle's forces overran the whole of Lincolnshire and pressed steadily southward, the threat to the Eastern Association grew ever more formidable. In letter after letter, Cromwell strove to awaken the committees of each county to their common danger. 'If I could speak words to pierce your hearts with the sense of our and your condition, I would . . . If somewhat be not done in this, you will see Newcastle's army march up into your bowels.'[38]

The successes of Newcastle, and his presence just across the Wash, put new heart into the Royalists of Norfolk. The King had many well-wishers in the western part of the county, and Parliament had several times attempted to quell the restlessness and disaffection in the town of King's Lynn. On 10 July orders had been sent to strengthen its fortifications, lest 'the Popish northern army' should attempt to force a passage into Norfolk. But the Royalists for some time past had been quietly concerting their measures, and now the moment had come. On 13 August the town declared its support for the King, and Sir Hamon L'Estrange was appointed as its Governor.

[37] Warwick, 246.
[38] Carlyle, *Cromwell*, i, 143 (Cromwell to the Committee of Suffolk, 31 July 1643); cf. iii, 315–6 (to the Deputy Lieutenants of Essex, 4 August 1643).

Nothing is known about the preparations made by Sir Hamon and his friends for their *coup de main*, or the way in which it was brought about. The leaders were a group of west Norfolk gentry —the L'Estrange family, Sir Richard Hovell of Hillington, the Mordaunts of Little Massingham—acting in concert with sympathizers among the townsfolk, who had secretly included Thomas Gurlyn the Mayor, Edmund Hudson the Mayor elect, and Francis Parlett the Recorder. Somehow a quantity of arms and ammunition had been assembled during recent months; and no doubt they took over, as soon as they were in power, the stock of Parliamentary arms in the town, and the cannon which had been sent there after Cromwell's visit earlier in the year. They extended the work on the fortifications which had lately been undertaken by order of Parliament. Houses which obstructed the defences were demolished; trees in the surrounding countryside, which might have afforded cover to the enemy, were cut down; and strenuous preparations were made to resist all attacks until Newcastle should march to the relief of the town, as he had undertaken to do. No active resistance seems to have been attempted by the Parliament's supporters within the town. Certain leading figures were confined under guard in their own houses, including the two Puritan members for the borough, John Percival and Thomas Toll. Their confinement does not seem to have been very rigorous, since Toll contrived to get out of a window and escape from the town by boat.

At first Manchester decided to blockade the town, rather than attempt to take it by force. He and Cromwell continued to send urgent messages to the committees of the Associated Counties for more troops, more arms, more supplies. While waiting for their arrival, he sent advance parties to secure the roads leading to Lynn, and set guards at the river bridges. Later in August he established his own headquarters at Setch Bridge, where the main road from the south crossed the little River Nar. Ships of the Parliament's fleet, under the command of his father-in-law the Earl of Warwick, were cruising in the Wash, and intercepted the sea-borne supplies on which the defenders of Lynn were relying. Only one vessel, laden with men and provisions, managed to slip through during the whole course of the siege. She 'vailed bonnet to the Parliament's ships', giving deceptive signals; while the

Lynn gunners, well aware of her identity, fired blank rounds at her till she came safely to the quayside.[39]

The first detachment of the besieging forces was a troop of horse from Essex. It was commanded by a captain named William Poe, who was sent by Manchester to block the approaches to the town until a larger force could arrive. On 19 August, 'it being six days since the Mayor of Lynn and that wicked crew declared themselves enemies to God and the Parliament', Poe addressed a long letter to the Deputy Lieutenants and Committee of his own county. He had much to say about the strength and consequence of Lynn, 'the people that are in it being the chief malignants and recusants in all these parts'. Sir Hamon L'Estrange, their Governor, had promised them a thousand pounds out of his own estate, and twenty other gentlemen by his procurement would raise as much more, with four or five troops of horse. They had in the town forty pieces of ordnance fully loaded, 'and may whom they please be furnished with many more out of their shipping.' In a postscript he added that they had 1200 muskets, 500 barrels of gunpowder with bullet answerable, and three or four troops of horse. 'It is their ungodly strength that they trust in, and not the strength of the Lord, wherefore (I hope) they will not long stand, for upon my knowledge they are cowardly cavaliers.'

He then described the skirmishing that had taken place between the defenders and his own troop. 'Having no relief either of horse or foot as yet, and the enemy ever since I came keeping me in alarm, or I them, my men and horses are quite spent; and (for two days and nights there being none on the east side of the town to keep them in awe) on the Lord's day in the afternoon they sallied out with two troops of horse, and two bodies of foot, having laid six score of musketeers in ambush to have cut me off, but the Lord so enabled me in his cause, that without the loss of one soldier's life, I made them retreat into the town, by giving fire upon them resolutely, whereupon they returned into the town with as much speed as their horses could carry them. Whereby you may perceive their cowardice: for before they marched out of town they swore by no small oaths that they would cut me and my troop as small as herbs to the pot, which I doubt not that they will do if they can take me.

[39] *Certain Informations*, 15 September 1643.

'I do therefore beseech you that you will speedily and cheerfully consider what is to be done in this great work, for the suppressing these wicked ones, against whom the Lord seemeth to fight, as by a particular accident may appear in the forementioned assault intended against me, for they having drawn a piece of ordnance to the end of the causeway to a little green where I was, in turning it about they overthrew it, and filled it so full of dirt that they could not discharge it; otherways you had had one servant and troop less . . . This last night they likewise sallied out with a great body of horse, intending to have taken me and my troop, as also three or four hundred beefs from Setch market, but by God's providence I prevented all, and made them again retreat, keeping them in alarm all night, which hath caused them to discharge above a hundred pieces of ordnance at the least, the bullets whistling about our ears but without further hurt, only my Lieutenant and three of my soldiers are taken prisoners by them, and I have taken some of them.'[40]

Throughout his letter Captain Poe—'your faithful servant and watchman till death'—sought respectfully but firmly to impress upon his superiors in Essex the urgency of sending reinforcements with the utmost speed. He hoped that the authorities of the Association, instead of attempting to starve out the defenders of Lynn, would 'speedily get good store of ordnance and plant them on every side of the town, playing upon them night and day, till they either yield it up or we beat it down'. The committees in the various counties no doubt did their best; but harvest was in full swing, recruitment and impressment were in consequence more difficult than ever, the unwillingness of men to march out of their own counties was matched by the reluctance of their masters to let them go. There were endless problems of organization and equipment. On 31 August the Committee of the Eastern Association at Cambridge wrote to the Deputy Lieutenants of Essex that 'some companies of foot are sent hither from you, but in so naked a posture, that to employ them were to murder them'.[41] A week later Manchester wrote in exasperation from his headquarters at Setch to Sir Thomas Barrington, a prominent member of the Essex committee: 'I have here divers men sent out of the county

[40] B.M. MS. Egerton 2647, f. 138.
[41] Ibid., f. 197.

of Essex, and as many of them I believe are run away as are come; and besides, those whom you have sent have no arms, no clothes, no colours, no drums, so as I confess to you I am more troubled to see these distractions than I can express to you.'[42]

Nevertheless he was able to tell Barrington in the same letter that 'I am gotten within musket shot of the town of Lynn'. This was on 7 September, and evidently referred to the southern and eastern defences of the town, for several days earlier his troops had occupied the village of West Lynn, just across the Ouse and within easy range of its crowded houses. A battery was planted on the river bank, 'which kept the town in continual alarms, and did so terrify the people with their shot and granados, that they durst hardly abide in any of their houses that were towards that side, the shot flying daily into the houses in the Tuesday market-place, and other places'. We are told by one eyewitness that the granadoes did not in fact do as much damage as might have been expected. 'To speak truth, there was some defect in them, so that they did little, only falling among a timorous people.' The morale of a civilian population, whether timorous or not, was unlikely to stand up to a bombardment of this kind indefinitely. Many of the ordinary men and women in the town, moreover, were indifferent to the contest or actively in favour of the Parliament. Yet they had to stand the same incessant fire as their Royalist neighbours. On Sunday, 3 September, according to another contemporary account 'in the afternoon, and in the middle of the sermon, came a shot of eighteen pound weight in at the window over the west door of St. Margaret's Church, and took the middle pillar a great part off, and broke it in many hundred pieces, dispersing them in all directions, all over the church. One piece of the stone fell into a seat at the lower end of the church, where five men sat, and split the board before them, on which they laid their books; but no harm was done to them. The preacher, a reverend divine named Mr. Hinson, left his sermon and came out of the church, and all the people departed in a most confused manner; some leaving their hats, some their books, and some their scarves; but, praised be God, no further hurt was done to any person'.[43]

[42] Ibid., f. 229.
[43] Richards, *History of Lynn*, 758-9. Quoted by Richards from 'a certain manuscript account of the town' of which he gives no further details.

The garrison put up a gallant defence, and made numerous other sallies besides those described by Captain Poe. On one of these occasions they burnt some houses, including an almshouse known as the Hospital, in the nearby village of Gaywood, lest the besiegers should take up quarters there; and it was alleged afterwards that they had intended to set fire to the whole place. They sent back defiant replies to every summons to surrender. On one occasion the answer was signed with twenty-five names, including those of the Mayor and Recorder. 'We send our names,' they wrote, 'lest you should forget to plunder us when you have taken our town.'[44] But the days passed, and there was no sign of Newcastle's promised march to their relief. He had in fact decided against a further advance southward, so long as the Parliamentarian stronghold of Hull, where the Hothams had been replaced by the formidable personality of Fairfax, remained uncaptured and a menace to his rear. Cromwell, who appears to have superintended the placing of the ordnance at West Lynn,[45] now moved northwards to attack him, taking as a part of his force the horse and dragoons upon whom Manchester had been relying for help in the siege.

Manchester mentioned this loss in his next letter to the Essex committee, in which he acknowledged the arrival of 330 men from that county, but with arms sufficient for only 200. 'I hope you will be mindful of yourselves and your own safety,' he wrote, 'as to hasten hither all the force you can, with money and arms, for otherwise they are by far more dreadful to me than any enemy whatsoever.'[46] Further reinforcements continued to reach him as September wore on, however poorly equipped; and at last he resolved to take the town by storm. Boats were prepared for an assault from the river, though under considerable difficulties: so accurate was the fire of the defenders that they were able to send their cannon-shot three times through the same port-hole. Cartloads of ladders were got ready for the attack from the land, which was to be delivered at the south and east gates; and a new battery was established south of the town to cover the attacking forces,

[44] *Certain Informations*, 15 September 1643.
[45] Cromwell is mentioned as having done this both in *Certain Informations* and in *Mercurius Civicus*.
[46] B.M. MS. Egerton 2647, f. 241.

in addition to the cannon which were continually firing from West Lynn.

All these preparations were strenuously resisted by the defenders, and there was some loss of life, although the number of casualties is unknown. The only full contemporary narrative of the siege is an anonymous pamphlet, which I suspect to have been the work of one of Manchester's chaplains, possibly the Rev. Simeon Ashe who preached the thanksgiving sermon in St. Margaret's when all was over.[47] This account states that 'in this violent playing with cannon and small shot we believe above eighty lost their lives on both sides'. On the other hand it has been pointed out that according to the parish registers only two soldiers were buried at St. Margaret's during the weeks of the siege, and one at St. Nicholas'. The matter must be left in uncertainty.[48]

The Hall Books at Lynn, the records of the proceedings of the civic body, have nothing whatsoever to say about the progress of the siege. On 29 August, the feast of the Decollation of St. John the Baptist, the Town Council met and elected Edmund Hudson to be their Mayor as from the feast of St. Michael next ensuing. Francis Parlett was re-elected as their Recorder, and William Leake as their Town Clerk. The two members of Parliament, Percival and Toll, rather surprisingly appear to have been present in their places as aldermen at this meeting—at any rate they were not marked as absentees, as they were at the next meeting on 8 September, so presumably at this date they had not yet been placed under house arrest. On the second occasion a little routine business was done about loans. There is not a word to suggest that Manchester was steadily pressing the siege, or that granadoes were falling hourly on the town. Nor is there any mention of the fact that the besiegers had succeeded in diverting the water-supply. 'The pipes that carried them fresh water are cut off,' a Parliamentarian news-sheet recorded, 'and the fresh river by Kettle Mills is turned another way.'[49]

Finally Manchester sent word that the town would be stormed

<hr>

[47] *A brief and true Relation of the Siege and Surrendering of King's Lynn to the Earl of Manchester* (1643). I have made use of this narrative throughout the foregoing pages, except where otherwise indicated.

[48] Hillen, i, 366.

[49] *Certain Informations*, 15 September 1643.

on Saturday, 16 September, unless the garrison surrendered by nine o'clock that morning. He warned them further to send the women and children out of the town before the general assault began. But on the Friday morning a message was received that the defenders were willing to capitulate, 'not as fearing the taking of the town, but to avoid the effusion of blood'. So peace returned to Lynn. The guns no longer boomed out across the sluggish river; and their silence told the fenland villages to the west and the farming uplands to the east that the siege was over.

Eight commissioners were appointed by either side to meet at Gaywood the same evening to arrange the terms of surrender. Manchester's nominees included Sir John Palgrave and Cromwell's brother-in-law Colonel Valentine Walton, as well as Parliamentarians from the Lynn neighbourhood such as John Spelman of Narborough and Gregory Gawsell of Watlington. Among the representatives of the defenders were Sir Hamon L'Estrange, Sir Richard Hovell, Edmund Hudson the Mayor-elect, Francis Parlett the Recorder and William Leake the Town Clerk. After many hours of parleying, broken only by a pause for dinner, certain conditions were agreed. The town, with all its ordnance and arms, was to be delivered up to Manchester. The 'gentlemen strangers' should have liberty to depart from the town, each with his horse, sword and pistols. The townsmen were to enjoy all their former rights and privileges, with full liberty of trading. Prisoners on both sides were to be returned. The commissioners would signify to Parliament, and to the Earl of Warwick, the wishes of the town as to certain of their ships which Warwick had captured in the Wash, 'and to that they can give no other answer'. In order to prevent plunder, a levy was to be raised within the town for a payment to all officers and soldiers of the besieging forces. Perhaps the most important article to the garrison was the sixth: 'That neither the person nor estates of any inhabitants, gentry, or strangers, now residing in Lynn, shall be hereafter molested for any thing past, or done by them, since the Earl of Manchester's coming into these parts.'[50]

Although it was agreed that Sir Hamon L'Estrange and others should remain as hostages until these conditions had been performed, the surrender was not accomplished without some further

[50] *Relation*, 4. Rushworth, III, ii, 283–4.

trouble. The townspeople of Lynn had longed to see an end of the siege; but the soldiers of the garrison felt very differently. A few shots were still fired from the defences, and ditches were cut with a view to flooding the siege-works at the flow of the spring tides. The Mayor and Aldermen also caused some delay by raising procedural difficulties. Manchester began to grow impatient, and his officers 'drew all our horse and foot into meadows, which we put into such a posture as might be most terrible to the enemy, making a large front, when God knows what depths they stood, then beating the drums and sounding the trumpets, as if we had been presently to march into the town'. At dusk this imposing array, under the command of Colonel Francis Russell, marched to the east gate, only to be told that 'the season of the night would not permit to open the great gate, and they must therefore be content to march one by one at the wicket'. Fearing that by morning the resolution of the defenders might have stiffened once more, the Colonel decided to take the risk of entering by the wicket-gate. In the meantime dissension had arisen among the troops of the garrison, some urging that the articles of surrender should be accepted, others insisting that 'they would not condescend nor obey, nor should the Mayor's and commissioners' acts bind them, crying *Shoot, shoot*'. All this led to a two hours' wrangle at the gate, in the darkness of the summer night. At one point a voice within the town shouted 'Give fire!', bringing dismay to some of Manchester's rustic levies. 'This being in the dead of the night, made some of the forward countrymen and others on horseback, who rid by the side of the foot that marched, to fall off their horses, and some into the ditch, so terrible was the word, *Give fire.*'[51]

At last this farcical scene came to an end. The unruly soldiers were pacified, and at dawn Colonel Russell and his troops entered the town. The south gate was secured; watches were set at other important points; and a force of horse and foot was quartered in the Tuesday market-place. 'In our passage through the town, not one man appeared, only the women, who for the general cried *God bless us*, whether for fear or love, you may guess.' At nine o'clock Manchester marched into the town with his own bodyguard, and took up his quarters in the house of Alderman Toll.

[51] *Relation*, 7.

Sermons were preached in St. Margaret's Church by his chaplains both morning and evening on that day; and he arranged that henceforward, 'for the better and more orderly government of the soldiers, and content of the people', they should be able to listen to a sermon every morning at eight o'clock.[52]

So ended the only episode of the war in which gunfire was heard and blood was shed on Norfolk soil. If Newcastle had risked a determined southward thrust, had relieved Lynn and used the town as a base for further operations, the whole course of the war might have taken a different turn. His decision to attempt the reduction of Hull and leave Lynn to its fate may in all the circumstances have been prudent; but to many it seemed that a great opportunity was thrown away. To the Royalist elements within the Eastern Association the surrender of Lynn was the final disaster. It put an end to all their hopes, and they could make no further organized endeavour to assist the cause of the King.

6

For a short time Manchester acted as Governor of Lynn. He then set out for Lincolnshire with the greater part of his troops, and joined with Cromwell and Fairfax in the operation which culminated in October with the victory at Winceby and the relief of Hull. Lincolnshire reverted to Parliamentarian control, and became the seventh county to join the Eastern Association. On Manchester's departure from Lynn, Colonel Valentine Walton succeeded him as Governor of the town. He was a brave soldier and a strict Puritan, very much in sympathy with his brother-in-law Cromwell, and in years to come a trusted member of the Protector's immediate circle.

The first consequence of the siege was the raising of the levy required from the town under the seventh of the articles of surrender, ten shillings a man for each of Manchester's foot soldiers, and a fortnight's pay for each of his officers under the rank of captain. Manchester reckoned the amount at £2300; and at the first Council meeting after the siege was raised, on 28 September, it was ordered 'that the same assessment be entered into debate instantly and performed accordingly by such equal ways as shall be thought most fitting'. Edward Hudson retained his office as the newly-elected Mayor; but in December letters were received from Francis Parlett the Recorder and William Leake the Town Clerk, 'upon their own request' asking for discharge from their offices. Both men had been prominent on the Royalist side during the siege, and their resignations were probably forced upon them. The Recorder was soon succeeded in office by the ubiquitous Miles Corbett.[53]

Colonel Walton now set to work to repair the effects of the siege, and to ensure that compensation was paid to those who had suffered damage. In this aim he was vigorously supported by the two members of Parliament, Percival and Toll, and of course by Miles Corbett. The sixth article of the terms of surrender had provided that the defenders should not be molested for anything that had occurred 'since the Earl of Manchester's coming into these parts'. The phrase was distinctly ambiguous, since the town had been seized and prepared for action some while before Manchester arrived on the scene. Moreover, the printed account of the siege expressly mentioned that during the negotiations Manchester's representatives had warned the defenders that 'as for freedom from ordinances of Parliament, they must expect no such thing'.[54] Whatever may have been intended by the commissioners, besiegers and besieged, as they sat round their conference-table at Gaywood on that September evening, both Houses of Parliament passed the following decisive order on 9 December. 'Forasmuch as the Earl of Manchester, in his articles of agreement with the town of King's Lynn, remitted their offence in reference to himself and his army, while he lay before the town, but touched on no private injuries done by the malignants to the well affected: it is this day ordered by the Lords and Commons, that such persons as did take any of the goods of the well affected by themselves, or such as they appointed, or did any damage to their houses, or mills, or any other ways, shall make restitution to all such well affected persons as have been damnified, according to the greatness of their losses; and that Colonel Walton, Governor of King's Lynn, Mr. Percival and Mr. Toll, Members of the

[53] King's Lynn Hall Book, 28 September, 11 December 1643.
[54] *Relation*, 4.

House of Commons, shall examine what damage hath been done to the well affected, and appoint such as have done them injury, to make them reparation accordingly, and if any of them shall refuse to make such reparation, that the said Governor, Mr. Percival and Mr. Toll shall have power to sequester so much of the estates of such malignants, as will make them reparation, and assign it to those that have been damnified.'[55]

It could be convincingly maintained that all this damage to the well-affected was done on the orders of Sir Hamon L'Estrange, in his capacity as Governor of the town during the period of the siege. On him the responsibility could conveniently be laid, especially as he was by far the wealthiest man among the defenders. His fine house, rich manors, prosperous sheepwalks lay only a few miles from Lynn. He was the obvious victim for exaction. His estate was already under sequestration, and the sequestration was now rigorously enforced. During or shortly after the siege, Hunstanton had been plundered of 1600 sheep, all the corn and most of the horses. Now, for years to come, Sir Hamon was never to be free from claims arising out of 'the unjust and tyrannical oppression of Mr. Toll and others of his faction in Lynn concerning the siege'.

The phrase is taken from one of the account-books kept by his wife. She had been Alice, daughter of Richard Stubbe of the neighbouring parish of Sedgeford, a woman of unconquerable spirit, his lifelong companion and support. During his absences from home during the summer, and throughout the period of the siege, she had remained in charge at Hunstanton. In the weeks of the siege, the life of the household and estate continued as it had done for the whole of her long married life. Sheep were being washed and clipped, servants were paid their wages, two pairs of new shoes were bought for Mary Ramsey. There were purchases of hawking gloves and salad oil, bone lace for a band and cuffs, taffeta and silk and ribband for a dress. The sole reference to the siege was a payment 'for horsemeat at Lynn for 6 horses, 3 weeks & 5 days, £3-6-8'. But now the claims for compensation against Sir Hamon began to pour in, and were recorded by his wife with outspoken and indignant comments.

The wrongs of the two imprisoned members of Parliament,

[55] Husband (1646), 396.

Percival and Toll, were assuaged by the payment of substantial damages, and further damages were also secured by their wives. A very heavy sum, in modern money, had to be paid 'to Mr. Seafowl and James Pope, sequestering traitors', for the burning of the hospital at Gaywood, and likewise for the loss of another almshouse in Lynn, although Walton the Governor had himself carted away and used all the materials. Thomas May, who later succeeded Hudson as Mayor, had to be lavishly compensated for unspecified losses 'sustained as they falsely suggest by the command of Sir Hamon L'Estrange'; and a similar payment was made to another member of the Corporation, Bartholomew Wormell. William Johnson's mill had been set on fire, and he received full compensation; so did John Johnson for his house which had been pulled down; so did Robert Clarke because his haystack had been burnt; so did the inhabitants of Setch for damage to their bridge. As late as 1650 the troubles of the L'Estranges were not yet over. The insatiate Mr. Toll was still making heavy demands, which they were obliged to meet as best they could. In the words of Lady L'Estrange, they were 'over-powered by the times'; and by sequestrations, forced levies and assessments, the plundering of their stock, and the claims arising out of the siege, their estate suffered damage which was never fully repaired.[56]

7

During these summer weeks of 1643, as the threat to the Eastern Association loomed large and then receded, emissaries from Parliament were in Edinburgh negotiating an alliance, long projected and sorely needed, with the Scots. For their military support the Scots exacted their price, the uniting of the two nations by a religious compact, the Solemn League and Covenant. It was finally signed in London at the end of September. The signatories vowed to 'endeavour the preservation of the reformed religion in the Church of Scotland, in doctrine, worship, discipline and government, against our common enemies', and 'the reformation of religion in the kingdom of England and Ireland, in doctrine, worship, discipline, and government, according to the

[56] N.N.R.O., L'Estrange MSS., P. 7 and P.10.

SIR HAMON L'ESTRANGE
from a painting by John Hoskins, in the possession of the Corporation
of King's Lynn

word of God, and the example of the best reformed Churches'. They would further 'endeavour to bring the Churches of God in the three kingdoms to the nearest conjunction and uniformity in religion, confession of faith, form of Church government, directory for worship and catechizing, that we, and our posterity after us, may, as brethren, live in faith and love, and the Lord may delight to dwell in the midst of us'.

Although the wording was somewhat nebulous, the imposition of a Presbyterian form of church government was clearly indicated. There could be no uncertainty about the second clause, which finally swept away the episcopal structure of government in the English Church. 'We shall in like manner, without respect of persons, endeavour the extirpation of Popery, Prelacy (that is, Church government by Archbishops, Bishops, their Chancellors, and Commissioners, Deans, Deans and Chapters, Archdeacons, and all other ecclesiastical officers depending on that hierarchy), superstition, heresy, schism, profaneness, and whatsoever shall be found to be contrary to sound doctrine, and the power of godliness.'[57]

The Solemn League and Covenant was duly subscribed or 'taken', in the prescribed form, by the majority of Members of Parliament and other prominent persons. There were those whose ideas of a reformed religion did not follow Presbyterian lines; but many future Independents nevertheless accepted the Covenant for the sake of the Scottish military aid that accompanied it. Others no doubt felt like John Selden: 'Now oaths are so frequent, they should be taken like pills, swallowed whole; if you chew them you will find them bitter: if you think of what you swear, 'twill hardly go down.'[58]

To many more the Covenant brought an agonizing crisis of conscience. Innumerable clergy in particular found the second clause impossible to reconcile with the vows they had taken at their ordination, and the whole spirit of the Church in which they ministered. On 2 February 1644 it was ordained by Parliament that the Covenant should be taken by all men above the age of eighteen. The local Committees, having taken it themselves, were to tender it to all ministers; and the ministers in their turn were to tender it to their parishioners. Every minister was to 'read the

[57] Husband (1646), 425.
[58] Selden, 87. Wedgwood, The King's War, 274.

whole Covenant distinctly and audibly in the pulpit, and during the time of the reading thereof, the whole congregation to be uncovered, and at the end of his reading thereof, all to take it standing, lifting up their right hands bare, and then afterwards to subscribe to it severally, by writing their names (or their marks, to which their names were to be added) in a parchment roll, or a book, wherein the Covenant is to be inserted, purposely provided for that end, and kept as a record in the parish'.[59]

In parishes where the minister was of Puritan sympathies, the Covenant was duly tendered and signed. For example, at St. Laurence in South Walsham—the church now in ruins of the pair which stand in the same churchyard—the Rev. John Baker recorded in the register how his parishioners did 'enter into a mutual and solemn League and Covenant, and each one for himself, with his hands lifted up unto God most high', accepted the Covenant clause by clause. Mr. Baker signed the articles first, and 62 of his parishoners followed him, 18 of whom signed their names and 44 made their marks.[60]

Sometimes a note of reservation was sounded. At Breccles the vicar signed without demur; but his leading parishioner, John Webb, wrote that 'I subscribe to so much of this Covenant as I already know, or shall hereafter know, to be agreeable to the word of God, the laws of this kingdom, and my oaths formerly taken'.[61] In many parishes, however, the minister absolutely refused to tender the Covenant to his people. It was one of the offences most frequently cited in the campaign against the clergy of Royalist sympathies which now began, and which will be described in a later chapter.

Another move in that campaign was the ordinance 'for the utter demolishing, removing, and taking away of all monuments of superstition or idolatry'.[62] This was passed by Parliament on 28 August; but the details of its enforcement in the eastern counties by Manchester, and the actual work of destruction as reflected in the journal of William Dowsing, belong to the following year and will also be considered in a later chapter. Already a

---

[59] Husband (1646), 420–1.
[60] N.A., i, 286.
[61] N.A., viii, 313.
[62] Husband (1646), 307.

good deal of random iconoclasm had occurred; and in places where Puritan feeling was especially strong, or a certain type of enthusiast was in control, the ordinance was promptly obeyed, sometimes with an excess of zeal. For example, it contained a specific provision that no harm was to be done to any monument or representation of a dead person, of whatever degree, 'which hath not been commonly reputed or taken for a saint'. Such precautions were frequently not observed; and moderate Parliamentarians began to view the activities of their more fervent brethren with considerable disquiet.

The mood of these moderates was reflected in a letter which Thomas Windham addressed from Felbrigg to Sir John Potts on 10 December. It seems that Windham had been accused of undervaluing his estate in connection with the levy imposed earlier in the year for the prosecution of the war. In fact his father, who still lived on at a great age at the family home in Somerset, retained some financial interest in the Norfolk estates on which he had established Thomas, his second son. Potts had evidently come to Windham's support.

Honoured Sir

I thank you for those kind favours which I lately received from you in the way of justice, to rescue me from the injury of that monster Report, which in this wicked age often takes the upper hand of Truth. Our joint affections, leaning on the same pillar of constancy to religion and the commonwealth, I doubt not shall always preserve our neighbourhood unto the mutual comfort of our families. My personal estate I have given up at two thousand pounds, which is one more than I know I am worth, my estate in lands to the uttermost, during my father's life. The oppression practised by Jubs and his associates is very odious, their fury in churches detestable. Mr. Coke and Mr. Sotherton are in the morning for Cambridge to represent those grievances which nothing but our own firm union (who have served the state in times of most danger) can withstand. In this, as I shall continue ever to serve my country, so God willing entirely remain

Your servant to be disposed

THOMAS WINDHAM.[63]

[63] B.L. MS. Tanner 62, ff. 426–7.

Moderate men, in fact, were beginning to have second thoughts. The war was bringing a heavy and increasing burden of taxation, special assessments for various military objectives, the requisition of horses, the impressment of men, a general dislocation of affairs. In default of a speedy victory, they cannot have expected it to be otherwise. But now, as in every revolution, events were moving too quickly, the enthusiasts and the extremists were beginning to gain the upper hand. The identity of 'Jubs' is uncertain; but there was at this time a Captain John Jubbs in Sir Miles Hobart's regiment, who probably became the Lieutenant-Colonel John Jubbes who expressed violently anti-monarchical sentiments at the critical Army Council of 1 November 1647. He was just the kind of man to display detestable fury in churches. Equally we do not know the nature of the grievances which John Coke and Thomas Sotherton were going to represent to their colleagues on the Committee of the Eastern Association at Cambridge. But the whole letter is eloquent of the misgivings already felt at this stage by the more moderate Parliamentarians.

That arch-moderate, Sir John Holland, was especially uneasy over the sequestrations and other penalties imposed upon the local Royalists, so many of whom were his kinsmen and friends. During the summer he had been 'in a course of physic' at Epsom, and had then withdrawn to recuperate at the house of the Earl of Northumberland at Petworth in Sussex. He and Northumberland had been colleagues in the commission sent by both Houses of Parliament to treat with the King at Oxford earlier in the year. Soon after the siege of Lynn he was summoned by Parliament from this retreat, and ordered to go down to Norfolk to enforce the ordinance of sequestration against several of his neighbours, and in particular his cousin Thomas Knyvett and his old friend Sir William Paston. He begged to be excused from this distasteful duty, in a speech of which his own copy survives. With all respect to the Speaker and to the House, 'Truly, Sir,' he said, 'I could never prevail with myself to be active in what is against my own heart and judgment, and this is some part of my condition touching what this order enjoins; besides that I observe that I am likewise expressly commanded to put in execution the ordinances of sequestration against all those gentlemen that were at Lowestoft, at Lynn, at Mr. Holl's house, together with those that are at present in

Holland and other parts beyond the sea, amongst whom there are, Sir, those to whom I have the nearest relations of blood and friendship beyond any other person of your committee in the county—such and so great engagements as I profess it's a very hard choice to want myself, or be instrumental to make them do so: wherefore, Sir, I beseech you spare me this employment, put me not upon so great a strait.'

His request was put to the vote, and it was decided by a majority that he must go down to Norfolk and carry out the instructions of Parliament. But in the end he had his way. A few months earlier he had settled the embarrassing problem of his Papist wife by sending her and their children across the sea to the Low Countries. Lady Holland was expecting another child, and he obtained leave to spend six weeks with her. This was, in his own words, 'afterwards protracted by several motions at several times to two years'.[64] He was able to avoid the later stages of a contest for which he had increasingly little heart, and did not return to England until the closing months of the war.

So the year 1643 drew to its end, with the nation weary and perplexed, the opposing forces still evenly balanced, and little prospect in sight of a decisive victory or an early peace.

[64] B.L. MS. Tanner 321, f. 8.

CHAPTER XI

The Bishop and the Cathedral

I

It will be remembered that the newly appointed Bishop of Norwich, Joseph Hall, arrived at his cathedral city soon after the Whitsuntide of 1642, having undergone some turbulent passages in Parliament and a period of confinement in the Tower. At Norwich he was agreeably surprised by the measure of respect with which he was received; and he preached, the day after his arrival, to a large and attentive congregation.[1] He continued to preach, and to carry out his episcopal functions, throughout the months that followed, 'till the times, growing every day more impatient of a Bishop, threatened my silencing'.[2]

The period of anxious uncertainty which followed the outbreak of war was rendered still darker by the loss of his youngest son Edward, who died on Christmas Eve. The sorrowing parents commemorated him by a small brass tablet, placed inconspicuously in the concavity of a pillar in the Cathedral choir. The tablet records that he was a candidate for holy orders and learned beyond his years, which only numbered twenty-two. Only a few months later the brasses in the Cathedral, a numerous and magnificent array, were to be ruthlessly torn up and sold by the cartload for scrap metal. So thoroughly was the work carried out that the inscription to Edward Hall, and one other small inscription in the Jesus Chapel, were the sole survivors in the whole great building. This may have been accidental; or it may be that some gleam of consideration was shown for the aged Bishop, even though the same forces were then engaged in driving him from his Palace.

The Bishop was able to pursue his course in comparative peace, 'though with some secret murmurs of disaffected persons', until

[1] See p. 133.
[2] Hall, *Works*, i, li.

the spring of 1643, when Parliament issued its ordinance of sequestration on 1 April. The purport of this ordinance has already been described. Briefly, it established committees in every county, with powers to seize and sequester the entire property—money, lands, revenues, rents, goods and chattels—of all persons who were, or could be suspected of being, in opposition to the Parliament. The Bishops, with Joseph Hall among them, were expressly listed by name in the forefront of the document, as prime delinquents.[3]

The Bishop's chronology of his misfortunes in his tract *Hard Measure* is not wholly clear, and it may have been before the passing of this ordinance that 'the first noise of my trouble' occurred. 'One morning, before my servants were up, there came to my gates one Wright, a London trooper, attended with others, requiring entrance, threatening if they were not admitted to break open the gates; whom I found at my first sight struggling with one of my servants with a pistol, which he had in his hand. I demanded his business at that unseasonable time; he told me he came for arms and ammunition, of which I must be disarmed. I told him I had only two muskets in the house, and no other military provision. He not resting upon my word searched round about the house, looked into the chests and trunks, examined the vessels in the cellar. Finding no other warlike furniture, he asked me what horses I had, for his commission was to take them also; I told him how poorly I was stored, and that my age would not allow me to travel on foot. In conclusion he took one horse for the present, and such accompt of another, that he did highly expostulate with me afterwards, that I had otherwise disposed of him.'[4]

Soon afterwards the Bishop experienced a more formal visitation, when a party of local Puritans, who had been named in the ordinance as sequestrators for Norfolk and Norwich, presented themselves at the Palace. This delegation consisted of the two Sheriffs of Norwich, John Greenwood and John Rayley; Alderman John Tolye, who had been Mayor in 1638; and Thomas Sotherton, a member of a family which had provided Norwich with many civic dignitaries in the past, but which had recently

[3] Husband (1646), 12-16.
[4] Hall, *Works*, i, lii.

established itself in the countryside at Taverham. They told the Bishop that by virtue of the recent ordinance they must seize upon the Palace and all his estate, both real and personal; and shortly afterwards they sent underlings—one of whom, as he noted sardonically, had been burnt in the hand for felony—to value his goods. This work they carried out 'with all diligent severity, not leaving so much as a dozen of trenchers, or my children's pictures, out of their curious inventory'. They even wished to include the wearing apparel of the Bishop and his family; but he appealed to Tolye and Rayley, who interpreted the ordinance on this point in his favour. All his other goods, his library of books and his household stuff of every kind, were appointed to be exposed to public sale. 'Much inquiry there was when the goods should be brought to market; but in the mean time Mrs. Goodwin, a religious good gentlewoman, whom yet we had never known or seen, being moved with compassion, very kindly offered to lay down to the sequestrators that whole sum which the goods were valued at; and was pleased to leave them in our hands for our use, till we might be able to repurchase them.' As for the books, 'several stationers looked on them, but were not forward to buy them; at last Mr. Cook, a worthy divine of this diocese, gave bond to the sequestrators, to pay to them the whole sum whereat they were set, which was afterwards satisfied out of that poor pittance, that was allowed me for my maintenance.'[5]

In the meantime the revenues of the see had been impounded by the sequestrators—not only the current income, but certain arrears which the Bishop had 'in favour forborne' to some tenants, but which had then been 'treacherously confessed' by the ungrateful debtors. The income from his modest private estate was likewise seized. Nothing whatever was allowed for his maintenance and the support of his family, and he found himself absolutely without funds. He therefore addressed himself to the Committee in session at Norwich, and was able to obtain an allowance of the sum which had been proposed the year before by Parliament as his particular allotment, four hundred pounds a year.[6] This concession was largely due to the sympathetic attitude of Sir John Potts and Sir Thomas Wodehouse, who happened to

[5] Ibid., li.
[6] See p. 132.

be present at this meeting of the Committee. They invoked the authority of Manchester, 'who was then conceived to have great power in the matter of these sequestrations', although he did not yet hold the dominant position to which he was appointed later in the year. Manchester thought the proposed arrangement 'very just and reasonable', and instructed the Committee to set aside certain of the episcopal manors in order to produce the annual four hundred pounds, and to confiscate the remainder. This was 'answerably done under the hands of the whole table'.[7]

2

The Bishop now thought himself secure of a reasonable mainten-ance, small though it was in comparison with 'that plentiful estate which I might have had'. But such a concession to a bishop, though reasonable enough in the eyes of moderates such as Potts and Wodehouse, was unacceptable to the more extreme elements in their party. One such extremist was Miles Corbett, who had now made himself powerful on the central Committee for Seques-trations which sat in London. Corbett seems always to have been particularly harsh towards Royalists connected with his own county, as we shall see later in the case of Thomas Knyvett. He was able to persuade the London Committee to reverse the decision which the Norfolk Committee had made. Word was sent down to Norwich that the Bishop was not to be accorded any favourable treatment, but that Mrs. Hall could apply for the fifth part, which might be granted for the support of a sequestered cleric's wife and family.

Mrs. Hall duly made her application, and after a long delay it was granted. But the weeks passed and no allowance was received, nor was any account rendered. Eventually the officials employed by the Norfolk Committee produced an account, 'but so confused and perplexed and so utterly unperfect, that we could never come to know what a fifth part meant'. It would appear that the Bishop and his wife were obliged in the end to accept substantially less than their fifth part; and every sort of difficulty was raised over the pittances which they eventually received. 'Whilst I received

[7] Hall, *Works*, i, lii.

nothing, yet something was required of me. They were not ashamed, after they had taken away and sold all my goods and personal estate, to come to me for assessments and monthly payments for that estate which they had taken, and took distresses from me upon my most just denial, and vehemently required me to find the wonted arms of my predecessors, when they had left me nothing.'[8]

Subjected to all sorts of 'insolences and affronts', and living in conditions of impoverishment and discomfort, the Bishop remained in his Palace for several more months. On one occasion a riotous mob came late at night and tried to force the locked gates, while others climbed over the walls and attempted to break into the house, on the pretext of searching for Royalist delinquents whom they suspected the Bishop of harbouring. He continued to ordain ministers and to institute to livings, until the universal taking of the Covenant was ordered by Parliament on 2 February 1644. This afforded his enemies an opportunity for further persecution, and they seized their chance after he had conducted an ordination service in the chapel attached to the Palace. 'Certain forward volunteers in the city, banding together, stir up the Mayor and Aldermen and Sheriffs to call me to an account for an open violation of their Covenant. To this purpose divers of them came to my gates at a very unseasonable time, and knocking very vehemently, required to speak with the Bishop. Messages were sent to them to know their business; nothing would satisfy them but the Bishop's presence; at last I came down to them, and demanded what the matter was. They would have the gate opened, and then they would tell me. I answered that I would know them better first; if they had anything to say to me I was ready to hear them. They told me they had a writing to me from Mr. Mayor, and some other of their magistrates. The paper contained both a challenge to me for breaking the Covenant, in ordaining ministers, and withal required me to give in the names of those which were ordained by me both then and formerly since the Covenant. My answer was that Mr. Mayor was much abused by those who had misinformed him, and drawn that paper from him; that I would next day give a full answer to the writing. They moved that my answer might be by my personal appearance at the

8 Ibid., lii–liv.

Guildhall. I asked them when they ever heard of a Bishop of Norwich appearing before a Mayor; I knew mine own place, and would take that way of answer which I thought fit: and so dismissed them, who had given out that day, that had they known before of mine ordaining, they would have pulled me and those whom I ordained out of the chapel by the ears.'[9]

Another excuse for trouble-making was provided by the ordinance for destroying superstitious and idolatrous ornaments in churches, which had been passed by Parliament in September 1643. Soon afterwards the Bishop received a visit from Thomas Toft, one of the new Sheriffs, and a former Sheriff named Matthew Lindsey, 'attended with many zealous followers'. They came to inspect the chapel of the Palace and 'to look for superstitious pictures, and reliques of idolatry, and sent for me, to let me know they found those windows full of images, which were very offensive, and must be demolished'. They were assured that the figures represented 'some ancient and worthy Bishops' such as Ambrose and Augustine; but the visitors insisted that they were all Popes, and an opinionated young man named Townsend maintained that all diocesan bishops were Popes. In the end the Bishop 'obtained leave that I might with the least loss and defacing of the windows give order for taking off that offence, which I did by causing the heads of those pictures to be taken off, since I knew the bodies could not offend'.[10] His attempt to save the windows was of no avail, since they and the building which contained them were completely wrecked in the years to come, and his successor at the Restoration was obliged to demolish the ruins and erect an entirely new chapel.

3

During the same months the Bishop was obliged to witness the spoliation and desecration of the Cathedral just beside his Palace, to listen to the smashing of glass and the shouting of the mob, all of which will presently be described in his own memorable words. 'Still yet,' he wrote in the concluding page of *Hard Measure*,

[9] Ibid., liv–v.
[10] Ibid., lv.

'I remained in my Palace, though with but a poor revenue and means; but the house was held too good for me.' As might have been expected, Miles Corbett was foremost in the campaign to evict him. It was determined, at his instigation, that the Palace would be convenient for the daily meetings of the Norfolk Committee, 'being a place both more public, roomy and chargeless' than the house at present devoted to that purpose. The Bishop at first attempted to resist, and then pressed for time to find some other abode, but 'Mr. Corbett was impatient of my stay there, and procures and sends peremptory messages for my present dislodgement'. Eventually 'out we must, and that in three weeks' warning by Midsummer Day then approaching'. Once again they were helped by a local sympathizer; a neighbour in the Close, a widower named Mr. Gostlin, offered to vacate his house for them.[11] One wonders if this was William Gostlin, the Mayor who had been displaced for his Royalist leanings the year before, and who by now had been released from his confinement at Cambridge.

Even during this summer of 1644, when his Cathedral stood disused and desecrated, and the Puritan faction was engaged in turning him out of his dwelling, the Bishop continued to preach when opportunity offered. Even the most fanatical of his opponents may have hesitated to provoke popular feeling too far by silencing him altogether. On Whit Sunday he delivered a sermon in the Green Yard, the open space between the Cathedral and the Palace; and he preached again, in continuation of the same discourse, in St. Gregory's Church in the following month. His text on both occasions was *Grieve not the holy Spirit of God, by which ye are sealed to the day of redemption*. He spoke of 'these heavy judgments, under which we have lain thus long, groaning and gasping, to the pity and astonishment of our late envying neighbourhood: even the destroying and devouring sword'. And he exhorted his hearers to penitence and prayer, to fortitude in this time of tribulation, to patient submission under the divine chastisement which the sins of the people had brought upon their once happy land.[12]

It is not certain how long the Bishop and his family occupied Mr. Gostlin's house in the Close. Within a year or two they had

[11] Ibid., lvi.
[12] Ibid., v, 489-503, 504-15.

moved to the village of Heigham, just outside the city, and settled in the quiet riverside house which later became the Dolphin Inn. It was not an episcopal property, despite the name of 'Bishop Hall's Palace' which was subsequently attached to it. It had been built in the previous century by a family named Browne, and they probably still owned it.[13] The Bishop used to speak of it deprecatingly in his letters to Archbishop Usher as his *tugurium* or *tuguriolum*, his little cottage;[14] and it was certainly less commodious than his palaces in Exeter and Norwich. It survives today, much reconstructed after severe damage from German bombs; and the visitor may feel that the Bishop, after the persecution he had undergone in Norwich, was fortunate in finding himself so pleasant a retreat.

In comparison with some of his fellow bishops—with Laud, facing trial and execution in the Tower, or Wren, destined to be confined there for eighteen years—Hall was indeed fortunate. He enjoyed personal freedom, some liberty of preaching, a considerable measure of local respect. In 1648 his temporal and real estate was discharged from sequestration, and life was easier thereafter for him and his devoted wife. At his death in 1656 he left bequests which in the circumstances of the times were not inconsiderable. But he had undergone great indignity and humiliation, and his closing years were very different from anything that he might have anticipated in happier days. He did not repine. His life was an example of piety and humility. He used to preach occasionally in the little parish church of Heigham, with the same eloquence and fervour which he had displayed before King James and King Charles at Whitehall, or before the assembled learning and piety of the Synod of Dort. At other times he took his seat in the congregation and listened to the discourses of the parish clergyman. When that clergyman, the Rev. John Whitefoot, came to deliver his funeral sermon, he recalled 'how often we have seen him walking alone, like old Jacob with his staff, to Bethel, the House of God'.[15]

---

[13] Rye, *Monographs of Norwich Hamlets*, 182–3.
[14] Parr, *Life of Archbishop Usher* (1686), 516, 528, 554.
[15] John Whitefoot, *Death's Alarum* (1656), 69.

4

The Cathedral, and all that it represented, had long been an offence to the Puritans of Norwich. With its wealth of colour and ornament, the monuments and brasses, the painted glass, the images and carvings, it stood as a constant reminder of Popery. Popish, too, were the services conducted within its walls—the ceremonial, the vestments, the singing and chanting of the choristers, the detested music of the organ.

The ordinance of 23 September 1643 was therefore a welcome measure. It was aimed specifically at things which the Puritan mind regarded as idolatrous—altar-rails, altar-steps, crucifixes, crosses, candlesticks; any representation of the Trinity, or of the Virgin Mary, or of the Saints; all inscriptions with prayers for the dead, or otherwise tending to superstition. All such objects were to be removed or defaced before 1 November. But no monument or inscription to a dead person of whatever degree, who had not been 'commonly reported or taken for a saint', was to be harmed.[16] In fact little distinction was observed, by parties of eager iconoclasts, between ornaments of a Popish tendency and those which, as Bishop Hall pointed out, were purely decorative.

He began his famous description of the fate of the Cathedral by contrasting it with the comparative leniency exercised in his chapel, where the visitors allowed him to remove merely the heads of the objectionable figures in the windows. 'There was not that care and moderation used in reforming the Cathedral Church bordering upon my Palace. It is no other than tragical to relate the carriage of that furious sacrilege, whereof our eyes and ears were the sad witnesses, under the authority and presence of Lindsey, Toft the Sheriff, and Greenwood. Lord, what work was here! What clattering of glasses! What beating down of walls! What tearing up of monuments! What pulling down of seats! What wresting out of irons and brass from the windows and graves! What defacing of arms! What demolishing of curious stonework, that had not any representation in the world, but only of the cost of the founder, and skill of the mason! What tooting and piping upon the destroyed organ pipes! and what a hideous

[16] Husband (1646), 307-8.

Vera Effigies Reverendi Do[mi]
Josephi Hall Norvici nuper Episco:
I. Cross fecit
for Nat: Brooke at the Angell in Cornhill

JOSEPH HALL, BISHOP OF NORWICH
from an engraving prefixed to his *Select Thoughts*;
or, *Choice Helps for a Pious Spirit* (1654)

triumph on the market day before all the country, when in a kind of sacrilegeous and profane procession, all the organ pipes, vestments, both copes and surplices, together with the leaden cross which had been newly sawn down from over the Green Yard pulpit, and the service-books and singing-books that could be had, were carried to the fire in the public market-place, a lewd wretch walking before the train, in his cope trailing in the dirt, with a service-book in his hand, imitating in an impious scorn the tune, and usurping the words of the Litany used formerly in the Church! Near the public cross, all these monuments of idolatry must be sacrificed to the fire, not without much zealous joy in discharging ordnance, to the cost of some who professed how much they had longed to see that day.'[17]

The Green Yard has now completely vanished. It lay between the Cathedral and the Palace, and had been used as a public preaching-place for at least two centuries. Its central feature was a pulpit raised on several steps of stone, covered with lead and surmounted by the cross which was now sawn down and destroyed. Covered seats had been built against the wall of the Palace for the Mayor and Aldermen, 'so that they were not offended by rain', and it was customary for the Bishop and his Chancellor to listen to the sermons from one of the Cathedral windows. There were galleries along the north wall of the Cathedral for the Dean and prebendaries, and for 'gentlemen and the better sort'. Less important people could sit on forms in the yard itself, paying a penny or a halfpenny for their places. Schoolboys might stand on the pulpit steps. Soon after the removal of its cross, the pulpit itself was removed to a position outside St. Andrew's Hall, and the public sermons of Puritan divines were henceforward preached there.[18] The other fixtures of the Green Yard were dismantled. It does not appear to have reverted to its ancient use after the Restoration, and the area lay derelict until it was taken into the Palace grounds by an eighteenth-century Bishop.

On the next Guild Day, in the spring of 1644, Bishop Hall described the desolate state of the Cathedral, 'now open on all sides to be filled with musketeers, waiting for the Mayor's

[17] Hall, *Works*, i, lv.
[18] Browne, *Works*, iii, 141.

return, drinking and tobacconing as freely as if it had turned alehouse'.[19] The civic service was on this occasion held in the church of St. Peter Mancroft, where the newly installed Mayor, John Tolye, heard the incumbent, the noted Puritan preacher John Carter, deliver his famous sermon entitled *The Nail hit upon the Head, and driven into the City and Cathedral Wall of Norwich*.

Another witness who viewed with sorrow the desecration of the Cathedral was Dr. Thomas Browne. He was on terms of friendship with the Bishop, and acted as his physician throughout his declining years. In his *Repertorium*, written many years later, he gave additional details of what was done during 'those unhappy times'. He estimated the number of brasses 'torn up and taken away' at one hundred. Looking at the indents of splendid figures and lengthy inscriptions that still remain all over the Cathedral, one can well believe it. He confirmed the Bishop's account of the destruction of the organ, and the bonfire of the organ-pipes and copes; and he specifically mentioned the breaking-up of the tomb and alabaster effigy of Bishop Scambler of unhappy memory. But his most important details relate to the rearrangement of the choir, for such services as the Mayor and Corporation now thought fit to attend. Everything was done in deliberate contempt for traditional Anglican usage. The pulpit was placed against one of the south columns, adjacent to Bishop Overall's monument. The seats for the aldermen were ranged at the east end, within the sanctuary; and the Mayor's seat was erected where the high altar had formerly stood. As a result the tomb of the founder and first bishop of the See of Norwich, the Norman prelate Herbert de Losinga, which stood in front of the high altar, was found to be an inconvenient obstruction. Accordingly, in the words of Browne, 'it was taken down into such a lowness as it now remaineth'.[20] Another probable survival from these stormy years is the bullet which may still be seen embedded

---

[19] I have followed the 1837-9 edition of Hall's *Works* in printing 'the Mayor's return', assuming that these musketeers were on duty as some sort of bodyguard on Guild Day. But the first edition of *Hard Measure*, in *The Shaking of the Olive Tree* (1660), prints 'the Major's returne'. Since the word *Mayor* is spelt correctly elsewhere in the tract, the soldiers may have been awaiting the return of their commanding officer.

[20] Browne, *Works*, iii, 123-4, 128, 138-40.

in the rich medieval decoration of Bishop Goldwell's monument in the choir.

5

The ordinance of sequestration had included the property of all Cathedral Chapters, and the incomes of the Dean and his six prebendaries were thus seriously reduced. They all held country livings in addition to their Cathedral stipends; and from some of these also they were presently to be ejected. For reasons outlined in the next chapter, in which the fortunes of the parochial clergy are considered, it is a difficult task to follow the course of any sequestered minister's life between his ejectment and the Restoration. So much could happen during that long stretch of years, so many changes of circumstance might occur. The following account of the fates of the Dean and his colleagues is therefore tentative, and liable to correction.

Of the prebendaries, Edmund Porter was deprived of his livings of Hevingham in Norfolk and Heveningham in Suffolk, and underwent several months of imprisonment; afterwards he lived in Essex and later in Norwich, and was restored to both his parishes at the King's return in 1660. Foulke Roberts lost his rectory of St. Clement in Norwich, but retained his vicarage of Trowse until his death in 1650. Samuel Garey was ejected from Icklingham in Suffolk, and died in 1646. Edward Young lost two rectories in Essex, but recovered one of them later, and was restored to the other in 1660. Nicholas Howlet seems to have retained his rectory of Winterton until his death in 1652, and was in any case a man of substantial private means. John Spendlove, on the contrary, was deprived of his benefices of Skeyton and Stratton Strawless, and fell into great poverty. Although he regained his livings after the Restoration, he was frequently imprisoned for debts incurred during the period of his sequestration.[21]

The Dean, Dr. John Hassall, was rector of two livings, North Creake and Brancaster. According to Walker 'he was reduced to

---

[21] These details are taken from Walker's *Sufferings of the Clergy* (1714), with additions and corrections from A. G. Matthews' invaluable *Walker Revised* (1948).

such extreme poverty, that one of his daughters, not many years since, was maintained by the charity and relief of the parish'.[22] Yet Thomas Thorowgood, in his *apologia* previously mentioned, affirmed that 'when the Dean of Norwich, Dr. Hassall, was in danger to lose his benefice of Brancaster, I did twice preserve him as his own letters testify'.[23] And it appears from his will, which incidentally mentions no daughter, that he was still rector of North Creake at his death in 1654.[24] It was humiliating and uncomfortable for a Dean and Doctor of Divinity, who had once been chaplain to a Queen and had expectations of a bishopric, to end his days in the obscurity of a country parish; but it seems possible that Walker's account of his penury was somewhat exaggerated.

Furthermore, it appears that the Dean and Chapter continued to function, in however subdued and restricted a fashion, for some years after the desecration of the Cathedral and their own sequestration. In May 1644 the Dean, according to the Chapter book, 'admonished Martin Carlton, one of the singing-men, for his very peremptory and irreverent speeches and carriage towards him'. In 1646 they granted an exhibition at St. John's College, Cambridge, to John Porter, one of the sons of their colleague Edmund Porter. In 1648 they allotted to Mr. Porter the house occupied by their late colleague Samuel Garey. All through these unsettled years they were still conducting a much-diminished volume of business—assigning leases, presenting to rectories and vicarages, granting tenancies of houses in the Close. It was only in May 1649 that the last Chapter meeting is recorded, *infra precinctum ecclesiae cathedralis*. Edmund Porter presided as Vice-Dean, and of the prebendaries only Foulke Roberts and John Spendlove were present. The Dean had by then retired to North Creake, and the meeting was held by his consent, under his signature and seal. Their sole business was to seal the presentation of Thomas Briggs to the vicarage of Hempstead. There were no meetings of the chapter thereafter, and nothing but blank pages in the book.[25]

As for the Cathedral itself, there were times during the coming

[22] Walker, *Sufferings*, II, 56.
[23] N.A., xxii, 327.
[24] *Walker Revised*, 268.
[25] Williams and Cozens-Hardy, *Norwich Chapter Books*, 1566–1649 (N.R.S., 1953), 83–6.

years when it narrowly escaped further injury and possible destruction. To many Puritans the great building was an idolatrous pile of valuable materials, stone and lead and timber, which might well be dismantled and put to more profitable uses. In 1650 the authorites of Great Yarmouth petitioned the House of Commons to that effect. They began with a long and obsequious preamble to the glory of the Rump Parliament—'our God hath broken the snare, and we are delivered to praise his name, who hath gathered together this Honourable House as so many choice arrows into his quiver to smite through the hearts and loins of his and his people's enemies.' They then prayed that 'you will be pleased to grant us such a part of the lead and other useful materials of that vast and altogether useless Cathedral in Norwich, towards the building of a work house to employ our almost starved poor, and repairing our piers, or otherwise as you shall think fit and sufficient'.[26]

The Cathedral was spared on this occasion, but there were further attempts to destroy it during the Commonwealth years. A member of the Corporation named Christopher Jay, who was Sheriff of Norwich in 1653 and Mayor in 1657, asserted after the Restoration that he had been instrumental in saving it from destruction and had spent large sums of his own money on its repair. He made certain claims upon the Dean and Chapter, and the matter was referred to the arbitration of the Bishops of Lincoln and Exeter. Their verdict was that 'the said Mr. Jay in the late disordered times, when endeavours were used to demolish the Cathedral Church of Norwich, had not only prevented the same, but disbursed considerable sums of money in the needful repairs of that Church, which would otherwise have fallen into very great decay, if not utter ruin'. King Charles II therefore commanded that 'he should be fully repaid those disbursements, with interest for the same and with an acknowledgement of his good service to the Church therein'.[27] And thus the magnificent fabric was preserved during those troubled years, battered and desecrated but not essentially harmed.

[26] H.M.C., Great Yarmouth Corporation, 320.
[27] B.L. MS. Tanner 134, f. 140.

CHAPTER XII

The Parish Clergy

I

The fortunes of the parish clergy, like those of the Cathedral clergy, are difficult to pursue. It was not until sixty years had elapsed that any sustained attempt was made to record them. In 1714 an Exeter rector named John Walker, fired by the emotions of the Sacheverell trial, and deeply resentful of Calamy's account of the nonconformist ministers ejected on 'Black Bartholomew's Day' in 1662, published his *Attempt towards recovering an Account of the Numbers and Sufferings of the Clergy of the Church of England . . . who were Sequestered, Harassed, etc., in the late Times of the Grand Rebellion.* Persecution is detestable, from whatever quarter it comes. But after fully discounting Walker's political and doctrinal bias, it must be admitted that he proved beyond doubt that the ejected Royalist clergy were far more numerous than Calamy's sufferers, and that the cruelties and indignities which many of them underwent were considerably more severe.

Nevertheless, sixty years is a long time. Walker's researches occupied him for a full decade; he examined countless archives, registers and other documents, and corresponded with every chapter and college in the land. But few eyewitnesses had survived, and not a great number even of the children of the suffering clergy. His accounts were inevitably affected by the lapse of years, by hearsay and legend, by the political views or personal resentments of the narrators.

It must be remembered, further, that the disturbed period of the Church lasted for the greater part of twenty years, until the Restoration in 1660. During that time all kinds of vicissitudes occurred in civil and ecclesiastical government. The two elements within the victorious Puritan party, the Presbyterians and the Independents, broke violently asunder. Individuals underwent unexpected conversions; conviction or expediency brought about surprising changes of heart. Clergy expelled from livings for their Royalism suddenly appear in other livings under Puritan patronage. By contrast a Puritan gentleman from Suffolk, Gibson Lucas, could seek ordination from the ejected Bishop Hall, coming to him 'like Saul in his scarlet, for that was his habit', but thereafter proving himself 'a sackcloth prophet, continuing a diligent and zealous preacher of the Gospel'.[1]

Despite the researches of Walker, and of his invaluable reviser the late A. G. Matthews, one still comes across clerics who do not figure in their pages, yet who appear to have been ejected or otherwise molested. Alexander Shipdham of Blofield is mentioned by neither; yet an eighteenth-century record describes him as 'a venerable person, turned out by Cromwell's troopers'. Actually he was only appointed to Blofield in 1646, and would seem to have weathered all storms for ten years or so, after which he did encounter some trouble and disappears from the parish registers until the Restoration.[2] John Novell of Northwold is recorded on his wife's memorial slab to have 'suffered many hardships under the tyranny of Cromwell (the so-called Protector)'; but Walker and Matthews know nothing of him. Robert Mihill's tablet in the church of Potter Heigham states that he 'suffered much in the Oliverian times for his loyalty to his Prince, and for his great piety, charity and sufferings was beloved in his country'. Yet he seems to have held his benefice continuously from 1627 until his death in 1664. What then were his sufferings? Occasionally one begins to suspect an element of exaggeration or even of invention in the woes thus posthumously recorded.

But when every allowance has been made, the treatment of the Royalist clergy still remains a cruel and a sordid business. The details in the ensuing pages have been taken, in almost every case, either from the manuscript accounts supplied by eyewitnesses to Walker when he was compiling his book, or from John Nalson's extracts from the proceedings of Manchester's committees. They tell a melancholy story, in which, as in every war or revolution, the innocent were the sufferers—the wives, the children, the peace-loving parsons who accepted penury and humiliation rather

---

[1] Hall, *The Shaking of the Olive-Tree* (1660), preface, unpaged. For Lucas's membership of various committees in Suffolk, see Husband (1646), 284, 567, 605, app. 11.
[2] Harrison, *Postwick and Relatives*, 11. Information from the Rev. R. S. C. Baily.

than forsake the principles to which they had vowed to be faithful.

A few clergymen of conspicuously Royalist sympathies were summoned to appear before Parliament at an early stage, in some cases even before the outbreak of the war. They had been denounced as too outspoken in their comments on the new régime, or as observers of ceremonies now disallowed, or as defaulters in their contributions to Parliamentarian funds. The earliest of these in Norfolk appears to have been Nathaniel Flick of Hardingham, who was accused in February 1642 of uttering opprobrious words against the Earl of Essex and the Earl of Warwick. He was followed later in the year by Dr. Edward Franklin of Great Cressingham, Thomas Reeve of Aldborough and Colby, Thomas Coleby of Cawston and Hamond Claxton of Holt. Of the whole group, only the last suffered serious penalties at this stage, being placed in confinement in the Bishop of Winchester's house and later in the Clink. He was released in a few weeks' time; and he and his fellows remained in their livings until the systematic campaign against the 'scandalous' or 'malignant' clergy began early in 1644. Then they were all ejected, and their estates sequestered.[3]

On 22 January, Parliament issued an ordinance which placed Manchester in absolute control of the destinies of the clergy in the Eastern Association and the University of Cambridge. According to the preamble, complaint had been made by the well-affected that 'the service of the Parliament is retarded, the enemy strengthened, the people's souls starved, and their minds diverted from God's cause by their idle, ill-affected and scandalous clergy'. Manchester was therefore to appoint committees in each county, who were empowered to call before them any minister whose loyalty to the Parliament was suspect, or against whom testimony might be brought by 'the oaths of such persons as shall and may be produced to give evidence against them'. They might further administer the Covenant to any person, 'upon such penalties as are or shall be assigned by the Parliament in this behalf'. The second clause of the Covenant, with its complete renunciation of the episcopal form of church government, was alone sufficient to ensure its rejection by any cleric faithful to his ordination vows. On receiving an adverse report on a minister from one of these

[3] C.J., ii, 455, 850, 895. Shaw, ii, 298–9. *Walker Revised*, 265–7, 272.

committees, or a notification of his refusal of the Covenant, Manchester was empowered to eject him from his living and to sequester his entire property, reserving only a fifth part for the benefit of his wife and children.[4]

Manchester duly appointed his commissioners for Norfolk and Norwich.[5] They included men of distinction such as Sir Thomas Wodehouse, Sir John Hobart and Sir John Potts; but it is significant that these leading figures played little part in the actual business of the committees. They had other and more urgent work on hand; and since they were essentially moderate in their outlook, they probably found such duties highly distasteful. The names appended to the examinations of the delinquent clergy, in almost every case, are those of men of lesser standing and more extreme views. Robert Jermy of Bayfield, Tobias Frere of Roydon, Robert Gooch of Earsham, Matthew Lindsey and John Greenwood of Norwich—these were the commissioners who sat in judgement, day after day, on the incumbents of parish after parish. They were all enthusiastic Puritans, obscure men savouring the enjoyment of power for the first time; and some of them were to figure conspicuously in Norfolk during the Commonwealth years.

There were usually a few parishioners who were ready to testify against a minister of Royalist sympathies, some from sincere religious and political conviction, others as a result of private quarrels or local feuds. Even so, Manchester was leaving nothing to chance. In his instructions to the commissioners, he told them it was 'not fit that the party accused should be present at the taking of the depositions, because of the discountenancing the witnesses'. The accused was, however, allowed a copy of the depositions, 'if he will pay for it', and might offer a defence at a second meeting a fortnight later. Furthermore, 'it being found by sad experience that parishioners were not forward to complain of their ministers, although they were very scandalous', the commissioners were instructed 'to call unto them some well-affected men, within every hundred, who having no private engagements, but intending to further the public reformation, were to be required and encouraged by the committees, to inquire after the doctrines, lives and conversations of all ministers and schoolmasters, and to

[4] Husband (1646), 415-6.
[5] The names of the commissioners are given in B.L. MS. Walker c. 5, f. 58.

give information to the committees, both what could be deposed, and who could depose the same'.[6]

The Norfolk committee was appointed early in March, and its work went busily forward in the ensuing months. The hostile or disgruntled parishioners duly testified against their ministers, and their depositions were carefully recorded. Certain stock accusations were constantly repeated—observing and urging Bishop Wren's injunctions; reading the Book of Sports; insisting on the people receiving the sacrament at the altar-rails; preaching in the surplice; bowing at the name of Jesus. These would be followed by more personal charges—swearing, drunkenness, frequenting alehouses and taverns, keeping company with malignants, using ill words against the Parliament.

It is clear, from the depositions, that many of these clerics were spirited and outspoken men. Richard Plummer of Sustead and Alby had called his well-affected neighbours 'Parliament rogues, roundheads, rebels to the King and traitors'; and when called upon for his weekly assessment, he had retorted, 'What, shall I pay money only to maintain rebellion?' Richard Anguish of Starston had preached vigorously on behalf of the King and against the ordinances of Parliament, saying that the demolishing of monuments in churches was a sin as ill as sacrilege, and 'this taking up of arms was as bad as the powder plot'. William Barwick of Hempnall had said at the outset of the troubles, 'I will be for the Commission of Array, for that is set forth by the King, and if there be any disturbance in the country I have a gun at home, and powder and bullets, and will defend myself as well as I can.' Parliament, in his view, was 'but a company of factious fellows, and he knew of no good they did, except it were to destroy a kingdom . . . and were about to make apron elders, waistcoateers and petticoateers to be governors'.

Stephen Hurry of Alburgh seems to have been particularly at odds with his female parishioners. He told Judith Muriell 'that it were a good turn if she and the Scots were hanged together, and that the Scots were rebels, rogues and knaves'. When Elizabeth Skeet informed him that she intended to give her ring towards the contributions levied in aid of Fairfax's army, he replied that 'if she

[6] Manchester's instructions and covering letter are given in Walker, *Sufferings*, 117–8.

did she might have a rope'. After his sequestration he lived at Pulham St. Mary, and was evidently a man of some private means, since at his death in 1647 he left £5 to Bishop Hall, £5 to Chancellor Corbett, and £3 apiece to twelve of his sequestered brethren. John Lewthwaite of Rockland St. Peter and Stow Bedon had said in his pulpit 'We have a merciful King, which is forced to take up arms to fight to maintain the true Protestant religion'. When two godly ministers were appointed by the committees to preach in his church, his wife told the bystanders that 'her husband would not have any skip-jack come in his place'. Lewthwaite was in any case a marked man as one of Bishop Wren's commissioners. He had to face such accusations as 'wearing a corner cap with a tassel on the crown'; and had not only read the Book of Sports, but 'hath stood by them that played and said to them *Well played*, some of his own family being among them'. Like many of his fellows, he had refused to take the Covenant or to tender it to his parishioners.

It may be recalled that the misdoings of the Rev. Nicholas Sherwood, and the accusations brought against him by his parishioners at Earsham, had caused much anxiety to Bishop Wren and Chancellor Corbett. His leading adversary at that time, Robert Gooch, was now one of the committee which sat in judgement on him; and Robert Gooch the younger was one of the eleven witnesses. Every sort of charge was produced against him. He was scandalous for incontinency, a man of a turbulent spirit, an alehouse haunter, a gamester and a swearer. He refused to preach more than once on a Sunday, 'saying of those that preached twice a day that they prated once'; yet he railed at those of his parishioners who went to hear sermons in other churches, saying it was a sin. Although his private morals had incurred the censure of Bishop Wren, he was stigmatized nevertheless as 'a strict observer of Bishop Wren's injunctions, going up to the communion table railed in, bowing at the name of Jesus and causing the children in their catechizing to do so'. Needless to say he was ejected and sequestered, in common with his more seemly brethren.[7]

Nalson's notes of the proceedings of Manchester's committees do not show whether any of the clergy attended at the second

[7] The last four paragraphs are based on John Nalson's transcripts of the proceedings of Manchester's committee in Norfolk, in B.L. MS. Walker c. 6, ff. 44-9.

meeting, at which they were given an opportunity to rebut the accusations against them. In view of the spirit of the times and the temper of their judges, there would have been little purpose in doing so. Against name after name appears the curt entry 'ejected and sequestered'; and that was the fate of many more whose cases do not appear in Nalson's transcripts. Walker preserved a number of other accounts of the treatment of the Norfolk clergy. Several of these were supplied by Robert Thexton, the son of one of the sufferers, Thomas Thexton of Trunch and Gimingham, and himself an eyewitness of what occurred in that north-eastern corner of the county. The younger Thexton related how Robert Le Neve, vicar of Scottow, was present at a christening dinner when a round pudding appeared on the table, and a jovial parishioner named John Edwards exclaimed, 'I think we have got a roundhead here'. These words were reported to the committee by two other parishioners, named Bush and Brown, as being uttered by the vicar himself, even though Edwards protested that the fateful remark was his own; 'upon which,' according to Thexton, 'and for no other crime that was objected, the said Le Neve having a wife and five or six small children, and nothing but that small living to support them, was sequestered and turned out of it, and denied the liberty of keeping a school.'[8]

Richard Howes, rector of Knapton, 'a person of very reputable character both for learning and sobriety of life', was haled before the committee and summarily ejected. He was confined, on some unknown pretext, in the gaol at Aylsham, where his name appears later in 1644 at the head of a petition urging the removal of a disorderly fellow-prisoner to the castle at Norwich. This character, Thomas Turner, was 'a very profane ill-mouthed and ungodly person and very dangerous, insomuch as he fileth his irons put upon him for his most vile and notorious actions, in breaking open doors and locks, and most absurdly abusing us . . . and also in threatening to pull down and lay waste or burn down the prison-house where we are, for that he affirmeth there is neither God nor devil, heaven nor hell'. The more tractable inmates of Aylsham gaol would be glad to see the last of him.[9]

Many more examples could be cited of the stupidity, the

[8] B.L. MS. Walker c. 5, f. 46.
[9] H.M.C., Lothian, 86.

intolerance, and often the deliberate cruelty of the zealots who dominated these committees. Robert Thexton's own father, after remaining unmolested for some time 'by the great interest and reputation he had among the gentry about him', was finally ejected from Trunch and Gimingham through the enmity of two local Puritans, and even had to compound for a fraction of the fifth part of his stipend which should have been allotted to him for the support of his family. Robert Blofeld of Thorpe by Norwich, 'a sober and grave divine', with a wife and seven small children, was sequestered of both his livings and for a while imprisoned in Norwich gaol. His half-brother, Thomas Blofeld of Aylmerton, was likewise sequestered, and was forced to subsist upon the charity of friends until the Restoration. Dr. Edward Franklin of Great Cressingham, who had been summoned before Parliament at the outset of the troubles, was ejected and harassed from place to place, 'till at last the house wherein he was with some others of the same malignancy as himself, was beset by some of Oliver's soldiers who were in quest of him, and he endeavouring to make his escape over the garden pales on the backside of the house, hung himself upon a pale which ran into his groin, of which he soon after died'.[10]

Edmund Duncon of Swannington and Wood Dalling, as one of Bishop Wren's commissioners, was yet another victim of sequestration. He was a friend of Nicholas Ferrar of Little Gidding, and in 1633 had been sent by Ferrar to visit the dying George Herbert. He returned bearing the manuscript volume of poems which Herbert had entrusted to him, and which Ferrar soon afterwards published as *The Temple*. Duncon thus reported the poet's words of farewell: 'Sir, I pray deliver this little book to my dear brother Ferrar, and tell him, he shall find in it a picture of the many spiritual conflicts that have passed betwixt God and my soul, before I could subject mine to the will of Jesus my master; in whose service I have now found perfect freedom; desire him to read it; and then, if he can think it may turn to the advantage of any dejected poor soul, let it be made public; if not, let him burn it; for I and it are less than the least of God's mercies.'[11] My narrative is necessarily concerned with the prosaic realities of the

[10] B.L. MSS. Walker c. 1, ff. 85, 225: c. 5, f. 46.
[11] Izaak Walton, *Lives* (ed. Zouch, 1796), 377–8, 385–7.

seventeenth-century church, the struggle between the Laudian and Puritan points of view; but the mention of George Herbert is a reminder of the spiritual forces in which both sides passionately believed, 'the Christian plummet sounding heaven and earth'.

Walker's papers contain three accounts related by eyewitnesses with particular vividness—the stories of Christopher Barnard of Dickleburgh by his daughter, of Thomas Reeve of Aldborough and Colby by his son, and of Thomas Campbell of Swafield by his younger neighbour Robert Thexton. The narrative of Barnard's daughter, Mrs. Rudkin, is in the wavering hand of a very old woman. Her father, she wrote, was 'a faithful and learned pastor, a painful labourer, holy in his conversation by which he constantly and daily preached, as well as by precepts in the pulpit, and well beloved by his parishioners, who thought it a judgement upon them when the soldiers dragged him away to carry him to Norwich Castle; but his beloved flock followed him and rescued him and hid him a long time after, but he lost his living of £200 a year. He had a wife and ten young children to bring up when he was carried before the Earl of Manchester, who proferred him his own preferment if he would take the Covenant and preach up their damnable cause; but he like a good and loyal subject slighted the offer, choosing rather to suffer affliction with the righteous than enjoy the pleasure of sin for a season, looking unto that God whom he trusted in his own good time would restore the King and the Church to their right'. His house was rifled of its plate, linen and other goods, although the troopers were again hampered by the resistance of the devoted parishioners of Dickleburgh, who even managed to get some of his corn out of his barns, threshed it secretly for his benefit, and carted the rest away to a safe place during the night. Mr. Barnard was to be reinstated at the Restoration and lived for twenty years thereafter. When he died in 1680 he had been rector of Dickleburgh for almost sixty years, including the sixteen years of his sequestration; and his ledger stone may still be seen in the chancel of his church.[12]

Thomas Reeve of Aldborough and Colby, as a notable local Royalist, had been summoned to appear before Parliament in November 1642; and although he came to no harm on that

[12] B.L. MS. Walker c. 1, ff. 44-5.

occasion, at some later date he thought it wise to leave his parishes and go into hiding. His case came before the committee in session at Aylsham on 15 May 1644, the same day as that of his neighbour Richard Plummer of Sustead and Alby. Reeve was accused of being absent from his cures for twelve months, refusing to take the Covenant, paying no assessments and encouraging his parishioners to do likewise, neglecting the fast days, being formerly an observer of Bishop Wren's erroneous injunctions, 'and also was superstitious, for he stood to prove the real presence of Christ in the Sacrament'. In a long statement which he supplied to Walker, his son John Reeve said that his father was forced to absent himself from his livings for two years, 'because he would not take the Scotch Covenant'; and told the story of the ill-treatment of his mother by John Reymes of Overstrand, a local Puritan squire of small estate who had lately become a member of some of the Parliamentary committees. 'One Major Reymes, his neighbour, having raised a troop of horse for Parliament, got a warrant from the committee of sequestration at Norwich to take away the said Dr. Reeve's cattle and to bring him prisoner to Norwich gaol, which he executed with all the rigour he could, searching the bed, where the wife of the said Dr. Reeve had lain in but three days, for the said Dr. Reeve; and when the women rebuked him for his barbarity, telling him he acted more like a beast than a man, he drew his sword and stabbed it through the bed in several places, pretending to stab the said Dr. Reeve as hid in the bed; after that he caused all his troopers to pull the bridles off their horses and whip them round the garden to tread all underfoot; after that he brake open the barn doors, and turned the whole troop to the stacks of corn to fill their bellies. Some few days after he came with another warrant, and brake open the doors with a plough share (being denied to open) and turned my mother and six children into the street, and brought carts and carried away my father's library and all the household goods, and sold them for what he pleased and gave no account to the Committee.'

We are not told what happened next to Mrs. Reeve and the children; but her husband's misfortunes continued. After having 'lain obscure' for three years in all, he attempted to join the King at Oxford, 'and within seven miles of that place was taken

prisoner by a troop of the Parliament's horse, and stripped naked
in very cold weather and his clothes ripped, all in pretence to
search for a letter, instead of which they met with nigh three-
score pieces of broad gold which were quilted into several places
for his support, but could get none of them again. Then he was
brought prisoner to London where his countryman Miles Corbett
(who was afterwards one of King Charles's judges) sat Chairman
of the Committee, who pretended at first to send him in exchange
to Oxford, but after that told him, that he knew him to be an old
malignant and promised to see him hanged, so sent him prisoner
to the Gatehouse'. According to his son he remained in 'that
noisome place' for three years; but when Miles Corbett was sent
in 1650 as one of the Commissioners to Ireland, the intercessions
of many friends brought about his release. After eight years
sequestration, his personal estate was released to him in 1652. He
did not return to his Norfolk parishes at the Restoration, but
accepted preferment elsewhere, which he held until his death
in 1672.[13]

The story of Thomas Campbell, rector of Swafield, was told by
Robert Thexton, the son of his companion in misfortune, the
minister of Trunch and Gimingham. 'Being sequestered by the
Earl of Manchester, he was forced from his rectory of Swafield
to retire to a neighbour village called Bradfield, to live in a poor
cottage, where visiting him in a very cold frost and deep snow I
found him at his study, reading of Gerhard's *Harmony*. He was
with his wife and four children, without fire or firing. I being
dry and weary with a long walk, asked him for a draught of beer.
He carried me to his window and showed me a watercourse, and
told me, if I were dry, thereof might satisfy myself; for he had no
other liquor to drink for some months past. I then asking for a
morsel to eat, his reply was he had neither bread, or butter, or
cheese, or fish, or flesh in his house; and he had wanted all these
and firing also, for many weeks. I wondering how he could
subsist, he led me to an old churn, and opening it I saw two or
three very great dumplings. He said they were barley dumplings;

[13] B.L. MSS. Walker c. 1, f. 78–9; c. f. 6, 49. There are a few minor chronological
discrepancies in John Reeve's account, though nothing to invalidate the general
truth of the story. His father was not a Doctor at the time of these events, though
he may have received a Doctorate after the Restoration.

and I perceived they were coarse and brown, and as cold and hard as vehement frost could make them; and he told me that he lived only on such provision, and water from the little run of water, for many weeks. I seeing his wants, told him I wondered at it, and feared that if I should fall under such circumstances and wants, I should I feared sink under it. He replied with a surprising cheerfulness, that I was a fool, I wanted experience, for if ever God called me to suffering, he would enable me to bear with courage and contentment—and other discourse to this purpose. His carriage was not abject, or dejected, but held with a heroical Christian bravery: or if that had been his wedding day, and he had then been joined to the greatest fortune and most pious mate in the world.

'This Mr. Campbell had been a soldier under Gustavus Adolphus in the German wars: a stout, prudent, honest man: a very good scholar in most parts of learning: very hospitable while he held his livings: very patient, and cheerful, after he was sequestered: a perfect honest man in all his dealings. . . . He died a year or two after the Restoration: and his memory is yet grateful among the neighbours.'[14]

2

Such was in general the spirit of the sequestered clergy. There were, of course, a few individuals to whom the term of 'scandalous' could fairly be applied, and for whose removal there was possibly some justification. Nicholas Sherwood of Earsham would seem to fall within this category. But the vast majority of the ejected clergy were virtuous and conscientious men, who would not be false to their principles and their beliefs. A few fortunate individuals found temporary refuge in the Royalist areas, or a more permanent shelter in the houses of friends. Penury awaited the rest, and long imprisonment was the fate of some. Their wives and children had to subsist on the 'fifths' due from their intruded successors, often irregularly paid, sometimes withheld altogether. All this was suffered, with what patience they could

[14] Robert Thexton's account of Thomas Campbell is in MS. Walker c. 1, f. 108. There is also a paraphrase of this account, with a few unimportant differences, in MS. Walker c. 5, f. 46.

muster, by innumerable clerics all over the land, who by complying with the times and taking the Covenant could have preserved
themselves and their dependants from a seemingly endless
nightmare of poverty and humiliation.

A few of the sequestered clergy appear to have retained some
contact with their former parishes. There must have been well-
wishers who sought to mitigate their lot—old friends and associates, devoted parishioners like Barnard's at Dickleburgh,
charitable people of neutral or secretly Royalist persuasion. Even
the intruded Puritans who occupied their livings may not in
every instance have been unkindly.

One of those who long remained in contact with his former
parish was Nethaniel Gill, the rector of Burgh-next-Aylsham. He
was the younger son of Dr. Alexander Gill, a famous High Master
of St. Paul's School. He only received three lines of print from
Walker, who could obtain no information about him and his
troubles. Oblivion seemed to have claimed him entirely. But he
had confided to the parish register of Burgh sufficient details of
his life and opinions to bring him before us once more as an
obstinate, masterful and decidedly original character.

He was admitted to the living of Burgh in 1638, on the presentation of the widow of Chief Justice Coke. He recorded the circumstances with some pomp in the register at Burgh, which soon
began to blossom with strange flowers of Latin and Greek, with
elaborate synonyms and euphuistical paraphrases. A child was
never just baptized: he was *aqua tinctus*, *hydrobaptizatus*, *Christi
membrum factus*, *Jordanizebatur*, or even *Antiochiebatur*. Similarly, a
man and woman were *concarnati*, *concatenati*, *una caro facti*, *arctis-
simo familiaritatis jugo conjugati*. And a deceased person was not
simply buried: he or she was *vermibus esca datus*, *sarcophago con-
tentus*, *brevi urna contenta*, *terrae et corruptioni nupta*, *cælicolata*.

Gill was also fond of punning on the names of his parishioners,
as when he buried a man named John Crow and described him as
aquila cælestis factus. It was only when describing the less virtuous
members of his flock that he sometimes descended to very plain
English, as when he committed to the earth 'Baseborne, the
bastard child of the whore Parnell Reade', and poor Rose Ives,
who was 'nor widow, nor wife, nor maid'. He took such pride in
his birth, and the family coat of arms, that he usually added after

his signature in the register the description *presbyter et armiger*, and sometimes πρεσβύτερος καὶ ὁπλοφόρος.

Naturally he watched the increasing troubles in the nation with profound misgiving. There is no indication that he took any part in the little rising at Aylsham in the spring of 1643. But when writing of that year in his register, he described it as 'Anno spreti Regis Caroli, et blasphemati Jesu Christi (tryumphantibus daemone, Kimboltono, Pymmo) tertio παρθενοτοκίας [*sic*] 1643.'

This forbidding trinity—Satan, Manchester and Pym—continued to triumph; and in 1644 Manchester ejected Gill from the living of Burgh. Unfortunately no record of the proceedings in his case appears to be preserved; but his cure was sequestered, and a temporal estate of some value as well. He signed the register at the close of 1644 as 'Nathaniel Gill quod θεοφόβος, φιλοβασιλεὺς ecclesia pulsus'—driven from his church because he feared God and loved the King—and repeated the statement in an outburst of defiant Latin verse.

Driven from his church, Gill still remained in his parish or somewhere not far away. He kept the registers in his own possession. He continued to baptize and marry the members of his former flock with the forbidden ceremonies of the Church. In fact he seems to have acted, for several years after his ejection, in complete defiance of the new order. Clearly his parishioners were entirely in sympathy with him, and he was able to carry on his work with the connivance of the churchwardens, whom he made a point of naming in the register with some such formula as *Nathaniel Gill presbyter armiger sui ipsius vicegessit permissu inferiorum.* His activities did not pass unnoticed by the local Parliamentarians. Early in 1647, for example, he was in trouble with four other sequestered clergy, including Blofeld of Aylmerton and Plummer of Sustead and Alby, for preaching in churches in spite of their deprivation.[15] It is surprising that the committees did not take a stronger line against him. But the register shows conclusively that year after year *Nathaniel Gill curæ inservivit adhuc sequestratus*; that child after child was *signo crucis baptizatus sicut meus est mos* or *secundum Lyturgiam Anglicanum in alvum ecclesiæ admissus*; that couples were *cum annulo matrimoniati*; and that this stalwart and uncompromising man, through sheer force of character and the

[15] *Walker Revised*, 264.

loyalty of his former parishioners, continued to administer all the sacraments of his Church long after they had been forbidden.

Of course it could not last. The imprisonment and presently the execution of the King were sadly recorded in the register; but it was not until 1651 that the authorities at length put an end to his defiance, and he was obliged to retire to Bungay in Suffolk. What he did there, or how he subsisted, we do not know. The only relevant entry in the register runs: 'During the time of anarchy, till the King's happy return, I being at Bungay, and not admitted into my living, I knew not, I heeded not, what was done.' He must have taken the register with him, since no one else wrote in it during those years, and we therefore do not know the name of the Puritan who must have been intruded into his living. At last the long period of tribulation came to an end, and he was able to inscribe the joyful words: 'Nethaniel Gill (after seventeen years sequestration, by traitors, rebels, Anabaptists, Quakers, and Presbyterians) was restored to his rectory of Burgh and preached on Christmas Day 1660. Δόξα Θεῷ.'

He celebrated the first year of his return by a complete repair of his parsonage and the chancel of his church, with its lovely Early English arcading and leafy carvings. The work, he recorded, was done at his sole and great charge, 'though he had all that time been sequestered for loyalty to King Charles the First'. In 1663 he became rector of the prosperous town of Aylsham, with its busy market and its spacious church. He held it in plurality with Burgh; but at Burgh he remained, faithful to his old parish. There his grandchildren were baptized; there he was buried on an April day in 1669; and there survives the register which contains the story of his eccentricity, his obstinacy and his courage.[16]

3

Reference has already been made in connection with the sack of Norwich Cathedral, to the ordinance of Parliament dated

[16] For a fuller account of Gill, from which much of the above is repeated, see my book *A Norfolk Gallery* (1948), 111-5. See also N.A., ix, 37-58. The parish registers of Burgh and Aylsham, which contain Gill's entries, are still in good preservation.

28 August 1643, 'for the utter demolishing, removing, and taking away of all monuments of superstition or idolatry'.[17] Towards the close of the year it was brought to Manchester's notice that this ordinance was not being properly obeyed. There had already been a certain amount of random iconoclasm, carried out by local Puritan extremists or detachments of unruly troopers. But such activities were viewed with little favour by numbers of people who were broadly in sympathy with the new régime. We remember the complaint of Thomas Windham, a Puritan himself, in his letter to Sir John Potts of 10 December 1643: 'The oppression practised by Jubbs and his associates is very odious, their fury in churches detestable.'[18] Nor were many parishioners, whether squires like Windham or humbler members of the congregation, easily reconciled to the spoliation of their own churches by ordinance of Parliament. Windham was active enough in enforcing in his neighbourhood the taking of the Covenant, with its emphasis upon the uprooting of the relics of Popery and superstition. But he took good care that no harm came to the splendid brasses of the Felbrigg family in his parish church, although the Felbriggs were in no way his kindred, and despite the Popish supplications for the souls of the dead with which they were inscribed.

So in many parishes the ordinance was wholly or largely disregarded. The Virgin and the Trinity remained unmutilated in the windows of painted glass; apostles, saints and martyrs stood unharmed in the panels of the screens; the angelic host still spread their wings in the magnificent timber roofs. Such indifference to the behests of Parliament could not be allowed to continue. Manchester therefore issued, on 19 December, a commission to a rather obscure Puritan enthusiast, William Dowsing of Laxfield in Suffolk, empowering him to visit in person or by deputy the churches within the Eastern Association and make certain that the necessary destruction was properly carried out. After a brief rehearsal of the contents of the ordinance, the commission proceeded: 'And whereas many such crosses, crucifixes, and other superstitious images and pictures are still continued within the said Associated Counties in manifest contempt of the said ordi-

---

[17] See pp. 220-1. The text of the ordinance is in Husband (1646), 307–8.
[18] See p. 221.

nance, these are therefore to will and require you forthwith to make your repair to the several Associated Counties, and put the said ordinance in execution in every particular, hereby requiring all Mayors, Sheriffs, Bailiffs, Constables, Headboroughs and all other His Majesty's officers and loving subjects to be aiding and assisting unto, whereof they may not fail at their peril.'[19]

This commission was addressed to Dowsing 'and to such as he shall appoint'; and its wording seems to imply that his responsibilities extended over all the Eastern Association. But our knowledge of his personal activities is confined to Suffolk and Cambridgeshire, since he left daily journals of his trail of destruction in both counties. We know also the names of some of the deputies whom he appointed in Suffolk, including a certain Francis Jessopp of Beccles, to whom the hundred of Lothingland was entrusted, and who was described by the indignant vicar of Lowestoft as 'a wretched commissioner, not able to read or find out that which his commission enjoined him to remove'.[20] But there seems to be no record of how the horrid work was carried out in Norfolk, or who was entrusted with the task.

Dowsing's journal of his doings in Suffolk is a most lamentable document. From January 1644 onwards he and his myrmidons journeyed from parish to parish, smashing the stained glass, tearing down the images, ripping up brasses, converting screens and organ-cases and altar-rails into firewood, erasing pious inscriptions, demolishing the crosses on roofs and porches, ordering the levelling of altar-steps. Sometimes he was able to deal with four or five churches in a single day. At Clare, for example, 'we brake down 1000 pictures superstitious; I brake down 200; 3 of God the Father, and 3 of Christ, and the Holy Lamb, and 3 of the Holy Ghost like a dove with wings; and the 12 apostles were carved in wood, on the top of the roof, which we gave order to take down; and the Sun and Moon in the east window, by the King's arms, to be taken down'. At Stoke-by-Nayland, 'we brake down an 100 superstitious pictures; and took up 7 superstitious inscriptions on the grave-stones, *ora pro nobis*, etc.' At Stradbroke, '8 angels off the roof, and cherubims in wood, to be broken down; and 4

[19] Dowsing, *Journal* (ed. Meadows White), 7.
[20] Suckling, ii, 102.

crosses on the steeple; and one on the church; and one on the porch and 17 pictures in the upper window; and *pray for such out of your charity*; and organs, which I brake'.[21]

Occasionally there was some attempt at resistance. At Ufford a united front of churchwardens, constable and sexton denied the keys of the church to the visitors, and succeeded in keeping them out of the building for two hours. At Covehithe the people refused to help them to raise the ladders to destroy the glass in the windows and the cherubim in the roof. At Great Cornard a valiant churchwarden named John Pain refused to pay the fee which Dowsing exacted from every parish, and was haled off by the constable to appear before the Earl of Manchester.[22] In most cases, however, the required noble (six and eightpence) was meekly paid to the iconoclasts; and at Cambridge each college was expected to render a tribute of forty shillings for their unwelcome services.

We have no such picture for Norfolk. But there can be no doubt that similar activities were carried out, with equal vigour and brutality, in the sister county. In April 1644 the churchwardens of Bressingham paid six shillings to a certain Captain Gilley 'for the viewing the church, for abolishing superstitious pictures'. They also paid John Nunn three shillings and fourpence for two days' work in taking down glass and pictures, and filing the inscriptions off the bells.[23] I have not come across Captain Gilley elsewhere, but presumably he was one of Dowsing's deputies for Norfolk. At Loddon the churchwardens paid a glazier named Rochester six shillings for 'defacing the images in the church' and mutilating the noble seven-sacrament font.[24] There are no doubt other instances yet to be discovered in churchwardens' accounts, and perhaps the names of other paid iconoclasts besides that of Gilley.

Broadly speaking it may be said that the same measure of destruction took place in Norfolk and Suffolk alike. There are the same evidences of damage in both, the same absence in church after church of the decoration and furniture that must once have

[21] Dowsing, *Journal*, 16–17, 24.
[22] Ibid., 22, 26, 29.
[23] Blomefield, i, 69–70.
[24] N.A., ii, 64.

been there. There are the same exceptions, the same inexplicable survival of objects against which the Parliamentary ordinance was specifically directed. It has been suggested that the complete preservation of the seven-sacrament fonts at Gresham and Sloley, when so many others were hopelessly mutilated, may have been due to the churchwardens encasing the figures in plaster so that they presented a plain surface to the visitors. There were odd instances of compromise, as at Trunch and Burlingham St. Andrew, when the faces of saints in screens were obliterated with heavy scratches, and the figures themselves allowed to remain. But how did it come about that the angelic figures at Ranworth have survived totally unharmed in their splendid setting? Why are the apostles still at Beeston Regis, and the martyrs and doctors at Ludham, and the royal saints at Barton Turf? Were the wonderful roofs at Knapton and Cawston and Necton, crowded with cherubim and seraphim, spared merely because of the absence of ladders? Why did no one destroy the glass in the great chancel window at East Harling, or that at Ringland, much of which was only dispersed a century after these troubled times?

Most remarkable of all, perhaps, is the case of the glass at St. Peter Mancroft in Norwich. This glorious array of 'superstitious pictures' has come down to us largely intact, with its stories of the infancy and the passion of Jesus Christ, the series of scenes of the life and death of the Virgin Mary, the life of Saint Peter, the life of Saint John the Evangelist, with other saints and martyrs in truly 'Popish' abundance.[25] Yet St. Peter Mancroft was a severely Puritan church, with that pre-eminent Puritan the Rev. John Carter in charge of it throughout these years. There are of course stories, here and at East Harling and elsewhere, of the glass having been removed and buried until safer times. This could possibly have happened in a remote country parish, but in the largest church in Puritan Norwich it is improbable in the extreme. A tentative explanation is that St. Peter was a church in whose governance the parishioners had an unusually large voice; and that a natural impulse of parochial pride may have led them to preserve their own church from the fate that had overtaken the

[25] For the glass in these churches and elsewhere in Norfolk, see Christopher Woodforde, *The Norwich School of Glass-Painting* (Oxford, 1950), esp. Ch. III.

Cathedral. Just as at remote Felbrigg the Puritan Thomas Windham had saved the brasses of the Felbriggs from harm, so in busy Norwich the people of Mancroft may have stayed the hand of the despoiler.

4

The more intractable Puritan clergy, who had been ejected during Bishop Wren's episcopate or had retired abroad, were able to return with honour under the protection of the Long Parliament. William Bridge of St. Peter Hungate, who had settled at Rotterdam as minister of the English dissenting church, was invited to become the town preacher of Great Yarmouth, and established himself there in 1641. His friend John Ward of St. Michael at Plea shared with him the duties of the church at Rotterdam; but he fell out with Bridge and the majority of the congregation, and was deposed. Their disagreement was apparently on the vexed question of prophecy—should the private members of the church be permitted to prophesy 'after the Brownists' way', as Ward advocated, or should they be restrained from this exercise? After his deposition Ward returned to England and ministered at Colchester.[26]

Two of Wren's most stiff-necked adversaries, Jeremiah Burroughs and William Greenhill, did not return from Holland to their parishes in the Norwich diocese, but were summoned to minister at Stepney, where they attained great popularity. Burroughs was the morning and Greenhill the afternoon preacher, and they became known to their admirers as the morning and the evening star.

Another prominent Norwich Puritan, Thomas Allen of St. Edmund's, had emigrated in 1638 to New England. There he distinguished himself as 'a pious and painful preacher', and married the widow of the founder of Harvard College. He remained in America until 1651, when he returned to take charge of another Norwich parish, St. George Tombland. The story of Robert Peck of Hingham, who crossed the ocean to the township of the same name which had been founded in Massachusetts, was

[26] C. B. Jewson in N.A., xxx, 333–6. Browne, 112–4.

told in an earlier chapter. He came back to resume charge of his old parish in 1646, and died there ten years later.[27]

Other Puritan clergy, of varying degrees of prominence and conviction, were appointed to livings made vacant by the ejectment of their Royalist incumbents. For example Paul Amyraut of Wolterton, who had been deprived by Bishop Wren, was installed in the important benefice of East Dereham, from which John Bretten, its vicar for more than twenty years, had been ejected. His neighbour Thomas Case of Erpingham, who had been deprived by Wren at the same time, did not return to his Norfolk parish. A long and eventful career awaited him, as a chaplain in the Parliamentarian army, then rector of a large London parish, and finally an enthusiastic advocate for the return of Charles II.[28]

Case's successor at Erpingham, Thomas Hobbys, who was collated to the living by Bishop Montagu in 1640, remained there through all the changes of fortune in church and state until his death in 1674. A true Vicar of Bray, he recorded in his parish register in 1645 the abolition of the Prayer Book (*Exiit Liturgia Anglicana*) and its return seventeen years later (*Liturgia Anglicana restaurata est*) with the same unruffled calm. After his death his successor wrote in the register that Hobbys *hanc Ecclesiam in dubiis plerumque ac turbidis temporibus annos triginta tres moderate rexit*. There were many others who found themselves able to pursue the same moderate path—for example John Robinson of Elsing, who was presented to the living in 1617 by the Protestant wife of the Catholic Sir Anthony Browne; proved himself learned, pious and eloquent; 'successfully refuted both Romanists and schismatics'; and died in 1667 after half a century of tranquil possession of his benefice.[29]

5

On 12 June 1643 an ordinance was passed by the Lords and Commons 'for the calling of an assembly of learned and godly divines to be consulted with by the Parliament, for the settling of the government of the Church'. Such an assembly had first been

[27] S. E. Morison, *The Founding of Harvard College* (1935), 364, 394.
[28] A. G. Matthews, *Calamy Revised*, 10, 104.
[29] N.A., i, 290-1; vi, 206-9.

mooted early in 1642, when Parliament ordered the nomination
of two suitable divines by the knights and burgesses of each
county. On that occasion the Norfolk members put forward the
names of two leading Presbyterian clergymen, John Arrowsmith
of King's Lynn and Thomas Thorowgood of Little Massingham.
In the summer of 1643, when the negotiations with the Scots were
at a critical stage, the summoning of a larger and more influential
body, strongly Presbyterian in complexion, was an important and
necessary step.

This Westminster Assembly of Divines, as it was called, included a small number of the laity. Manchester was one of the ten
peers named. No one from Norfolk or Suffolk was among the
twenty laymen. The Norfolk divines whose names had already
been brought forward, Arrowsmith and Thorowgood, were of
course included, together with William Bridge of Yarmouth and
Henry Hall, Bachelor of Divinity, the rector of St. Andrew's in
Norwich. The last-named died in London shortly after his
appointment to the Assembly. Of former East Anglians the twin
stars of Stepney, Jeremiah Burroughs and William Greenhill, and
Thomas Case, once of Erpingham, were also members.[30]

The eloquence of these divines was an important weapon in the
struggle. We have already listened to William Bridge encouraging
the volunteers at Yarmouth; and similar exhortations poured forth
from the ministers in cities and towns and villages, from the chaplains in camp and in the field. But the leading Puritan clergy had
special responsibilities in this direction. From February 1642 onwards a fast was appointed on the last Wednesday of every month;
and Parliament listened to a sermon composed for the particular
occasion by some eminent divine, which was afterwards printed
at the request of the House. Professor Trevor-Roper has shown,
in a masterly essay, how these 'fast sermons' were used as an
instrument of policy by Pym and the other Parliamentarian leaders.
The preachers were selected with care; their texts and subject-
matter were prearranged; and it was thus contrived that, in the
words of Clarendon, 'the auditors might judge and commonly
foresaw what was like to be next done in the Parliament or
Council of State'.[31]

[30] Husband (1646), 208–10. Blomefield, iv, 301.
[31] H. R. Trevor-Roper, *Religion, the Reformation and Social Change*, 294–344.

One of these sermons was preached before Parliament by John Arrowsmith on 25 January 1643. It was entitled *The Covenant-Avenging Sword Brandished*, a reference to the text from Leviticus on which Arrowsmith based his discourse, *I will bring a sword upon you, that shall avenge the quarrel of my covenant*. The title-page bore a further text, *I came not to send peace, but a sword*; and in all respects the sermon was a sanguinary and intemperate performance. In Professor Trevor-Roper's words, 'its message was that bloody civil wars were peculiar signs of God's blessing on a country'. He points out that it was preached just before the unsuccessful negotiations with the King at Oxford, and was therefore 'singularly inappropriate to the opening of a peace-treaty'; but that Pym wished to present a firm front, was suspicious of the King's good faith, and was 'determined to negotiate only from the appearance of strength and radical resolve'. Arrowsmith was briefed accordingly; and hence his emphasis on blood and the sword, on warlike resolution, and on the irreclaimable wickedness of the malignants.[32]

This sermon of Arrowsmith's was a rich storehouse of Puritan invective, as indeed were his other writings. Parliament had converted England into a rich vineyard, had gathered out malignants as stones, had planted it with men of piety as choice vines, and 'made a winepress therein for the squeezing of delinquents'. Nor were the malignants alone assailed. In the nation as a whole 'Bibles lie moulding in corners, while lascivious stories and playbooks (the Devil's best catechisms, out of which his children learn satanical principles) are even worn out with over-diligent perusal'. His eloquence did not go unrewarded. In the following year he was promoted from his cure at Lynn to the mastership of St. Catherine's Hall at Cambridge, from which Manchester had lately ejected the Royalist master, Dr. Beale; and five years later he achieved the still more exalted position of Master of Trinity.[33]

A few weeks later the fast sermon was preached by William Bridge of Great Yarmouth. This discourse likewise was carefully suited to the moment, when the Queen was just about to arrive with reinforcements from Holland. Bridge's offering to Parliament, *Joab's Counsel and King David's Seasonable Hearing It*, was

---

[32] Ibid., 310–11.
[33] *The Covenant-Avenging Sword Brandished*, 3, 23. D.N.B. *sub* John Arrowsmith.

based on that monarch's ill-judged indulgence to his family. 'If the Queen of your bosom,' Bridge exhorted King Charles, 'stand in competition with your kingdom, you must not love her better than us, than it.' And he quoted the story of a Turkish sultan who slew his Queen in the presence of his subjects, to demonstrate 'how little I regard her in comparison with you'.[34]

Other divines with East Anglian connexions likewise preached before Parliament. Thomas Case's sermon was entitled *God's Rising, His Enemies Scattering*; William Greenhill's was *The Axe at the Root*. Thomas Thorowgood of Little Massingham struck a somewhat milder note with *Moderation Justified*, which he preached early in 1645 on the text from St. Paul's Epistle to the Philippians, *Let your moderation be known unto all men, the Lord is at hand.* Thorowgood remains a perplexing figure. He may have been a genuine Puritan moderate; or he may have been, as the course of his life rather suggests, an exceptionally dexterous time-server. The elaborate exercise in self-justification, which he addressed after the Restoration to the first Lord Townshend, in his capacity as Lord Lieutenant of Norfolk, was mentioned in an earlier chapter, with reference to his claims to have aided Royalist clerics and harboured Royalist fugitives. This document also had much to say about his views and conduct in matters of religion.

The whole of Thorowgood's plea to Townshend, at a time when 'heinous misrepresentations' were being made against his past behaviour, was based on the consistency of his moderation. He had seen no evil, he said, in attending the Westminster Assembly, 'for the divines by the act were called, not to determine but to be consulted with, as shall be most agreeable to the word of God'. That was true enough: the Assembly had no powers of legislation, and in fact the Commons overrode its advisory functions when it suited them to do so. He had some reservations about taking the Covenant, 'which I sub-signed, but after the rest, and not till I had given in my reasons especially in reference to episcopacy, for I presumed the King's Majesty and his posterity were well fenced therein.' One wonders if Townshend, who had been a child at the time of the Covenant, was familiar with its exact wording. During the debates of the Assembly, Thorowgood claimed, he had named divers learned and pious bishops with

[34] Trevor-Roper, op. cit., 312.

honour. This had not gone down at all well. 'In the Lords' House one of the officers was violent against me and drew blood from me, and being blamed for it he said I was a malignant, for he saw me talking to two of the most malignant doctors.'

As for his fast sermon, 'I am sure some of the House stared sufficiently upon me at the very reading of the text; my friends of the royal party did not believe at first that such a scripture had been sounded in the ears of the Commons in that juncture of affairs, when the mastery of the Army began to work.' The sermon did indeed contain a few vague aspirations towards a reconciliation between Parliament and King, provided always that such a reconciliation could be achieved without a return to the old evils of prelacy. But it was by no means so fervent a plea for moderate courses as Thorowgood would have liked Townshend to believe. In his *apologia* he claimed that the sermon was 'serious against church robbing and sacrilege, and suffering the fabrics of our churches to decay. It called for more charitable respect to episcopal men and their families, yea it inclined to moderation even unto papists'. Perhaps he relied on the unlikelihood that Townshend would examine the sermon carefully, even if he perused it at all. Most of it was in fact well attuned to the ears of the Parliament, such as the passage which, far from condemning sacrilege in churches, warmly applauded the destruction of their furnishings. 'I am glad for my part, they are scoured of their gay gazing, and I marvelled a great while since, how and why the organs grew so many, when the very homilies accused them for defiling God's house.' His protest about the decay of churches was dictated by considerations of comfort rather than of reverence. 'It was accounted a sin to be covered in them; and it is now a punishment in them not to be covered, a punishment by the wind and weather, from the roof and windows.'[35]

In fairness to Thorowgood, it may well have taken some courage to speak of moderation at all in the pulpit at the opening of 1645. But his subsequent career shows that the sermon in no way damaged his prospects as a rising Puritan divine. During that career, he told Townshend, he was able to give assistance to the former rulers of the Norwich diocese and chapter, Bishop Hall

[35] Thorowgood, *Moderation Justified, and the Lord's Being at Hand Improved* (1645), 16.

and Dean Hassall. He claimed further that many of the humbler sequestered ministers 'have publicly acknowledged my helpfulness, for my soul did sympathize in their miseries and the sad sufferings of their wives and children, and so much notice was taken of it that I was openly called the malignants' advocate for my solicitude in recovering the fifth part for them'. But he came to no harm. His vicissitudes during the Commonwealth and thereafter are outside the scope of this book. It is enough to say that he surmounted all difficulties, survived all revolutions, and died in great prosperity as rector of Great Cressingham in 1669. Looking back over his life, he concluded that his adversaries were envious of him, 'as if there had been somewhat of the serpent in me, that I have suffered no more and not been quite undone in these overturning times'. Let those adversaries remember the Master's precept, *Be wise as serpents and harmless as doves*. 'It hath been my study also and prayer to keep a good conscience; and if I have failed to any man in dovelike innocence, I will not only be sorry for my fault, but thankful to a friendly reprover.' And there let us leave him.[36]

[36] N.A., xxii, 311–37.

CHAPTER XIII

The Puritan Ascendancy

I

After the autumn of 1643 the Royalists of Norfolk could do no more. During the year they had made three attempts at concerted action—the gatherings at Lowestoft and at Augustine Holl's house at Heigham in March, and the seizure and siege of Lynn in August and September. All these enterprises had failed, two of them ignominiously. Henceforward they were powerless. The tides of the war rolled to and fro across the kingdom, but always further away from the territory of the Eastern Association.

Within that territory, the burdens of the war pressed heavily upon all classes. The voluntary contributions at the outset of the war had long since been replaced by compulsory assessments of ever-increasing harshness. In March 1643 an ordinance was issued 'for the speedy raising and levying of money for the maintenance of the army raised by the Parliament, and other great affairs of the Commonwealth'. The county of Norfolk and the city of Norwich were together required to pay the weekly sum of £1250; and a powerful committee was named to organize and enforce this levy.[1] In May came a further ordinance, more specifically directed at those who had not yet contributed, 'or if they have, yet not in any reasonable measure answerable to their estates'. The same committee was now empowered to exact from those reluctant donors an amount up to a fifth part of their yearly revenue in land, and up to a twentieth part of their personal estate and their goods and chattels. Distresses might be levied, houses broken open. There were penalties for concealment and subterfuge.[2]

Only a few months later, in October of the same year, it was found necessary to raise a loan of £66,666 13s. 4d. 'for the better enabling of our brethren of Scotland, for our assistance and

[1] Husband (1643), 932–47.
[2] Husband (1646), 169–75.

defence, in this common cause of religion and liberty'. The Scots had in fact made such a payment one of the conditions for their entry into the war. This loan was levied by compulsion upon the rich and reluctant—those whose estates exceeded £1000 in value— but was otherwise voluntary. The assessment for Norfolk and Norwich was £6000.

An so it continued, seemingly without the prospect of an end. In January 1644 the weekly assessment for Norfolk and Norwich was raised from £1250 to £1850. All this was in addition to occasional levies for special purposes within the Eastern Association, and to emergency demands for arms and more particularly for horses. The estates of active Royalists living within the eastern counties mostly remained under sequestration until the compounding system was introduced towards the end of the war. It was reckoned that in September 1644 one-eighth of the entire county was still under sequestration.[3] The committees also dealt rigorously with passive Royalists or persons of neutral sympathies, those described in one ordinance as men 'who have not either upon this or the like occasions of money heretofore manifested their good affections to the public'. But these constant exactions grew burdensome in time even to the most committed Parliamentarians.[4]

Along with the raising of money went the impressment of men. Voluntary enlistment, and the assembling by wealthy gentlemen of their own troops of horse or foot, soon proved inadequate. As had already been mentioned, the trained bands were not under any obligation to march beyond their county boundaries. So in August 1643 it was ordered that 20,000 soldiers should be impressed within the six counties of the Eastern Association, together with as many gunners, trumpeters and surgeons as should be required. By the following January it was publicly announced that the six counties, together with the more recently associated county of Lincolnshire, had raised 14,000 horse, foot and dragoons. There was a great deal of wastage, however, partly by casualty and disease, but still more through desertion. When the New Model Army was raised in 1645, further impressment took place; but even so its commander, Sir Thomas Fairfax,

[3] B.M. Add. MS. 15,903, f. 40.
[4] Husband (1646), 371–4, 413, 492, 551, 607.

complained bitterly of 'the difficulty of raising recruits in the Associated Counties, which are so populous, and their suffering men that run from the Army to return and continue unquestioned among them'.[5]

Like the rank and file of all armies in all wars, these men left no individual record behind them. Siegfried Sassoon wrote of the thousands of 'intolerably nameless names' inscribed on the Menin Gate. Of the men who struggled and prevailed at Marston Moor and Naseby, we do not know even the names. Only occasionally, in parish accounts and similar documents, do we come across some trace of their existence; and the details are confusing enough, since seventeenth-century churchwardens and constables were neither very literate nor very methodical.

Many of them were unwilling soldiers, like those paraded by Justice Shallow before Sir John Falstaff in a play first acted barely fifty years earlier. Whole classes and categories were exempt from service, including any person, or the son of any person, rated in the subsidy books at five pounds in goods or three pounds in lands. The menial servants of peers and members of Parliament were specifically exempted;[6] and local justices and committeemen likewise took good care of their own servants and farmhands. Most young men of martial temperament and adventurous spirit had already volunteered. Those impressed by Parliamentary ordinance either went reluctantly and with resentment, or had decided that army pay and the chance of some plunder were preferable to such wages as they might obtain at home. Sometimes a parish took the opportunity to get rid of a bad character. The churchwardens of Swaffham in 1643 paid the wife of a man named Balls one pound 'when her husband was in the jail 10 weeks', and another pound 'when her husband was gone for a soldier 20 weeks'.[7] The parish constable of East Barsham even received specific instructions from the Deputy Lieutenants to choose for impressment 'idle serving men, and such other able persons as live dissolutely or idly without employment'.[8]

It was the task of the parish constable to convey the men thus

[5] Firth, *Cromwell's Army*, 15–21, 35–6. Husband (1646), 288–9, 413, 623.
[6] Husband (1646), 623–4.
[7] Rix, *The Pride of Swaffham* (1950), 38.
[8] H.M.C., le Strange, 101–2.

impressed to the appointed place of mustering, and where necessary to keep a very strict watch upon them. Thus at Gissing the
constable, George Kerrison, conveyed to Thetford the 'two
pressed soldiers' of that parish, Roger Strong and Richard
Pattericke; and his successor Thomas Rix expended two shillings
'for firing, candle, house-room and lodging when James Tofts
was impressed, three days'.[9]

None of the men impressed at Gissing appears to have given
any trouble; but it was a different story a few miles away at
Stockton. Here, as in many small parishes, the duties of churchwarden and constable were carried out by the same man. In
1643–4 the posts were jointly filled by Arthur Shelton and
William Woodroofe; and the names of the two pressed soldiers
from Stockton, John Bird and John Rivett, frequently appear in
their accounts. Shelton paid Bird one shilling for his press money,
seventeen shillings for cloth and other materials for a new suit,
five shillings for making the suit and turning an old doublet,
2/10 for a pair of shoes, 2/3 for a pair of stockings, 3/4 for a new
shirt. He also gave him 1/2 at the christening of his child. But
Bird remained unreconciled to his lot. Shelton paid 11/– 'for
keeping of the said Bird after he was pressed four days, and for
two men to look to him all the while'; and there was a further
entry of 2/6 'to Thomas Goslen, John Bellard, and Richard
Rivett also, for looking to the said Bird to keep him in awe'.
Woodroofe's accounts show payments for conducting Bird and
Rivett to Thetford, where the army received them.

A year later the accounts of John Pratt, 'churchwarden, over-
seer and constable', show two new 'town soldiers', Robert Seaman and William Bettes. Bird and Rivett had both become
casualties. Rivett returned home wounded after some unspecified
action: there is mention of a sickness of seventeen weeks, and
Mr. Jenny, a surgeon from Bungay, coming to minister to him.
John Bird likewise 'returned home maimed from Naseby fight'.
The churchwardens attempted to console him by the gift of
4½ lbs. of cheese, which cost them ninepence. And so John Bird
disappears from history.[10]

Scarcely more is known about the individual rank and file of

9 Gissing Town Book. Extracts kindly supplied by the late Eric Pursehouse.
10 Town Books of Stockton, quoted in N.A., i, 182–7.

Cromwell's own regiment, the Ironsides—it was a Royalist nickname, at first for Cromwell himself and in later years for his soldiers, and none was ever better deserved. The Maiden Troop under Robert Swallow, first raised by the subscriptions of the young men and girls of Norwich, retained its identity and its East Anglian complexion for many years to come. Two Norfolk privates in Major Swallow's troop died on service in Scotland in 1655, and their wills have survived. Robert Wildman from Wymondham, sick in body but well in mind, declared his last wishes in the presence of Nicholas Spilman, corporal, and William Whitaker, private soldier, both of the same troop. Gregory Ellis of Northrepps bequeathed his property mainly to the sons of his brother John, and to John himself his silver buttons and a silver hatband. His horse, accoutrements and pistols were to be sold to defray the charges of his burial. He gave all his clothes to William Sprint, 'my loving friend and fellow soldier in the same troop', together with three roe-skins: and a stag's skin to George Clarke, also of the troop.[11]

The long service of another Norfolk soldier, Edmund Peckover of Fakenham, is attested by the certificate of good conduct given on his discharge, a document still in the possession of his descendants.

'These are to certify whom it may concern that Edmund Peckover, gentleman, served as a soldier in the troop of William Colman, major; after him Joseph Blisett, captain, had and hath still the command of the same troop under command of the Right Honourable Lieutenant-General Charles Fleetwood, whom is Colonel in the service of the Commonwealth; both in England and Scotland, from the year of our Lord one thousand six hundred and forty six until the year one thousand six hundred fifty and five: during which time he behaved himself faithfully and honestly, as become a soldier. In witness whereof we have hereunto set our hands and seals this sixth of August 1655.

JOSEPH BLISETT.
HUGH PARRYE.'[12]

[11] N.A., v, 213-4.
[12] Kingston, 355-6. I recopied the document in 1949, when it was in the possession of the late A. P. D. Penrose, whose mother was a member of the Peckover family.

2

The coming of the Scots led to momentous events during 1644. The whole aspect of the war in the north was changed; and the Marquis of Newcastle, on whose southward advance in the previous summer the Royalists of East Anglia had placed such hopes, found himself in April closely besieged by a combination of English and Scottish forces in the city of York. In June these forces, under Fairfax and Leven respectively, were reinforced by Manchester's army of the Eastern Association, with Cromwell in charge of the cavalry. At the beginning of July they shattered the army of Prince Rupert, who was advancing to the relief of York, in the savage battle of Marston Moor. This virtually put an end to the Royalist cause in the northern counties of England. York surrendered a fortnight later. Newcastle himself took ship and retired abroad.

The town of Newcastle had been under siege by the Scots since January, and did not capitulate until October. This was a serious matter for London, since virtually its entire coal supply came from Newcastle by sea. Newcastle coal came likewise to Norwich, along the river from Yarmouth. At some time during 1644—the date is uncertain—a subscription was raised in Norwich 'for raising money towards regaining the town of Newcastle'; and the subscription list happens to have survived among the city archives. The citizens are listed, ward by ward, and a surprising number of them are recorded as having 'denied to contribute any money for the purpose before mentioned'. This need not in all cases be regarded as an indication of Royalist sympathies. Allowance must be made for the close-fisted, the hard-up, and those who felt that the frequent obligatory levies were more than enough. Even so, it is remarkable that so many citizens in a Puritan-dominated community flatly declined to spare a few extra shillings in support of the Parliament at this critical juncture. The list must have included all the merchants and tradesmen of any substance, together with a sprinkling of private residents and a few widows. Yet in fact there were only 212 persons who subscribed a total of £516, as against 252 who refused to subscribe at all.

The largest subscriber was Sir John Hobart, who paid £40. He was living in his great house at Chapel Field, and may already have made Blickling over to his daughter and her husband, his nephew and namesake. Most subscriptions however ranged between £5 and 10/-. Naturally the leading Puritan aldermen and councillors subscribed largely—Smyth, Toft, Lindsey, Rayley, Greenwood. Likewise there are several known Royalists among those who refused—William Gostling the Mayor deposed in 1642; John Osborne, Joseph Payne, Francis and Thomas Cory, most of whom had been in trouble in 1643. Dr. de Laune, the pastor of the Walloon church, also declined to pay. But the most interesting name in this list of the 'deniers' is that of Doctor Browne, then living in the ward of North Conesford.[13]

3

Thomas Browne was born in 1605. After several years of medical study abroad, at the universities of Montpellier, Padua and Leyden, and an uncertain period of practice in England, he finally settled at Norwich in 1637. Four years later he married Dorothy, daughter of Edward Mileham, a gentleman living at North Burlingham. In December 1642, a few months after the outbreak of war, a London bookseller published, without his authority, a volume entitled *Religio Medici*, which he had written a year or two before he came to Norwich and which had hitherto been circulated only in manuscript copies.

Despite the anxieties of the war, this exploration of his own mind by an unknown provincial doctor was received with interest and warm approval. In 1643 the same bookseller issued an authorized version with Browne's corrections and some additions. Further interest was roused by the printing of the admiring if occasionally critical *Observations* on the book by Sir Kenelm Digby, written while that volatile character was a prisoner of the Parliament. Next year a Latin translation, printed at Leyden,

---

[13] N.A., xv, 149-60. The list is included in a volume of miscellaneous accounts among the Norwich Corporation MSS. It bears the date of 1643, in what appears to be a later hand. In the absence of other indications, I have assumed that it belongs in fact to 1644.

established Browne's reputation throughout the European world of learning.

No book could have been less in tune than *Religio Medici* with the angry times in which it first appeared. Although composed in the sixteen-thirties, it never touched on the political issues of those years—monarchy, prelacy, power. And in its portrayal of one man's religion, the consistent emphasis was upon the virtues of tolerance and charity. Browne had arrived in Norwich in time to witness the closing stages of Bishop Wren's drive against the Puritans. Now he was living in the midst of the Puritan counter-persecution. Mrs. Bennett, in her illuminating study of Browne's writings and thought, has remarked that in 1643 he included in the authorized version of his book a paragraph which had not appeared in the manuscript copies or the unauthorized issue, condemning the folly of mutual intolerance among Christians. ' 'Tis true we all hold there is a number of elect and many to be saved; yet take our opinions together, and from the confusion thereof there will be no such thing as salvation, nor shall any one be saved . . . Thus whilst the mercies of God do promise us heaven, our conceits and opinions exclude us from that place. There must be therefore more than one Saint Peter; particular churches and sects usurp the gates of Heaven, and turn the key against each other; and thus we go to Heaven against each others' wills, conceits and opinions, and, with as much uncharity as ignorance, do err I fear in points, not only of our own, but one another's salvation.' Surely Mrs. Bennett is right in suggesting that this passage was prompted by the increasing animosities of the war.[14]

On the strength of his refusal to pay the Newcastle subscription, Browne has sometimes been regarded as an ardent Royalist, only precluded by circumstances from active support of the King. There is no reason to accept this view. He remained throughout his life on equally friendly terms with Puritan families like the Hobarts and Royalist families like the Pastons. They were all his worthy and honoured friends. Although he was repelled by iconoclasm, as by every other form of intolerance, he aimed to pursue a moderate path to the end of his days. His dislike was reserved for the fickle and irresponsible multitude. 'Neither in the

[14] Joan Bennett, *Sir Thomas Browne* (1962), 94. Browne, *Works*, i, 67.

name of multitude do I only include the base and minor sort of people; there is a rabble even amongst the gentry, a sort of plebeian heads, whose fancy moves with the same wheel as these; men in the same level with mechanics, though their fortunes do somewhat gild their infirmities, and their purses compound for their follies.'[15]

So he devoted the years of the war to compiling an enormous treatise, *Pseudodoxia Epidemica: or Enquiries into very many received Tenets, and commonly presumed Truths*, which was more conveniently known, both in his time and ever afterwards, as *Enquiries into Vulgar Errors*. He was already the foremost local physician, famed throughout East Anglia, constantly summoned to the sick-beds of wealthy patients all over Norfolk and Suffolk, and practising in Norwich among rich and poor alike. His literary work, he explained in the preface, had to take second place to his professional duties, being 'composed by snatches of time, as medical vacations, and the fruitless importunity of uroscopy would permit us'. In consequence 'perhaps it hath not found that regular and constant style, those infallible experiments and those assured determinations, which the subject sometime requireth, and might be expected from others, whose quiet doors and unmolested hours afford no such distractions.'[16]

We do not know when he began to write *Vulgar Errors*. It is undoubtedly based on notes and extracts which had been accumulating during many years. But he must have worked upon it throughout the war, since it was licenced in 1645, and published during the following year, when the war had come to an end. Again the book bore no trace of the disturbed times in which it was composed. Like *Religio Medici* it was instinct with tolerance and humane wisdom, a world away from the vociferous pamphlets and furious sermons which were pouring from the press throughout those years. It was written in the same incomparable style, though often with a richer texture which foreshadowed the splendours and obscurities of his later works. It contained humour as well as humanity, wit as well as eloquence, passages full of extravagance and fantasy.

Night after night, when the city gates were shut and the streets

[15] Ibid., i, 71.
[16] Ibid., ii, 4.

were silent, Browne worked at his huge task. His speculations ranged over scripture and mythology, the created world and the world of illusion, history ancient and modern, the sciences and the arts. Galen and Hippocrates, Aristotle and Pliny were his favourite sources, to be cited or to be contradicted; but there were countless other authorities on the shelves of his crowded study. Seldom has a writer been more lavish in his quotations. The basilisk and the unicorn were his subjects, the kingfisher and the hare, the mandrake and the mistletoe, Balaam's ass and the wandering Jew, Methusaleh and Pope Joan. It was an extraordinary book to have been completed at the climax of a civil war, and published at its close; and it was the only significant work of art, of any kind, that was achieved in East Anglia during those troubled years.

4

Although the victory at Marston Moor brought control of the north, the Parliamentary cause did not prosper during the remainder of 1644. Far away in Scotland, the Royalists of that country rallied under Montrose and embarked on a series of dazzling successes. In the west of England the King's own forces penned the army commanded by Essex into the Cornish peninsula. Essex escaped by sea, but the infantry under Philip Skippon were compelled to surrender. Having given up their arms and ordnance, they were allowed to march back as best they could to their distant bases.

In the army of the Eastern Association, serious disagreement now developed between Manchester and Cromwell. Hitherto they had acted in harmony, with Cromwell serving loyally under Manchester's command. They were neighbours and friends, with the same Huntingdonshire background; and during the opening years of the Parliament and the war their outlook had been the same. But they were men of very different temperaments, and the contrast grew more evident under the stress of war. Manchester began to hesitate and to draw back. He still believed in the possibility of accommodation with the King, combined with the abolition of episcopacy and the establishment of that Presbyterian form of government which he so fervently desired. Cromwell thought of nothing but the urgent and victorious prosecution of the war. He did not share Manchester's view of the monarchy as an institution; and although he had taken the Covenant, his religious views leaned towards Independency rather than Presbyterianism. Anger flared up between them. There were wrangles and recriminations, with Cromwell deploring Manchester's lethargy, and Manchester accusing Cromwell of insubordination and faction.

Their conflicting views were expressed during an altercation at a council of war shortly after the second battle of Newbury. Cromwell and his supporters were eager to follow up their advantage and defeat the King, decisively and finally, before the arrival of certain French troops which were believed to have been sent to reinforce him. Manchester refused to engage in any further pursuit. Cromwell's own version of the words that passed between them was given in evidence at a subsequent inquiry. 'The Earl answered . . . "that if we should beat the King never so often, yet he would be King still and his posterity, but if he should beat us but once we must be hanged and our posterity undone", or words to that effect; to which this examinant [Cromwell himself] replied, "that if this principle was true it condemned all our former fighting as foolish, and was an argument against fighting in the future, and a ground for making a peace how dishonourable soever".'[17]

Their subordinates likewise took sides; and the army of the Eastern Association was now divided, both over the prosecution of the war and on matters of religion, since the cleavage between Presbyterians and Independents steadily widened. Cromwell openly attacked Manchester in the Commons in November, and Manchester denounced Cromwell in the Lords. In December there was introduced into Parliament what came to be known as the Self-Denying Ordinance, by which no member of either House should hold military office. This meant that both Manchester and Essex would have to resign their commands, being unable to divest themselves of their peerages: while Cromwell would be able to resign his seat in the Commons and retain his army command. In the end the Ordinance was modified, so that members of

[17] C.S.P.D., 1644/5, 151. See also Bruce, *Quarrel between Manchester and Cromwell*, passim.

either House, having laid down their commissions, might be reappointed if both Houses thought fit. Its effect, however, was the eventual withdrawal of Essex and Manchester, and the formation of the New Model Army under the command of Fairfax and Cromwell.

While these high matters were under debate, a curious minor episode was taking place in Norfolk. Sir Hamon L'Estrange's youngest son Roger, after fighting beside his father throughout the siege of Lynn, had made his way to the King at Oxford. He was an enthusiastic, hot-headed, plausible young man; and throughout his long life, which lasted into the next century, he was perpetually evolving ambitious schemes and failing to bring them to fruition. At Oxford he managed to convince the King and his advisers, contrary to all the evidence, that a spirit of resistance was still strongly alive in Norfolk, and particularly in the town of Lynn. Rather surprisingly, he further persuaded them that he was the most suitable person to organize and lead an uprising of the loyal subjects of that region. Towards the close of 1644, therefore, the King gave him the following commission.

'CHARLES R.

'We having received from our trusty and well beloved Roger L'Estrange, declarations of the good affections of divers of our well affected subjects of our counties of Norfolk and Suffolk, and particularly of our town of Lynn, we have thought fit forthwith to return our royal thanks unto our said well affected subjects; and particularly to give our said trusty and well beloved Roger L'Estrange these encouragements to proceed in our service, principally in the work of reducing the said town of Lynn.

'1. That in case that attempt shall be gone through withal, he the said Roger L'Estrange shall have the government of the place.

'2. That what engagements shall be made unto the inhabitants of the said place, or any other persons capable of contributing effectually to that service, by way of reward, either in employment in his Majesty's navy, or forts, or in moneys, not exceeding the sum of £5,000, the service being performed, shall be punctually made good unto them.

'3. That they shall in this work receive what assistance may be given them from any of our nearest garrisons.

'4. That when our said town shall be reduced unto our obedience we shall forthwith send thither such a considerable power, as shall be sufficient to relieve and preserve them; we being at present (even without this) fully resolved to send a considerable power to encourage our faithful subjects in those parts, and to regain our rights and interests there.

'Given at our Court at Oxford, this 28th of November 1644.

'By his Majesty's command,

'GEORGE DIGBY.'[18]

Armed with this remarkable document, Roger L'Estrange set forth single-handed to restore the town of Lynn, and the surrounding countryside, to the obedience of the King. He went straight to Appleton Hall, a lonely house belonging to William Paston, a kinsman of Sir William Paston of Oxnead, some six miles to the north-east of Lynn. Paston was a noted Royalist and recusant, and was apparently away from home at this time, possibly in prison. After being welcomed by Mrs. Paston at this safe retreat, L'Estrange sent for a certain Leaman, 'a sea-captain belonging to Lynn', with whom he had had some previous acquaintance at Oxford, and whom he believed to be, if not a convinced Royalist, at least a man who could easily be bribed. He showed Leaman his commission, and offered him £1,000 and substantial promotion if he would assist in forming a party within the town and delivering it up to the King. Leaman agreed to the suggestion, and promised to return to Appleton next day to discuss matters further. He then went back to Lynn and told the Governor, Colonel Valentine Walton, exactly what had occurred. On Walton's instructions, he returned to Appleton next day as had been arranged, taking with him one Corporal Hagar, disguised as a seaman, and purporting to be 'a man for their turn . . . a poor man living in Fishers-End in Lynn, and kept an ale-house, and was £40 the worse for the Roundheads'. Hagar asked to be satisfied of L'Estrange's authority to act as he was doing; whereupon he took the King's commission out of a hole in the canopy of his bed, read it to them, and put it in his pocket. In the meantime a Lieutenant Stubbing and five soldiers, all dressed as poor seamen, came to the house and pushed their way into the courtyard, asking

[18] Rushworth, III, ii, 805.

for alms. Mrs. Paston went upstairs and told L'Estrange that there were six poor seamen from Lynn begging down below. He sent them down a shilling and a request to go away; but they all rushed up the stairs, arrested and searched L'Estrange, found his commission and carried him off in custody to Lynn. A few days afterwards he was sent up to London to be tried for his life as a spy.

His father of course fell at once under suspicion, although it is unlikely that he was privy to his son's hare-brained scheme. The old Cavalier was now anxious only to live quietly, to rebuild his shattered estate, and to obtain if possible some remission of the heavy claims brought against him by those who had suffered damage during the siege of Lynn. Nevertheless his wife's accounts mention his expenses when he 'was taken and carried to Lynn and there retained ten days about receiving of his son Roger, and divers days at Lynn attending that before he was discharged'.[19]

The whole affair was a humiliating fiasco, which was frequently to be brought up against Roger L'Estrange by his adversaries in the political and personal controversies of later years. There can be no doubt that he had made a rather poor showing; and that, entrusted with an important duty by his King, he fell easily into a very simple trap. On the other hand, he had no reason to doubt the good faith of Leaman, whom he would hardly have approached in this way if he had not known him in the past as a staunch Royalist. His failure was the result of inexperience and a sanguine temperament; and he very nearly paid for his errors of judgement with his life.

The distinction between military duty and espionage is particularly hard to define during a civil war; and in the course of 1644 the Parliament had acted severely in certain cases whose rights lay along this delicate margin. The ordinary course of civilian life was inextricably tangled up with the war. At first both sides had made concessions, so that under certain conditions ladies might visit their husbands, children might obtain the blessing of their dying parents, lawyers might consult their clients and stewards receive orders from their masters. But by 1644 the increasing bitterness of the war, and certain breaches of faith that had occurred, brought this easy-going traffic to an end.

[19] N.N.R.O., L'Estrange MSS., 7.

Parliament had clearly laid down that 'whatsoever persons shall come from Oxford or any part of the King's army to London or the parts adjacent, or to any part of the army under the command of the Earl of Essex, etc., without the warrant of both Houses of Parliament, shall be apprehended as spies and intelligencers, and proceeded against according to the rules of war'. Moreover the King's party had adopted a policy of tampering with the governors of important towns and men in similar positions of trust; and Roger L'Estrange's commission was typical of many that were issued by the King in varying circumstances during this time. On several occasions during 1644, and especially towards the close of the year when L'Estrange's attempt in Lynn took place, exemplary justice was meted out by sentence of court martial in cases of this type. Sir Alexander Carew, governor of the fortress-island of St. Nicholas in Plymouth Sound, was detected in corresponding with the enemy and in conspiring to deliver up his island to the King. He was tried by court martial at the Guildhall in November, and beheaded in the following month. Early in December the same court sat in trial on Sir John Hotham, the governor of Hull. He had declared his support for Parliament even before the actual outbreak of the war, and had closed the gates of the town against the King; subsequently he turned against his new masters, and had conspired to surrender Hull to the Royalists. He and his son were also condemned, and were executed at the beginning of January. In comparison with these distinguished traitors, Roger L'Estrange was small game; but the Parliamentary leaders were determined to put an end to treachery and espionage behind their lines, and he was tried in the Guildhall by court martial just as Carew and the Hothams had lately been tried, and with the same end in view.

The trial opened on 26 December. The case of the Judge-Advocate, Mr. Mills, was simple enough. L'Estrange's commission was not the commission of a soldier, but 'a commission of bribery and corruption, being merely to make a party in the town by clandestine ways with baits and promises of money and preferment'; he had come with this commission 'into the quarters of the Parliament without drum, trumpet or pass, which alone brings him within the danger and penalty of a spy'; he had come without forces as an enemy, but 'all alone, in a secret clandestine manner, and made choice of a solitary place near Lynn, to obscure himself the better to effect his treacherous design'; in short, he was a spy and a traitor, and must suffer as such.

L'Estrange argued gallantly and volubly in his own defence. He maintained that his commission 'was the commision of a soldier, enabling him to raise and conduct such a party as should attempt the surprisal of the town'; that Appleton Hall was not garrisoned by Parliamentary troops, and so was not within the Parliament's quarters, nor was Leaman a member of the garrison; 'that he came as a fair and open enemy, never pretending to be any other than he was; and had no treacherous ends; and therefore being thus apprehended was by the laws and customs of war, a just enemy and prisoner of war'. After much argument the trial was adjourned until the 28th, when the court found him guilty 'as a spy and treacherous conspirator, in endeavouring to betray the town and garrison of Lynn'; and the President, Sir John Corbett, sentenced him to be hanged by the neck until he was dead.

His execution was fixed for 2 January; but he petitioned the House of Lords for a reprieve on the grounds of his youth and the hard measure he had received. He also addressed a personal appeal to the Earl of Essex, who was still, for a few months to come, commander in chief of the army of the Parliament. Although in strict justice his sentence was fully warranted, a good deal of compassion was aroused by his case, and particularly by the contrast between his offence and his past record and those of the Hothams, who were about to suffer the same penalty by a less ignominious means. Finally a letter arrived from Prince Rupert to Essex, one of those courteous interchanges which the circumstances of the war still allowed.

'MY LORD,

'The occasion of my sending unto you at this time is the report of one Mr. Roger L'Estrange, his being condemned to death at London upon a charge of having undertaken somewhat for the reducing Lynn to his Majesty's obedience. If the person be found guilty of any treachery as having been engaged anywise upon your side, I shall not interfere. But if not I should be sorry that any bloody example should be begun at this season, contrary to that fair quarter which hath hitherto been observed on His Majesty's part in this unhappy war. For a particular conclusion of which no man prays more heartily than

'Your Lordship's servant,
'RUPERT.'[20]

In the end the various appeals prevailed. L'Estrange was reprieved and was committed to prison in Newgate. He was visited there, before his reprieve was assured, by two of the Norfolk representatives at the Assembly of Divines, who were also neighbours of his father in west Norfolk—the Rev. John Arrowsmith and the Rev. Thomas Thorowgood. Though his life was still at stake, he staunchly resisted their persuasions that he should take the Covenant; and in general he maintained the attitude of unswerving loyalty to which he gave expression in the famous poem, 'Beat on, proud billows; Boreas blow', often entitled *Loyalty Confined* or *A Hymn to Confinement*. This excellent poem, so light-hearted and defiant, and in its concluding stanzas so fine an expression of the cavalier spirit, achieved a wide popularity, and was circulated in manuscript for several years before it could appear in print.

What though I cannot see my King
　　Either in his person or his coin;
Yet contemplation is a thing
　　Will render what I have not, mine:
My King from me what adamant can part
Whom I do wear engraven in my heart?

My soul's as free as the ambient air,
　　Although my baser part's immured,
While loyal thoughts do still repair
　　To accompany my solitude:
And though rebellion do my body bind
My King can only captivate my mind.

[20] The story of Roger L'Estrange's attempt on King's Lynn has been reconstructed from Rushworth, III, ii, 804-7, together with various autobiographical passages in his own writings. The account in Kitchin, *Sir Roger L'Estrange* (1913), 11-21, has also been used, but with some caution.

Have you beheld the nightingale,
  A pilgrim turned into a cage,
How still she tells her wonted tale
  In this her private hermitage?
E'en there her chanting melody doth prove
That all her bars are trees, her cage a grove.

  I am the bird whom they combine
    Thus to deprive of liberty;
  And though they do my corpse confine,
    Yet, maugre hate, my soul is free,
And though immured, yet here I'll chirp and sign,
Disgrace to rebels, glory to my King.[21]

L'Estrange remained in Newgate for more than three years, frequently petitioning for a rehearing of his case or for release on grounds of ill-health, but without success. Early in 1648, according to his own account, he made his escape 'with the privity of his keeper'. Clarendon, who disliked him, expressed it differently: 'being kept in prison till the end of the war, he was then set at liberty, as one in whom there was no more danger.'[22] Whatever the circumstances of his release, L'Estrange had lost none of his Royalist ardour; and he promptly engaged in a rising in Kent, one of the series of events known as the Second Civil War.

[21] The four concluding stanzas of the poem, taken from the late Norman Ault's *Seventeenth Century Lyrics* (1928). Mr. Ault's text was that of the earliest copy which he had been able to discover, a manuscript written about 1650. In this copy the poem is entitled 'Mr. Le Strange his Verses in the Prison at Linn'; but as he can only have been confined at Lynn for a very few days before being removed for trial to London, and the whole tone of the poem appears to suggest a protracted imprisonment, I assume that it was actually written in Newgate and probably after his reprieve.

[22] Clarendon, iii, 104.

CHAPTER XIV

The Puritan Victory

I

The year 1645 opened with the execution of Archbishop Laud on 10 January. After his four years of imprisonment in the Tower, and the destruction of all that he had striven to achieve in church and state, his enemies were still eager for his blood. Their vengeance was gratified, and the Church of England had a new martyr.

During February there was a final attempt at negotiation between King and Parliament. Their respective commissioners met at Uxbridge, and the hopes of moderate men on both sides were raised once more. But the King, with that strange optimism which only increased with his adversity, was determined to give no ground. His letters to the Queen, which were to fall into the hands of Parliament after Naseby and were then printed for all the nation to see, left no doubt of his resolve. 'There is little or no appearance,' he told her, 'but that this summer will be the hottest for war of any that hath been yet: and be confident, that in making peace, I shall ever show my constancy in adhering to Bishops, and all our friends, and not forget to put a period to this perpetual Parliament.'[1] The more forceful elements in the Commons were equally resolved to pursue the war to an end. The negotiations broke down, and the measures to create the New Model Army were carried through.

The idea of the New Model was by no means welcome to many of the officers who had hitherto been prominent in the Eastern Association. Local security and the defence of their own area still dominated their minds. These leaders of county committees had joined together for the protection of a particular group of counties, and were unwilling to campaign beyond their boundaries. Some of them were also uneasy about their personal dignity, and the appointment and promotion of their social

[1] *The King's Cabinet Opened* (1645), 7.

inferiors. It was to the Suffolk Committee that Cromwell had addressed his famous remark: 'I had rather have a plain russet-coated captain that knows what he fights for, and loves what he knows, than that which you call a gentleman and is nothing else.'[2] In the controversy between Cromwell and Manchester, the gentlemen of the committees were almost unanimous in their support of the Earl.

On January a remarkable conference of the Associated Counties took place at Bury St. Edmunds. The respresentatives from Norfolk were Sir John Palgrave, Sir Edward Astley, Thomas Sotherton, Robert Jermy, Robert Woods, John Spelman and Tobias Frere, together with John Greenwood from Norwich. There was a full day's meeting, at which every detail of the projected New Model was discussed. Might not the new army, whatever its disadvantages, be for the safety of the kingdom? 'To this it was replied that notwithstanding it might be for the safety of the kingdom, yet that was not our work.' Did the proposed incorporation of their own army into the New Model not impair the Association? 'Affirmed by the most that the consistence thereof was taken away, and by all that the ends and purposes thereof are abrogated.' After full discussion of these and many other questions, a letter was addressed to Parliament in which all their 'sad apprehensions' were recited. The reorganization of the army would 'take away from them not only the head and body of their strength designed, promised, and by ordinance settled for their mutual assistance, but also deprive them of means of future subsistence and consistence and so render their solemn promise of Association ineffectual, which God Almighty hitherto hath graciously honoured by witness of concurrence with success of victory to the army and general peace for the most part even to their borders, to the wonderment of all observers and envy of the enemy'. They would be 'left naked to the secret malignants at home and to the watchful enraged enemy abroad'. Recruits would be hard to obtain, 'especially to unknown captains and commanders'. They therefore offered certain suggestions designed to safeguard as far as possible their independence and freedom of action.[3]

[2] Carlyle, *Cromwell*, i, 154.
[3] Alan Everitt, *Suffolk and the Great Rebellion* (Suffolk Record Society, 1961), 33–4, 83–9.

Small account was taken of the apprehensions and objections that were raised by the local committees. The New Model came swiftly into being, with Sir Thomas Fairfax at its head. Essex withdrew into private life, and Manchester took little further part in military affairs. Cromwell laid down his commission, in accordance with the Self-Denying Ordinance; but the second place in the command, that of Lieutenant-General, was left vacant, and after an interval he was formally appointed to it. Philip Skippon was made Major-General. 'The new army consisted of eleven regiments of horse, each numbering six hundred men, twelve regiments of foot, each of twelve hundred, with a thousand dragoons, and a small train of artillery. About half the infantry was composed of men who had served under Essex, Manchester and Waller; the rest were pressed men, raised by the county authorities. Of the cavalry, more than half was drawn from the former army of the Eastern Association.'[4]

The ordinance establishing the new army was dated 15 February. A monthly assessment was levied for its expenses, and on this occasion the city of Norwich was for the first time assessed separately from the county of Norfolk. The county was required to find £7070 each month, and the city £366. The task of raising it was entrusted to a large committee, on which occurred the names of several men of Royalist or neutral sympathies who had now come to terms with the prevailing power. They included Sir William Paston, Sir William D'Oyly, John Buxton and Edward Heyward, all of whom have figured in this narrative in a different context. Five days later, another ordinance empowered the same committee to raise a further monthly levy in Norfolk and Norwich of £1825 3s. 4d. 'towards the maintenance of the Scottish army under the Earl of Leven'.[5]

There were further ordinances for the impressment of men, and Fairfax's complaint of their frequent desertions has already been quoted. In July there was yet another ordinance for the raising of 500 horse in the Eastern Association, 100 of which were to be provided by Norfolk.[6] A summons in connection with this ordinance, addressed by some of the committee on 18 July to Francis

---

[4] Firth, *Oliver Cromwell*, 117-8.
[5] Husband (1646), 599-615.
[6] Ibid., 687.

Neve, gentleman, of Witchingham, has been preserved. 'Whilst Sir Thomas Fairfax's army in the west pursue the enemy towards a happy conclusion of this unnatural war', Neve was required 'without delay to bring into the standing committee at Norwich the sum of one hundred pounds, where you shall have security from such of them as you shall choose as are not lenders themselves or not engaged to others that shall before you bring in their proportions required'. The eight gentlemen of the committee signed themselves 'your assured loving friends'; but there was a sting in the postscript. 'We expect your answer without delay after receipt of this letter, or otherwise we shall be enforced to return up your name and neglect to Parliament, which may turn to your trouble.'[7]

It was in no boastful spirit that they spoke of an approaching conclusion to the war. Just a month before, on 14 June, the New Model Army had won a splendid victory at Naseby. A long and desperate struggle ended in the complete rout of the King's forces. Several thousand prisoners were taken, together with the royal artillery and baggage-train, and all the King's personal papers. It was a triumphant success for the new policy, and for those who had advocated it and carried it through.

The two Norfolk veterans, Skippon and Astley, were opposed at Naseby as they had been in earlier battles. Skippon was badly wounded at the head of his own regiment. Astley had commanded the main body of Royalist infantry in the centre, who fought back grimly against the repeated attacks of forces which outnumbered them. He was always one of the mainstays of the royal cause, in victory or defeat.

As the reward of his services he had been raised to the peerage in November 1644 as Baron Astley of Reading, the town which he had captured and garrisoned in the previous year. The letters patent, still in the possession of his family, splendidly engrossed and bearing the Great Seal, give no indication that they were drawn up at Oxford at a time when the King could command only a fragment of his realm. They recite in detail Sir Jacob's early exploits under foreign powers, and in more recent years his fidelity to his own sovereign and his good services again the machinations of wicked rebels. All his actions are given—Edgehill (which is

[7] B.M. Add. MS. 27,447, f. 288.

called Kineton), Brentford, Newbury, the bridges of Gosworth and Cropredy, the surrender of Essex's army in Cornwall—*praeclara illa et insanguis prope Lestithiel in comitatu nostro Cornubia victoria.* And mention is also made of his son Sir Bernard, *re vera tali patre dignus*, who had greatly distinguished himself at the storming of Bristol by Prince Rupert in 1643.

In the autumn after Naseby, Bristol was once again besieged and taken, this time by the Parliamentarian forces under Fairfax. In the course of this siege, Sir Bernard Astley was wounded and made a prisoner, dying of his wounds at Bath ten days afterwards. His mother, the old Dutch lady Agnes Impel, was also in the besieged city; but she was given a safe conduct a few days before the final assault, and was able to make her way to Norfolk, to the house of her daughter and her Parliamentarian son-in-law at Hindolveston.[8] Her brother's death, and her father's continuing service in a defeated cause, must have intensified the conflict of loyalties that Elizabeth Lady Astley had to endure. Her husband, Sir Edward, was still with the Parliamentarian forces; but during the days before Naseby he was at Wisbech and Spalding, his regiment being part of the reserve forces which were securing the borders of the Eastern Association. He therefore did not confront his father-in-law in battle on this, or probably on any other occasion. Three of his letters to his wife have survived, designed principally to comfort and reassure her at this anxious moment. On the day of the battle of Naseby he wrote from Spalding that 'we lie here very secure from danger, having no enemy near us, and expect very shortly to be called home again. I prithee, sweet heart, trouble not thyself, for by the grace of God I make no question but to see thee very shortly'. As a result of the battle the war moved ever further westwards, and it is unlikely that he played much further part in it, or desired to do so.

2

In the course of the past three years, large gaps had occurred in the ranks of the Long Parliament. The members who joined the King at Oxford, or for other reasons had persistently absented

[8] Entries in Elizabeth Lady Astley's Bible at Swanton House, Melton Constable.

themselves, were disabled from sitting. Many others had died. By 1645 there were perhaps 260 members who attended the House of Commons regularly, and 200 vacant seats to be filled. Hitherto these seats had remained empty, even in the case of counties and boroughs where the Parliament was in absolute control. After Naseby, however, the House decided to recruit its numbers.[9]

Of the Norfolk members, Sir Edward Moundeford, one of the Knights of the Shire, had died in the spring of 1643; and John Percival, one of the members for King's Lynn, died some time during 1644. Sir Robert Hatton, who sat for Castle Rising, joined the King at the outset of the war, and was among the first of those declared in the autumn of 1642 to be disabled from sitting at Westminster. Richard Catelyn, one of the members for Norwich, had also been disabled from sitting in January 1644, after several warnings, owing to his prolonged absence from Parliament.[10]

Catelyn did not take his seat, as Hatton did, in the King's Parliament at Oxford; but it is evident that his sympathies were with the Royalist cause. He was still attending at Westminster in February 1643, when his colleague Harman reported to the Mayor of Norwich that they were jointly endeavouring to secure a reduction of the levy on the city.[11] But later that year he complained to the Corporation of Norwich about the burden of his Parliamentary duties, and their reply has been preserved. 'We received your letter,' they began, 'and are very sorry that you should take up occasion of such passionate expressions as are therein . . . As for your place, we know it hath been and is like still to be both painful, tedious and prejudicial to your own private affairs; yet you being designed thereunto, the burden must be undergone by you with a mind carried forward and led out rather to the public affairs of the kingdom than looking back upon your own private interests . . .' and much else to the same effect.[12] But despite these admonitions Catelyn ceased to attend Parliament. He withdrew to live quietly in his house at Kirby Cane, beside the ancient church with its round Saxon tower. His eldest son Thomas had openly espoused the cause of the King. We have already seen him involved

---

[9] Wedgwood, *The King's War*, 577–8. Brunton and Pennington, 21 ff.
[10] C.J., iii, 77, 140, 246, 374.
[11] B.M. Add. MS. 22,619, f. 49.
[12] Ibid., f. 76.

in the Lowestoft affair and as Knyvett's fellow-prisoner at Windsor; and he was killed at the second battle of Newbury. Richard Catelyn's estate was sequestered; and when, at the close of 1645, he applied to compound for it, he asked to be allowed to do so by proxy instead of going to London, 'being very infirm and unable to travel'. He mentioned also his second wife and her eight small children.[13]

There were thus four 'recruiters' to be chosen in Norfolk. The vacancies were declared in Parliament, and the writs issued at various dates towards the end of 1645. The new Knight of the Shire was that respected and influential figure Sir John Hobart, whose name had been in the forefront of all the county committees from their inception. He was an elderly man and perhaps already infirm, since he died less than two years after his election, in November 1647. He was also a staunch and convinced Presbyterian; and his choice by the gentlemen of the county indicates clearly enough the attitude of the majority on the great issues, religious and political, which were already beginning to divide the victorious party. Few men as yet consciously regarded themselves as committed Presbyterians or Independents; but the two antagonistic bodies of opinion were steadily growing, both in the army and in civilian life.

In normal times the borough of Castle Rising was under the control of the Howard family. But Lord Arundel was now an old and ailing man—he died in his exile at Padua in the following year—and his son Lord Mowbray was with the King's army. All their estates in East Anglia were under sequestration. They owned about thirty burgage-tenements at Castle Rising, whose occupiers were entitled to vote, and were accustomed to vote as the Howards directed them; but there appears to be no evidence as to who gave the voters their instructions on this occasion. Presumably such matters fell within the jurisdiction of the county sequestration committee. The new member was John Spelman of Narborough, a youngish man who had been active on the Parliamentarian side in western Norfolk throughout the war. His mother was the second wife of Sir John Potts; and he himself belonged to the same moderate and Presbyterian grouping.

A very different choice was made by the dominant faction in

[13] *Cal. Com. Compounding*, 942. M.I. in Kirby Cane Church.

Norwich. Thomas Atkins was a merchant with interests both in Norwich and London. He was Sheriff of Norwich in 1627 and one of its representatives in the Short Parliament, but he did not stand again for the Long Parliament. He was Sheriff of London in 1637, Lord Mayor in 1644, and a prominent officer in the City militia. In this last connection he became something of a figure of fun. While training in Tothill Fields he was 'troubled with a yearning in his bowels', which he was not able to control; and this unfortunate incident in so public a place led to endless ribaldry on the part of the Royalists.[14] His name became a proverb; and when Thomas Knyvett wished to chaff his friend John Buxton for timidity in the face of Parliamentarian threats to his estate, he described him as being 'almost dead, and ever and anon in Atkins' case, for fear of being catched'.[15] Nevertheless, and joking apart, Atkins was a formidable character—a rigid Independent in the years to come, and a vehement Cromwellian throughout the Commonwealth.

A situation arose over the seat at King's Lynn, left vacant by the death of John Percival, to which there seems to have been no parallel elsewhere. In December 1645 the town council applied to Parliament for a writ for the election of a new burgess. This was duly issued next month, when the Council chose Edmund Hudson, who had been their Mayor-elect at the time of the siege in 1643, and had then played an active part among the defenders. In fact, Lynn had the audacity at this unpromising time to elect as its 'recruiter' a man of known Royalist sympathies. His election appears to have been wholly disregarded by Parliament; probably Miles Corbett, now the Recorder of the town, made certain of that. Nothing further happened for a year, and then the town council despatched a letter to their Recorder 'to hasten the report to the House of Commons that hath lyen hidden there so long for the electing of a burgess for this borough, for that this house conceive that the town suffereth for want of one'. As a result of this, the Commons resolved that Hudson was an unfitting person to sit, in view of his having assisted in the Lynn rising, and issued a writ for the election of another burgess. Two further years elapsed before anything was done; and then, in September 1649,

[14] *Mercurius Aulicus*, 545.
[15] Knyvett, 123.

several months after Parliament had been reduced to the Rump, and the King had been put to death, that accommodating left-wing nobleman, William second Earl of Salisbury, was elected to represent the town of Lynn.[16]

3

Slowly the war drew to its expected close. All through the later months of 1645, and the opening months of 1646, the royal armies dwindled, the isolated and beleaguered garrisons surrendered. The western cities fell one by one—Hereford, Worcester, Chester —until only Exeter remained to the King, the sole city or sizeable town, apart from Oxford, that he could still call his own. The lesser strongholds were gradually reduced, and the scattered castles and country-houses which had held out for so long. On 14 March the gallant Hopton surrendered at Truro with the remnants of his once irresistible Army of the West. Exeter capitulated shortly afterwards.

Old Lord Astley was now the last of the Royalist commanders with a body of troops outside the radius of Oxford. Throughout the winter he had been endeavouring to rally a force along the Welsh border and the counties of the Severn. He had hoped to march with this force, some two thousand men, to the assistance of the King at Oxford. But on 22 March he was intercepted by Parliamentarian troops near Stow-on-the-Wold; his inexperienced Welsh recruits proved no match for seasoned cavalry, and he was obliged to surrender. It was the last serious action of the war. A contemporary account relates that since Astley was 'wearied in this fight, and being ancient (for old age's silver hairs had quite covered over his head and beard), the soldiers brought him a drum to sit and rest himself upon'. Seated comfortably on this drum, the cheerful veteran uttered words which the victorious officers grouped around him may well have recalled in the years ahead. 'You have now done your work, boys, and may go to play, unless you will fall out amongst yourselves.'[17]

[16] Le Strange, *Norfolk Official Lists*, 132. King's Lynn Hall Books. H.M.C., King's Lynn Corporation, 182.
[17] Rushworth, IV, i, 140–1. Vicars, *The Burning Bush* (1646), 399.

SIR JACOB ASTLEY
from a painting by Sir Anthony Van Dyck, in the possession of
Marguerite, Lady Hastings

Just a month later the King fled from Oxford in disguise, in circumstances which will be described in detail in the next chapter, and gave himself up to the Scottish army at Newark. Oxford itself surrendered in June. In the meantime Astley had been imprisoned in Warwick Castle. He was no less honoured and respected by his opponents than by his own friends; and when Fairfax was discussing the terms of the surrender of Oxford with Sir Thomas Glemham, the Governor of the city, it was agreed that Astley should be covered by the articles as if he had been amongst the garrison. These articles provided that the defenders of Oxford might pass unmolested, with their arms and equipage, 'to their houses or friends, without any prejudice to their friends for receiving them'. Easy terms were also laid down by which they could compound for their estates, and withdraw them from sequestration.

When a family had been divided in its political allegiance, no effort was spared by those on the winning side to succour their defeated relations. This was generally the case even in families with less intimate bonds of personal affection than the Astleys. If one member had imperilled a part of the family property by his adherence to the wrong cause, the property must be rescued from sequestration as soon as possible through the influence of his right-thinking relations. Thus we find John Coke of Holkham, as soon as the war was over, 'labouring what he can, as he sends me word, but he cannot as yet do any good', in aid of his Royalist brother Robert in Surrey; and no doubt he made similar efforts on behalf of his brother Henry in Suffolk.[18] With equal promptitude, and greater success, Sir Edward Astley hastened to the assistance of his father-in-law. At the beginning of July he wrote to his wife from Warwick, to say that he was going to Oxford 'to solicit my Lord's business' with Sir Thomas Fairfax—presumably to ensure that the provisions made on his behalf under the Oxford articles were duly carried out.[19] We learn from his daughter's Bible that 'my father the Lord Astley came from Warwick Castle to Hindolveston the 18th day of July 1646'. At Hindolveston they all settled down happily once more—the old Cavalier and his wife, their daughter and her Parliamentarian husband, and little Jacob their

[18] James, 83.
[19] Swanton House MSS.

grandson. Lord Astley was able in due course to compound for his estate, which lay not in Norfolk but in Kent, by the payment of a capital sum of two years' value. When the Second Civil War broke out in 1648, with risings in Kent and Essex, and stirrings of discontent in Norfolk, he was true to his parole and made no move. Two years later he returned to his home in Kent, where he died in 1652.

4

In the dedication of the printed version of his fast sermon before Parliament, quoted on an earlier page, the Rev. John Arrowsmith named 'the squeezing of delinquents' as one of the most commendable activities of his distinguished audience. Certainly the income from the sequestered estates of Royalists was a most important source of the sinews of war. So were the payments under the ordinance by which the 'fifth and twentieth part'—one-twentieth of the real and one-fifth of the personal estate—was exacted from the reluctant or recalcitrant. This ordinance was originally intended to apply to all persons alike, but it came to be increasingly used as a weapon against the 'malignants'.[20]

The county sequestration committees, whose task it was to collect this money, acted with varying degrees of severity. Their decisions were swayed by every kind of personal factor—jealousy and prejudice, favouritism and kinship, humanity and compassion. Old scores were often paid off, past kindness met sometimes with its reward. Some committee members acted with complete integrity, others with extreme self-interest. All tended to come under criticism either for leniency or harshness, for protecting their friends or oppressing their enemies.

The money locally collected was supposed to be sent up to London. So it may have been at the outset of the war, when in December 1642 the newly-established Committee for the Advance of Money wrote to Sir John Potts and the other Deputy Lieutenants of Norfolk, congratulating them on having raised £40,000 by loan, 'which would be a very seasonable supply', and instructing them to send it up promptly to Guildhall. 'This will be a very

---

[20] *Cal. Com. for Advance of Money,* xi.

acceptable service to both Houses of Parliament.'[21] But in fact a great deal of the money was required for local purposes, and especially for the equipment, arming and training of the militia. Some of the disbursements for these purposes by John Cory, the treasurer of the Norfolk Sequestration Committee, have already been mentioned. There was always much friction, and a good deal of overlapping and confusion, between the county committees and the major committees which sat in London—the Committee for the Advance of Money, and later the Committee for Compounding. Most formidable of all was the Committee for Examinations, an inquisitorial body set up early in the war for the detection and examination of delinquents, the chairman of which was the inevitable Miles Corbett.

The aim of any Royalist within the boundaries of the Eastern Association, once the hopelessness of his situation was made evident by the course of the war, was to extricate his property from sequestration on the easiest possible terms. The case of Sir William Paston has been described in an earlier chapter. There were several reasons why he was treated with comparative leniency. He had not actually borne arms against the Parliament; he had powerful friends to make representations on his behalf; it was desirable that he should transfer his still considerable local influence to the victorious cause, as in fact he soon did. At the end of January 1644 the Parliament further sought to detach lukewarm or war-weary supporters from the Royalist cause by what came to be known as the Declaration of Both Kingdoms.

This was an offer of amnesty, accompanied with mitigated penalties, to those delinquents who, despite their reprehensible activities, 'yet are not to be reckoned amongst the prime authors of this unnatural war, nor amongst the malicious and desperate enemies of their religion and country'. Such persons were to 'withdraw themselves from that faction', confess their errors, and take the Covenant before 1 March. If they did so, their lives and persons would be secured, and they would be received into favour. 'But to the end that a just difference may be made betwixt such persons returning so late to their duty, and those that never departed from it, they must expect that . . . their estates in some proportion should be liable, and that as the wisdom and discretion

[21] Ibid., 3.

of the Parliament, or of such as shall be authorized by them (who will be as careful to prevent their ruin, as to punish their delinquencies) shall find and judge to be necessary for that end.'[22]

Many Royalists availed themselves of this offer, despite their scruples of conscience over the taking of the Covenant. Some were treated with leniency, others with what appears to have been unreasonable severity. One such case was that of Jeremy Beck, a young man studying law at the Inner Temple. His father had died at the beginning of the war, and he had inherited substantial property at Castleacre and lands also in Suffolk. He denied later that he had ever been in arms for the King, or had contributed to his cause. His sole delinquency, he said, consisted in going into King's Lynn at the time of the siege. He was one of those who sought to make their peace under the Declaration of Both Kingdoms. Nevertheless his estate appears to have remained under sequestration, with the Norfolk Sequestration Committee and the Committee for the Advance of Money both making heavy demands upon his dwindling resources. In September 1644 he was ordered 'to be committed to Lambeth House for threatening the officers with their lives, to remain till further order, and to be kept in custody meantime'. Later still he endeavoured to compound; but even in 1650 he was still unable to pay the sum demanded 'by reason of his great debts'. Matters were only settled in 1651 by the sale of his Suffolk estates.[23]

The ascertaining of the value of a large estate was often a most complicated process. Leases, mortgages, loans, debts, family settlements of every kind, all had to be taken into consideration. There were endless grounds for argument and dispute. The browbeaten Royalists, firmly convinced of the justice of their cause, resorted to concealment and subterfuge, and on occasion to downright lying. In consequence informers flourished, and were rewarded with a percentage of the value of such concealed property as they could bring to light. The case of Thomas Peck of Spixworth and his wife dragged on, like Jeremy Beck's, for year after year. Peck was in arms for the King, and one of the garrison of Basing House, which surrendered after a desperate siege in October 1645. His estate had been sequestered, and in July 1645

[22] Husband (1646), 417–20.
[23] *Cal. Com. for Advance of Money*, 438. *Cal. Com. Compounding*, 841–2.

was ordered to be sold; but later he was able to compound on payment of a fine of £900. In 1650, however, information was laid by one Armiger Warner that Henry Philpott of Thruxton in Hampshire owed Peck £1000, and that Peck had concealed this debt and had not compounded for it. In fact Philpott was Mrs. Peck's brother, and had vested this sum in three trustees for her benefit at the time of her marriage. This led to interminable disputes between Peck, Warner, the trustees and the Committee, and the matter was still unsettled as late as 1654.[24]

The troubles of these Royalists, and the anxieties and humiliations that beset them, are depicted with unrivalled clarity in the letters of Thomas Knyvett. It will be remembered that after the Lowestoft fiasco in 1643 he was imprisoned at Cambridge, and then transferred to Windsor Castle. Later in the same year he was released, but was not allowed to return to Norfolk, being kept under some form of surveillance first in London, and then at the house of his friend the dramatist Lodowick Carliell at Petersham. In the meantime his wife remained at Ashwellthorpe, endeavouring to manage his estate and deal with the countless problems that arose. Even before his property was placed under sequestration, the less dependable of his tenants saw how the wind was blowing, and broke their covenants or withheld their rents. 'I see there is no trust in any of these clunts,' he wrote in exasperation.[25]

Knyvett's letters to his wife vary in outspokenness. Some, which were sent by reliable private messengers, express with great frankness his views on the progress of the war and on his own predicament. Most of them are more cautiously worded. But by some mischance certain very imprudent letters, addressed to his wife and to his aunt Lady Bell, got into the hands of Miles Corbett and his Committee for Examinations. Corbett was also a member of all the Norfolk committees, and he saw to it that Knyvett's property was sequestered, in spite of some doubt whether such a course was justified in his case. Manchester himself wrote to the Norfolk committee asking that this should not be done. He pointed out that 'Mr. Knyvett, by your forbidding his tenants to pay him any rents, by which he might have supported his family, is reduced to greater exigencies and extremities than most of those

[24] *Cal. Com. for Advance of Money*, 358. *Cal. Com. Compounding*, 1793–4.
[25] Kynvett, 116.

whose estates are actually sequestered . . . I have much more reason to desire the same of you than formerly, having understood of the said Mr. Knyvett's innocency since my coming to London from Colonel Cromwell himself, who hath assured me that upon his coming to Lowestoft the same Mr. Knyvett did voluntarily yield himself without making any resistance, being not otherwise armed than with his sword he ordinarily wore'. But even Manchester's advocacy was of no avail. The Norfolk committee proceeded to enforce Knyvett's sequestration.[26]

There is a gap in Knyvett's letters to his wife from August 1643 until March 1644. During that period, after a struggle with his conscience of which there are several traces in his later correspondence, he brought himself to take the Covenant. But when the series of his letters was resumed, he was no nearer returning to 'that sweet place we had wont to call our own'. His sons, little more than boys, had made their way to Holland. Jack had become a soldier and was in Lord Craven's company: Tom, the younger, was engaged in some form of study. His wife was still at Ashwellthorpe with her daughters, coping valiantly with grasping officials and insubordinate tenants. Most of the Norfolk Royalists were in London, entangled like himself in the net of sequestration, and they were naturally much together. Sir William Paston and Sir Robert Kemp had returned from Holland; Sir Robert de Grey and Augustine Holl were still in trouble over their delinquencies in England. ' 'Tis pretty to hear the variety of all our fates since this time twelvemonth . . . God help us, we have all had our shares.' The sudden reversal of their fortunes and the interminable course of the war were wholly bewildering, both to himself and his friends, and to the country as a whole. 'Surely this history to after ages will seem rather a romancy, a feigned thing than a matter really acted. And, in my opinion, 'twill be much more for the credit of the nation to have it so construed than clearly believed, for the best excuse that can be made for us must be a fit of lunacy. The Lord God Almighty open all our eyes.'[27]

Sir William Paston was soon able to extricate himself from the toils—Knyvett called it 'a quick despatch'. He himself received no such advantage. It was rumoured that Cromwell 'had disclaimed

[26] Ibid., 36.
[27] Ibid., 129, 133.

his courteous testimony, saying I put a trick upon him at Lowestoft'. A local jackal in Norfolk, one Nathaniel Beadle, the solicitor
for the sequestration committee there, pursued him with especial
vindictiveness, reporting to London that he was favoured by the
more moderate Parliamentarians as their kinsman and friend, as
indeed he was. Sir John Holland, Sir John Potts, Sir Miles Hobart,
Sir John Palgrave are all mentioned in his letters as having spoken
in his favour, or otherwise seeking to ease his lot; and old Sir
Thomas Wodehouse was particularly helpful and kind. But the
moderates were losing ground. Worst of all, he wrote, 'my
Lord of Manchester's power is much spurned at . . . he is much
condemned for his favour and courtesy to gentlemen in
matters of sequestration, be it right or wrong. I fear we shall
have worse justice if his power be eclipsed, God in mercy
look upon us and defend us from the tyranny of hard-hearted
people'.[28]

But worse was yet to come. Knyvett's son Jack had written
from Holland a letter to one of his sisters about their father's
troubles, which had been intercepted and laid before Corbett.
'Our amiable countryman,' as Knyvett called him, pronounced
it to be 'stuffed with much malignancy', and vowed that 'in all his
life he never read such malicious, pernicious, malignant invective
against the Parliament and our religion'. Whether or not it contained any particular abuse of himself, Corbett used this unlucky
letter as a reason for intensifying his persecution of Knyvett.
'There are two strong drugs out of the devil's shop, malice and
lying,' wrote his victim. 'I hope 'tis a strong argument of God's
mercy and favour to me in the world to come, that suffers me to
be thus tormented by these evil spirits here.' He sought an interview with Corbett, who 'did intimate to me that there was enough
in those letters, if he should press it, to restrain me of my liberty
again . . . I durst not answer him in a way of argument, but gave
him thanks and the best satisfaction I could, though I bit my lip
for anger, not daring to justify myself in an honest cause.' Jack
also sent Corbett a humble letter of apology for the error of his
ways. 'Poor boy,' wrote his father, 'he is much dejected, I see, at
the sense and apprehension of the prejudice he hath done us by
his folly.' Sir John Potts and Sir John Holland repeated their

[28] Ibid., 133-4, 136, 138.

kindly offices, and continued to do their best to mollify the indignant Corbett.[29]

In the meantime Nathaniel Beadle was addressing to the London committee a series of vicious denunciations of the Norfolk committee whose servant he was, repeating his accusations against its members of favouritism and indulgence to delinquents on the grounds of 'kindred and friendship'. He did not actually name the moderates of the committee, Potts and Holland and Wodehouse and their associates; but their identity would have been perfectly clear to his correspondents in London. 'It is partly, as you say, their connivance and principally their partiality, but not as you say their timorousness, but rather as I may say their boldness to adventure to proceed contrary to the letter and intent of the ordinances: presuming that through their greatness and friends, and their plausible speeches and carriages and specious pretences, and other means that they can use, through the corruption of the times, they may do anything and never can be questioned, or not so as shall harm them.' Still less did he spare the characters of the Royalists themselves. Sir Robert Kemp, for example, was 'as notorious a delinquent as any in Norfolk and the most dangerous person, a kind of an atheist if not a papist as is confirmed, and if not so debauched and vicious as Mr. Holl, yet more able to do mischief'.[30]

At one time Knyvett considered bringing his wife to London to intercede with Corbett, since ' 'tis observed here that wives have far better success in their solicitations than we men'. Lady Kemp and Mrs. Holl had both secured some advantage for their husbands. The attractive Mrs. Holl, indeed, had obtained leave for her husband to go down to Norfolk to see to his affairs, a concession which Corbett firmly refused to grant to Knyvett. As the weeks passed, and one friend after another was either discharged from sequestration or received special favours of this kind, Knyvett began to fear that he might find himself 'the only object of pity and scorn in the county'. Baffled by Corbett's persistent hostility, 'I strive but like a bird in a net and more entangle myself'. In the end Mrs. Knyvett remained in Norfolk, while her husband continued his campaign, through his own persuasions

[29] Ibid., 139, 142, 147-8, 150.
[30] B.M. Add. MS. 5508, ff. 16, 23-4.

and the good offices of his Parliamentarian friends, to appease
their powerful enemy. 'It would be too great a happiness for me
to expect for us to live all together quietly. I will not despair, but
trust in God's mercy. Oh this cruel-hearted man Corbett, 'tis he
undoes me and obstructs all my happiness in these sad times. To
take delight to insult upon another's misery is not noble, scarce
Christian. God turn his heart.'[31]

The series of Knyvett's letters to his wife ends in July 1644.
But the lobbying by his friends, with Sir John Holland especially
active in his support, and his own humiliating efforts to placate
Corbett, continued unabated. Finally his case was fully heard on
23 August; and after the presentation of evidence on both sides,
and 'a full and serious debate of the whole matter', the sequestration of his estate was discharged. It may be that Corbett withdrew
his opposition, and stood neutral on the occasion, as he once
promised to do. Another factor may have been a feud which
arose between him and Beadle, which resulted at the end of the
year in Beadle being discharged from his office and imprisoned
until he produced his accounts.[32] At all events Knyvett was now
free to return to his much-loved home at Ashwellthorpe, and try
to repair his broken fortunes.

Knyvett's reunion with his wife, after these years of anxiety and
separation, was sadly brief, since she died at the end of April 1646.
His sons returned safely from Holland in due course, his daughters
married well, and family life continued at Ashwellthorpe despite
the injuries that his estate had suffered. But Knyvett himself did
not live to see the Restoration. Life was not always easy for him
under the Commonwealth, and at times of Royalist unrest in the
country he was still subjected to surveillance and some degree of
mulcting by the prevailing powers. He did not marry again, but
spent much time at the house of his elder daughter, the wife of
Sir John Rous of Henham in Suffolk. Ashwellthorpe in the meantime was left in the care of a steward; and it is evident that his
estate, never prosperous even in the years before the war, continued to deteriorate thereafter. He died at Henham in the summer
of 1658. His memorial at Ashwellthorpe bears an inscription of
which he would have approved:

[31] Knyvett, 151, 153, 155, 161.
[32] Ibid., 38, 41. C.J., iii, 728.

'Here lies loyal Knyvett, who hated anarchy,
Lived a true Protestant, and died with Monarchy.'[33]

5

The Declaration of Both Kingdoms had been effective in detaching a considerable number of supporters from the King. With the same object, during the later stages of the war, the system of compounding was introduced, whereby the estates of Royalists could be discharged from sequestration on the payment of a single substantial fine. An increasing number accepted this course as the hopelessness of the struggle became daily more evident. And most of those who were no longer in arms, but were living in Parliamentarian territory, were thankful to resume possession of what remained of their estates, however grievous the mulct that was laid upon them.

These composition payments varied greatly in severity, according to the measure of delinquency imputed to the applicant. They could be as low as one-tenth of the value of the estate, or as high as two-thirds. The would-be compounder appeared before the Committee for Compounding which sat at Goldsmith's Hall, bringing a certificate of the value of his estate from his own county committee. In the drawing up of these valuations, as in all their activities, the local committees were incessantly accused by the various interested parties of favour or lack of favour, of extortion, bribery, or excessive leniency. They themselves resented the usurpation of their authority by a remote committee in London, which had no first-hand knowledge of local circumstances, and might well be misled by a plausible delinquent. The Committee for Compounding tended to show especial harshness towards Papists, towards Members of Parliament who had sat in the King's Parliament at Oxford, towards ministers (because they had denounced the proceedings of Parliament from their pulpits), towards lawyers (because their legal training should have enabled them to make a better decision between the causes of the contending parties). There were frequent disputes as to whether a man was or was not covered by the articles of surrender of a town or

[33] Knyvett, 43-50. M.I. in Ashwellthorpe Church.

garrison, in which easy terms of composition were frequently stipulated.[34]

The compounders from Norfolk were a varied band. They included the yeomen and small landholders who had been concerned in the demonstration at Aylsham in the spring of 1643, and whose estates had been under sequestration ever since. For example Thomas Leman, the Aylsham attorney, 'begged to compound for delinquency in opposing, though only for an hour, the Parliament's forces, not knowing them to be such'. He met with the stern treatment often meted out to his profession, and was fined at one-third, having to pay £367. A fellow lawyer, Edward Colfer, was fined £940, later reduced to £320. Robert Burr 'begged to compound for delinquency in committing some rash act ignorantly', and pleaded his wife, his ten children and his many debts. He was fined £407, which was later reduced to £370. On the same day, 27 November 1645, Richard Curtis of Aylsham and Richard Allin of Tuttington were fined £20 and £20 respectively. They must all have travelled up from Norfolk together to face their ordeal.[35]

Youth and inexperience were frequent pleas in mitigation. Samuel Newsom of Norwich, 'being then not 21 years old, went into the King's quarters, where he remained four months, but was never in arms against the Parliament'. He was fined £200. John Barber, also of Norwich, 'being a minor at the beginning of the war, was unhappily drawn to take up arms for the King against Parliament, but laid down in January 1646. Leaving his small estate to the disposal of his brother, there was such spoil thereof that he could not raise money to compound earlier'. He was fined £63. The case of Sir Thomas Corbett, Miles Corbett's Royalist nephew, was not so easily settled. He too was a minor and a ward at the outbreak of the war, and never in full possession of his estates, which his father had left charged with a debt of £16,000. He joined the King at the outset of the war, was one of his lifeguard at Edgehill, and later captain of a troop of horse. He was fined £2010, which was later reduced to £1271 since he successfully claimed to be covered by the articles of the surrender at

[34] M. A. Everett Green. Prefaces to vols. i and v, pf *Cal. Com. Compounding*. Preface to C.S.P.D., 1649–50.
[35] *Cal. Com. Compounding*, 954, 993.

Truro in March 1646. He had in fact fought from the very begin-ning to the very end of the war. But he proved unable to pay this and other claims against his estate, and was still hopelessly enmeshed in sequestration as late as 1651.[36]

Several other Norfolk Royalists were in the surrender at Truro, and were able to take advantage of the articles. Sir Dru Drury of Riddlesworth was fined £957, at the rate of one-sixth of his estate; but under the articles this was reduced to £639 10s. 0d. John Hamond of Little Ellingham was fined £3717, one-half of his estate. This high rate was presumably due to the fact that he had been involved in the Lowestoft affair, and was imprisoned with Knyvett at Cambridge and Windsor. He must have rejoined the King after his release, possibly violating some undertaking not to do so. But under the Truro articles his fine was reduced to £1000. Also at Truro was Roger Castell of Raveningham, whose father of the same name had likewise been in trouble at Lowestoft. He was fined £30.[37]

The adventures of the compounders during the war had been as varied as their backgrounds and their circumstances. Captain Thomas Pigg of Walsoken had been taken prisoner by the Earl of Essex in October 1643, and exchanged at Burleigh House 'on a bond of £2000 never to bear arms again'. Arthur Heveningham, the Royalist brother of the vehement Parliamentarian William Heveningham of Ketteringham, was taken prisoner in the skir-mish at Langport in the summer of 1645. He owned nothing beyond an annual rent-charge of £200 on William's estate; and on this he was fined £400. William Edge of Oulton had been a surgeon in the King's army. After compounding for a fine of £40, he found himself unable to pay, and fled to Barbados, where once again he had to surrender when the island was captured in 1651 by Sir George Ayscue. On this occasion his fine was remitted and his sequestration discharged.[38]

A curious situation arose over the estate of Augustine Blome-field, a philanthropic Norwich merchant of Royalist sympathies who died while his property was under sequestration. He left his lands at East Winch and certain houses at East Dereham to the

[36] *Cal. Com. Compounding*, 909, 1193–4, 1958. *Cal. Com. for Advance of Money*, 784.
[37] *Cal. Com. Compounding*, 1297, 1322, 1393–4.
[38] Ibid., 928, 1312, 1517.

Great Hospital and the Children's Hospital in Norwich, and further bequests to the poor of Dereham. It fell to Matthew Peckover, the strongly Puritan mayor of Norwich at the time, to petition for the discharge from sequestration of the lands bequeathed for the benefit of his city by the benefactor to whom he was politically so strongly opposed. Peckover made this application in 1645, and Blomefield's executor sought at the same time to compound for the estate; but the matter still remained unsettled in 1652.[39]

In short, the whole process of compounding was a confused and unsatisfactory affair. If an estate was small and relatively uncomplicated in its financial structure, and the owner was able to pay his fine within a reasonable time, all might be well. But the larger estates, often burdened with settlements and trusts and not infrequently with formidable debts, could be the subject of endless argument between the committees and the unfortunate owners. Notable Royalists such as Sir Hamon L'Estrange, despite the articles of surrender at Lynn, continued in trouble far into the Commonwealth years. Augustine Holl was not yet out of the wood when he died in 1650, despite the very minor nature of his 'delinquency' in 1643.

The Catholic families met with still harsher treatment. The most conspicuous recusant group was established in west Norfolk, and was headed by the Bedingfelds of Oxburgh. Sir Henry Bedingfeld and three of his sons fought throughout the war in the King's army. The second son, Henry, was married to a niece of William Paston, the head of the Catholic branch of the Pastons at Appleton. One of Sir Henry's daughters was the wife of Colonel William Cobbe of Sandringham, also a Catholic and also serving in the royal forces. Another son-in-law, Colonel Robert Apreece, was shot in cold blood after the capture of Lincoln. The eldest son, Thomas, was wounded and taken prisoner at Lincoln, and in his own words 'for two years suffered loathsome imprisonment in the common gaol and was at length banished'. The second son, Henry, also went into exile after the end of the war. The third son, Edmund, entered religion and was a canon of Lierre in Belgium. William, the fourth son, served throughout the war, and was in trouble again during the Commonwealth years.

[39] Ibid., 1012.

The large Bedingfeld estates in Norfolk and Suffolk were placed under sequestration, and their beautiful moated house at Oxburgh was occupied and seriously damaged by fire. During the later stages of the war Sir Henry was amongst those excluded from pardon in the manifestoes of Parliament, and at its close he was imprisoned in the Tower of London for almost two years. Thence he addressed to his wife a series of meditations on the Passion, for 'your spiritual comfort in these most miserable and distracted times, which doth amaze the greatest spirits that now liveth'. There was a faithful steward named Henry Widmerpool, who seems to have maintained some degree of control during the absence of his master, and even managed secretly to collect some rents from loyal tenants. But in 1652 the estates were sold 'by the usurped power'. Details are lacking, but subsequent statements by members of the family placed the amount of which they had been 'damnified' at figures varying between £45,000 and £60,000.

The Suffolk estates of the Bedingfelds were sold 'to the then pretended President and Society for the Propagation of the Gospel in New England', and remained in the possession of that pious body. They were eventually able to repurchase the greater part of their Norfolk lands; and Sir Henry's grandson, after considerable expense 'in supplying the house with furniture that was burnt and making the house habitable', was able to reoccupy Oxburgh.[40] Members of the family are living there at the present day. But none of this could be foreseen by Sir Henry as he composed his sorrowful meditations in the Tower during the final months of the war, when the last scattered garrisons were surrendering, and an exhausted nation was wondering what the next turn of events might bring.

6

Although it is not strictly relevant to the narrative of events, one side-effect of the war perhaps deserves some detailed consideration. The concluding stages of the conflict witnessed an outbreak of trials for witchcraft, more especially in the eastern counties. The past century of religious and ideological struggle in Europe, as Professor Trevor-Roper has lately reminded us, had seen the

[40] *Bedingfeld Papers* (Catholic Record Society, 1909), 1–19, 37, 231–4.

most appalling and wholesale persecutions of supposed witches. During the Thirty Years War there was peace in England, and there were no executions for witchcraft in the period of King Charles's personal rule. Civil War on English soil brought witch-hunting in its train; and in the course of 1645 more so-called witches were executed in England than in any year before or since.[41]

A belief in witchcraft was deeply rooted in the popular mind. It was supported, moreover, by the authority of the scriptures and the law of the land. Some enlightened justices and churchmen may have had their private reservations; but few of them ventured openly to dissent when the populace were bawling the instruction delivered to Moses upon Mount Sinai, 'Thou shalt not suffer a witch to live'.

In the territory of the Eastern Association the witch-hunt was led by Matthew Hopkins, a Suffolk man who styled himself 'witchfinder general', and his lieutenant John Sterne. Hopkins is said to have been the son of the minister of one of the Wenhams, and to have practised as a lawyer at Manningtree in Essex. His activities are recorded in the fullest detail in the reports of the assizes held at Chelmsford in July 1645, when the dignitaries of Essex were headed by Robert Rich, Earl of Warwick, the eminent Presbyterian nobleman who figured in earlier chapters of this book. As the result of the denunciations of Hopkins and Sterne on this occasion, some twenty women were hanged at Chelmsford and Manningtree, or died in gaol.

Torture in the cruder sense, as practised on the continent, or in Scotland in the earlier years of the late King James, was no part of English procedure. Suspected witches were merely kept awake, night after night, under merciless interrogation by Hopkins and his colleagues; or, when necessary, subjected to the ordeal of 'swimming', being thrown into a river or pond and regarded as guilty if they floated and did not sink. Their bodies were searched for the hidden teats at which they were supposed to suckle their imps, and which the searchers usually managed to find. Hopkins repeatedly swore that his victims, during the night-long sessions when he 'watched' them, actually conjured their imps into his presence.

[41] Trevor-Roper, *Religion, the Reformation and Social Change*, 162–3.

Elizabeth Clarke of Manningtree produced Jarmara, 'like to a dog, which was white, with some sandy spots, and seemed to be very fat and plump, with very short legs, who forthwith vanished away': and Vinegar Tom, 'in the shape of a greyhound with long legs'. As Hopkins walked home from one of these vigils, his greyhound was bitten in the shoulder by a white thing like a kitling; and in his own yard he saw something like a cat, but three times as big, sitting on the strawberry bed. His friend John Sterne also saw Jarmara and Vinegar Tom, and another imp called Holt; but a fourth, Sack and Sugar, did not manifest itself. Anne West, Mrs. Clarke's neighbour, also had her set of imps; and both women suckled their imps, and each other's imps, at teats concealed in the private parts of their bodies. Mrs. Clarke further confessed that the Devil lay with her, 'in the shape of a proper gentleman with a laced band', half a night together. Most of the women further confessed to bewitching children, or causing the deaths of cattle and swine, or raising winds to sink fishing-hoys, or other unlikely misdemeanours.[42]

Similar trials, with the same hideous nonsense by way of evidence, took place next month during the Suffolk assizes at Bury St. Edmunds. Again a whole string of women and some men, driven crazy by enforced sleeplessness, made their pitiful confessions. Elizabeth Richmond of Branford, 'after six days watching', told how the Devil, claiming to be the prophet Daniel, embraced her, ordered her to forsake God and the Church, and enabled her to curse Goody Furnis so that she died within six weeks. Susan Marchant of Hintlesham described her imps Antony, Blackfest and Will, two like rabbits and one like a crow, by whose means she lamed her brother Geoffrey's cow. Others had imps in the form of cats, rats, mice, moles, toads, owls, blackbirds, chickens, turkey-cocks and a crabfish. The Devil had appeared to them in equally varied forms—a calf, a red-shagged dog, a black bee, a black boy, and a handsome young gentleman with yellow hair and black clothes.[43]

The list of those arraigned is far longer than the Essex list; and the number of those executed in Suffolk during this dreadful

[42] *A True and Exact Relation . . . of the late Witches . . . in the County of Essex* (1645), passim. L. L'E. Ewen, *Witch Hunting and Witch Trials* (1929), 65–9, 107–8, 231.
[43] Ewen, *Witch Hunting and Witch Trials*, 291–313.

summer was probably larger in proportion. Samuel Butler, writing of Hopkins and the witches in *Hudibras* not many years later, made Ralpho ask

> has he not, within a year,
> Hanged threescore of 'em in one shire?

This shire is supposed to have been Suffolk; and Francis Hutchinson, writing early in the next century, likewise gives the figure of sixty Suffolk victims.[44]

The Suffolk holocaust included one unusual victim in the person of an elderly clergyman, John Lowes, the vicar of Brandeston. He had been the incumbent of that parish for close on fifty years, and throughout that time had been at loggerheads with many of his parishioners, who described him as 'of a turbulent spirit, being possessed with an humour of a multitude of vexations'. As far back as 1615 he had been accused of causing death by witchcraft, and many other crimes had been laid to his charge during his long and quarrelsome career. Now the old accusation caught up with him, and he was subjected to the torment of being deprived of sleep for nights on end, while the invigilators 'ran him backwards and forwards about the room, until he was out of breath; then they rested him a little, and then ran him again'. He was put to the ordeal of 'swimming' at Framlingham, when his failure to sink convinced the spectators of his guilt. Finally he confessed the usual rigmarole—a pact with the Devil, a teat at which he suckled seven imps, the sending of his yellow imp 'to do all the hurt he could at sea between Yarmouth and Winterton', the sinking of a fine new vessel at Landguard Fort near Harwich. He was duly convicted, and hanged in a batch with sixteen women and another man, according to one account reading his own burial service and committing his own body to the ground.[45]

Much less is known about the activities of the witch-hunters in Norfolk. There were contemporary reports that 40 witches were arraigned in the county, and 20 executed, during the summer of 1645; but in fact there appears to be no record of any assize at

[44] *Hudibras*, II, iii, 143-4. Hutchinson, *Historical Essay concerning Witchcraft* (1718), 37. Ewen, in *Witchcraft in the Star Chamber* (1938) puts the number at almost 70.
[45] Ewen, *Witchcraft in the Star Chamber*, 44-54; *Witch Hunting and Witch Trials*, 300-1. Hutchinson, *Historical Essay concerning Witchcraft*, 66-8.

NORFOLK IN THE CIVIL WAR

Norwich that repeated the horrors enacted at Bury St. Edmunds and Chelmsford.[46] In this same year of 1645, however, the Corporation of Great Yarmouth resolved that 'the gentleman, Mr. Hopkins, employed in the county for discovering and finding out witches, be sent for to town, to search for such wicked persons, if any be, and have his fee and allowance for his pains, as he hath in other places'. He succeeded in discovering a considerable number of witches, and sixteen of them, all women, were duly hanged. From an entry in the Corporation accounts we learn that the women who searched the suspects for their hidden teats were paid a shilling a day for their pains.

Next year King's Lynn followed the example of Yarmouth. The council resolved that 'Alderman Thomas Rivett be requested to send for Mr. Hopkins the witch-discoverer, and his charges and recompense to be borne by the town'. Two Lynn women had already been hanged for witchcraft the year before, without the assistance of Hopkins. There appears to be no record of his activities when he visited the town.[48]

The reign of Hopkins was as brief as it was bloody. Protests began to be voiced; and in anticipation of the 1647 assizes at Norwich, certain questions were drawn up for the consideration of the judges, expressing well-reasoned doubts about 'this torturing witch-catcher' and all his works. Hopkins at once published the questions, together with his own rejoinders, which would hardly have brought conviction to any unprejudiced mind. The pamphlet was adorned with a woodcut showing him interrogating two witches, together with a selection of their imps; and the title-page bore the grim old text *Thou shalt not suffer a witch to live.*[49]

In August of this same year Hopkins died, and was buried at Mistley, close to Manningtree. According to Butler he was himself accused of witchcraft—

'Who after proved himself a witch,
And made a rod for his own breech'—

---

[46] Notestein, *History of Witchcraft in England* (1911), 200–1, 403–4.

[47] Manship, 273–4. Palmer, *Perlustration of Great Yarmouth*, ii, 145–6. H.M.C., Great Yarmouth Corporation, 320.

[48] Richards, *History of Lynn*, 1200–1.

[49] *The Discovery of Witches . . . now published by Matthew Hopkins, Witch-finder* (1647), passim.

and this statement was repeated by Hutchinson, who asserted that some gentlemen, out of indignation at the barbarity of Hopkins, put him to the swimming test, whereupon he floated on the surface as witches were supposed to do. 'That cleared the country of him,' in Hutchinson's words. There is nothing to suggest, so far as I know, that he suffered the fate of his victims.[50]

[50] *Hudibras*, II, iii, 153-4. Hutchinson, loc. cit., 65-6. The statement in the D.N.B. that Hopkins was hanged appears to be due to a misreading of Hutchinson's text.

CHAPTER XV

The King's Journey

I

'Dear heart,' the King had written from Oxford to his Queen in France at the beginning of 1646, 'I desire thee to take notice that with the year I begin to new number my letters, hoping to begin a year's course of good luck.'[1] Few hopes can ever have withered more swiftly. There were no visible grounds for the King's optimism, and the year proved disastrous to him from the very outset. Nevertheless, throughout the months which saw the final collapse of his military power, he had been engaged in a series of negotiations with his opponents and his few potential allies. Messages had gone out from Oxford to the Parliament, to the City of London, to the leaders of the Scottish army in England, to the Queen for transmission to the rulers of France. With his cause in hopeless ruin, Charles still retained one unique asset, his personal position as the lawful ruler of England, Scotland and Ireland—the imponderable but enormous prestige of the Crown and the royal lineage.

He might yet be able to take advantage of the divided purposes of the Parliament and the Scots, and contrive to play them off one against the other. Monsieur de Montreuil, the emissary sent by Cardinal Mazarin as his special representative with the Scottish government, had come to Oxford bringing definite offers from the Scottish leaders; and since Parliament continued to reject the King's terms, his thoughts turned more and more towards an escape from beleaguered Oxford to the Scottish camp outside Newark. On the other hand, the Scots continued to place at the head of their demands the establishment of Presbyterianism throughout the kingdom; and that was a concession which Charles was determined not to make. He wrote to the Queen on 3 March: 'For the Scots, I promise thee to employ all possible pains and

---

[1] *Charles I in 1646*, ed. John Bruce (Camden Society, 1856), 1.

industry to agree with them, so that the price be not giving up the Church of England, with which I will not part upon any condition whatsoever'; and the same resolve—'the saving of the Church wherein I have been bred'—occurs in letter after letter. He described to the Queen, from day to day, the bargaining of the Scots, the relentless approach of the Parliamentary forces, his own anxieties and indecisions, the whole confused and treacherous situation. He was 'absolutely resolved, God willing, never to fall into the rebels' hands, as long as I can by any industry or danger prevent it'; but as April advanced, he still found himself unable to accept the Scottish terms, and the position remained one of complete deadlock.[2]

In his deepening perplexity he came to an unexpected decision, which he communicated to the Queen in his letter of 22 April: 'To eschew all kind of captivity, which, if I stay here, I must undergo, I intend (by the grace of God) to get privately to Lynn, where I will yet try if it be possible to make such a strength, as to procure honourable and safe conduct from the rebels; if not, then I resolve to go by sea to Scotland, in case I shall understand that Montrose be in condition fit to receive me, otherwise I mean to make for Ireland, France or Denmark, but to which of these I am not yet resolved; desiring, if it may be, to have thy judgement before I put to sea, to direct my course by. In the meantime, I conjure thee, by thy constant love to me, that if I should miscarry (whether by being taken by the rebels or otherwise), to continue the same active endeavours for Prince Charles as thou hast done for me, and not whine for my misfortunes in a retired way, but, like thy father's daughter, vigorously assist Prince Charles to regain his own.' In a postscript he warned his wife that 'if thou hearest that I have put myself into Fairfax's army, be assured that it is only to have the fittest opportunity for my going to Lynn in a disguise, if not by other ways'.[3]

It is unlikely that Charles really supposed that he could 'make a strength' in the neighbourhood of Lynn. After the failure of the uprising at Lynn in 1643, and Roger L'Estrange's abortive attempt to seize control of the town in the following year, a strict control had been kept upon the Royalists of western Norfolk. They were

[2] Ibid., 22–3, 35.
[3] Ibid., 38.

in no condition to take any concerted action whatsoever. But Lynn, rather than the closely watched southern ports, would have been a possible choice for the King to make as his means of escape from the country, should he decide to join Montrose in Scotland, or to seek refuge in some foreign land. At all events he now had the project of a secret flight from Oxford fixed firmly in his mind, with Lynn as his first objective. And so it came about that although he had never set foot in Norfolk during all the marching and campaigning of the past four years, he was now to enter the county as a harassed fugitive, during the last days of freedom from captivity that he was ever destined to know. [4]

2

For a few more days he waited at Oxford. He wrote privately to Ireton, offering under certain conditions to surrender to Fairfax's army—presumably in order to put the 'rebels' on a false scent, as he had suggested in his recent postscript to the Queen. Ireton forwarded the letter to Cromwell; no reply was returned to the King, and Parliament issued orders that no officer of the Army was in any circumstances to listen to overtures for peace from any quarter. A message was also conveyed to the Scots through Montreuil, to the effect that the King was prepared to make his way to the Scottish army if his conditions, particularly as to liberty of conscience, were faithfully observed. By this time the Parliamentary forces were attacking Woodstock; and on 25 April Charles made to Colonel Rainborough, their commander, certain overtures which were again ignored. On the 26th he heard from Montreuil, who was with the Scottish leaders outside Newark, that they were prepared to receive him and were even sending troops to assist him on his journey. Montreuil was still somewhat vague as to the conditions upon which he would be received; but his message finally determined the King to leave Oxford before

[4] The narrative which follows is based principally on the examinations of Michael Hudson, printed in Francis Peck's *Desiderata Curiosa* (1779 ed.), and H.M.C., Portland, i (1891). John Ashburnham's *Narrative of his Attendance on King Charles the First* (1830) has also been used. A few other sources have been indicated in the footnotes.

Fairfax's advancing army cut off every possibility of escape.

On Sunday evening, 26 April, he summoned his Council, and told them that he had determined to go to London. If they heard nothing of him in a fortnight or three weeks, they were to surrender Oxford on the best conditions they could obtain. He appears to have said nothing about his intention of joining the Scots, knowing that his Council would oppose such a course; and according to Clarendon 'it was generally believed, that he had not within himself at that time a fixed resolution what he would do'.[5] He may have anticipated some message, from Parliament or from the City, which would have justified his going to London; he may have intended to make straight for Lynn and escape by sea; he may have been in a state of complete irresolution.

Charles then dismissed his Council, and sent word to two of his most trusted personal attendants, John Ashburnham and Dr. Michael Hudson, that certain plans, already laid, were to be carried out. 'Jack Ashburnham', a Sussex gentleman and Member of Parliament for Hastings, had been a Groom of the Bedchamber and fully in the King's confidence for many years past. He was prominent in advising the King to leave Oxford, in opposition to Secretary Nicholas and others who thought the risk of capture and possible maltreatment by Parliamentary forces was too great to be taken. Michael Hudson came from Westmorland, had been a 'poor serving child' at Queen's College, Oxford, and subsequently became a Fellow of that house. For some years he held the living of Uffington near Stamford in Lincolnshire, but was ejected as a Royalist. During part of the war he had been employed in Newcastle's army as 'scoutmaster general', and had acquired an intimate knowledge of the roads and byways over large tracts of the English countryside. Later he joined the King at Oxford, and became one of his chaplains. He was greatly liked and trusted by Charles, 'who used to call him his *plain-dealing chaplain*, because he told him his mind when others would, or durst not'. He had already been sent with messages to Montreuil at the Scottish camp, and had made himself familiar with the country between Oxford and the district in which the Scots were quartered. He had come to the conclusion that the Parliamentary horse were too numerous and active in this area for the King to be able to escape

[5] Clarendon, iii, 17.

to the Scots under the protection of an armed bodyguard; but he was confident that 'he might pass what way he pleased in a disguise as a private man'. And he was perfectly right; in the long journey which they were about to undertake, they passed through no fewer than fourteen posts of their enemies without detection and almost without challenge.

Later on that Sunday evening Hudson came to Ashburnham's chamber, bringing a pass which he had obtained from a gentleman who had received permission of the Parliament to go to London to compound for his estate. Horses had been chosen and saddled, and all other necessary preparations made. About midnight the King came into the room. They disguised him as a servant; and his hair was cut and his beard trimmed by the inexpert hand of Ashburnham. The others were dressed as private gentlemen of some means, and carried pistols as well as swords. Presently the Governor of Oxford, Sir Thomas Glemham, was summoned, and was told that the King was leaving the city. He went back for his keys, and let the little party out of the east gate, accompanying them for a short distance, and then returning with the King's orders to keep the gates closed and to allow no one to enter or leave Oxford for five days.

They heard a clock strike three as they rode in the darkness over Magdalen Bridge, Ashburnham and Hudson in front, the King as their servant a little distance behind them. 'Farewell, Harry!' Glemham had called out as he left them, for the benefit of any inquisitive loiterers who might have been within earshot at that unlikely hour. They passed a guard of Parliamentary dragoons at Dorchester without any examination, and answered without difficulty the questions of a small party of horse at Bensington. At Henley there were no questions when they had shown their pass and given a small gratuity to the corporal of the guard; and they adopted the same procedure at several other places. From Nettlebed to Slough they were accompanied by one of Ireton's troopers; he rode beside the King, and seemed impressed by the lofty air with which the pass was displayed and gratuities bestowed upon the guards. Finally he asked the King if Ashburnham was not a member of the House of Lords; to which the supposed servant replied that his master was merely one of the lower house. After passing through Maidenhead and Slough, they turned towards

Uxbridge and so to Hillingdon, where they arrived between ten and eleven, and dismounted at a tavern kept by one Teasdale. Here they remained for almost three hours, while the King, vacillating and perplexed, debated whether he should enter London or strike northwards to Lynn. It is possible that he had expected to receive, at Hillingdon or some other point along the road, a message from London which would have encouraged him to enter the city. But no such message had reached him; and early in the afternoon he resolved to set off again in the direction of Norfolk. They passed through Harrow and Edgeware, and then through St. Albans. Soon after they had left the latter town, they were alarmed by a gentleman on a fine horse who came galloping furiously after them. Fearing that they had been recognized in St. Albans, the King and Ashburnham drew off the road while Hudson turned to confront the pursuing horseman, who turned out to be quite harmless and very drunk. They got rid of his company as soon as possible, and rode on to Wheathampstead, where they spent the night.

Charles had now determined to make a final approach through Montreuil to the Scottish leaders. Next morning, 28 April, they left Wheathampstead at daybreak. As they rode along towards Baldock, it was arranged that Hudson should be sent to Montreuil's quarters at Southwell, and that the King and Ashburnham should ride on to Downham Market in Norfolk, and stay at the White Swan in that town until Hudson rejoined them. If he brought satisfactory terms from the Scots, they would then make their way to the Scottish army; if the terms were not acceptable, they would go on to Lynn and endeavour to get a passage by sea, either to Montrose in Scotland or to some foreign country. At Graveley the King gave Hudson a letter for Montreuil, 'wherein he expressed his departure from Oxford, and desired him to make an absolute conclusion with the Scots; and if they would give such assurance for honourable conditions for him, as should satisfy him (concerning the particulars whereof the King had given me instructions) then he would come to them; if not, he resolved to dispose otherwise of himself upon my return'. Bearing this letter, Hudson set off north-westward on his long ride to Southwell, while the King and Ashburnham went on at a slower pace towards Norfolk. They spent the night of the 28th at the common inn of a little village near Newmarket, and reached the White Swan at Downham Market next day.

3

The narrative of the King's journey has thus far been derived from the statements made by Hudson after his capture by the Parliamentary authorities a few weeks later. During his various examinations, he was more than willing to describe how easily they had passed through the unwary guards and outposts of their enemies; but he had no intention of incriminating any Royalist sympathizers with whom the King may have made contact in Norfolk or elsewhere. Clarendon states vaguely that Charles had 'wasted time in several places, whereof some were gentlemen's houses, where he was not unknown, though untaken notice of'.[6] We have seen also that he had talked of 'making a strength' in the neighbourhood of Lynn; and this at least suggests that he knew who were his supporters in that region, and expected some assistance from them. It is certain that one Norfolk gentleman, Ralph Skipwith, who lived at Snore Hall in the parish of Fordham, was in frequent contact with him after he had arrived at Downham Market; and there may have been others in the secret. But, thanks to Hudson's steadfast reticence during his examinations, further details are lacking. We are now obliged to fall back on a somewhat confusing report by two members of the House of Commons, Miles Corbett and Colonel Valentine Walton, who were hurriedly sent down to Norfolk when Parliament received news that the King was suspected to have been in the county. It will be remembered that Walton had been appointed Governor of Lynn after its capitulation, and Corbett had replaced the Royalist Recorder. They took up their quarters at Lynn, and the results of their inquiries were embodied in a report to William Lenthall, the Speaker, dated 11 May.

'Since our coming to Lynn,' it began, 'we have done what service we were able. We have taken some examinations, and it doth appear to us, that Mr. Hudson, the parson that came from Oxford with the King, was at Downham in Norfolk, with two

---

[6] Clarendon, iii, 17.

other gentlemen upon Thursday the last of April.' On this point they were incorrectly informed; it is clear from other sources that Hudson spent the whole of 30 April in consultation with Montreuil and the Scots, and did not rejoin the King in Norfolk until the evening of 1 May. 'We cannot yet learn where they were on Friday night,' the report continues: 'but Saturday morning, the 2nd of May, they came to a blind alehouse at Crimplesham, about eight miles from Lynn.' From one of Hudson's statements which will be quoted later, it seems certain that the party spent Friday night at the village of Mundford; and it is probable, though Hudson did not mention it, that they went on to the little alehouse at Crimplesham next day. 'From thence Mr. Hudson did ride on Saturday to Downham again, and there two soldiers met with him, and had private speech with him. Hudson was then in a scarlet coat. Then he met with Mr. Ralph Skipwith of his former acquaintance, and with him he did exchange his horse; and Skipwith and the said Hudson did ride to Southery ferry, a private way to go towards Ely; and went, by the way, to Crimplesham, and there were the other two, one in a parson's habit, which by all description was the King. Hudson procured the said Skipwith to get a grey coat for the Doctor (as he called the King) which he did. And then the King put off his black coat and long cassock, and put on Mr. Skipwith his grey coat. The King bought a new hat at Downham, and on Saturday went into the isle of Ely. Wherever they came, they were very private, and always writing. Hudson tore some papers when they went out of the house. Hudson did inquire for a ship to go to the north, or to Newcastle, but could get none. We hear at the same time there were six soldiers and officers, as is thought, at Oxburgh at another blind alehouse.[7]

There are several confusions and discrepancies in this report. It is impossible, for example, that Hudson can have gone to inquire for a ship: Lynn was the only place where such an inquiry could have been made, and his recorded movements do not allow him the time to visit that town. Possibly Ashburnham or Skipwith may have gone on this particular errand. Nor did Corbett and Walton, so lavish of minor details, hear of an incident which subsequently amused the Parliamentarians so much that it even

[7] Peck, *Desiderata Curiosa* (1779), 349–50.

found a place in the sober pages of Rushworth—that the King, evidently dissatisfied with Ashburnham's efforts at Oxford, had his hair cut again at Downham, and that 'the barber found much fault with the unevenness of his hair, and told him, the barber that last trimmed him, was much to blame for it'.[8] But on the whole their account, taken in conjunction with Hudson's various statements, does provide a fairly coherent narrative of what probably took place.

Hudson, in the meantime, had reached Southwell on the Wednesday morning, and at once delivered his message to Montreuil. The next two days were occupied with consultations between Montreuil and the Scots, at the end of which Montreuil told Hudson that the Scots would agree to the King's terms, but would not enter into any written undertaking. This did not satisfy Hudson, who insisted, 'to avoid mistakes, that the particulars might be set down in writing, lest I should afterwards be charged with making a false relation'. The propositions were then written down, either by himself or by Montreuil, and Montreuil once again submitted them to the Scots. According to Hudson, the propositions were:

'1. That they should secure the King in his person and in his honour.

'2. That they should press the King to do nothing contrary to his conscience.

'3. That Mr. Ashburnham and I should be protected.

'4. That if Parliament refused, upon a message from the King, to restore the King to his rights and prerogatives, they should declare for the King; and take all the King's friends into their protection. And, if the Parliament did condescend to restore the King, then the Scots should be a means, that not above four of them should suffer banishment; and none at all, death.'

The Scots once again 'seriously protested' that they agreed to these propositions and undertook to carry them out; and Montreuil now seems to have been satisfied that they would honour their undertakings. He wrote a reassuring note to the King, which included the sentence 'I desire your Majesty so much to trust me as to believe them'. Hudson thereupon left Southwell on Wednesday night on the long ride to Norfolk. He was with the King on

8 Rushworth, IV, i, 267.

Friday evening, gave him Montreuil's note and told him the whole story of the negotiations; upon which the King resolved to set out for the Scottish camp next day.

Hudson did not meet the King at the White Swan at Downham Market, as had been previously arranged.[9] In one of his examinations he explained that during their stay at Downham 'the King and Ashburnham had like to be discovered by a barber who said that their hairs were cut with a knife'; and that they had decided to leave Downham in case the man's suspicions had been aroused. As he rode towards Downham, he had been met by Skipwith, who had been sent by the King with the cryptic message that 'if he had any friends at Downham they were gone to Mundford to the Cherry'. It must have been at the little village of Mundford, therefore, that the King received Montreuil's message from Hudson, and that he took the momentous and final decision to surrender himself to the Scots. Ashburnham urged him to try once more to get a passage by sea to Newcastle; but Hudson pointed out that the 'news books' telling of their departure from Oxford had already reached Norfolk, and that they would be watched for and apprehended at any port, as a warrant from the Parliamentary authorities had to be produced by anyone intending to travel by sea. The King agreed that a journey by land to Southwell was their best and safest course.

Next day, Saturday 2 May, Hudson relates that 'the King sent me back to Downham from Mundford for a coat and sword, and I had it of him for him'. This roughly coincides with the report of Corbett and Walton; and we may also accept their statement that the King, who at some unspecified time had changed his servant's disguise for a clerical gown and cassock, now donned Mr. Skipwith's grey coat and made other changes in his attire in the alehouse at Crimplesham. It was probably here, also, that Hudson exchanged his horse, worn out with the hard riding of the

[9] The *Diary* of the Rev. William Stukeley, M.D., the antiquary, contains this passage under the date of 26 August 1746: 'The Rev. Mr. Shipley, of Downham, visited me. He says the White Swan Inn remains there, and they have a perfect memory of King Charles I lying there in 1646. There is some of the King's handwriting on a quarry of glass remaining in a window, and a walk by the town side, called the King's Walk, from his walking there whilst waiting for Dr. Hudson's return from Southwell, where he went to make a bargain for the King's coming to the Scots.'

previous day, for a fresh horse of Skipwith's. From Crimplesham
the party made for Southery Ferry, where they crossed the Ouse
and struck into the road which ran to Huntingdon, through the
south of the Fens, by way of Littleport, Ely and Earith.

Skipwith in the meantime returned to Snore Hall, and had
probably heard that the King had reached the Scottish army in
safety before his own part in the affair became known to the local
Parliamentarians. He was then arrested and brought before
Corbett and Walton, who reported that 'he offered himself freely
to us, and made free discovery to us'. They examined him at
great length, and then committed him to the custody of the
Mayor of Lynn, from which he was in due course released. They
extended their inquiries to all the known Royalists of the district,
especially those whose houses the King might have visited.
Suspicion was naturally directed towards Sir Hamon L'Estrange,
as the most prominent supporter of the King in the Lynn neighbourhood. As it happened, Sir Hamon was in London throughout
these weeks. He was engaged in one of his many attempts to
persuade the authorities to relax or modify the demands made
upon him as the result of the siege of Lynn. But his wife's
account-books contain an entry of a payment to Markant and
Constable, two of his servants, 'for their charges at Lynn when
Mr. Miles Corbett did send for my sons and them, to examine if
King Charles had been at our house'.[10]

4

It is idle to speculate on the King's thoughts during those extraordinary days, as he passed disguised as a serving-man within
sight of his Castle of Windsor, and caught a glimpse of his capital
city from Harrow Hill, and gazed from the tree-shaded churchyard on the hill behind Downham Market across the vast desola-
tion of the Fens, and rode in the soft spring weather through the
little Norfolk villages. His past life had become a story of tragic
failure. He was now journeying into a dangerous and incalculable
future. But no disaster could shake his religious faith; he was conscious that, for all his follies and mistakes, he had steadfastly

[10] N.N.R.O., L'Estrange MSS., 10.

upheld against every temptation the integrity of his Church; and it is not surprising that at this dark time his thoughts turned to a nearby community of Anglican dévots whose house he had visited more than once in earlier days.

In 1625 Nicholas Ferrar, a successful young merchant and politician, prominent in the affairs of the Virginia Company, had withdrawn from the world and had settled with other members of his family in the manor-house of Little Gidding in Huntingdonshire. Here they had established a religious community, in which continual worship, prayer, fasting and almsgiving were combined with the daily routine of a large and prosperous country family. In addition to their constant and strict observance, the inmates of Little Gidding were noted for the *Harmonies of the Gospels* and similar works, exquisitely written and arranged, which were greatly valued by the eminent churchmen and laymen to whom they were presented: while the needlework bookbindings embroidered by the ladies of the community were famous all over England. The 'Arminian Nunnery', as it was named by its Puritan foes, aroused much interest and curiosity. Charles had visited the Ferrars in 1633, and had subsequently accepted a *Harmony of the Gospels* executed and bound in their most elaborate style. 'How happy a King were I,' he had said to Laud, 'if I had many more such workmen and women in my kingdom! God's blessing on their hearts and painful hands!' Again in 1642, on his way northward to York after his breach with Parliament had become irreparable, he had spent a few happy hours in the tranquillity of Little Gidding. Now once more, as he rode with his two companions towards the Huntingdonshire uplands, he decided to visit the home of these loyal recluses.

Nicholas Ferrar, the guiding spirit of the community, had died some years before; but his brother John was still living there with some of his family. At an unknown date during these troubled years the place was raided and despoiled; it may have happened before the King's visit, but the scanty evidence seems to suggest that it took place later, perhaps even as an act of reprisal if his presence there came to be publicly known. Parliamentarian troopers broke into the house and plundered the farmstead; the little church was desecrated, and sheep roasted at a fire built from the broken fragments of the organ; Nicholas Ferrar's books and manuscripts were destroyed, and his furniture and plate carried away. But all was quiet when the King 'came very privately and in the night to Gidding'; and John Ferrar received him with all duty and loyalty at the house which he had last visited with his son the Prince of Wales and a throng of courtiers and attendants.[11]

Three hundred years afterwards, the King's visit provided one of the themes in the poem of *Little Gidding*, the last and perhaps the greatest of T. S. Eliot's *Four Quartets*. The figure of Charles appears early in the poem—'If you came at night like a broken king'—and one recalls that as he rode sadly towards Gidding the hedges were 'white again, in May, with voluptuary sweetness'. But it is later, in the long meditation of the third section of the poem, that Charles's journey to the place 'where prayer has been valid', to kneel for awhile in the Ferrars' little church, is given its full significance.

> If I think, again, of this place,
> And of people, not wholly commendable,
> Of no immediate kin or kindness,
> But some of peculiar genius,
> All touched by a common genius,
> United in the strife which divided them;
> If I think of a king at nightfall,
> Of three men, and more, on the scaffold
> And a few who died forgotten
> In other places, here and abroad,
> And of one who died blind and quiet,
> Why should we celebrate
> These dead men more than the dying? . . .
> We cannot revive old factions
> We cannot restore old policies
> Or follow an antique drum.
> These men, and those who opposed them
> And those whom they opposed
> Accept the constitution of silence
> And are folded in a single party.[12]

It is the final comment on the tragedy of the Civil War.

[11] D.N.B. *sub* Nicholas Ferrar.
[12] T. S. Eliot, *Little Gidding*, section III.

The day had been a long and weary one for the King, perhaps the most exhausting of all his journey. He had ridden across the Norfolk heathlands and wastes, across the Isle of Ely with the Cathedral soaring above the endless levels, across the meadows and the wooded uplands of Huntingdonshire. No doubt he would have been thankful to pass the night in the quiet sanctuary of Little Gidding. But by this time all England knew that he had left Oxford for an uncertain destination; and there was a risk that watch might be kept on so well known a Royalist house. About ten o'clock that night, therefore, the party left Gidding and went to a house in the neighbouring village of Coppingford. Hudson had passed through Coppingford the previous day on his way from Southwell to Norfolk, accompanied by one John Browne, an innkeeper of St. Ives, an old acquaintance whom he had met by chance at Melton Mowbray. Browne had been left at Coppingford, no doubt in order to arrange a lodging for the King, and he was waiting to receive the travel-stained party when they arrived. The house at Coppingford was so small, according to Hudson, that 'the King and we with my host and hostess and two children were by the fire in the hall; there was no other chimney in the house'.

Here they spent Saturday night, and remained for the whole of the next day. They did not go to church that Sunday, but Hudson read prayers to the King. They sent from Coppingford to the faithful Mr. Skipwith for another horse, which was brought to them at Stamford on the following day. On Sunday afternoon they sent John Browne before them to Stamford, to make arrangements for their reception; they themselves left Coppingford about six o'clock, and arrived at Stamford about nine. When subsequently examined by the Parliamentary authorities, Browne said that he himself put up at the Falcon Inn, but the King and his two companions 'lodged at a gentleman's house in Stamford whose name this examinant knows not'. Hudson stated that their host at Stamford was a Mr. Cave, and that 'the King was at no gentleman's house but Mr. Cave's in Stamford in all his journey'. They spent the Sunday night at Stamford, and remained there next day until eleven o'clock at night. Then they set out for Southwell; and after travelling all night they arrived at Montreuil's lodgings at seven o'clock on the morning of Tuesday, 5 May.

5

The King's journey was over. Never again, except for a few days after his flight from Hampton Court in 1647, was he able to move about his kingdom as a free agent. He had only been at Southwell a few hours when the commissioners of the Scottish Estates arrived. They lost no time in making a variety of demands upon him, including the taking of the Covenant. No such terms had been mentioned in the course of his negotiations with Montreuil. Acceptance of the Covenant, with its denial of episcopacy and endorsement of the Presbyterian system, was an impossible condition, and he rejected it firmly. Three days later the Scots removed him to Newcastle. There he remained, continually subjected to the importunities of their preachers and a variety of minor humiliations, until they handed him over to Parliament early in the next year.

Ashburnham and Hudson were both allowed to accompany him to Newcastle. But the Scots, anxious on certain points to conciliate Parliament, asked the King to dismiss Ashburnham, who was among the prominent Royalists who had been excepted from pardon in earlier negotiations. It was further hinted that both Ashburnham and Hudson were in danger of being handed over to Parliament if they remained. The King therefore sent Ashburnham abroad, describing him in a letter to the Queen as 'Jack Ashburnham, who at this present is the most (and with the greatest injustice) persecuted of all my servants, and merely for his fidelity to me'.[13] He reached France in safety, and was able to give the Queen all her husband's private messages and to explain all his most secret hopes and fears. In 1647, when the King was in the power of Parliament, he was allowed to return to England and resume his attendance upon him. He accompanied him in his flight from Hampton Court in November of that year, the escape which ended ignominiously in his imprisonment in the Isle of Wight. He was removed from attendance on the King at the beginning of 1648, and was never allowed to see him again. Under the Commonwealth he was subjected to repeated persecution and imprisonment; but at the Restoration he received his old post of

[13] *Charles I in 1646*, 39.

Groom of the Bedchamber, became once more a notable figure at Court, and lived in prosperity until his death in 1671.

For Hudson a harsher fate was reserved. When it became clear that he was in danger if he remained at Newcastle, he begged the King not to send him abroad but to allow him to go to London, as he thought he could do some service there. He reached London in disguise, and soon afterwards tried to go to France to consult the Queen, but was apprehended at Sandwich early in June. His examinations by the Parliamentary authorities, which were numerous and protracted, furnish most of the known facts about the King's journey from Oxford; but they incriminated no one and gave away no vital information. He remained in confinement until November, when he broke out of prison. Retaken early in 1647, he was firmly incarcerated in the Tower, where he occupied his time in composing a treatise on the Divine Right of Government. Once again the indomitable clergyman managed to escape, disguised as a hawker with a basket of apples on his head, in 1648, during the Second Civil War. He gathered together a small body of Royalists from Lincolnshire and the adjacent counties, and declared for the King. Their headquarters was Woodcroft House, about seven miles from Stamford, from which they made many sorties against the local Parliamentary troops. Eventually Woodcroft House was surrounded by the enemy, and an entry was forced into it. Fighting desperately at the head of his little garrison, Hudson was forced up to the roof of the house, and then over the battlements. He clung to a projecting water-spout, but his hands were cut off at the wrists and he dropped into the moat. He managed somehow to paddle himself to the bank of the moat, but no quarter was given to him; he was knocked on the head with the butt of a musket.[14]

[14] Peck, *Desiderata Curiosa*, 378-9.

CHAPTER XVI

The Royalist Reaction

I

The war had come to an end with the victors deeply divided, both in religion and in politics. The Presbyterian majority in Parliament was confronted by a sizeable minority of members who may be broadly described as Independents. In the Army the situation was reversed. Many of the officers of the New Model had been drawn from among the people. They felt no love for the gentlemen of standing who had commanded the Parliament's forces, none too efficiently, during the earlier stages of the war, and who from their seats in Parliament still controlled the country. Amongst the rank and file there was a widespread mood of discontent with the social order. Officers and men alike, they knew that the war had been won, and the King defeated, by their own efforts; and they were determined that their voice should now be heard. From Cromwell downwards, the Army had come to regard the dominant majority in Parliament with profound mistrust. Sir Jacob Astley did not have long to wait for the fulfilment of his prophecy that the victors would fall out amongst themselves.

One of the first measures of Parliament, during the summer of 1646, was the attempted imposition of a Presbyterian system upon the nation. An ordinance of the previous year had already directed each county to prepare a scheme of division into classical presbyteries by districts, and this order was now repeated. The instructions to the Mayor, Sheriffs and Aldermen of Norwich were in the following terms:

Gentlemen,

The Parliament being desirous above all things to establish truth and righteousness in these kingdoms, towards which the settlement of a church government is very conducible, and hath resolved to settle a presbyterial government in the kingdom for the better effecting whereof, you are required with the advice of godly ministers and others to consider how the county and city of Norwich may be most conveniently divided into distinct classical presbyteries, and what ministers and others are fit to be of each classis, and you are accordingly to make such divisions and nomination of persons for each classical presbytery: which divisions, and persons so named for every division, you are to certify to this House with all expedition.

I am your very loving friend

W. LENTHALL, Speaker.[1]

No doubt these orders were carried out, both in Norwich and in the county. But no details of the divisions, or of the persons chosen to form each classis, have survived. The lists for Suffolk were printed at the time, and show the county as divided into fourteen classes, each containing a single hundred or a group of hundreds. The names of several members of Parliament, and others of the leading gentry, are among the select number of the elders of the classis within whose area they resided. Six or eight ministers were included in each classis, and a substantial number of lesser gentry were associated with them. Presumably the same pattern would have been followed in Norfolk. In any case, except in London and in Lancashire, the Presbyterian system never seriously functioned, and was soon abandoned.[2]

All through the summer and autumn of 1646 the King remained at Newcastle, resisting the unceasing efforts of his Scottish custodians to persuade him to accept the Covenant. Deprived even of the faithful companionship of Ashburnham and Hudson, he wrote to the Queen that 'there was never man so alone as I . . . all the comfort I have is in thy love and a clear conscience'.[3] He rejected the terms brought by a body of commissioners from Parliament—the taking of the Covenant, the abolition of episcopacy, renunciation of the control of the militia by the Crown. He watched the growing power of the Independents against the Presbyterians, and rejoiced in the division of his enemies, even though he must have recognized the greater menace of the

---

[1] Norwich Corporation Records, 7K., f. 34. Blomefield, iii, 390.

[2] Shaw, ii, 27-8, 423-31.

[3] *Charles I in 1646*, 46.

Independent temper. Rumours of Royalist stirrings also came to his ears. But at the close of 1646, when it was certain that neither the Scots nor the English could bend him to their will, an accommodation was reached between them. The Scots agreed to withdraw to their own country on receiving the money which they claimed from Parliament for the payment of their troops. The sum was fixed at £400,000. At the end of January 1647 the King was formally handed over as a prisoner to an English guard, under the command of Philip Skippon.

Parliament had selected Holdenby House in Northamptonshire for the King's residence. There he was installed, under guard but in considerable state; and there he remained for some months, while the feeling between Army and Parliament grew daily in intensity. Among the members deputed by Parliament to attend upon him at Holdenby was Sir John Holland, who had now returned from his sojourn in the Netherlands. The demeanour of Sir John and two others was distinguished by the King, according to Sir Philip Warwick, 'from those who less observed him'; although even they, added that ardent Royalist, 'had entertained an office which unbecame gentlemen of free minds'.[4] Finally, on 3 June, he was removed from Holdenby by Cornet Joyce, acting against the authority of Parliament but undoubtedly on the instructions of Cromwell. He was now the prisoner not of Parliament but of the Army, which marched slowly on London. It entered London in August, and came to a temporary accommodation with Parliament, from which some of the more combative Presbyterians had now withdrawn. The King was lodged, still under guard, at Hampton Court.

The seventeenth century loved metaphors drawn from its favourite pastimes. Clement Walker, himself a Presbyterian member of Parliament, described the two factions at this juncture 'as it were in a cockpit pecking at one another'. The pecking was to continue for some time yet; but the Army was destined to prevail, and Walker was to write of 'Independency triumphant, rousing itself upon its legs, clapping its wings, and crowing in the midst of the pit, with its enemy under its feet'.[5] In the meantime the

---

[4] Warwick, 297. Holland had himself protested in Parliament against his nomination for this duty, but was over-ruled (B.L. MS. Tanner 239, f. 17).

[5] Walker, *History of Independency* (1660), 27.

more radical elements of the Army showed increasing militancy. Their demands went far beyond the dissolution of Parliament and a fresh election. Republicanism was in the air. The soldiers brought forward their grievances through the mouths of their chosen 'agitators'. The ideas of the Levellers, with their threats to property and order, were spreading through the ranks.

In this atmosphere the Army debates took place during the winter months. On these occasions Cromwell, who had in effect become the leader of the Independents in Parliament, entered into the fullest consultation with the diverse elements of the Army, officers and troopers alike. It was at the first of these debates, held in the parish church of Putney, that John Jubbes from Norfolk, now a Lieutenant-Colonel, made a memorable intervention. He began, as did many of the speakers, by enlarging on his religious views. 'Truly I do not know how to distinguish whether the Spirit of God lives in me or no, but by mercy, love and peace; and on the contrary whether the spirit of Antichrist lives in me, but by envy, malice and war. I am altogether against a war if there may be a composure possible, so that the Englishman may have his privileges.' He then brought forward certain queries, wherein he 'desired satisfaction for the preventing of the effusion of blood'. Could the Parliament be purged of its actively Presbyterian members, 'and still continue a House'? If so, 'whether the major part of the remainder be such persons as are desirous of giving satisfaction to our or the kingdom's just desires?' Would such persons 'declare the King guilty of all the bloodshed, vast expense of treasure, and ruin that hath been occasioned by all the wars both of England and Ireland?' Blunt questions of this kind led towards conclusions that Cromwell and his chief associates must already have been pondering in their hearts.[6]

Shortly after the debates at Putney the King escaped from Hampton Court together with three courtiers, including John Ashburnham who had accompanied him on his earlier flight from Oxford. He made his way to the Isle of Wight, and finally surrendered himself to Colonel Robert Hammond, the Governor of the island, who installed him at Carisbrooke Castle. The menacing tone of the Army debates had come to his ears, and he had received a letter threatening his life. Cromwell may have deliberately

[6] Woodhouse, 99–100. Gardiner, iii, 234.

afforded him the opportunity of escape. Such at least was the view of the poet Andrew Marvell a few years later. Hampton Court, he wrote, revealed the full measure of Cromwell's statecraft,

> Where, twining subtle fears with hope,
> He wove a net of such a scope
> That Charles himself might chase
> To Carisbrooke's narrow case.[7]

At Carisbrooke the King was treated with respect by Colonel Hammond, whose wife was John Hampden's daughter and therefore a kinswoman of Cromwell. He might without much difficulty have escaped to France; but he now preferred to live under Hammond's easy surveillance, endeavouring to play off the Army against the Presbyterians, and the Scots against both.

The whole country was in perplexity and discontent. Something of the mood is reflected in a letter written by Thomas Knyvett to the younger Sir John Hobart on 11 February 1648. Sir John had now succeeded his uncle and namesake in the baronetcy and the ownership of Blickling; and it is surprising, in view of his family tradition as well as his future career, to find him addressed in such frank terms by a noted Royalist. He was to marry as his second wife the widow of Colonel Hammond, the King's warden at Carisbrooke; and he pursued the resultant connection with Cromwell to the extent of becoming a member of his House of Lords. But all this lay a long way ahead. Evidently in 1648 his fear of Independency and social unrest brought him into sympathy with Knyvett's point of view.

'Worthy Sir,' wrote Knyvett, 'the scene of our sad distracted commonwealth's affairs alters almost every day.' Although it was now generally known that the King had been treating at Carisbrooke with the Scots Commissioners, and that an intervention on his behalf by a Scottish army was planned, Knyvett felt that he could never welcome the aid of so treacherous a nation. 'For though I know our English rulers now stink in the nostrils of all loyal true-hearted subjects, yet, sure I am, I shall join with the cunninger traitors of the two; and therefore let Presbyterians and

---

[7] Andrew Marvell, *An Horatian Ode on the Return of General Cromwell from Ireland* (1650).

Independents fight till I part them. But it is so far from coming to that, as it is now noised up and down, that a reconciliation and compliance is a-working between the two factions; which, if once composed, the next effect sure must be a marriage between a Presbyterian incubus and an Independent succubus, to beget a new generation of devils for the next Parliament; or rather for the continuation of this, so well grounded in diabolical principles.'[8]

2

With Presbyterians and Independents at loggerheads, and the King in effect the prisoner of neither party, Royalists all over the country began to take heart once more. Even in the regions which had been most Parliamentarian in sympathy, a reaction began to develop in their favour. The currents of popular opinion are always mysterious in their working. 'Though we had peace,' wrote Selden, 'yet 'twill be a great while ere things be settled: though the wind lie, yet after a storm the sea will work a great while after.'[9] This was emphatically so in the city of Norwich, and especially among the artisans and apprentices, who hitherto had not had the opportunity or perhaps the inclination to express their views. Like the private soldiers of the Army, but in a different direction, they now made their grievances known. A long period of discontent culminated in a riot to be known in Norwich history and legend as 'the great blow', which convulsed the city in the spring of 1648.

This Royalist demonstration was to a large extent the result of years of frustration and boredom. In the now distant sixteen-thirties, life in Norwich had not lacked colour and enjoyment even for the humblest citizen. The Guild Days, when the Mayor rode in procession after his election, were celebrated with pageantry and side-shows, the streets adorned with garlands and streamers, Snap and Dick Fool raising laughter all along the route. There were stage-plays, shows of tumblers and freaks, the Florists' Feasts with their songs and masques. Christmas was kept with the traditional mingling of reverence and gaiety, religious observance and family happiness. All this had long since been

[8] Knyvett, 42-3, quoted from Cary, *Memorials of the Civil War*, i, 376-8.
[9] Selden, 147.

NORFOLK IN THE CIVIL WAR

swept away. On the Christmas Eve of 1645 the Mayor had sent special directions to ministers and churchwardens that they were to have no sermons nor communions in their churches next day, and that all shops were to be set open as usual.[10]

For the younger element in the city, the mass of apprentices just growing into manhood, the festival of Christmas and the gaieties of Guild Day were distant memories; but they were memories which they, and many of their elders, delighted to recall. The Puritan clergy in their sermons, and in particular the vociferous John Carter at St. Peter Mancroft, did their best to discourage such backward glances. Four years earlier Carter had preached his celebrated sermon, *The Nail hit on the Head, and driven into the City and Cathedral Wall of Norwich*, in which he assailed the Mayor and Corporation on the grounds that their government of the city was lax and indulgent. The rule of the godly, he proclaimed, should be far more severe.

The new Mayor of 1647 was John Utting, a man of moderate opinions, and regarded with mistrust in consequence by the more austere Puritans. At his installation on Guild Day the sermon was again preached by John Carter, and was entitled *The Wheel turned by a Voice from the Throne of Glory*. It was openly directed at Utting and those of his colleagues who shared his views. The magistrates were the wheels, Carter pronounced, and they should turn in accordance with the divine command. Yet they had suffered fish to be sold in the streets on the sabbath day, and had rebuked a godly minister who had dared to protest. 'Oh that these rusty and ill-shaped wheels were filed, or oiled, or removed, and better put in their room!' Still worse, malignant clerics were bringing back the old superstitions. 'O Wheels have you not eyes! Do you not see what abundance there are of these? Why do you let them lie so quietly? Oh Wheels! turn over them: either mend them, or remove them, or break them.' As as for the chief wheel, the unfortunate Mayor—'O Wheel! with all your weight, turn over idolaters, heretics, blasphemers, schismatics, sabbath-breakers: suppress them, and make much of them that fear the Lord . . . O Wheel! O Wheel! never leave turning, and turn all wheels to bring more faithful and able ministers into the city . . . O Wheel put on: to settle church government, to settle the union of parishes, to

[10] Norwich Court Book 1634–46, f. 405. Blomefield, iii, 392.

procure pastors for every flock, to see the sabbaths of the Lord sanctified. O Wheel lift up God, lift up Christ on his throne, and the Lord will lift you up higher.' This outpouring was published with a dedication to Utting, full of ironical undertones, and with a note addressed 'To those magistrates in the city of Norwich, who were so highly offended and exasperated at this sermon'. For good measure *The Nail hit on the Head* was reprinted at the same time.[11]

Utting's sympathies, as those of so many throughout the kingdom at this juncture, may indeed have been turning towards the King. The leading Puritans in Norwich were no doubt aware of the gathering Royalist reaction; and the publication of Carter's sermons may have been part of a campaign to discredit the Mayor and his supporters. Certainly the suspicions of his adversaries were not lessened later in the year, when the apprentices of the city assembled in the Castle Yard and petitioned him that the festival of Christmas might be observed according to the ancient forms.

However much he may have sympathized privately with their request, it is unlikely that the Mayor felt able to grant it. Such a concession, at a time of nation-wide tension, would have been highly imprudent. Even so, the Puritan faction presented him a few weeks later with a counter-petition, urging 'a more speedy and thorough reformation'. They emphasized that some of the ejected clergy had been allowed to preach in the churches of Norwich, whilst their own godly ministers were discouraged and slighted. In some cases the Directory, the manual issued by the Assembly of Divines, was being ignored, and the Prayer Book and the old ceremonies were being brought back into use. There were still images that had not been destroyed—a crucifix on one of the Cathedral gates, another on the free-school, a figure of Christ on the church of St. George Tombland. They demanded that the various ordinances of Parliament for silencing ejected ministers, for abolishing idolatry, and for defacing images should henceforward be strictly enforced. Although this document was signed by a number of substantial citizens, Utting disregarded it as he had done the petition of the apprentices.

His opponents then took action. A party of them, including Thomas Ashwell, one of the Sheriffs, rode up to London and

---

[11] *The Nail and the Wheel* (1647), 90, 97-9.

laid their grievances before Parliament. On Saturday 22 April, a pursuivant arrived in Norwich, with orders to take the Mayor into custody and convey him to Westminster, there to answer the charges against him. A former Mayor, an elderly man of strong Puritan sympathies named Christopher Baret, was appointed to act as his deputy; and he and the Corporation were enjoined to take care 'that the orders and ordinances of Parliament be duly and punctually observed, and not slighted as formerly'.[12]

3

The community of Norwich, even after the disruptions of the war years, retained a deep sense of civic loyalty and pride. The Mayor represented, in the eyes of the citizens, the rights and privileges which they derived from their ancient charter. When they took their oaths as freemen they had sworn 'to support their Mayor and to keep him in the city during his year'; and they remembered that oath now. They remembered also how their Mayor of 1642, William Gostlin, had been deprived of his office and for a time imprisoned. Deep feeling had been aroused, even though opinion in Norwich had then been weighted strongly on the other side. Now that a Royalist reaction was gathering strength, a repetition of the outrage caused still greater indignation. Many people of moderate views felt disposed to support Utting, in addition to those of Royalist sympathies or otherwise disaffected towards the Parliament. The apprentices were enthusiastically on his side, a body of tough and active young men with a natural intolerance of constituted authority, by no means a negligible factor in disturbed times. There had been serious rioting by the apprentices of London earlier in the month. Now it was their own turn.

As soon as the news of the Mayor's deposition reached Norwich, his sympathizers drew up a petition to Parliament, 'testifying

[12] The ensuing pages are largely based on the depositions of those concerned in the riot (Norwich Corporation Records, 12b). They were used by Walter Rye in an account of the riot in his appendix to his *History of the Bethel Hospital in Norwich* (1906), which I have also consulted. The version in Blomefield, iii, 393-6, also draws upon these depositions, although he seems to have had access to some other contemporary account which I have not traced.

his good government and behaviour'. They circulated it throughout the city, and obtained a great number of signatures. During Sunday, 23 April, all sorts of rumours began to spread, and the people became restive. Groups started to shout abuse at the Puritan aldermen, and threatened to hang Sheriff Ashwell and the pursuivant upon the Castle mound. When it was reported that the Mayor was to be carried away secretly in the night, they locked all the city gates and took away the keys. Towards midnight a great multitude assembled in the Market Place, some of them with arms. A password, 'For God and King Charles', was given out; and a Royalist spokesman told them that 'if they suffered the Mayor to be carried away, they would have a governor put in (as was done at Lynn) and then all would be tried by martial law; and then we had as good be free of Catton, as free of the City, for freemen would have no freedom at all in any choice.'

The Mayor did everything possible to calm the tumult. He assured his well-wishers that there was no likelihood of his being taken away during the night, and begged them to disperse. But on Monday morning the people assembled once more, in still larger numbers and in a more threatening mood, in Chapel Field. Thence they moved to the Market Place, where the pursuivant was lodging at the King's Head; and when, about ten o'clock, it was rumoured that he was about to depart with the Mayor in his custody, they were with difficulty prevented from attacking the house. The Mayor in person tried to appease them. But they continued to shout that they would purge the Bench of Aldermen and the Common Council; that they would 'pluck the Roundheads out, and put such honest men in, as would go to Church and serve God'. Finally it was thought best for the pursuivant to leave the city unaccompanied by the Mayor. Some of the more responsible citizens managed to smuggle the terrified official out of his lodging, and escorted him a couple of miles beyond the gates, after which he made his way back to his masters at Westminster. The Mayor, although technically deposed from his office, continued his efforts to pacify the rioters.

But the situation was now getting completely out of hand. The crowd began to attack the houses of the leading Puritan aldermen, and especially that of Ashwell the Sheriff, whose information to Parliament had brought about the removal of the Mayor. They smashed Ashwell's windows, broke open the doors, and searched the house for arms—of which, since he was a captain of the militia, there was a considerable store. Some handed the arms out of the windows to their comrades; others drank the Sheriff's beer and devoured his brawn and his pies. They then attacked the houses of Thomas Kett, another of the party who had ridden to London to denounce the Mayor, and of a former Mayor and prominent Parliamentarian called Adrian Parmenter, whose wife's hasty distribution of food did not avert considerable damage. Other houses were entered, and the more purposeful of the insurgents collected and distributed all the arms they could find; but there was also a good deal of indiscriminate looting and destruction.

As the day wore on, the position grew still more serious. Many of the poorer citizens and apprentices had at first regarded the affair as a glorious day's holiday, as an opportunity to shout and halloo for King Charles and against the Roundheads, to break the windows and drink the strong beer of the Puritan merchants whose rule they found so oppressive. But the authorities had already sent for help to the nearest military force, a body of cavalry stationed at East Dereham under the command of Colonel Charles Fleetwood: and word was brought to the rioters, about three o'clock in the afternoon, that the troopers were on their way. Fleetwood was absent from Norfolk at the time; but his second-in-command had at once dispatched a troop of horse and a portion of another troop to Norwich. The news only served to stiffen the determination of the crowd, and they swore to resist the troopers at all costs.

They would need a far larger supply of arms than they had yet obtained; and there was in Norwich one ample store of arms, which they now resolved to capture. Not far from the church of St. Peter Mancroft, on the site of the present Bethel Hospital, there stood a large house which served as the headquarters of the County Committee and as its arsenal. It was known to contain a store of arms and ammunition of all descriptions; and its garrison numbered two or three men only, who were probably caretakers rather than guards, and can in any case have scarcely anticipated an attack from an angry mob. Nevertheless, when the crowd began to surge round the 'Committee House' these defenders bolted the doors and barred the windows; and one of them discharged a firearm through a window and killed a boy. This was the first loss of life, and it infuriated the rioters, who stormed their way into the building and began to remove the contents of the arsenal. Muskets, pistols, swords, pikes, armour and bandoliers were handed out to the jostling crowd in the street; and bundles of official documents were flung from the windows and trampled in the gutter.

At the height of the tumult round the Committee House, the first of the troopers came riding into the city. They were a small force by comparison with the angry crowd, who thought they could easily deal with them. The two parties, Royalist citizens and Parliamentarian troopers, joined in a confused mêlée up and down St. Stephen's and the neighbouring streets. Reinforcements arrived for the soldiers. More and more arms were looted from the Committee House, to replace the pitchforks and spits and other improvised weapons of the rioters.

The loading of seventeenth-century firearms was a cumbrous business, involving coils of 'match' and a good deal of loose gunpowder. The powder-barrels stored in the Committee House had been hastily broken open, and a proportion of their contents dropped about the rooms. One of the mob afterwards described how he had filled his hat with gunpowder swept up from the stairs. Another rioter was seen 'very busy with a lantern in his hand'. It was inevitable that sooner or later the heat of such a lantern, or some even less adequately shielded flame, would come into contact with the scattered powder, and thence with the great powder-casks stored in the cellar. Suddenly, as the struggle continued to rage outside, the entire Committee House blew up with a tremendous explosion, killing a number of people and injuring many more, shattering the windows of several churches and innumerable houses, and showering debris all over the city.

4

The investigation of this affair occupied the magistrates of Norwich for many days afterwards; and the volume in which the depositions were taken down is still preserved amongst the city archives. All sorts of people were examined, in no particular order. Troopers, rioters and independent witnesses follow one another in bewildering succession; and it is difficult to make out, from these crabbed and crowded pages, the principle on which the magistrates committed certain individuals for trial and allowed others to go free. Some of the accused men may already have been regarded as notorious trouble-makers in the city. And after all the riot, in itself a sufficiently grave matter, had culminated in 'the great blow' with its alarming toll of lives. The ringleaders would now have to face the charge, not merely of riot and plundering, but of murder.

The general effect of this mass of depositions is as confusing as the riot itself must have been to most of the witnesses and participants. Men and lads and even some women, who had joined in the fray with no thought of the serious developments that would ensue, are now desperately anxious to exculpate themselves. Indignant troopers are still sore from their bruises. There are hints of political prejudice, suggestions of malice between neighbours. Margaret Brady reports Richard Turrell as saying, when asked if the sermon were done, 'No, Church is done, but he thought sermon would never be done, and if sermons were done it would be a better world than it is'. Jonathan Lambe makes it clear that he is 'burthened in conscience', before he gives the evidence which will help to bring Henry Goward to the gallows. Samuel Wilkinson describes how Thomas Balden rushed past his house with a pitchfork in his hand, bawling against the 'trooping rogues' who were riding into the city—'we will have the gates shut up and take them alive—now for these roundheadly rogues and whores!' Occasionally a deposition or a group of depositions will bring a particular episode into view, with its group of shouting and gesticulating actors; and then they relapse once more into the general turmoil.

One such episode, typical of many, is described in the depositions of two of the troopers, John Cornelius and Thomas Scott. It involved a couple named John and Margaret Secker, and also a certain Martin Morley, a mason who was later to execute remarkable mural monuments in the churches of Felbrigg and Foulden. Cornelius made no fewer than four depositions. In the first he stated that as he was riding down St. Stephen's Street 'one John Secker came forth with a watch bill and strook violently at this

338

informant therewith, and had not this informant warded off the blow this informant doth verily believe his head had been cliven in pieces'. In his second deposition how in the same street, near the house of Lady Frances Hobart—where the Assembly House now stands—a butcher named Worsley followed him 'with a great club in his hand', together with Risbrooke a watchmaker and Morley a mason. As the struggle swayed to and fro, 'the said Worsley with his club did strike down this informant's mare, and so he and his mare both fell, whereupon he and the said Worsley together with the said Morley and Risbrooke having staffs in their hands fell upon this informant and did beat him very much and had killed him had not relief come in and rescued him'. The third deposition relates to an unsuccessful assault upon him by one William Pratt with a fork. The fourth brings Mrs. Secker into the picture—'the woman now present who confess herself to be Margaret the wife of John Secker came running out with a spit and ran the same into the ribs of his horse, her husband then being fighting with him with a halbert.'

Nor was Cornelius the only victim of Mrs. Secker and her spit. The second trooper, Thomas Scott, deposed that he was 'charging through the White Swan back lane, and when he came against the Lady Frances' gate he was dismounted by the rioters, who presently after did get up behind one Thomas Sissen his fellow trooper of Captain Sanckey's troop, and coming riding down against St. Stephen's church was both of them beaten off their horse and was then wounded in several places by a little woman in a red waistcoat with a spit in her hand, and being so wounded, seeing a door open at Thomas Toller's he would have gone in to shelter himself, but when he was going in the said Thomas Toller and his wife did thrust out this informant and would not suffer him to remain in their house, but thrust him out, and exposed him after he was wounded, and could not well go, to the fury of the said rioters'.

At her examination Mrs. Secker would not admit any of this. 'She saith that upon Monday last in the afternoon Goodwife Wilson and Sotherton's wife in St. Stephen's street cried out for arms, whereupon this examinate brought a spit in her hand to the door, and when she came there Martin Morley, mason, took it out of her hand and did run down in the street with it, but what he did she know not nor what further became of him or the spit, for she hath it not again. And she denies that she did run at any trooper or trooper's horse with her spit, or any other weapon, or did hurt or wound any trooper at all.'

In the same fashion Thomas Toller absolutely denied that he had turned the wounded trooper from his door. He had gone to work at John Peck's before five o'clock in the morning, and had continued working there until seven at night, 'except when he was sent to Ben Baker's in the White Lion lane to buy some biscuits to be sent into the country, and was not gone above a quarter of an hour but did not come amongst any of the mutinous company.' When he left off work he went to see the damage done by the explosion to St. Stephen's church, and the ruins of the Committee House, and then returned home; but by that time the riot was long since over. He had never refused shelter to any trooper, nor had any trooper sought it. At this point the deposition is much frayed and torn; but it would seem that some other trooper had accused Toller of wounding him, and had identified him by his hands, which were 'dyed with the colour of yarn'. There must have been many other men in the crowd whose hands bore the stains of their trade as dyers. Toller continued to maintain his innocence.

In the end not one of the people involved in this particular episode was committed for trial. In spite of the statements of Cornelius, the husband of Margaret Secker does not even seem to have been examined; nor was the wife of Thomas Toller; nor were Worsley, Morley and Risbrooke. Probably they had all borne reasonably good characters hitherto, and were not the sort of people whom the magistrates wished to see punished. None of them was accused of plundering, and none had been seen on the premises of the Committee House. At all events their part in the riot was overlooked, and they sink once more into oblivion.

Very different was the treatment accorded to those considered by the authorities, rightly or wrongly, to be the ringleaders. One of these was a saddler named Henry Goward. Two men, Nathaniel Elmer and the conscience-burthened Jonathan Lambe, deposed that during the fatal afternoon they heard Goward say 'It were a good turn to go and blow up the Committee House upon the Roundheads'; and both had seen him prominent among the rioters. A little later Thomas Yonges heard Goward inviting the mob to advance on the Committee House and help themselves to the arms stored there. (Yonges was anxious to save his own skin; he confessed he had taken a pistol from the arsenal, but had brought it away before the house was fired, and later gave it to Goodwife Baxter.) An inn-keeper's wife named Ursula Moore laid information that on the Sunday night, when she and her husband were in bed, Goward and other company, to the number of twenty, came to her door. They were making a great noise in the street, and bore halberts in their hands; 'and the said Goward did say to her before she opened the door, that they were watch-men for King Charles and Mr. Mayor.' There was also a mysteri-ous gentleman in a black suit, who asked the others not to disclose his name. They spent half a crown in drink at her house, and Goward paid the reckoning.

These appear to be the only references to Goward in the depositions. Further evidence may have been brought against him at his trial, although it seems most unlikely that he or anyone else deliberately planned the blowing-up of the Committee House. Whatever the facts of the case may have been, he was regarded as one of the chief fomenters of the riot, and in due course he was condemned and executed.

5

Among the throng of excited apprentices, shouting up and down the streets for King Charles and confusion to the Roundheads, was a youth named Charles Porter. He was the son of the Rev. Edmund Porter, one of the former prebendaries of the Cathedral and rector of the parish of Hevingham, who had been ejected from his preferments in 1644. His son Charles, now apprenticed to a Norwich tradesman, lived to be a distinguished lawyer and Lord Chancellor of Ireland. He was a social and convivial person-age—'his person was florid', according to Roger North, 'and his speech prompt and artificial'—and in later years he was fond of recounting to his dinner-table companions the part which he had played in this riot of long ago.

This was his version of the story as he related it to Roger

North. 'He was the son of a prebend in Norwich and a 'prentice boy in the city in the rebellious times. When the Committee House was blown up, he was one that was very active in that rising, and after the soldiers came and dispersed the rout he, as a rat among joint-stools, shifted to and fro among the shambles and had forty pistols shot at him by the troopers that rode after him to kill him. In that distress he had the presence of mind to catch up a little child that, during the rout, was frightened and stood crying in the streets and, unobserved by the troopers, ran away with it. The people opened a way for him, saying, 'Make room for the poor child'. Thus he got off and, while search was made for him in the market-place and thereabouts, got into the Yarmouth ferry and at Yarmouth took ship and went into Holland, there being an opportunity of a ship then going off; and he was scarce out at sea before the pursuit came down after him; so narrowly he escaped hanging at that time. In Holland he trailed a pike and was in several actions as a common soldier. At length he kept a cavalier eating-house; but, his customers being needy, he soon broke and came for England, and being a genteel youth, was taken in among the Chancery clerks.'[13]

The story is so vividly told that one hesitates to cast any doubt upon it. Charles Porter may indeed have met with the adventures which he describes. Yet it is curious that throughout the volume of depositions, in which the names of scores of the rioters occur, there appear to be no accusations whatever against him. If his part in the affair had been so conspicuous that it was necessary to pursue him to Yarmouth, surely his name might be expected to appear somewhere in the depositions. The volume does contain, however, the examination of an apprentice named Charles Porter; and he signed it in a clear and educated hand, the hand of a youth who had received good schooling. The great majority of the examinants either signed their evidence in a laborious scrawl or, still more often, affixed their marks. There may have been two apprentices named Charles Porter involved in the riot. They may both have been young men of good education. Nevertheless the coincidence does seem a little peculiar.

This Charles Porter had been observed to have a gun in his possession, and was under suspicion of having taken the gun from

[13] *Lives of the Norths,* i, 381–2.

the Committee House. In his examination before the justices he explained his possession of the gun in this way: 'He saith upon this day fortnight his master sent him to Thomas Barber of Magdalen Street for money, and the said Barber told this examinate that if he would buy a carbine he could help this examinate to a good pennyworth, and thereupon the said Barber went with this examinate to a soldier of Captain Blissett's troop at the Bull who had the said carbine, and this examinate did buy it for eight shillings, and the said Barber told this examinate it was now a vacant time, he might kill pigeons with it.' He did not carry the gun home, but sent it by a hostler to a person or place whose name is illegible. 'Upon Thursday last this examinate charged the same with powder, and as he was about to let it off his master came to the door, and thereon he went and set it in at Gibson's the cobbler's.' This story was corroborated by Gibson's wife. Nothing is said in the examination about any part which Porter may have played in the riot; and it would seem that the justices were satisfied by his explanation about the gun. It is all very different from Lord Chancellor Porter's heroic reminiscences; and probably we shall never know whether there were two Charles Porters or one.

6

The destruction which resulted from the blowing-up of the Committee House was immense and widespread. Estimates of the number of deaths vary greatly. In the first excitement people talked of two or three hundred; but later an official report to Parliament put the total at about forty. Many others must have been injured. Considerable damage was done to the churches of St. Peter Mancroft and St. Stephen's, and to their windows in particular. At both the churchwardens' accounts show heavy payments to glaziers, masons and carpenters, and special parish rates had to be levied to meet them. At St. Peter Mancroft it was necessary to shore up the tracery of the great east window, and during the next few years it was entirely renewed. The work was entrusted to the mason Martin Morley, who had been implicated in the riot, and he received the substantial sum of £55.[14] It is

[14] Woodforde, *The Norwich School of Glass-Painting* (1950), 17.

astonishing that the splendid medieval glass, which had been spared by the iconoclasts, survived this catastrophe also.

All over Norwich private householders mournfully surveyed their roofs, their windows, their ceilings—as their successors were to do in those same streets after the German air-raids three centuries later. Emergency measures were taken against the weather and the danger of thieves. Women and children were given shelter by neighbours whose houses had suffered less. The atmosphere is vividly preserved in two letters which have by chance survived. The first was written, on the evening of the riot, by a prominent citizen named Joseph Payne to his brother-in-law Richard Bensly in London. It will be noticed how warmly he commends the Mayor for his conduct throughout the whole business.

'Brother, our kind loves remembered and to all good friends . . . I must tell thee of the unhappiness befell our city this present day by an unruly multitude met together to prevent our Mayor going to London, who was sent for by a messenger from the Parliament. The Mayor used much diligence to preserve this messenger from danger, which was done, and he gone safe and well towards London this morning. After this the multitude goeth to Sheriff Ashwell, from thence to Mr. Kett's, so to Alderman Parmenter's where much mischief was done but not bloodshed, for the Mayor used what diligence he could to assuage their fury. The rout being gone from Mr. Parmenter's, the Mayor goeth to the Hall to consult with his brethren what course to take; then the people goeth to the Committee house (I mourn to tell you) where the magazine of powder that was there was fired, blew up the house where tis reported that at least fourscore are slain and divers wounded; they are now pulling the mangled bodies out of the rubbish. At the very instant of this miserable accident cometh a troop of horse riding into the market which then very easily dispersed the rest. Sam Gosling is slain by one of the troopers, going into the street with his cloak on, as I hear . . . The break of the air with the powder have blown most of the glass out of Mr. Hobart's house and mine and out of the church, a great deal of damage done to the city. Now at present, blessed be our God, the city is quiet and a watch set of the trained men to guard the city.

'I pray go see my noble friend Mr. John Hobart, his lodging is at Mrs. Bagnall's house at the Flower de Luce court in Fleet Street, present my service to him and her and his children's duties, tell him they be all very well but something affrighted with this day's distraction. They shall lodge at my house until I see the city a little settled, and at present we have stopped up his windows with boards as well as we could; as soon as we can we shall get them mended. Desire him not to be troubled at any thing, what I can do for him or his I will.'[15]

The second letter was written three days later by Justinian Lewyn, a lawyer who lived, like Bishop Hall, outside the walls of Norwich in the village of Heigham. It bears no address, but from internal evidence it was almost certainly addressed to the John Hobart mentioned in the previous letter.

'The tumult is over, but the evil consequents thereof I fear are of longer date, for now an inquisition is on foot *nodum in scirpo querere*, and God knows what will be the issue of it. Much mischief came of the blowing up of the Committee House, and of larger extent than could easily have been imagined, for your house in St. Gregory's had a share in it where most of the windows are shattered—to the so great affrightment of your little family, that they fled for sanctuary this night to your neighbour Mr. Payne, and the next morning I fetched them to Heigham, where, I hope, they shall remain in safety till your return. Your house in St. Giles his parish fared much worse, where your tenant, whom I understand would not quit possession by fair means, is unhoused by this accident. I took care to board up the windows of your lower rooms in your dwelling house, and I hear that Dr. Bing hath not been wanting to you at the other, but taken order to preserve what tile and glass there could be saved.'[16]

A letter written to the Speaker of the House of Commons on 4th May by the Deputy Mayor, old Christopher Baret, has also survived. He takes the credit for the pursuivant's escape entirely to himself, and makes no mention of the Mayor's efforts to appease the tumult—indeed he contrives to insert several hints to the Mayor's disadvantage. At the time of the tumult Utting's mayoralty had only a few more weeks to run, and an ironmonger named

[15] B.L. MS. Tanner 57, f. 35.
[16] B.L. MS. Tanner 311, f. 36.

Roger Mingay had already been chosen as his successor; but Baret and his supporters called an emergency meeting of the common council, which revoked Mingay's nomination and elected a more reliable Parliamentarian, Edmund Burman, in his stead. This was done by virtue of a special by-law, which had been much opposed by 'licentious and refractory persons'—in other words by the Royalist sympathizers in the Corporation, who must now have been too subdued by the recent events to offer much protest. It is not surprising that the election went off, in Baret's words, 'with that quietness and peaceableness as was wonderful'—especially as a troop of horse had been drawn up outside.

Having described these manœuvres, Baret goes on to tell the Speaker of the particular solicitude shown by the Almighty, at the time of the explosion, towards the supporters of the dominant régime. 'We have, in the great sense of the Almighty's goodness to this poor city and his infinite deliverance of us, in a word Sir give leave abruptly to say, not an honest man slain. In the blowing up of the house there were 3 families in it consisting of as I am informed 24 persons, divers neighbours next of many persons all overwhelmed in the same ruins, some lying above 4 hours buried are alive, all miraculously preserved, not one slain, all the other dead, we hear not of one in the house escaped alive, above 40 persons already taken up, how many more shall [be] we know not, besides broken shattered pieces blown far and nigh, abundance. For this we have appointed a day of thanksgiving to Almighty.'[17]

The phrasing and punctuation are somewhat vague, but the meaning is clear enough. And it is endorsed by some observations of the Rev. William Bridge, in a sermon preached before the House of Commons on 17 May. 'Ye have heard,' he told the assembled Members of Parliament, 'ye have heard of the lamentation of Norwich. There was a generation of men that rose up and threatened to destroy the godly party there, but the Lord so ordered things in his providence that those whom they threatened to destroy were preserved and the destroyers perished, nigh two or three hundred (if relations be right) blown up with powder or spoiled, and three godly families consisting of about twenty persons in several rooms of the house that was blown up were

[17] Ibid., f. 38.

all preserved, and not a bone of them broken, whilst the others flew up in the air, as spectacles of divine anger, as if God should speak from heaven. These are the people whom I would have preserved, and these are the people that I would have punished.'[18]

The Corporation of Norwich resolved that a day should 'be set apart and kept as a solemn day of thanksgiving for God's deliverance from the rebellious company of people that did rise against them'. They would attend at the Cathedral in full state, with the aldermen in their scarlet gowns. The Rev. John Carter was desired to preach there in the morning, and the Rev. John Collinges in the afternoon, for which they were to receive twenty shillings apiece. The great pieces of ordnance were to be shot off. Special peals were rung in the churches: at St. Peter Mancroft one Thomas Bubbins received 7s. 6d. 'for ringing on the thanksgiving day for the great deliverance from the Blow'. The corporation did everything possible to show its gratitude to 'the several troops of horse now in this city', and the sum of £250 was voted 'for repair of loss of horses and arms, and healing of wounded men'.[19]

John Utting, the delinquent Mayor, made his way to London, hopefully bearing with him the petition attesting to his good conduct which his supporters had circulated and signed. But the Second Civil War was about to break out in Kent and Essex; and the Parliament, faced by an uprising of great potential danger, had no time to concern itself with the aftermath of a minor demonstration which had been successfully quelled. It was ordered that Utting should be confined to his house at Brandon Parva; and nothing more was apparently done about him for many months to come. His misdoings were investigated in the course of 1649, and in September of that year a committee reported to the House upon his case. By that time Pride's Purge had eliminated several local members who might have spoken on his behalf, and he was treated with considerable severity. The report put the worst construction on all his actions; he was accused of organizing the petition in his own favour, encouraging the rioters, and ordering the gates to be shut against the troopers. It was added, for good measure, that he had embezzled some of the city funds. In all this he had been greatly countenanced by Alderman John Tolye.

[18] William Bridge, *Christ's Coming Opened.* (1648), 11.
[19] Norwich Assembly Book 1642-68, f. 62. Woodforde, *ut supra*, 17.

Now John Tolye was one of the most respected of all the Norwich citizens. He had been twice Mayor, in 1638 and 1644, and had represented the city in the Short Parliament. Many of the depositions relating to the riot had been taken in his presence and bear his signature. He had concurred in the earlier measures of the Parliament, and had sat on various Parliamentarian committees. But he was a man of moderate views; his sympathies had by now veered away from the dominant power; and he was for that reason, and perhaps also because he was one of the richer citizens, to be Utting's fellow-scapegoat. Parliament, on the strength of the committee's report, resolved that both were delinquents within the ordinance of sequestration. They were sent for in custody, and on 9 October were brought into the House by the Serjeant-at-Arms. Utting was fined £500 and imprisoned in the Fleet for six months; Tolye was fined £1,000 and imprisoned for three months; both were disabled from bearing any office under the Commonwealth. Neither lived to see the end of the Commonwealth, and no doubt they felt the effect of these heavy fines to the end of their days.

As for the rioters who had been committed to prison, they remained crowded together in the Castle throughout the stifling summer and the chilly autumn. In accordance with a disagreeable Puritan foible, they were purposely brought to trial upon Christmas Day. Nine were acquitted; twenty-four were fined £30 and sentenced to remain in prison until their fines were paid; eight were condemned to death. They were Christopher Hill, a brazier; Anthony Wilson, a blacksmith; William True, a dyer; Henry Goward, a saddler; Edward Gray, described as an 'oatmeal-maker'; two brothers, Thomas and John Bidwell, labourers; and Charles Emerson, whose occupation is not recorded. These eight men were hanged in the Castle Ditches on 2 January 1649, in company with two old women convicted of witchcraft.

They were ordinary small tradesmen and artisans, who had blundered into an ill-conceived demonstration against the dominant power. They had engaged in looting and rioting; the murderous explosion at the Committee House was laid to their charge; and by the laws of the land they were justly condemned to die. But a little scrap of evidence, suggesting the sympathy with which some and perhaps many of their fellow-citizens regarded them, lies hidden in the parish register of the church of St. Lawrence. 'January 2nd 1648–9. Buried Charles Emerson, executed in the Castle Deekes as one of the pretended mutineers when the then Committee house was blown up with 80 barrels of powder.' The implications of words alter with centuries; but it seems probable that this use of 'pretended' means that the incumbent of St. Lawrence, even in that intolerant time, was confiding to the pages of the register his belief that Charles Emerson and his companions had not deserved so harsh a fate.[20]

7

The Second Civil War was an outbreak of sporadic risings, with no coherent Royalist strategy and no effective direction or leadership. There was serious trouble in Wales and in the north of England early in the spring, and the expected Scottish invasion materialized in July. Welsh supporters of the King were dispersed at St. Fagan's in May, and Cromwell won his memorable victory over the Scots at Preston in August.

The eastern counties, so successfully dominated by the Parliament throughout the earlier war, were in a restless state. The riot at Norwich was only one of several similar demonstrations, though none had such catastrophic results. On 4 May two thousand men from Essex marched to Westminster, claiming to represent thirty thousand inhabitants of the county, and petitioned Parliament for the return of the King and the disbanding of the Army. On the 12th a riot at Bury St. Edmunds began with the setting-up of a maypole, with a large assemblage dancing and shouting 'For God and King Charles'. They seized the powder magazine and began to put the town into a posture of defence; but the local trained bands, assisted by troops sent by Fairfax and Fleetwood, managed to restore order, and two townsmen and two horses were the total casualties. A similar gathering was easily dispersed at Thetford. A little later there was fighting in the streets of Cambridge. 'The royal townsmen assisting the scholars of their party which drew into a body, charged with much gallantry, and after a long and hot dispute, the victory first one side and then on the

[20] E.A., iii, 34.

other, at last the Parliamenters prevailed, and the other left the field.' The siege of Woodcroft House in Northamptonshire, with the death of the King's chaplain and companion Michael Hudson, has already been described.[21]

Towards the end of May there was a general rising in Kent. The county had always contained a substantial number of Royalist sympathizers, and had long been restive, with a number of minor outbreaks; but its division into local groups and interests had prevented any concerted action. Nor was the pattern very different in this more serious revolt. From the first there was disunity between the various sections, and all was over in less then a fortnight. Fairfax and his troops had little difficulty in gaining the upper hand, and after one sharp action at Maidstone most of the Royalist forces melted away. The residue crossed the Thames and joined the fresh revolt which had just broken out in Essex.

A conspicuous figure in the Kentish rising was Roger L'Estrange, not long released from prison. In the rather chilly words of Clarendon, he 'retained his old affections, and more remembered the cruel usage he had received, than that they had not proceeded as cruelly with him as they might have done'. He was the friend and mentor of an enthusiastic young Royalist named Edward Hales, and through him was enabled to play an active part throughout the rising. Both from his own subsequent *apologia* for his doings in Kent, and from Clarendon's disapproving account of them, one derives the impression that the rebellion virtually centred around him.[22] But it is unlikely that the gentlemen of Kent were much disposed to follow the lead or even to listen to the advice of an outsider. We are warned by Dr. Alan Everitt, in his admirable volume on Kent during this period, that L'Estrange 'consistently exaggerates his own importance . . . he was a dominating figure among the "foreigners" who joined the rising, but their importance was marginal, not central, to the action as a whole'.[23] After the collapse of the revolt L'Estrange prudently retired abroad, and did not return to England for several years.

[21] Kingston, 255–65.

[22] Roger L'Estrange, *His Vindication to Kent, and the Justification of Kent to the World* (1649), *passim*. Clarendon, iii, 104–6.

[23] Alan Everitt, *The Community of Kent and the Great Rebellion*, 238n.

The rising in Essex began on 4 June at Chelmsford, where the County Committee was meeting to discuss the general situation. The Committee had ruled Essex with a heavy hand during the past years, and had incurred much enmity. Their meeting was invaded by an angry crowd, who bore them off as prisoners. The Royalists throughout the county rallied together, and were joined by some of the trained bands and presently by the men who had crossed from Kent. The whole force then established itself in Colchester, where it was besieged by Fairfax. The siege lasted for more than two months, bringing privation and famine to the luckless inhabitants. A woman who escaped from the town with her five children, but was turned back again by the besiegers, told them that 'could they get but dogs and cats to eat, it were happy for them, but all the dogs and cats, and most of the horses, are near eaten already'.[24] At the end of August the town was literally starved into surrender. The ugly mood of the Second War was exemplified by the summary trial, and immediate execution by a firing squad, of two of the Royalist commanders, Sir Charles Lucas and Sir George Lisle, and the shipping of many prisoners as slaves to the West Indies.

The Suffolk trained bands played a part in the reduction of Colchester, but in Norfolk all the available forces were needed to watch the ports and the coast. Nine ships of the fleet had mutinied, and joined with the Royalist ships which were based on Holland. The Prince of Wales left France to command the fleet so formed, and Lynn and Yarmouth were both likely ports for a landing. Fairfax wrote from the siege of Colchester to warn the bailiffs of Yarmouth of the danger threatening them. He was sending a body of horse to stand by, but not to garrison the town. Parliament reinforced his warning—'we conceive you cannot but be sensible of the danger your town is in, by reason of the ships revolted; if they should make their descent there, and surprise your town, it would not only be a very great prejudice to the public, but might bring the same misery upon the place which the land forces of the enemy have done upon Colchester'. They had ordered Captain Brewster's company from Suffolk and another company from Norwich to draw into the town, 'not with any intention to make a garrison, but to preserve you from surprise

[24] Rushworth, IV, ii, 1232.

of the enemy, and from the mischief and misery that will attend it'.[25]

Nothing could be more unwelcome to a town like Yarmouth than the prospect of a garrison of soldiers, and both Fairfax and the Parliament were at pains to reassure them accordingly. At the end of July the Prince's ships did appear in Yarmouth roads, and summoned the town to surrender. One of the ships, incidentally, was commanded by a sworn foe of Yarmouth, the freebooting Captain Thomas Allin from Lowestoft, whose activities were described in an earlier chapter. The force sent by Fairfax, under a Major Jermy, 'a faithful and stout commander', probably Robert Jermy of Bayfield in Norfolk, had to take prompt action. There was some Royalist feeling within this very Parliamentarian town, and a Captain Johnson organized some sort of demonstration. A mob assembled, 'throwing up their caps, and crying *For Prince Charles and Captain Johnson*'. Jermy was denied the use of the ferry-boat, or any other boats, to cross the Yare, and was obliged to swim his troop of horse across. The Prince had sent a trumpeter with his order to surrender, and some of those who accompanied the trumpeter were detained and interrogated. The bailiffs sent back a message to the Prince, in which they 'modestly excused' themselves from complying with his orders, together with a gift of provisions. He threatened to sink some ships to block the harbour, but finally sailed off southwards to the Downs without any further action. Thereafter the town authorities and Jermy's soldiers had little difficulty in restoring order.[26]

Yarmouth, however, continued to be regarded as a vulnerable point. Soon after the surrender of Colchester, and the final collapse of the Royalist reaction, Cromwell sent Ireton down to review the position. Installed in Sir John Wentworth's house at Somerleyton, Ireton received a deputation from Yarmouth. Despite their protests he insisted on the garrisoning of the town, which was duly enforced to the great displeasure and expense of its people. Fairfax also made a tour of inspection in the eastern counties, in the course of which he visited both Yarmouth and Norwich. At Somerleyton he had 'great entertainment', and was shown 'the greatest varieties for ponds, water-works, groves,

[25] Manship, 389–90.
[26] Rushworth, IV, ii, 1206–7. Manship, 384.

conveniences of coy-ducks, that are to be seen in the kingdom of England'. At Norwich the mayor, sheriffs and aldermen received him in their scarlet gowns, 'with extraordinary expressions of their joy at his coming thither; and feasted him, with all his company, in an extraordinary manner; there appeared love in a high degree.'[27]

Apart from the rioting in the towns. Norfolk remained quiescent during the Second Civil War. The known Royalists of the county were closely watched, but they made no move. Most of them had by now compounded for their estates, and compounders were required to take an oath that they would be faithful to the Parliament henceforward. Three years afterwards an informer alleged that Sir Robert Kemp had entertained and assisted with horses the soldiers in the garrison of Colchester; but the matter does not seem to have been pursued further.[28] The only Norfolk participants in the war were younger sons with little to lose, such as Roger L'Estrange and Edmund Hobart of Holt. The latter, a member of the sole Royalist offshoot of that extremely Puritan family, later applied to compound, and admitted that 'being very young, and having no estate, he was drawn into both wars'. In order that he might 'live quietly by his labour', he begged to compound for his wearing apparel, which was valued at £5. Fined at the rate of one-sixth, and so required to pay 16s. 8d., he was one of the smallest fish caught in the widespread net of the Committees.[29]

It is unlikely that Sir Hamon L'Estrange took any pride in his son Roger's efforts to uphold the King's cause at Lynn and more recently in Kent. He had hoped to live quietly at Hunstanton, and to preserve his diminished estate from further spoliation. Roger's activities, and the notoriety that had attended them, brought the name of L'Estrange before the public once more, just at a time when all Royalists were under suspicion. The fact cannot have been unwelcome to Sir Hamon's local enemies, and probably gave them an excuse for harassing him over a very trivial occurrence.

A party of Royalist prisoners, who were being conveyed across the Wash from Lynn to Boston, overpowered their guards and

[27] Manship, 390–1. Rushworth, IV, ii, 1263.
[28] *Cal. Com. for Advance of Money*, 475.
[29] *Cal. Com. Compounding*, 2906.

ordered the keelman of their boat to take them on to Scarborough. The man told them that this was impossible, but that he would land them at Heacham, whence they could make their way to the house of a noted Royalist who would be willing to help them. When they arrived at Hunstanton under the guidance of the obliging keelman Sir Hamon, made wise by events, refused to see them. In fact he sent for Toby Pedder, the chief constable of the hundred, and advised him to report the affair to his superiors, and to use his own discretion about hindering the prisoners' escape. Later they were all recaptured. On the way back to Lynn they and their guards came again to the outer court at Hunstanton, and asked for a drink on that hot summer's day. Sir Hamon's butler gave them drink, without his master's orders but with his subsequent approval. As Sir Hamon said later, 'I may safely justify that charity to a Turk'. In the far-off days of peace, Toby Pedder had received his office through Sir Hamon's influence; but now he had become a self-important busybody, and he reported the little act of kindness to higher authority, as the granting by his old patron of clandestine favours to soldiers of the King's party. Sir Hamon, in his explanation of the affair, was properly contemptuous of Toby Pedder, 'whom I made not chief constable to repay me with malice and ingratitude for the many favours which he and his predecessors have received from me and mine'.[30] Nothing further seems to have happened to Sir Hamon on this occasion. Toby Pedder continued to flourish, and during the Commonwealth years received further promotion, becoming noted in north-west Norfolk as an exceptionally active and officious Justice of the Peace.

[30] H.M.C., le Strange, 103.

CHAPTER XVII

The Death of the King

I

The Second Civil War finally confirmed Cromwell and the Army in power. The Royalist attempts had failed hopelessly. The victory over the Scots had been complete. In the minds of the leading Independents, and of many of their supporters both in Army and in Parliament, the conviction steadily grew that there could be no further negotiations with the King. In their eyes, the events of the last few months had revealed to the whole nation the true measure of his falseness and duplicity. It was evident that he cared nothing for the suffering and bloodshed that he had brought upon his people. He would still intrigue to recover the authority of his crown, to disregard his promises and to break his pledges, so long as he remained alive.

In the meantime the Presbyterian majority in Parliament had themselves been negotiating with the King. Their commissioners held long discussions with him throughout the autumn at Newport, where he had lately been moved from Carisbrooke. At one time he led them to hope that he would accept their proposals, or some modification of them; but in the end, even in this hour of imminent danger, he rejected any accommodation. 'My Lords,' he said to them in farewell, 'you cannot but know that, in my fall and ruin, you see your own, and that also near to you. I pray God send you better friends than I have found.'[1]

For many months past the King had been, in the view of the extremists in the Army, the Man of Blood, the author of all the woes that had fallen upon the land. Now even the more responsible elements, officers and men alike, were urging with ever greater insistence that 'the King be brought to justice, as the capital cause of all'. Such was the first demand of the remonstrance, largely the work of Ireton, which they addressed to

[1] Charles I, *Works* (1662), 424.

355

Parliament on 20 November.[2] The talks at Newport finally broke down on the 24th. A few days later the Army marched on London, and took control at Westminster, surrounding the Houses of Parliament. A detachment was sent down to the Isle of Wight, which removed the King across the Solent to closer confinement at Hurst Castle.

Fairfax, still the titular Lord General, was a fine soldier but a perplexed and indecisive politician. He was able to exert little influence on the events which followed. Cromwell was still in the north, perhaps lingering there deliberately; and his son-in-law Ireton was the driving force during these critical days. The Presbyterians in Parliament, ignoring the soldiery outside, determined to resume negotiations with the King, and carried a motion to that effect. When the members sought to enter their House on the morning of 6 December, they found the approaches guarded by a strong body of troops. At the door of the House stood Colonel Thomas Pride, with a list in his hand. Ireton and his associates had decided that Parliament should be purged of all members who might be likely to oppose their policies; and the list contained the names of those whom they proposed to exclude from further participation in the business of the House. Nearby stood Lord Grey of Groby, the son of the Earl of Stamford and a member of the House since its inception. It was his business to point out to Pride the members who were to be excluded. The larger number of these were simply turned away by the soldiers, and prevented from entering the House and taking their seats. Forty-one, the most militant or otherwise objectionable of the Presbyterians, were taken into temporary custody. The Rump, as the survivors soon came to be called, alone remained of the most memorable Parliament in English history. The Army and the Independents had triumphed, and there was now no power in the land that could obstruct their will.

2

Since the first election, at the end of 1645, of 'recruiters' to fill the vacant seats in the House of Commons, there had been further

[2] Rushworth, IV, ii, 1331.

changes in the Parliamentary representation of Norfolk. Old Sir John Hobart, who was chosen in 1645 to replace Sir Edmund Moundeford as one of the knights of the shire, died in 1647. His place was taken by Sir John Palgrave of North Barningham, who had commanded one of the Norfolk regiments from the outset of the war, and had especially distinguished himself at the siege of Newark. In choosing him, the gentlemen of Norfolk once again showed their preference for a candidate of conservative and Presbyterian leanings. Sir John can have had no sympathy for the political outlook of the Army under Cromwell and Ireton.

Richard Harman, member for Norwich since the outset of the Long Parliament, died towards the end of 1646. He had never been a conspicuous figure, but he served the city faithfully and well, and was their sole representative for some years, since Richard Catelyn had deserted the House long before his actual expulsion. A number of his reports from Westminster to the Mayor and Corporation of Norwich have survived.[3] His successor was a Norfolk lawyer named Erasmus Earle, a native of Sall, and married to Frances Fountaine of a Puritan family in the same parish. The year after his election he became a Serjeant-at-Law, and also Recorder of Norwich. One of his first duties in that capacity was the trial and sentencing of the participants in the riot described in the previous chapter. He was an able lawyer, but noted for parsimony and covetousness. When the future Lord Keeper Guilford, as a young barrister, asked him how he kept his accounts, his reply was: 'Accounts, boy? I get as much as I can, and I spend as little as I can; and there is all the account I keep.'[4] This policy enabled him to acquire the beautiful house and fine estate of Heydon, close to his birthplace, where his descendants still remain.

Five Norfolk members figure in the various contemporary lists of those who were excluded in Pride's Purge. They were the two knights of the shire, Sir John Potts and Sir John Palgrave; the two members for Castle Rising, Sir John Holland and John Spelman; and Framlingham Gawdy, one of the members for Thetford. All these belonged essentially to the Presbyterian group. They were men of old family, substantial estates, conservative instincts.

---

[3] B.M. Add. MS. 22,619 *passim*.
[4] *Lives of the Norths*, i, 53.

They would have vehemently opposed the measures that the Army and the Independents were now determined to carry through. None of the five, however, was included among those especially obnoxious Presbyterians who were taken into custody by the Army, and detained in some cases for a considerable time.[5]

Although the name of the other member for Thetford, Sir Thomas Wodehouse, does not figure in any of these lists, there is a strong probability that he had by now withdrawn altogether from the service of Parliament. He was an old man, described as 'fettered with arthritic pains'; and he had acted with studious moderation throughout the war. The career of Sir Thomas Wodehouse in Parliament was described in a most convincing way by his son Sir Philip, in a long rhymed history of the Wodehouse family which he appears to have written during the Common-wealth years.

> At length is called that fatal Parliament
> To King and kingdom. Thither is he sent
> A member, where he stoutly acts for right
> And laws of kings and subjects, 'gainst the might
> Of Court-Leviathans who would pull down
> The pale between the people and the Crown.
> Thus far went he. But other bigot fools
> Ran to extremes, and pulled up all the dools[6]
> Of government. They brought in anarchy
> In kirk and lay: that brought in tyranny.
> This 'tis for faction, interest and blind zeal
> To be reformers of a commonweal.[7]

The position of a moderate in the Long Parliament could not be more clearly defined.

[5] The lists are printed in Cobbett's *Parliamentary History*, iii, 1248-9; *A List of the Members . . . secluded*, N.D., reprinted in Somers' *Tracts* (ed. 1811), vi, 37-43; and *A Brief Narrative . . .* (1660). Only the names of Palgrave and Spelman are common to the three lists; but there can be no doubt that all five were in fact disabled from sitting.

[6] The word dole or dool is defined by Forby in his *Vocabulary of East Anglia* as 'a boundary mark in an unenclosed field'.

[7] I have transcribed this poem, most of which is also printed in Blomefield ii, 556, from a copy among the Swanton House MSS. in the handwriting of Sir Philip Wodehouse's daughter, Blanch Lady Astley.

Another probable absentee from Parliament was Edward Owner, one of the members for Great Yarmouth. He too was elderly and perhaps ailing, since he died in 1650. In religion he had always been a staunch Presbyterian, and it is likely that he would have adhered to the Presbyterian group in politics. But nothing is heard of him at this time.

At King's Lynn one of the seats was still vacant, since the House had not admitted Edmund Hudson owing to his involvement in the rising of 1643. The other member, Thomas Toll, was not among those excluded in the Purge, but continued as a member of the Rump. So the only Norfolk members now left with a voice in Parliament were Toll for Lynn, Miles Corbett for Yarmouth, and Thomas Atkins and Erasmus Earle for Norwich. Other members of the Rump with Norfolk connections were William Hevening-ham of Ketteringham, who sat for Stockbridge in Hampshire, and Cromwell's brother-in-law Valentine Walton, the governor of Lynn, who represented Huntingdonshire. In 1646 General Philip Skippon had been brought into Parliament as a 'recruiter' for Barnstaple in Devon, a little borough with which he had no personal connection. He too continued to sit with the Rump.

3

Cromwell returned to Westminster the day after Pride's Purge, for the first time since the outbreak of the Second War. Later in the month the King was brought up from Hurst Castle to Windsor. It was now made evident to the nation and the world that he would be put on trial for his life.

No such outcome of the war had been even remotely con-templated by the Puritan gentlemen who first opposed the King in the House of Commons and in the field. They had taken up arms in order to limit his personal rule, to ensure the downfall of his advisers, to combat the menace of Popery, to assert the authority of Paliament in church and state. When his defeat was certain, they believed that he would submit to their demands. They had not foreseen his unyielding determination to retain what he regarded as his divinely granted prerogatives. Nor had they anticipated that in consequence the control of affairs would fall into the hands of their more revolutionary colleagues. Potts, Holland, Wodehouse and the rest—they were obliged to watch helplessly as those whom they regarded as 'bigot fools' pursued their extremist policies to the end.

On 25 December, no longer to be known or celebrated as Christmas Day, a petition of 'the well affected gentlemen, and others the inhabitants of the county of Norfolk and county of the city of Norwich' was presented to the House of Commons, 'and very gratefully accepted'. No details have survived as to how it was organized, and by whom it was presented in the absence of most of the Norfolk members—probably by Miles Corbett, the senior Norfolk member of the Rump. 'After a vast expense of blood and treasure for many years' continuance,' the petition began, 'we have expected a firmer establishment of our native liberties; but by the just hand of God upon us for our old and new provocations in our unchristian divisions, and abominable self-seeking that is amongst us, even of all conditions, and through the restless malice of our secret and open adversaries, we are under the shadows of hope cast back into as great fears and dangers as ever.' The Norfolk petitioners therefore offered certain requests to the House 'for the redress of present, and prevention of future evils'. The first of these was 'that present inquiry be made, who have been the chief instruments of the King in the former or this latter war, and the late inviting and bringing in the Scots; and that he himself, and all such as have been the most notorious incendiaries and instruments in shedding blood, may without further delay be brought to due and impartial justice'.[8]

On 1 January 1649 the Commons passed an ordinance for the trial of 'Charles Stuart, the now King of England'. He was charged with 'a wicked design totally to subvert the ancient and fundamental laws and liberties of this nation, and in their place to introduce an arbitrary and tyrannical government'. He had prosecuted this design 'with fire and sword, levied and maintained a cruel war in the land against the Parliament and Kingdom, whereby the country has been miserably wasted, the public treasure exhausted, trade decayed, thousands of people murdered, and infinite other mischiefs committed'. Therefore a body of commissioners was appointed to sit in judgement upon him. It

[8] Rushworth, IV, ii, 1372–3.

was further declared that 'by the fundamental laws of this realm it is treason for the King to levy war against the Parliament and Kingdom of England'. The ordinance was then sent up to the Lords, a shrunken remnant of that House, sixteen in all, with Manchester acting as Speaker since there was no Lord Chancellor. The lords 'stuck much' upon the declaration that the King had been guilty of treason, since the sovereign could not commit treason against the Parliament which he alone had the power to summon or dissolve. In the end they refused to have any part in the trial; whereupon the Commons resolved that they alone, 'being chosen by, and representing the people, have the supreme authority of this nation'.[9]

The commissioners thus appointed were 135 in number, although in the event more than fifty of them refused to sit. Among those named were most of the members of Parliament who afterwards sat in the Rump, but not all: of the members from Norfolk, Thomas Toll and Erasmus Earle were not in the list. Miles Corbett and Thomas Atkins were appointed, as were William Heveningham, Valentine Walton and Philip Skippon.

During the months of the Second War Skippon had acted as commander-in-chief of the London militia. It was largely due to his skill and vigilance that Royalist feeling in the City had not erupted in more formidable demonstrations. More recently he had been of great assistance in reassuring the London trained bands when the Army ousted them and took control of the capital early in December. In fact he served the Army as well in politics as he had done in battle. But his Independency was of recent growth, and was never extreme. 'He hath gotten a vast estate,' wrote a hostile pamphleteer, 'hath been of all parties, first a Presbyterian, till Philip Nye opened his eyes, and showed him the way to worldly greatness.'[10] He certainly amassed a good deal of property, including the Bishop's Palace in Norwich. He was to bequeath the Palace to his unmarried daughter; but fortunately for her prospects he altered this to a money bequest, shortly before his death in March 1660.[11] But he followed the example of another great soldier, Fairfax, in refusing absolutely to sit in

[9] Ibid., 1379-83.
[10] *The Mystery of the Good Old Cause* (1660).
[11] Quarles, *History of Foulsham*, 94-5.

judgement on the King. Both were named prominently in the list of commissioners, and neither obeyed the summons.

Thomas Atkins also appears to have refused to sit.[12] But the other commissioners with Norfolk connections—Corbett, Walton and Heveningham—duly took their seats in the court in Westminster Hall. According to one account the Commons sent Corbett to Windsor, to inform the King of his impending trial. They could hardly have chosen a more disagreeable messenger.

4

The trial of the King, which opened on 20 January, has often been described, most recently in a memorable book by Dame Veronica Wedgwood.[13] I can only refer the reader to her scholarly and dispassionate yet deeply moving narrative. It is sufficient to say here that the King steadfastly refused to allow that the court, or any earthly court, had power to try him. He regarded himself as in the hands of a lawless tribunal. If he admitted its legality, he would be delivering his people over to a tyranny whose end could not be foreseen. 'For the charge,' he said, 'I value it not a rush. It is the liberty of the people of England that I stand for. For me to acknowledge a new court that I never heard of before, I that am your King, that should be an example to all the people of England for to uphold justice, to maintain the old laws; indeed I do not know how to do it.' And again: 'It is not my case alone, it is the freedom and the liberty of the people of England; and do you pretend what you will, I stand more for their liberties. For if power without law may make laws, may alter the fundamental laws of the kingdom, I do not know what subject he is in England that can be sure of his life, or any thing that he calls his own.'[14]

Legality was on his side. The more eminent and reputable lawyers in the land, many of whom had bitterly opposed the King throughout the past years, refused to countenance the trial in any way. When John Bradshaw, the President of the Court, asserted

---

[12] He is mentioned as having sat by Walker, *History of Independency*, ii, 123, but his name is not in the lists in Rushworth, IV, ii, 1395, 1416.

[13] C. V. Wedgwood, *The Trial of Charles I* (1964).

[14] *State Trials* (1719), i, 512, 514.

that the prisoner was charged with treason and other crimes 'in the name of the people of England', a masked woman in the gallery cried out: 'Not a half, not a quarter of the people of England. Oliver Cromwell is a traitor.' It was later discovered that she was Lady Fairfax, the wife of the General who had done so much to bring about the downfall of the King, and was now dismayed at this outcome of all his efforts.[15] But Bradshaw continued to press home what he and his associates regarded as their moral justification for the trial. 'There is a contract and a bargain made between the King and his people . . . whether you have been, as by your office you ought to be, a protector of England, or the destroyer of England, let all England judge, or all the world that hath looked upon it.'[16]

Throughout the week of the trial, the King behaved with superb courage and dignity. The harassed and fugitive monarch was transformed, by the nobility of his bearing, into a new image, Charles the Martyr. Memory is short; and the weakness and obstinacy of the King, his shifts and errors, the endless suffering of the war began to seem of less account. In all the history of England, no sovereign had been put to death by trial and sentence of his subjects. It was a deed without precedent; and its horror was intensified by the resignation with which the King submitted to his fate. The outcome of the trial was inevitable. The court gave sentence that 'the said Charles Stuart, as a tyrant, traitor, murderer, and a public enemy, shall be put to death by the severing of his head from his body'.[17] The execution was carried out, on a scaffold outside the Banqueting House at Whitehall, on the afternoon of 30 January.

Royalists throughout the kingdom had watched the trial with the profoundest grief. Thomas Knyvett's mother wrote to her sister Lady Bell of 'the sad condition of our good but most distressed King. God in mercy for our blessed mediator's sake comfort him and deliver him now in his great extremities. We must expect a bloody and tyrannical government'. She wrote again, after the execution, of 'that horrid act of murdering our good King—whose heart cannot but mourn that consider his innocency

[15] Wedgwood, *Trial of Charles I*, 154-5.
[16] *State Trials*, i, 518.
[17] Ibid., i, 520.

and their cruelty?[18] Nor was distress confined to the Royalists. The Presbyterian clerics preached and petitioned vehemently against the trial. Thomas Thorowgood, when 'that calamitous day' of the execution approached, 'did solemnly fast and pray with the little company in my family'.[19] As for Sir Thomas Wodehouse, according to his son in the poem quoted earlier, the shock of the King's death shortened his own life.

> He lived well nigh two climacterics o'er
> His great one, and well mought have lived more
> Had not that hellish act (the horridest
> This world did ever see, but killing Christ)
> So smote his soul, that he ne'er joyed good day
> Here-hence, as to a friend he did bewray.[20]

William Heveningham had sat in court during the greater part of the trial, and was present on the last day, when sentence was pronounced. He asserted long afterwards that he 'did refuse to consent to his Majesty's death by holding up his hands as the rest did'; and in common with several others he certainly refused to sign the death-warrant, 'although he was pressed thereunto with much importunity by Serjeant Bradshaw, the then President'.[21] Walton and Corbett both signed the fatal warrant. Eleven years later, at the Restoration, Heveningham was among those of the King's judges who surrendered. The two others fled abroad. Walton went first to Hanau in Germany, and then disappeared altogether. There is a vague story that he supported himself as a gardener in Flanders, but even the date of his death is unknown. Corbett settled in Holland, but was kidnapped there with two other regicides in 1662, and brought back to England to stand his trial.

Heveningham was condemned to death, but reprieved. 'My Lord,' he pleaded, 'in 1649 we were under a force, under the tyranny of an Army; they were our masters: for a malicious and a

---

[18] B.M. Add. MS. 27,400, ff. 31, 32.

[19] N.A., xxii, 328.

[20] Swanton House MSS. (unpublished passage). A climacteric is the seventh year. The great climacteric is the age of 63 (nine times seven). There is slight poetic licence here, but Sir Thomas in fact died in his middle seventies.

[21] H.M.C., House of Lords, 86.

traitorous heart I had not.'[22] Afterwards he petitioned repeatedly
for pardon. He was responsible, he said, for the wife and six
children of his Royalist brother Arthur, now deceased, 'who was
so fortunate as to serve the late King in all his wars'. He even
went so far as to maintain that 'your petitioner never appeared in
the pretended High Court that sat upon our late gracious sovereign, but with firm resolutions to save his most precious life, as
far as his utmost endeavours could extend'.[23] His own life was
spared, and his estates, forfeited to the Crown, were eventually
restored to his family; but he remained in confinement until his
death eighteen years later. His grave, without his name or other
inscription, and identifiable only by his armorial bearings, may
still be seen in Ketteringham Church.

Corbett was a man of stronger fibre. To friends who visited
him in the Tower after his trial and sentence, he explained in
detail the legal reasoning and the spiritual prompting which had
jointly impelled him along his chosen path through life, and
especially with reference to the trial of the King. As a lawyer he
had satisfied himself in his own mind 'of the lawfulness of the
fact, as well as of the power by which it was done'. Nevertheless
he had hesitated, since his nephew Sir Thomas Corbett, to whose
estate he was heir, was an enthusiastic Royalist and might cut off
the entail. But 'conscience wrought much with him, and would
not suffer him,' he said, 'to be quiet night nor day'; and God
frequently brought to his mind the text from Revelations that
*the fearful and unbelieving shall have their part in the lake of fire and
brimstone*. So he had signed the death-warrant 'with a free and
resolved mind, and blessed God that he had conquered his
cowardly spirit'. And now, the day before he went to the gallows
at Tyburn, he affirmed once more that the execution of the King
was 'a necessary and public act of justice', and that 'if all that hath
been done were to be acted over again, he would do as he had
done, and would not abate an inch of it'.[24]

But the imprisonment of Heveningham and the execution of
Corbett were far in the future on that January day in 1649. The

[22] *Trial of the Regicides* (1679), 312.
[23] H.M.C., House of Lords, 129, 158.
[24] *Speeches, Discourses and Prayers of Barkstead, Okey and Corbett* (1662), 31-4. No
printer's name or place of publication is given, and the pamphlet was printed
surreptitiously and perhaps abroad.

English people, stunned and bewildered, waited to learn what lay ahead. They were to endure eleven years of incessant changes in government, experimental Parliaments, oppressive military rule, a Lord Protector, and in the end something perilously near to anarchy. The Commonwealth had begun.

Bibliography

No period of English history has been more closely studied in recent years than the first half of the seventeenth century. I would like to acknowledge a particular debt to the works of certain historians—to the late Godfrey Davies's *The Early Stuarts* (1936); Dr. Christopher Hill's *Puritanism and Revolution* (1958) and *Society and Puritanism in Pre-Revolutionary England* (1964); Professor J. P. Kenyon's *The Stuart Constitution* (1966); Mr. Ivan Roots's *The Great Rebellion* (1966); Professor H. R. Trevor-Roper's *Laud* (1940), *Historical Essays* (1957) and *Religion, the Reformation and Social Change* (1967); and Dame Veronica Wedgwood's *The King's Peace* (1955) and *The King's War* (1958).

As was indicated in the preface, my book aims to be a narrative of events and not an interpretation of motives. Nevertheless I have studied, I hope not without profit, the discussions of the period in *Past and Present*, and the controversy which Professor J. H. Hexter has described as the *Storm over the Gentry*.

My only predecessor in this local field was Alfred Kingston in his *East Anglia and the Great Civil War* (1897), which covered the whole area of the Eastern Association. I have found this work helpful in many particulars. I am indebted also to Dr. Alan Everitt's *Suffolk and the Great Rebellion* (Suffolk Record Society, 1960). I am grateful to Mr. D. W. Boorman for allowing me to consult his unpublished thesis *The Administrative and Disciplinary Problems of the Church on the Eve of the Civil War*.

My principal manuscript sources have been the Tanner and Walker Manuscripts in the Bodleian Library, and the Harley, Egerton and Additional Manuscripts in the British Museum. Local manuscript material has included documents in the possession of Marguerite, Lady Hastings and the Earl of Leicester; the L'Estrange papers in the custody of the Norfolk and Norwich Record Office; and the archives of the Corporations of Norwich, Great Yarmouth and King's Lynn.

In my quotations, both from printed and manuscript sources,

I have modernized the spelling and occasionally the punctuation. In a few places I have also thought it permissible to replace *country* by *county*, where the latter was quite clearly the meaning of the writer.

The following abbreviations have been used in the footnotes:

B.L.	Bodleian Library.
B.M.	British Museum.
C.J.	*Commons' Journals.*
C.S.P.D.	*Calendar of State Papers (Domestic).*
D.N.B.	*Dictionary of National Biography.*
E.A.	*The East Anglian.*
H.M.C.	Historical Manuscripts Commission.
L.J.	*Lords' Journals.*
N.A.	*Norfolk Archaeology.*
N.N.R.O.	Norfolk and Norwich Record Office.
N.R.S.	Norfolk Record Society.

Several references are made in the footnotes to each of the following sources. Works less frequently used are not included in the list, but are cited in the footnotes by their full titles.

AUBREY. John Aubrey. *Brief Lives and other Selected Works.* Ed. Anthony Powell. 1949.

BLOMEFIELD. Francis Blomefield. *An Essay towards a Topographical History of Norfolk.* 11 vols. 1805.

BROWNE. John Browne. *History of Congregationalism in Norfolk and Suffolk.* 1877.

BROWNE, *Works. The Works of Sir Thomas Browne.* Ed. Sir Geoffrey Keynes. 4 vols. 1964.

BRUNTON AND PENNINGTON. D. Brunton and D. H. Pennington. *Members of the Long Parliament.* 1954.

Cal. Com. Advance of Money. Calendar of the Proceedings of the Committee for Advance of Money, 1642–56. Ed. Mary Anne Everett Green. 3 vols, 1888.

Cal. Com. Compounding. Calendar of the Proceedings of the Committee for Compounding, 1643–60. Ed. Mary Anne Everett Green. 5 vols. 1889–92.

CARLYLE, *Cromwell.* Thomas Carlyle. *The Letters and Speeches of Oliver Cromwell.* Ed. S. C. Lomas. 3 vols. 1904.

CLARENDON. Edward Hyde, Earl of Clarendon. *History of the Rebellion and Civil Wars in England.* 3 vols., 1702–4.

D'EWES, *Autobiography.* Sir Simonds D'Ewes. *Autobiography.* Ed. J. O. Halliwell. 2 vols. 1845.

D'EWES, *Journal. The Journal of Sir Simonds D'Ewes.* Ed. Wallace Notestein. 1923.

EVELYN. John Evelyn. *Diary.* Ed. E. S. de Beer. 6 vols. 1955.

FULLER, *Church History.* Thomas Fuller. *The Church History of Britain.* 1655.

FULLER, *Worthies.* Thomas Fuller. *The History of the Worthies of England.* 1662.

GARDINER. S. R. Gardiner. *History of the Great Civil War.* 3 vols., 1886–91.

GERARD. John Gerard. *The Autobiography of an Elizabethan.* Tr. Philip Caraman. 1951.

GILLINGWATER. Edmund Gillingwater. *Historical Account of Lowestoft.* 1790.

HALL, *Works. The Works of Joseph Hall, D.D., successively Bishop of Exeter and Norwich.* Ed. Peter Hall. 12 vols. 1837–9.

HERVEY. Mary S. F. Hervey. *The Life, Correspondence and Collections of Thomas Howard, Earl of Arundel.* 1921.

HILLEN. H. J. Hillen. *History of King's Lynn.* 2 vols. 1907.

HUSBAND (1643). *An exact Collection of all Remonstrances, Declarations, Votes, Orders . . . between the King's most excellent Majesty and his High Court of Parliament.* Ed. Edward Husband. 1643.

HUSBAND (1646). *A Collection of all the public Orders, Ordinances and Declarations of both Houses of Parliament.* Ed. Edward Husband. 1646.

JAMES. C. W. James. *Chief Justice Coke: his Family and Descendants at Holkham.* 1929.

KEELER. Mary Frear Keeler. *The Long Parliament: a Biographical Study of its Members.* 1954.

KINGSTON. Alfred Kingston. *East Anglia and the Great Civil War.* 1897.

KNYVETT. Thomas Knyvett. *The Knyvett Letters (1620–1644).* Ed. Bertram Schofield. 1949.

LAUD, *Works. The Works of Archbishop Laud.* Ed. W. Scott and W. Bliss. 7 vols. 1847–60.

Lives of the Norths. Roger North. *The Lives of Francis North, Baron Guilford; Sir Dudley North; and Dr. John North.* Ed. Augustus Jessopp. 3 vols. 1890.

MANSHIP. Henry Manship. *History of Great Yarmouth.* Ed. C. J. Palmer. 1854.

MASON. R. H. Mason. *History of Norfolk.* 1884.

MOENS. W. J. C. Moens. *The Walloons and their Church at Norwich.* (Huguenot Society, 1887–8.)

RICHARDS. William Richards. *The History of Lynn.* 1812.

ROUS. John Rous. *Diary.* Ed. Mary Anne Everett Green. 1856.

RUSHWORTH. John Rushworth. *Historical Collections.* 7 vols. 1659–1701.

SELDEN. John Selden. *Table Talk.* Ed. Sir Frederick Pollock. 1927.

SHAW. W. A. Shaw. *A History of the English Church during the Civil Wars and under the Commonwealth.* 2 vols. 1900.

SUCKLING. Alfred Suckling. *The History and Antiquities of the County of Suffolk.* 2 vols. 1846.

SWINDEN. Henry Swinden. *History and Antiquities of Great Yarmouth.* 1772.

WALKER, *Sufferings.* John Walker. *An Attempt towards recovering the Numbers and Sufferings of the Clergy.* 1714.

Walker Revised. A. G. Matthews. *Walker Revised.* 1948.

WARWICK. Sir Philip Warwick. *Memoirs of the Reign of King Charles I.* 1701.

WOODHOUSE. A. S. P. Woodhouse. *Puritanism and Liberty: being the Army Debates (1647–9).* 1938.

Index

Hobart, Edmund, 353
Hobart, Lady Frances, 39–40, 339
Hobart, Sir Henry, Chief Justice, 38–9
Hobart, Sir James, 38
Hobart, Sir John, 33–5, 39, 81, 93, 150–1, 154, 172, 241, 269–70, 288, 357
Hobart, Sir John the younger, 270, 330–1
Hobart, John (of Norwich), 344–6
Hobart, Sir Miles, 39, 172, 202, 221, 297
Hobbys, Rev. Thomas, 258
Hogan, Sir Thomas, 154, 172, 188
Holkham, 47, 153, 176
Holl family, 46
Holl, Augustine, 99, 151, 176–9, 186, 222, 264, 296, 298, 303
Holland, Sir John, 34, 47–8, 93, 108–13, 116–18, 134, 144, 149, 163, 192, 198, 297–9, 328, 357; his moderating influence, 48, 118, 177–8, 222–3, 299; his speeches, 112–13, 119–21, 146–147, 222–3
Holland, Lady (née Alathea Panton), 48, 108, 121, 223
Holt, 72, 152–3, 240, 353
Honingham, 177–8
Hopkins, Matthew, 305–9
Horsham St. Faiths, 23, 72
Hotham, Sir John, 202, 211, 278
Houghton, 23, 153
Houghton, Robert, 167–9
Hovell family, 154
Hovell, Sir Richard, 207, 213
Howard family, 18, 26–7, 31, 288
Howard (see under Arundel, Mowbray, Northampton)
Howard, William (later Viscount Stafford), 32, 55

Howes, Rev. Richard, 244
Howlett, Rev. Nicholas, 153, 235
Howmans, Rev. Roger, 101
Howse, John, 117–18
Hudson, Rev. Michael, 313–25 *passim*, 327, 349
Hurry, Rev. Stephen, 84, 242–3
Hunstanton, 27–8, 40–1, 156, 217, 354

Impressment of soldiers, 265–7, 283–4
Independency, development of, 238, 326, 328–9, 356
Ipswich, 53, 57, 58, 63, 68–9
Ireton, John, 312, 352, 355–7

James I, King, 32, 36–7, 54, 66, 104, 321, 305
Jay, Christopher, 237
Jegon, John, Bishop of Norwich, 24, 51–2
Jegon, Robert, 52, 194
Jenkins, John, 28, 41
Jerningham family, 49
Jermy, Francis, 172, 198
Jermy, Robert, 172, 241, 283, 352
Jessopp, Francis, 254
Jocelyn, Torrell, 198
Jones, Inigo, 27–8, 43, 55
Jubbs, John, 221–2, 253, 329

Kemp, Sir Robert, 93, 135, 151, 155, 176, 184, 194, 197, 296, 298
Kenninghall, 26–7, 33, 145–8, 175–6
Kerdiston, 155
Kett, Thomas, 336, 344
Ketteringham, 44, 365
Kimberley, 28, 34, 41
Kimbolton (see under Manchester)

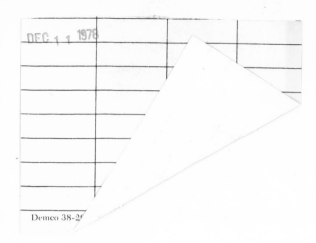

DEC 1 1 1978

Demco 38-2

942.062
K51n

23379